PRAISE FOR LUC

'Lunatic and splenetic and distinctive...
may be some sort of genius.'   —*Telegraph*

'A true original.'   —*Guardian*

'Ellmann's comedic brilliance is sui generis on any continent.'
                                                               —*Paris Review*

'In a class of her own.'   —*Cosmopolitan*

'If there were a laureate for anger, it should go to Lucy Ellmann.'
                                                      —*Scotland on Sunday*

'A CAPITAL case of comic genius.'   —*Independent*

'Funny, angry, sarcastic and utterly individual.'   —*Observer*

PRAISE FOR *DUCKS, NEWBURYPORT*

**WINNER OF THE 2019 GOLDSMITHS PRIZE • WINNER OF THE
2020 JAMES TAIT BLACK PRIZE FOR FICTION • SHORTLISTED
FOR THE 2019 BOOKER PRIZE • SHORTLISTED FOR THE
ORWELL PRIZE FOR POLITICAL FICTION • SHORTLISTED FOR
THE SALTIRE PRIZE FOR FICTION**

'That rare thing: a book which, not long after its publication, one
can unhesitatingly call a masterpiece.'
               —Erica Wagner, chair of the judges, the Goldsmiths Prize

'The unstoppable monologue of an Ohio housewife in Lucy Ellmann's
extraordinary *Ducks, Newburyport* is like nothing you've ever read before...
Audacious and epic.'   —2019 Booker Prize jury citation

'In her latest novel Lucy Ellmann doesn't just carry on as before: she
doubles down, doubles up and absolutely goes for broke... Success?
Failure? Triumph.'   —Ian Samson, *Guardian*

'Extraordinary... astounding... amazing... one of the outstanding books of the century, so far.'   —Declan O'Driscoll, *Irish Times*

'The time and care that [Ellmann] lavishes on her narrator seem like their own form of political speculation — that every individual is owed an unending devotion, and that such devotion, applied universally, might change the fate of the world.'   —Katy Waldman, *New Yorker*

'Ignore the laundry. Let this novel open like an oubliette under your feet.'
                    —Parul Sehgal, *New York Times*

'Ellmann adeptly riffs on a vertiginous range of subjects... all the while carefully avoiding the didacticism that would warp the novel into either a soapbox or a gallows. Her heroine's anger burns cleanly, refusing the easy conflagration of self-righteousness. The cumulative effect is devastating. This is a powerful and deeply felt indictment of American moral failure, a fearful, dazzling bloom of conscience... A grand mimetic achievement.'
                    —Dustin Illingworth, *Nation*

'A sublime literary enactment of how guilt, grief, rage, regret, compassion, and every other emotion swirls and ebbs in unbalanced defiance of rational logic... If art is measured by how skillfully it holds a mirror up to society, then Ellmann has surely written the most important novel of this era.'   —Emma Garman, *Paris Review*

'Sei Shonagon [and] Walt Whitman... are the intellectual company Ellmann keeps... *Ducks, Newburyport* [is] as accumulative, as pointed, as death-addled, as joyous, as storied, as multitudinous and as large as life.'
                    —Martin Riker, *New York Times*

'Timely, fresh... and possibly one of the most important books of the decade.'   —Alexandra Marraccini, *Los Angeles Review of Books*

'Effervescent... Ellmann has made a case that a richer, less regimented language leads to a more vibrant and capacious mind, and has thus crafted the entrancing *Ducks, Newburyport* into a celebration of all that words, and the minds they build, can contain.'
                    —Sebastian Sarti, *Chicago Review of Books*

THINGS
ARE
AGAINST US

ALSO BY LUCY ELLMANN

Sweet Desserts
Varying Degrees of Hopelessness
Man or Mango? A Lament
Dot in the Universe
Doctors & Nurses
Mimi
Ducks, Newburyport

THINGS

ARE
AGAINST US

Lucy Ellmann

GALLEY BEGGAR PRESS

First published in 2021 by Galley Beggar Press Limited
37 Dover Street, Norwich, NR2 3LG

Text design and typesetting by Tetragon, London
Set in Zuzana Licko's Filosofia, a 1996 Bodoni revival

Printed and bound by CPI Group (UK) Ltd, Croydon CR0 4YY

Sections of this book have previously appeared, in modified form, in various
publications. For a full list, please refer to the 'Sources' section at the end of the book.

A CIP catalogue record for this book is available from the British Library.

Papers used by Galley Beggar Press are from
well-managed forests and other responsible sources.

ISBN 978-1-913111-13-7

www.galleybeggar.co.uk

For Claire Lucido

All of life is pandemonium. With plague in our midst, every-thing feels like an emergency. I'm jittery, can't tolerate the least upset. So what else is new?

In times of pestilence, my fancy turns to shticks. They seem almost *innocent* to me, my scruples and my scorn, now that the whole human experiment seems to be drawing to a close.

Still, let's complain.

TABLE

OF DISCONTENTS

THINGS ARE
AGAINST US

You have to watch THINGS. THINGS are always making trouble, getting out of hand, trying to take advantage. THINGS do not have your best interests at heart. THINGS have their own agenda. THINGS care only for other THINGS. THINGS favour THINGS. THINGS indulge THINGS. THINGS prioritise THINGS. THINGS let THINGS get away with THINGS.

I speak as someone who is always losing THINGS, dropping THINGS, tripping over THINGS, breaking THINGS (even bits of my own body: bones, teeth, heart). Coming a cropper over THINGS. Okay, I'm accident-prone. But still, THINGS have a lot to answer for. The obstinacy, the indifference, the incorrigibility of THINGS! The recalcitrance of THINGS. So many disobedient and unbiddable THINGS. THINGS deceive you. THINGS perplex you. THINGS run out on you. THINGS look graspable when they aren't. THINGS slip out of your hand. THINGS look solid and steady when in fact they're wobbly: you step on the THING and you tip off.

Clothing rebels against the wearer. Socks won't stay up. Scarves are strangly THINGS. Hat brims blind you at crucial moments so you miss THINGS. Buttons try not to button THINGS. Pockets hide THINGS, or all too eagerly develop holes, defeating the whole purpose of a pocket, a THING designed to be a closed space with an opening at the top or maybe the side, but never the bottom. And who in hell invented the zipper? Like the atom bomb, not a good idea. Zippers can go badly wrong. Eventually, they *all* give out. Scary THINGS, zips.

THINGS disappoint us. Drawers stick so you can't get THINGS out of them or into them. Machines conk out. Rugs fade. Clothes shrink. Bookshelves fall on people; they are lethal THINGS. THINGS fall off hangers, and people fall off ladders. Ladders are dangerous THINGS. THINGS don't stay put. THINGS are never the right way up. THINGS get mouldy, THINGS break, THINGS drip, THINGS make odd noises, THINGS inexplicably collapse, THINGS move around in the night! THINGS get untidy. It is so hard to keep THINGS in order.

A kind of violence is done to us by THINGS all the time, unwieldy THINGS that awkwardly escape us, trick us, creep up on us. Soap slips from your grasp in the bath and you can't find it in the dark. The soap is dissolving while you splash around singeing your hair on the candle and getting water on the floor. All the tranquillity of bathing is upset by this dopey wrestling match. You catch hold of the soap briefly, then it slides away again! Giving up on the whole THING, you attempt to get out of the bath, a tricky THING at the best of times. Now you step on the slimy soap in the bottom of the tub, which causes you to slip. You grab the shower curtain, which tears right off its rail. You land on your slippery ass in the bathtub

and the momentum and curvature of the tub somehow combine to propel you right out on to the floor, where you lie, all
wet and winded, seeing stars. This is a typical example of the
anarchy of THINGS. The enmity of THINGS. The conspiratorial
manoeuvrings of THINGS.

They may not always cause major calamities, but they suggest an underlying hostility. All I'm saying is that, if THINGS
can go wrong, they will. THINGS let us down. THINGS fail us.
Plumbing! What could be a more intimidating THING than that?
THINGS outwit you, THINGS flood your kitchen and then act
all innocent. THINGS pester you, THINGS try to bring you
down. And these various cumulative outrages committed by
THINGS are like little crimes against us, filling us with distrust
of the whole wide world, both the man-made THINGS and all
its other sweet parts. The unseen rock that jolts the foot, bird
shit on the head (odd that this doesn't happen *more*), three
buses at once...

Matches won't light – or else they explode, sending burning particles on to your hand or clothes or eyes. Fireworks are
notorious for boomeranging back onto the fuse-lighter. Rugs
grab you and knock you over whenever they can. Needles prick
you. They sit in the sewing box waiting patiently to prick you
some day. These THINGS never give up hope of a good prick.
Thimbles are merely an annoying collector's item, no help at
all. Use the wrong utensil when cooking spaghetti and you get
no end of trouble, a real show of resistance. The particular
pillowcase you wanted to find somehow manages to hide from
you, cleverly camouflaging itself amongst other pillowcases.
You thought you had THINGS sorted, huh? Once you find it,
the pillow tries every trick in the book to prevent itself being
inserted into the appointed pillowcase. Like a wild stallion, it

rears and leaps. Fitted sheets never fit. And duvet covers? Their deviltry is legendary.

THINGS fall into disarray – so fast! It's not fair. Pieces of paper frequently evade control: they either pile up threateningly, disappear unexpectedly, or give you a paper cut. They like to form themselves into unfathomable wads and cascading fans. They drift to the floor and you slip on them. Unopened envelopes are accusatory THINGS that emit unremitting waves of neglect and distrust.

You fill a hot-water bottle and then can't find the stopper THING. It has impishly hidden itself. When you finally spy it, cowering idiotically behind a bunch of dirty mugs, you reach for it with one hand, your other hand still holding the boiling hot hot-water bottle. The stopper now rolls off the counter on to the floor, clever THING. In your effort to retrieve the THING, you inevitably scald yourself.

Try dropping merely a small single piece of cardboard into the recycling bag. Will it go in with no trouble? Like hell it will. It always falls outside the recycling bag and goes straight down a crack in the floorboards. This is how we begin to realise THINGS are against us. In fact, it's possible THINGS really kind of hate us.

We all know about toast falling buttered side down. That is a cliché of the ill will of THINGS. But either way up the toast lands is not good! Why is it any better for it to fall butter side up? Okay, the floor might not get as greasy, and you won't have to mop all the butter up. But you've still got a dirty piece of toast on your hands, your buttery hands. Out it goes. Yeast has died for nothing. What a THING, what a THING.

THINGS get you coming and they get you going. THINGS go around and THINGS come around. When THINGS *can* mess with you, they will. THINGS are not shy. Some THINGS seem especially out to get you. Is it just clumsiness, or a jinx? You get out of bed on the wrong side and are at war with THINGS the rest of the day.

You try to cut up your salad and the choicest piece of lettuce falls to the floor.

The radish flies across the room.

You start the dishwasher, but then find a stray spoon.

When you open the dishwasher to place it carefully in the cutlery basket, the spoon falls to the side of the basket and ends up in the yucky murky detergent pond at the bottom of the dishwasher.

Out of fastidiousness or self-preservation, you naturally hesitate to delve into this swamp.

But you dutifully reach for the spoon anyway.

In bending over, your Kleenex, which was handily tucked in your armpit, replaces the spoon in the icky water.

Now your dishwasher has a soggy Kleenex in it and your sciatica's coming back.

It's so unseemly. So many stealthy attacks going on, cruel, cunning little acts of malice perpetrated upon us by THINGS. Some might say it's just not your day. I would say it's those pesky THINGS again. THINGS are out to get us.

Why do I always, always, pull the wrong cord on the blind, may I ask, making the darn THING go up instead of down, or vice versa? It's not just fifty per cent of the time that this happens, or even seventy-five per cent, it's *every time*. It isn't a nice THING about THINGS, that THINGS behave this way. It isn't kind. THINGS fall suspiciously often. THINGS are always testing us, testing, testing. Of course, gravity is an aid to THINGS in these plots and betrayals. THINGS take advantage of gravity too much. Gravity is helpless against THINGS. Centrifugal force is also a THING.

I guess I have a THING about THINGS. But why is it ovens get dirty so fast? Ovens do these THINGS to humiliate us. Why does jam get mouldy? Why do closets become impenetrable miasmas of junk? Why do people get locked out of their own houses? All the time! Of all the crazy THINGS. Keys are tricky THINGS. Why do the wheels break off your brand-new wheelie suitcase on its very first outing? Why do ankles get themselves sprained? Why so much dust and rust? THINGS are decaying all around us.

It is odd that we all own plastic feather dusters. What a strange THING to buy.

Then there's the way THINGS go missing. Those lost socks. Belligerent socks are racing to get away from us! Also pens, pencils, matches, hats, gloves, credit cards, and lemons (there are always fewer lemons lurking around the house than you thought). Is it because we just have too many THINGS in general, and THINGS feel crowded out, unwelcome? Do THINGS fear obsolescence? Surely that is their primary terror. If so, we must pity THINGS. It is the only THING to do.

If you have the right ingredients on hand when a THING goes missing, you can appeal to St Fanourious, saint of lost THINGS. You bake him a fanouropita out of a magical seven THINGS, or nine THINGS (always including lemon, flour, and sugar – this is why not having lemons at all times is a bad THING). Put the fanouropita by an open window. After invisibly partaking of the THING, St Fanourious will supposedly help you find whatever THING it is that you lost. Curiously, fanouriously, this cake remedy THING sometimes seems to work. But otherwise, all you can do is hope your lost THING miraculously appears again when the gods are feeling more forgiving about THINGS. Or when the THING itself relents. Because it's probably not the gods that are against us, but THINGS themselves.

A plastic takeaway container, used for storing dried thyme, falls to the floor as you rummage through your crazy mixed-up herbs and spices. It scatters little dried leaves of thyme everywhere, just everywhere. These THINGS are on the floor, on the counter, in the dishwasher, probably in the bathtub. On every THING. Sharp little barely visible thyme leaves will keep turning up for centuries after your demise, accusingly tickling the feet of your descendants — all because you once dared do such a THING as rummage through the cupboard in search of some THING in there. Thyme leaves are extremely punitive THINGS.

Some people are more trusting of THINGS, and yes, I'm speaking here of my own dear husband, who will leave a glass of water, or the iPad, or our ancient dearly beloved salt bowl, right at the edge of a rickety table. I often find the teapot on the corner of the cutting board, giving it a vertiginous view of the three-foot drop below. Or pots are set to boil on the stovetop with their handles sticking straight *out*. The trusting fellow clearly has greater faith in THINGS than I have. In fact, he seems remarkably confident that he'll get away with these little dares without incurring the bad-tempered revenge of THINGS. Less convinced, I am forever shoving endangered THINGS inland from precipices about the place, and correcting the suicidal tendencies of THINGS. My position is, why take a chance on THINGS looking after themselves? THINGS are erratic, THINGS are unpredictable. THINGS are sometimes out-of-sorts. Lead THINGS not into temptation. You can lead THINGS to water but don't let them think.

What does it mean though, more profoundly, if all the innocent-looking THINGS in the world are actually determined to let us down? Because, if *inanimate* THINGS have it in for us, just think how much animosity *animate* THINGS must be feeling towards us – our contemporaries, I mean, the birds, the bees, giant killer hornets, snakes and snake-like THINGS. Spiders. This is why the hostility of THINGS is so unnerving. It rouses our fear of all kinds of other potential slights, carried out by stronger or sneakier THINGS.

How many thousands of tales of animal revenge are there? We unconsciously suspect animals will turn on us any minute. That would be bad enough. But what if *botanical* THINGS started acting up too? It would not be a nice THING to be attacked by a tree. (As lumberjacks well know.) And then there are all the poor vegetal THINGS which we are so used to bending to our will. Without a qualm, we grow these THINGS and pluck these THINGS and transport these THINGS and wash these THINGS and chop these THINGS and mash these THINGS and boil these THINGS and bake these THINGS and butter these THINGS and gobble them up. Or chomp their little heads off raw, poor THINGS! (Vegan recipes are often very complicated THINGS.) Any minute now, plants will turn out to be sentient THINGS, with all kinds of THINGS on their minds, and that'll give everybody a bit of a turn. Veggies will then feel as bad about THINGS as carnivores do. What if cauliflowers organised a walk-out sort of THING and leapt right out of your mouth, waving their pom-poms? What if carrots objected to being grated, or were hurt by our laughter when they come out of the ground cross-legged, with a penis, apparently doing a jig?

A carrot, a cauliflower, and a radish go into a bar.

Barman says: 'What the hell do you guys want?'

The carrot replies: 'No crudités, please.'

We're all fully accustomed to the disobedience of comput-ers. Those THINGS were sent to thwart us. But it's scarier to be attacked by familiar THINGS that supposedly belong to you and obey your will. Your tried and trusted toothbrush, a blanket, your own front door, or your phone wire, tangling itself up into a knot when you aren't looking.

And then, what a THING the *body* is. It works one day and not the next. Maybe it's okay for your first few decades or so (though even children get sick) but in old age it becomes a THING of terror. This is how most people end their days, finally succumbing to THINGS, including their own bodies. THINGS start taking it out on you. THINGS become useless, unreachable, untenable. THINGS like care homes are mooted. THINGS fly at you, THINGS block your path, THINGS drag you down. THINGS start to perplex you, escape you. Your dotage is a prime time for losing THINGS: you lose your way, your libido, your spectacles, your wits, your friends, your finances, muscle tone, and a lot of other THINGS besides. Your aim is off. You find it hard to navigate your way around. You forget which THING you went to the next room for. You forget the THINGS you were about to say. THINGS get you down. THINGS just don't go right.

THINGS start being against you, though, from *babyhood*. As an infant, THINGS are not in your favour. Hand-eye coordin-ation is a difficult THING, and you have no control over your environment. You find THINGS bewildering. For newborns, THINGS are also out of focus. Being a baby is a pretty frus-trating THING. This must be when you first begin to suspect that THINGS are shifty and unreliable. No wonder babies cry so much over every little THING.

23

We're probably best able to fend off the malevolence of THINGS in our twenties and thirties. At this point, many treacherous THINGS wait in abeyance, semi-contained, unable to take their full toll. But let your guard down even for a second, even in your prime, and THINGS will try to scupper you, no matter how resilient you think you are to THINGS. Your alarm clock will often disturb a good dream. At other times, its battery will die and you'll miss an appointment. The milk goes off. A water pipe will whine, or burst, and there's not a THING you can do about it. No matter how old you are, grapefruit will always spit in your eye. Those THINGS have an uncanny aim.

What better proof the spitefulness of THINGS than a viral pandemic? Viruses aren't even *alive*, in any sense that we can understand. They are just THINGS, THINGS which thrive on scuppering other THINGS. THINGS that long for chaos, THINGS that drive you crazy. Viruses want to bother us. They're bullying, troubling, thuggish THINGS, and their whole THING is to get us down. They are very determined little THINGS, and the THING they want to cause is disaster.

So THINGS, it must be said, are against us. But it's mutual. Humans are hostile to many THINGS, maybe even *most* THINGS. Our relationship with THINGS is discordant and haphazard. Our attitude to THINGS is intrinsically ungrateful. We're forever choosing this or that THING to be for, and ruling out a whole lot of other THINGS we don't like. Yes, we say, to sunsets; no to hurricanes. Yes to sunsets improved by hurricanes... Yes to cars, no to roadside weeds. Yes to pandas, no to mole rats. Yes to kittens, no to wolves. We've said no to wild THINGS till we're blue in the face – when *we're* the worst of them.

Are birds so bothered by THINGS? They don't seem it. When you're building a nest, stuff must go wrong all the time. No nails or glue available. If you drop THINGS, they land miles below. Twigs must sometimes refuse to be woven the way the bird planned. A cotton wool ball the bird carefully carried to the nest is whipped away by a breeze, an egg falls out, a cuckoo or cowbird baby is born. It's a tricky THING, at the best of times, bringing up young THINGS at a great height on a platter of grass in the crook of a tree branch. But birds soldier on, patient and forgiving towards THINGS. Birds just let THINGS be. Birds get on with THINGS. They don't dwell on THINGS, the usurpations committed against them by THINGS they can't control. Or I sure hope they don't, because it blights your life, having this THING about THINGS.

We bear grudges, and often take it out on THINGS: slamming doors, violently thwacking THINGS with a stick. We waste THINGS like water and plastic bags, and use up too much loo paper, just for the hell of it. We are mean to THINGS. We hurl THINGS when petulant, we squeeze THINGS harder than strictly necessary, we ignore THINGS, junk THINGS, fly-tip THINGS, refuse to clean or tend THINGS or repair THINGS or recycle THINGS. We disobey the clear will of THINGS. And with 3-D printers we even downgrade the organic integrity and traditional nature of THINGS!

All these little comebacks we have against THINGS – our revenge against THINGS for all the THINGS THINGS have dumped on us. And then, in the calm after the storm, we try to make THINGS up with THINGS, try to get along with THINGS again for a while if we can. But the rapprochement soon dissolves into some sort of sordid kind of stand-off THING, with each side doing little THINGS that eat away at bonhomie. THINGS have their own agenda, and it's rarely our kind of THING.

THINGS probably started it, but we've carried on the fight: polluting THINGS, shooting THINGS, refuting the basic nature of THINGS. Lugging poor old boulders all the way to Stonehenge… We're always wrecking THINGS, exploiting THINGS, belittling THINGS, dislodging THINGS, exacerbating THINGS, delaying THINGS, extinguishing THINGS. We are so ignorant of THINGS. We just don't fit into the grand scheme of THINGS, and THINGS know it.

So it's understandable THINGS might take the hump.

THE UNDERGROUND
BUNKER

On January 6, 2021, the USA imploded. Trump's rabid followers, a lynch mob sporting Nazi slogans, nooses, Confederate
flags, guns, spears, explosives, and plastic zip-tie handcuffs,
attempted a coup. They rioted, assaulted police and reporters,
broke into offices and scared politicians half to death with the
threat of assassination. They erected a gallows outside the Capitol
building, sprayed gas at opponents, and desecrated a public
landmark with pee and shit and blood and spit. They killed one
police officer by beating him with flags and a fire extinguisher.
With others they took selfies. To cap it off, they participated in
a superspreader event during a pandemic. All because their
leader, a delusional mass murderer (who let thousands die from
Covid-19) wanted to continue illegally as president. And what a
president. The MAGA hats and Trump brand are now signs of
infamy. But those treasonous bums had the time of their lives!

Still, Americans blather on about how great America is. They'll salute their ruined nation till the whole place is awash in corpses, swastikas, and radioactive waste. They'll be clinging to the roof, barbecuing steaks up there, talking god and cars and UFOs and QVC jewellery lines until there's nothing left alive but a few DDT-resistant bugs.

Americans are acutely unaware of the past and the future. Also, the present. History is infinitely malleable for them. So is reality. Are they just undereducated, indoctrinated, chronically indifferent, hypnotised, or too damn busy makin' a buck? Consumed by consumerism, they wallow in army fatigues and self-regard, coveting the next dynamite Apple doodad or an AK-47, plasma screen and some Nikes. They have worried everybody and *ruined the earth*, all so that they can prance around, effect insouciance, drink beer, watch football, guzzle Sloppy Joes and Oreos, wear pro-Auschwitz sweatshirts, make pipe bombs, absorb incessant rock music, object to positive discrimination and the public display of female nipples, wonder whether the mailman has shut the mailbox properly, and choose a new euphemism for excretion yearly.

Dazed and furious, they wrestle with a world of distraction and fake facts, their minds ravaged by malign corporations, PFAs, PCBs, dioxins, cocaine, caffeine, and any creed on offer – American god-lust is among the many forms of self-sabotage that gave us this male-order muppet show in the first place. The US is now the worst Boy Scout jamboree or jerk circle in history.

MEN HAVE GLORIED IN THIS. Men with their hierarchies, their secret handshakes, gang warfare, ownership, privilege, entitlement, and extra helpings of roasted meat. They glory in death, and the chastening of women. Women are exhausted!

Fifty women a day are shot dead in America by so-called part-ners. How can women thrive in such a society?

Not just in America but elsewhere too. What have we got to show for putting up with thousands of years of male rule? On the plus side, Roman mosaics, rocking chairs, and the Chrysler Building. On the minus? Fascism, poverty, carnage, the Large Hadron Collider, tornadoes, tirades, Boogaloo Bois, Three Percenters, Elk reunions, the internal combustion engine, and oceanic levels of plastic.

Patriarchy has trashed the place. Wildlife is pretty much finished now. Walruses drop helplessly to their deaths from iceless rocks. Soon there will be no orangutans. There are now *queues* on Mount Everest. Next thing you know, everyone will insist on riding the Loch Ness monster.

Men have wrecked everything of beauty and cultivated every-thing putrid on the face of the earth. Not *all* men, of course, yeah, yeah, yeah, I know I'm generalising. But it's for a good cause: sanity. Men have a death wish. Violence is not just a drug for them, it's a security blanket.

Men learn early on to mock the female body. Girls are mocked for *menstruating*, which they cannot help, and breastfeeding too is frowned on by many a well-fed man. Everything women do is taboo. Anything men can do, women can do better – but somehow, everything women do, men say *stinks*.

Men couldn't oppress us any better if they really did get together in an underground bunker and plan the whole thing out. Which I half-suspect they do. How else would they all come up with the same identical thoughts on high heels, inflatable sex dolls, and the pay gap? (Though Trump's taste in femininity always seemed a little corny.) In the absence of anything positive to contribute, male power rests on a tiresome combination of

volition, violation, and volatility, along with booze, biz, bellow-
ing, and boring the pants off you.

The United States of America has now reached a whole new
level of patriarchal absurdity. You mean they massacred the
Indians, enslaved the Africans, cut down all the trees, poisoned
all the rivers, and extinguished or imprisoned all the animals
for THIS, this hellhole of bombast and hamburgers and opioid
addictions and cardboard-box houses and pretend ideas? You
mean they used up all the oxygen on 4th of July firecrackers
and forcing kids to pledge allegiance to the flag every goddam
day, drank Coke till they choked, spat tobaccy till they puked,
fought cancer (but only for people with lots of money), nestled
in Nestlés, slurped slurpees, burped burpees, handed on herpes,
Tasered the wayward, jailed the frail and tortured about a million
billion chickens (then fried and ate them), just so people can
drive around and shoot each other and create GoFundMe sites
to pay the hospital bills?

Make America abate again.

TRAPPED
FAMILY FINGERS

When exactly did America give up on love of life? Are they the victims of some awful *experiment*? You almost expect the gigantic bald pate of a mad scientist to appear over the Rockies one day, checking on his helpless specimens, all stuck in their hamster wheels of indefatigable optimism.

Flummoxed by fake facts, Fox News, and the phoniest guy they could find for prez,[1] Americans rely on Disney for comfort, along with vaccine evasion, Vietnam bombing-raid re-enactments, and whole days devoted to YouTube gaming videos. For the few remaining centrists and liberals, there's a self-congratulatory movie now and then about Ruth Bader Ginsberg or the more prominent heroes of the Underground Railway — while everyone

---

[1] NB. This essay was originally written when the Trump regime was in full flower. Luckily, everything's fine now — apart from the lingering presence of guns, war, racism, sexism, fundamentalism, terrorism, democracy defilers, tornadoes, hurricanes, wildfires, forever chemicals, universal cerebral underdevelopment, and wretched TV series.

unites to await execution at church, the mall, the gas station, convenience store, or parking lot. Or, of course, at home.

When they tire of killing *each other*, they slaughter some Iraqis or Afghans. No wonder extraterrestrials haven't the stomach to visit the US any more.

Every child in America has now been drilled in how to climb under the desk when a shooting spree is going on. The latest idea for preventing school shootings is to train *dogs* to confront the gunman. The dog is supposed to make his or her way to the homicidal maniac, mid-rampage, and wrestle him to the ground. These are kamikaze K-9s, doomed from the start to be shot along with everybody else.

Or here's a good move: arm the teachers! This they've done and, as a result, children are now exposed to guns, gun threats, and gun accidents at school every day. Parents dutifully join campaigns for 'gun sense' while their kids have nightmares and panic attacks and try to run faster than a speeding bullet.

For extra protection (at least for the upper torso, if shot from the rear), your child can wear a bulletproof backpack:

THREE TIMES THE FUN!

BOOK BAG, LUNCH PAIL AND LIFE-PRESERVER, ALL IN ONE!

Or just pretend Sandy Hook and Parkland never actually happened. Then you don't have to doubt the American system at all.

Never in all this is the possibility of simply *banning all firearms* raised. Forget gun *control*, gun reform, gun sense. How about NO GUNS? There is no unassailable right to own a gun or be shot. Babies are not yet born armed.

But not to worry. Rube Goldberg's here and he's just turned on his think-faucet! Republican senator (A), on way to receive large cash donation (B) from NRA (C), slips on wife's alligator handbag (D), out of which flies cockatoo (E). While senator is out cold, bird spies blueberry muffin (F) on desk (G) and settles in for big breakfast. Scrabbling about, cockatoo upsets bottle of Kahlúa (H). Bottle spills, bird steps in puddle (I), and produces sloppy but legally 'X' on important document banning guns (J), which only required one more signature. Before senator (A) even regains consciousness, total ban on private ownership of guns in America has been instituted, and all guns (K) have been thrown into either Pacific (L) or Atlantic (M). Random child (N) is now able to attend random elementary school (O) in safety and learn alphabet (PQRSTUVWXYZ).

～

Freud said America was a big mistake, presumably because it was a place where the id was allowed to run rampant, from Columbus's outrages on through all the land-grabbing, massacres, slavery, greed, insensibility, Oscars ceremonies, and ice-cream sundaes. As Randy Newman put it:

> *Hide your wives and daughters, hide your groceries too,*
> *Great nations of Europe coming through.*

By the mid-1800s, the experiment had undeniably turned sour. Fanny Trollope was *appalled* by Americans, finding them not only cheerless, misogynistic, murderous, and unneighbourly, but so vulgar! They ate with their knives and she couldn't believe how much they spat. The only time they seemed to brighten up a bit was on Independence Day, or at least the *men* did ('women have but little to do with the pageantry, the splendour, or the gaiety of the day', she wrote):

> On the 4th of July the hearts of the people seem to awaken from a three hundred and sixty-four days' sleep; they appear high-spirited, gay, animated, social, generous, or at least liberal in expense; and would they but refrain from spitting on that hallowed day, I should say, that on the 4th of July, at least, they appeared to be an amiable people.[2]

Some spit, others are spat out. The go-getters go get, the rest get got. The US has long teetered on the verge of 'mobology' and is subject to the 'mobocratic spirit', as Lincoln put it.[3] America was always each man for himself, with a big investment in law-lessness. Abolition's still a work in progress.

Carlos Fuentes identified the 'anguish' intrinsic to the American way of life, the anguish of 'doing, getting things done, making it'. Failure, pretty much guaranteed in such a merci-less set-up, goes unloved. That's why Trump, one of the biggest failures of all time, tried to transmogrify his every fiasco into a supposed success.

Fear of failure drives Americans into uptight bubbles of ME, only relieved by the collective daily orgasm of consumerism. Shopping is proof of citizenship. This provides Americans with the *us* in US. (Undocumented 'Dreamers' just dream of buying stuff.)

Even the *niceness* of many Americans seems suspect, because you never know if it's just a precautionary kindness. What if all

---

2 *Domestic Manners of the Americans* (1832).
3 See Philip Gourevitch's remarkably prescient 'Abraham Lincoln Warned Us About Donald Trump' (*New Yorker*, March 15, 2016).

those chocolate chip cookies suburbanites offer each other are really SOS messages? Chip-on-the-shoulder cookies. What if American politeness stems from Stockholm syndrome: three hundred and thirty million captives, all being pleasant just to avoid being shot in the head?

'When terror descends' (as Edward Albee put it[4]), these helpless, cornered creatures easily swap democratic rights for gossip, lobbyists, peer pressure, Super PACs, gerrymandering, voting restrictions, that antique gewgaw the Electoral College, pre-election dismantling of the postal service and post-election dismantling of the vote count.

'I just want to find eleven thousand, seven hundred and eighty votes,' Trump boldly declared, two whole months after losing the 2020 election. Sad.

But there's an upside! All this powerlessness leaves more time for the ME stuff. Because, you know, there's like all this pop music to consider, cosmetics to apply, and foreign slave-labour jeans to purchase, so many beggars to belittle, billionaires to emulate, elders to ignore, and theories about the purifying effects of mindfulness or green tea to propound. So much purifying and putrefying going on. It's really very absorbing! Never mind what the police are doing just down the street to Black men who don't mow their lawns in the right direction.

∼

Patriotism, charity, and heroism have been replaced by one essential task: the moral duty to go to the gym. If only these people, so enamoured of exercise, would use their muscles for

4 *A Delicate Balance* (1966).

the greater good. Instead of scolding the sedentary, these eager beavers could help out a bit more. Plant trees, lug food to the poor, scoop plastic crap out of rivers, fortify cities against flood and fire. Forfeit their cars and run (if run they must) to work. *March* too, on Washington – and *stay there*, dammit, till all the nitwits depart.

But so much time is devoted to the self, there's none left for society. Americans count the calories, not the capitalists. Meanwhile, the ICE man cometh: Guantanamo wasn't enough for everybody, the Republicans now want *immigrants* incarcerated for life too.

At the sight of child prisons and all the screaming, self-described liberals cry out, 'This is not America, this is not who we are!' But it so clearly *is* who they are. Or what they became while drinking the requisite amount of sody-pop and gawping at their smartphones.

'Why can't I have anything just for me? Is that so selfish?'
'Actually, that's the definition of selfish.'[5]

Americans hardly think beyond the bounds of family. Thanksgiving and Xmas won out against the Covid scare. These are people drowning in family life, family fun, family businesses, family secrets, Family Paks of aspirin and burger buns, Family Size gallons of milk, beer, and OJ (the drink, not the felon), family cars big enough to shove trucks off the road, family pets, family movies, family vacations, family affiliations, family trees, family traits, family genetic diseases, family men, family matters, family favourites, family hunting trips, family vendettas, family murder–suicides.

---

5 A George and Jerry debate in *Seinfeld*.

Americans are trapped in trapped families – and the hills are alive with the sound of gunfire.

You'd think *mothers* might be awarded high status in such a family-oriented set-up, but women in America have no status at all. As we saw with the Brett Kavanaugh hearings, not only are some men called *Brett*, but American women never get a word in edgewise.

Professor Christine Blasey Ford offered the nation a lesson on integrity. It didn't take.[6] The US is really just one big internment camp for women, where they are gagged, cuffed, and detained, awaiting a (fair) hearing.

> *Kavanaugh good for Amer-ic-a.*
> *Women not heard in Amer-ic-a.*
> *Women not safe in Amer-ic-a.*
> *Women just slaves in Amer-ic-a,*
> *free to wait tables and shine shoes.*

America's no place for women. It's so depraved that a woman can't even work a shit job in a shirt store without having to choose one day if she wants to be sodomised or shot in the head. Whatever happened to compassion, or a sense of community? But *that* word is awkwardly close in sound to *communism*, which frightens Americans more than death itself. (And the intensity of that fear frightens everybody else!) All their help-thy-neighbour impulses quail at the mere hint of communism. Socialism too – though paradoxically they don't

---

6 She bravely testified to a Senate Judiciary Committee that Kavanaugh had sexually assaulted her when they were teenagers, and laughed at her. But Kavanaugh still won his place on the Supreme Court (though by just two votes, the smallest margin for a hundred and forty years).

mind socialist programmes like Medicare, state education, the fire service, search and rescue volunteers, national parks, and transport infrastructure. The latest nickname for protestors against climate change, people hoping to *preserve future life on earth*, is 'watermelons': green on the outside and red on the inside.

Nah, we don't want life on earth. Leave us alone.

∽

Just as Brexit is the apotheosis of age-old British self-hatred, America embarked in 2016 on its own act of self-immolation. The nation mulled things over, Stan Laurel-style, blinked its eyes, scratched its head, and decided to go for *more* corporate criminality, *more* exploitation, *more* inequity, *more* poverty, *more* sickness, *more* indifference, *more* conformism, *more* conservativism, *more* waste, *more* plastic, *more* violence. And astonishing levels of sadness. The mad scientist must be about to begin his vivisection. Obediently, the lab rats lounge before their big TV screens, munching apocalypse stew – dumbo gumbo – and railing against RINOs,[7] every house blazing with the sinister blue light of unreason.

What riches there once were, what beauties! Raindrops on roses and crop tops on cuties. Now it's just tear gas and water hoses, and Mexican children tied up with strings. *These* are a few of their favourite things. Quarry every mountain, wreck every stream.

---

7 Republican In Name Only: hated by fascist, white-supremacist Republicans; liked by over-optimistic Democrats.

Sure thing, ma'am, long as it's worth frackin'.

But wait! It's Rube again to the rescue! New president (A) clips previous president (B) on ass (C) with old boot (D) and makes reparations to Native Americans (E), African Americans (F), women (G), alligators (H), and oil-caked sea otters (I). He then reinstates US Constitution (J), establishes universal Medicare (K), defunds the police (L), distributes basic living wage to every citizen (M), bans guns (N), saves whales (O), opens all borders (P), dismantles nuclear plants (Q), discards nuclear weapons and weapons deals (R), undermines power of big tech companies (S), establishes Green New Deal (T), and erases student debt (U). What's more, he delightedly extracts Trump's back taxes (V) and catapults resultant dough into education (W), so scariest nation on earth (X) won't fall into drainage canal (Y) of vapidity (Z) ever again.

Wow, what a relief. I thought we were all goners.[8]

---

8 There may be hope yet for America: on January 15, 2021, the NRA went bankrupt.

THREE STRIKES[1]

I made nice.[2] It didn't work. Women are still oppressed, men still running the show, still running around raping, killing, and maiming women – raping, killing, and maiming *children* too

---

1 In baseball, three strikes and you're out. Out on your ass. The expression therefore has some bearing on the trajectory of this essay, my pitch being that men are swinging wild. The original idea for the piece came from reading Virginia Woolf's *Three Guineas* (Hogarth Press, 1938), to which I was alerted by a friend, the novelist Peter Burnett. But I couldn't refer to three letters, as Woolf does, since nobody *writes* letters any more; and I chose strikes to replace her guineas, since nobody knows what a *guinea* is any more either. Woolf is being ironic about money anyway. With eccentric thoroughness and wit, her essay considers various good causes to which three guineas could usefully be put: the prevention of war; rebuilding a women's college in Cambridge; or finding employment for women in the professions. She finally offers a guinea to each cause, this being all an 'educated gentleman's daughter' could afford. Woolf's three guineas thus become, in their paltriness, both a significant gesture in the right direction and an emblem of women's second-class status. The limitations imposed on women are the real subject of Woolf's essay. But there's something tenacious about the image of those three guineas. They can't be denied. It may be hard now to imagine behaving patronisingly towards Virginia Woolf – aren't we all supposed to be *afraid* of her? – but she was well aware of what both the 'intelligentsia and ignorantsia' put women through. In *Three Guineas*, she concludes that women are outsiders – but in a good way. So are the many footnotes in Woolf's essay. Footnotes are the outsiders within a text, and make obliging underdogs in an essay on female subordination.

2 As George Bernard Shaw said on his second arrival in America, 'I told you what to do and you haven't done it.' I put my solution to male violence towards women in the most palatable form I could think up, a romcom novel called *Mimi* (Bloomsbury, 2013) about a rich guy in New York who sees the light and becomes a champion of women. *Mimi*'s solution to the downward spiral of patriarchal insanity is: *hand over the money*. Transfer all wealth into female control. Not *half* of it, not fifty-two per cent either — ALL THE MONEY. Given the mean little way late capitalism works, a steady wholesale redistribution of wealth seems the simplest method of ensuring women get respected more, and raped and murdered less (femicidal violence being a five-thousand-year-old fad, embedded in women's low social status). Until we can return to a matriarchal form of socialism (or 'commonism', as another friend, the novelist John Aberdein, puts it) in which money has *no place*, we must in the short term put women in possession of serious wealth. This pro-female asset-reset, which in *Mimi* I dubbed the Odalisque Revolution, would be a peaceful form of male revolt — yes, it's *men* who will need to do the work here, if they want to join the Odalisque Revolution (women are automatic members). It could be progressed on an *individual* basis, in private, by any right-thinking man who's tired of hearing about women being deprived, denied, doubted, despised, derided, deluded, defamed, ignored, cheated, exploited, blamed, vilified, cajoled, threatened, violated, killed, overworked, messed with, ordered about, and ground into the dirt. It's not just about *money* though. The ultimate aim of the Odalisque Revolution is to start a new matriarchal era. Such a revolution seems to me a safe, sensible, efficient, and really rather innocuous solution to the devastation caused by male mayhem and wars and depredations of the environment. And yet hardly any men to my knowledge have followed my very clear instructions on how they can relinquish the unfair advantages so many claim to abhor. Only one person (the intrepid writer and critic Anthony Rudolf) has actually asked to have his Odalisque Revolution Mea Culpa Declaration stamped. The detachable certificate, once stamped, ensures membership of the Odalisque Revolution. It can be found at the back of any copy of *Mimi*, and all the contrite philogynist has to do is sign it and give everything he's got (or *most* of it: he can keep some petty cash, for pizza's sake) to a woman, or women, of his choice. The Declaration (see footnote 59), written in plain English, invites the signatory to admit that male property and power are ill-gotten gains, the products of men's ancient and misguided terrorist campaign aimed at the usurpation of women and, to redress this, the signatory pledges to hand over all his assets to women. Strangely enough, few besides my dear husband Todd McEwen have shown any sign of wholly acquiescing to my demands. No one has even asked me to defend my position. Instead, the usual male silence: the unspoken policy seems to be to deprive my wealth-redistribution idea of oxygen by not responding to it at all. Even some *female* reviewers surfaced to voice doubts, flinging around examples of unworthy female leaders such as Margaret Thatcher, Elizabeth I, and Lady Macbeth. Now, wait a minute! You're

41

(another way of attacking women). They're still waging war, spraying every living thing with pesticide, distributing micro-particles of plastic everywhere, eating huge pizzas,[3] and charging an awful lot for a haircut, highlights, and blow-dry. Or how about this new craze for murder-suicide, that apparently culpritless crime, whereby the execution of women and children is often transposed by police and news commentators into a mere 'tragic family incident'? Patriarchy did this.

These people hate us! These people are trying to kill us! I don't know why we're all so goddam *nice* about it, but nothing is ever done about the way men carry on. Instead, it's feminism that is for ever in retreat.

~ Pause to do the dishes. ~

When any outwardly positive step forward is made, say, toward equal pay or maternity/paternity benefits, something even worse always seems to happen to women on some other level. Patriarchal retribution is swift: for all the mild protests from women against the male bias of Oscar awards, topless photos on

---

telling me you object to joining other women in acquiring all the world's wealth, and thereby subverting the murderous course men have taken during the last five thousand years, because there have existed a few women, real or fictional, with anti-humanitarian sympathies? In other words, because a few creepy women rose to high office *within patriarchy*, you think women as a whole should never be given an even break. But can anyone truly believe women would make as big a mess of power as men have? Come on, who are you trying to kid? Enough of this. We've run out of *time* for ambivalence, hair-splitting, and coquettish self-abnegation. What we need NOW is a radical transfer of power.

3 Why *do* men like pizza so much? I think it's because the boxes look official, as if the guy has just come from some important meeting and he's got really important documents in there or something – whereas really, it's just a big hot slippery blop of dough covered with pepperoni, chicken tikka, and pineapple chunks.

Page 3 of the *Sun*, or nude photos of Jennifer Lawrence shared online, we now have a global rape crisis, with an accompanying boom in female self-harm. Sure, women are permitted to work (great, thanks a lot), and a few hard-working campaigners have managed to deny Britons some *Sun* fun (the exhausting Page 3 campaign eventually paid off, I believe). Women can now sue hackers over invasions of privacy, or even get a prettified portrait of a female novelist on to the ten-pound note (a lot of good this does Jane Austen, who really could have *used* ten quid). But then our punishment comes, in the form of some new, unexpected backlash, along with a multitude of malignant jibes and threats from Twitter trolls. As the much-hounded Mary Beard said in a lecture about men's determined efforts to ignore everything women have ever said over the last few thousand years, women 'pay a very high price for being heard'.[4]

The sources of female oppression are many. Self-inflicted saturation in porn has produced a whole generation of young men who apparently cherish, or at least accept, absurd ideas of pneumatic female torsos,[5] and male rights of domination.[6]

---

4 In the *London Review of Books* (March 20, 2014), Beard described what it's like never to feel you and your kind are properly represented in the culture. NB. America broke away from England for just such a reason: 'No taxation without representation.' Just saying.

5 Our inane absorption in youth and beauty has disenfranchised most of the female population. Never have the ideals of female appearance been so standardised: the self-airbrushed face, the nail polish, the long straight flowing hair, tight-ass jeans, and sassy short top are now compulsory, while the wrinkled, dimpled, frazzled, ex-Pilateased bodies of older women have become the world's last great expanse of uncharted territory.

6 One all too literal 'backlash' against female emancipation is the new allegiance to anal sex, amusingly aired in the aptly named movie *Damsels in Distress* (directed by Whit Stillman, 2012). Men's unwillingness to concern themselves with the clitoris and vagina is a new blight on our age. Corrective instructions on rimming, offered to 'analphobes', suggest any lack of interest in anal sex is inexcusable (adopting a

clockwise direction is highly recommended). And women's increasing dissatisfaction with their own genitals has kept pace with male oversights – when they're done waxing, plucking, and scenting themselves, the next step is creating the 'designer vagina'. Labiaplasty is a growing business, along with a belief that 'abnormal labia tissue' is a widespread problem. The fault is not with pudenda but with misogynists. By the sound of things, men seem to have become worse lovers than ever before (and, given the history of the missionary position, that's saying something!), piteously unaware of their true and ancient role, that of *pleasing women*. Women are not here for male pleasure – men exist to give *women* pleasure. Biology supports this, as Catherine Blackledge points out in *Raising the Skirt/The Story of V* (Orion, 2003/2020), a book highly recommended for anyone interested in female sexuality, or even those who are not – in fact it should be compulsory reading for anyone who purchases a 'sex arse', a rubber sex toy comprising a select portion of amputated torso. ('I voted Leave – but now my sex arses are stuck at customs!', cried a disappointed UK patriot experiencing Brexit shambles – *Sunday Sport Online*, January 2, 2021.) Penis construction throughout nature is oriented more toward *female* pleasure than male, since the quality of the *female* orgasm determines the male's reproductive influence. Even female fruit flies insist on orgasms! (They also have the most elaborate, spiralling vaginas. Who knew?) The vagina, Blackledge reports, is not a passive canal for receiving sperm and issuing offspring. It is an assessment station, selecting and expelling sperm – and one major deciding factor for sperm admission is the female orgasm. People wrongly believe the penis performs 'as a sperm placement tool, a rigid insertion device shaped to shoot sperm quickly and efficiently into the correct orifice'. This fails to explain the varied size and shape of penises, as well as the time and care males of many species take to prepare the female for sperm insertion, throughout courtship and mating behaviour (there's some kind of marsupial mouse that spends *five hours* thrusting – marsupials really know how to live). Despite the standard use of rape in war to secure a genetic advantage over enemies, female pleasure is, if not essential, highly recommended in the passing-on of men's genes. Rape doesn't pay, in the long run, says Blackledge. 'The important question for a male is not: Can I place my sperm inside this female? Rather the crucial question is: Can I persuade the female to use my sperm instead of some other male's?… The primary role of the penis is none other than to act as an internal courting device – shaped to provide the vagina with the best possible and reproductively successful stimulation.' The male orgasm is biologically necessary too, sure, but that's less of an influence on penis construction. All of which reminds me of a limerick:

> There was a young fellow named Prost
> Who tried to make love to a ghost.
> At the height of its spasm,
> The poor ectoplasm
> Cried 'Ah, now I feel it – almost!'

The consequences of recessions[7] are felt most by those already disadvantaged, particularly *women* – in the UK, through cuts to the NHS, rape crisis centres, women's refuges, Legal Aid and other vital services.

Police behaviour toward female victims of crime degrades us all,[8] as does the revealing take on women shown by most news organisations.[9] Despite the notorious 2012 gang rape and

---

7 Disasters caused by men, but borne by women. Men run the banks and building societies after all, the property market, the stock market, industries, Parliament, Congress, the internet, monopolies and corporations and all the other enterprises that keep economic downturns happening. Not only do men create these financial collapses, but they unfairly tend to withstand them better too. *Because they have all the dough!* We are all being crushed beneath their insane belief in growth and progress and maniacal lust for despoiling things. Since the Romans, patriarchy has proved to be the guarantee of a society doomed to implode. (But at least the Romans, before Christianity spoiled everything, had a lot of wine and sex. And chariots. It wasn't all bad.)

8 The accusation of *institutional sexism* must be added to the British police force's proven institutional racism. Only eight out of forty-three police forces in England and Wales respond adequately to instances of domestic violence, according to the 2014 estimate of their *own body*, Her Majesty's Inspectorate of Constabulary. Police behaviour towards purported victims ranges from unforthcoming to shameful. West Midlands police officers called one female victim a 'fucking slag'. 'He threatened to cut my womb out with a pizza cutter. When I spoke to the police, they just laughed,' recalled another abuse victim (*Progress Report on the Police Response to Domestic Abuse*, HMICFRS, November 2017). Predictably, domestic abuse committed by cops is widely covered up by their colleagues, and the victims and witnesses are arrested instead and intimidated. With domestic abuse now on the rise, due to Covid lockdowns, Greater Manchester Police have admitted that they ignored or *erased* seventy per cent of reports of domestic abuse reported during 2020. Not very nice of them. (NB. The police did nothing for years about reports of Jimmy Savile's crimes either. Wherever women are ill-treated, children will be too.)

9 When Phil Spector died in prison in January 2021, the death was largely reported as that of a big important gifted and famous music producer whose life happened to end in 'tragedy'. The tragedy was of his own making. He abused women all his life; he waved guns at people, particularly women who rejected him. He bullied his ex-wife, on pain of death, into accepting an old car and minimal alimony as part of the divorce settlement. And, finally, he shot an actress in the head, whom he'd just met, and then claimed she'd committed suicide in his house. Yet *Rolling Stone*

evisceration in India, quickly followed by a similar event in South Africa and the Steubenville case in Ohio – in which an unconscious sixteen-year-old girl was carried naked from party to party to be sexually preyed upon and peed upon (which some of the participants claimed to have believed was consensual sex) – doubt only seems to grow about what constitutes rape or whether it even exists.[10] The worse men behave, the more their crimes seem to get downgraded to minor misdemeanours. This perversity is necessary to maintain the perverse status quo, the mass delusion which holds that men are okay and women, in so many ways, aren't. How about the sex-slave trade, or the treatment of women and children in detention centres?[11] Such cruelties are not confined to the USA. The English family court system vilifies mothers, shrouds its own proceedings in secrecy, and often issues irrefutable orders, handing children over to

---

treated this recurrent behaviour as incidental, tweeting about 'Phil Spector, the famed "Wall of Sound" producer… whose legacy was marred by a murder conviction' (January 17, 2021). Some legacy.

10 Nitpicking about rape definitions is so wearying, especially when you need all your strength for fleeing rapists. Whoopi Goldberg added to the confusion in 2009 by declaring that Roman Polanski isn't guilty of 'rape-rape'. What, just 'rape' then? Trump seems even more oblivious to all the rape allegations against him, an invincibility that must give new vigour to millions of fellow rapists. In England and Wales, few sexual molestation victims expect any solution from the criminal justice system: rape prosecutions are at an all-time low. Recent figures suggest that only 1.5% of rape claims result in any charge at all (see Julie Bindel, *The Guardian*, January 24, 2021). That's a lot of consequence-free violation going on.

11 Intolerance toward immigrants and foreigners closely resembles the negative male treatment of women and animals and other groups that are left out of calculations except as objects of blame. According to Teresa Hayter, *all* border controls are counterproductive and unjust: 'Their object… is to exclude poor people, and especially black people. The denial of free movement across frontiers gives rise to some of the worst and most vicious abuses of human rights, and provides perhaps the most fertile terrain for the agitation of the far right.' From *Open Borders: The Case Against Immigration Controls* (Pluto, 2004).

unpredictable fathers.[12] The aim of all this is to traumatise women and subdue them. This is traditionally accomplished both through rape, but also through the labyrinthine workings of the justice system.

~ A pause to hang up washing. ~

This is a society that's failing women big time![13] A society in which men keep women in a simmering state of *terror*.[14]

---

12 The UN's Special Rapporteur Rashida Manjoo's statement on sexism in the UK (April 15, 2014) dropped like cool rain on a desert, and even managed to affront the *Mail* (or was it the *male*?). Amongst many acute observations about Britain's non-compliance with the Convention on the Elimination of All Forms of Discrimination against Women (to which, incidentally, the British government had already signed up), Manjoo raised concerns about the machinations of the family court system. She said it ignores 'children and women's safety when hearing applications for contact with estranged parents. ... Lawyers and magistrates have limited understanding of the dynamics of domestic abuse and force children and their mothers to enter into unsafe and inappropriate contact arrangements, which are mostly unsupervised. Shared parenting is increasingly seen as an appropriate, default position without the adequate consideration of the best interests of the child principle and ignoring the history of family abuse...' The best interests of children rarely seem much of a priority in Britain.

13 We think we treat women *okay*? Then why do they feel they have to wear six-inch heels to work? And that their only purpose in life is to sculpt their eyebrows, give good head, and learn to lap-dance? Why does Melania Trump have to organise those 'fucking' Christmas decorations? Why do some women feel they need plastic surgery in order to look like a Barbie doll? This form of self-mutilation is becoming the *norm*, and is now being sought at an earlier and earlier age (if you can afford it, that is; and, if you can't, you may well be fired, demoted, dumped, snubbed, harassed, or shunned). Discrimination on the basis of how you look has long been an effective repressive weapon against women. Every cosmetic procedure performed puts pressure on *other* women to submit to body enhancements. When the fact is, even if you miraculously manage to be whatever's considered beautiful in your era (the ideal is always changing), you'll *still* be stuck in a sexist society that hates you! Women's self-esteem is in *tatters*, smothered under a deluge of photoshopped celebs, the grotesqueries of the designer fashion parade, the realities of poverty, and a gushing river of porn and big-eyed, big-breasted superwoman types in films and cartoon animation, all geared

47

to prioritise male pleasure and artificial styles of female body. As a result of all this, there are girls on anorexic websites who *congratulate* each other for dying. Why is female life held so cheap? The young opera star Tara Erraught was described in the *Independent* as 'dumpy', by *The Times* as 'unbelievable, unsightly and unappealing', and by the *Financial Times* as a 'chubby bundle of puppy fat'. Ever considered focusing on the woman's *singing* ability? (See Susannah Clapp's great retort to these insults – *Observer*, May 25, 2014.) Why does female fat worry people so? Because it implies a freedom from constraint, a vice, a failure, a lack of decorum. But what heaven does slimness win you? As the novelist Elfriede Jelinek wrote, 'The slim ones, who have worked hard for their figure... climb up the mountains every day or climb the walls at home...' (*Greed*, 2006.) One defect of Susie Orbach's book *Fat is a Feminist Issue*, by the way, is that it offers diet advice: this seriously undermines the radicalism of its empowerment message. It's *fattism* that is the real feminist issue. Meanwhile, in 'The Obesity Era' (*Aeon* magazine, June 19, 2013), David Berreby suggests that being overweight may actually be caused by global *pollution* rather than shameful lapses in self-control. This places guilt back where it belongs, in patriarchy's lap, as the instrument of all this environmental destruction.

14 No one has so far questioned my use of the term 'terrorism' to describe all the really lousy stuff men do to women en masse as a gender – perhaps because the word is so self-evidently spot on. But it all depends on who's doing the defining. Men, the current controllers of language, seem reluctant to admit that all men in a patriarchal society are terrorists. Instead, they trip all over themselves trying to keep the definition of terrorism fuzzy. White American males rarely commit it, apparently. The police and media hesitate to name their barbaric acts 'terrorism'. Nobody even bothered to keep an eye on Anthony Quinn Warner, though his girlfriend warned police a year before his 2020 suicide bombing in Nashville that he was making bombs and plotting some destructive act. Instead, CNN reported after the incident, 'The man who detonated an RV bomb in downtown Nashville early Christmas morning was a loner with no significant criminal record and as yet no signs of a political ideology' (Eric Levenson, CNN, December 30, 2020). Here's what his ideology was: patriarchy. The US Department of Defense's dictionary of military terms defines terrorism thus: 'The calculated use of unlawful violence to inculcate fear; intended to coerce or to intimidate governments or societies in pursuit of goals that are generally political, religious, or ideological.' According to FBI special agent Doug Korneski, terrorism is 'the use of force or violence in the furtherance of a political or social ideology' (Levi Ismail, News Channel 5, Nashville, December 28, 2020). What is *male oppression* if not a coercive campaign that depends on propaganda, blackmail, and the calculated use of unlawful violence to further its ideology? Through violence, or the threat of it, patriarchal terrorists indoctrinate, malign, silence, subdue, guilt-trip, and murder. Misogyny can be *lethal*. Just because this particular terror agenda has been in play for thousands of years doesn't absolve it of criminality. ALL VIOLENCE IS A TERRORIST ACT. Unless committed in self-defence or to protect life. All violence

Yet how we bustle around, trying to *look* good, *be* good, restrain ourselves in all kinds of ways, contort ourselves and our own needs and beliefs in order to work within this set-up men have moulded to suit themselves, in which women are for ever doomed to be the losers, hangers-on, the butt of jokes – funny nutso floozies that we are.[15] The first suggestions the internet offers when you google the word 'women' are: women's clothing, women's shoes, women's dresses, women's trainers. Have we no other interests,[16] no other qualities, no depths? We certainly aren't supposed to.

---

aids patriarchy. And all violence is a hate crime against women, since *women* gave birth to the people being murdered or mutilated, and *women* are usually the ones left to tend the wounded and mourn the dead. Family annihilation, that euphemistic term for massacring the people closest to you whenever you feel like it, is a good example. Killing your family out of pique is not just an unfortunate offshoot of domestic disharmony, as in 'it takes two to tango' and other victim-blaming guff. It is an intimidating display of male power, a misogynistically motivated hate crime, an act of patriarchal terror. The truth will out. The *New York Times* has now introduced the clumsy term 'male supremacy terrorism' (March 17, 2021) and even Wikipedia has a page on 'misogynistic terrorism'.

15 In *The Kreutzer Sonata* (1889), Tolstoy's narrator Pozdnyshev complains bitterly that the whole world is *pro-woman* – essentially because women are big shoppers. There are all these products, he says, aimed at women: they may be hopeless at making money, but they sure can spend it. This picture of male victimhood is neatly contradicted later on though, when it emerges that Pozdnyshev has murdered his own wife in a jealous rage. Mrs Pozdnyshev has had her last spree.

16 Women have to be kept on their toes, worrying and consuming, to keep late capitalism afloat. So-called fashion is a way of corralling women's psyches into acquiescence, even to the point of personal financial ruin. There is continual pressure on women to throw out one set of clothes in favour of another, at great cost to the environment, or risk humiliation. Marks and Spencer released a self-satisfied ad campaign in 2014 called 'Leading Ladies', which involved well-known, middle-aged women like Emma Thompson, Annie Lennox and others, swanning about distractedly in M & S gear (*S & M* gear would have been more appropriate, given the slavish predicament of the fashion-conscious). Somehow, these celebs all seemed a lot more celebratable *before* they were roped into modelling those dopey black-and-white duds. Again, a vague 'advance' made by women (in this case, excelling as actors, artists, movers and shakers) is somehow twisted into its opposite,

49

~ Pause to mess — in vain — with my hair. ~

The media's harsh treatment of Mary Beard, Greta Thunberg, and others shows the high level of hostility directed at women whose achievements single them out from the crowd.[17] This,

---

in the service of commerce. So, instead of offering middle-aged women reason to feel somewhat proud of themselves for what they've accomplished through talent and hard work, M & S's 'Leading Ladies' adverts implied that whatever lofty things these high-flyers may once have had on their minds, what they *really* care about is towing the line in very conventional clothing. For marketers, respected public figures become just more gals on which to hang products. The hidden purpose of it all is to reduce any supposed independence in women to signs of compliance — in this case, compliance with the dictates of fashion. These 'Leading Ladies' weren't leading the way anywhere but the fitting room.

17 Gallantry is dead. In 2013, the BBC sports reporter John Inverdale felt his negative estimation of tennis star Marion Bartoli's feminine allure was required by the nation the day she won Wimbledon. Not very sporting of him. Here is Inverdale on the champion, in her moment of glory: 'I just wonder if her dad did say to her when she was twelve, thirteen, fourteen maybe, "Listen, you are never going to be, you know, a looker. You are never going to be somebody like a Sharapova, you're never going to be five foot eleven, you're never going to be somebody with long legs, so you have to compensate for that. You are going to have to be the most dogged, determined fighter that anyone has ever seen on the tennis court if you are going to make it," and she kind of is.' The message was clear: get back to your mirrors, girls. Because, however good you may be at something else, your only real function in life is to be found attractive by jerks like Inverdale. The BBC received seven hundred complaints about Inverdale's comments (and even a reprimand from Maria Miller, the Tory Secretary of State for Culture, Media and Sport — though what induced compassion in a Tory, I do not know). Inverdale apologised later for his obnoxiousness, and the BBC issued this grudging statement: 'We accept that this remark was insensitive and for that we apologise.' But what good was that? The damage was already done to the psyches of women and girls across the country! The last resort of the cornered misogynist is often hypochondria. Behind every male fist, every declaration of male displeasure, there is always the threat of self-pity. Inverdale claimed illness had interfered with his judgement. Harvey Weinstein succumbed to back trouble (after all his lively antics in hotel rooms too!), travelling to his 2020 trial in a wheelchair. And in June 2014, Michael Fabricant used novocaine confusion (he'd just been to the dentist) as his excuse for his threatening tweet about Yasmin Alibhai-Brown: 'I could never appear on a discussion prog with [her.] I would either end up with a brain haemorrhage or by punching her in the throat.'

after the centuries it took us to get the vote![18] This, after people have *died* to protect abortion rights. After governments across the globe have finally recognised the injustice of female circumcision.[19] What did all these struggles mean?

Not a goddam thing. The violence continues, as does the inequality, and the pay gap,[20] and the production of about a million Hollywood movies that don't pass the Bechdel test.[21] When we peer up through that glass ceiling what we see are the soles of a lot of big dirty men's shoes still galumphing around.[22]

18 While American women got there a little earlier, British women were only fully entitled to vote, at age 21, in 1928 – just ten years before the publication of Woolf's *Three Guineas*. (Women couldn't vote in Switzerland and Bangladesh until 1971, and in Iraq had to wait until 1980.)

19 Although the only FGM conviction to succeed in Britain so far occurred in 2019; three other cases ended in acquittal. Meanwhile, a form of *virtual* FGM goes on at Evangelical 'Purity balls' (now spreading to Europe from America). At these cheery gatherings, the sacrificial victim, a teenage girl, dressed all in white, pledges her virginity to her father (eeeugh!), in his capacity as 'High Priest in the home'. I am not kidding. Proffering her virginity to her dad for safekeeping, the girl effectively neuters herself (temporarily) for the sake, she's led to believe, of *another* bloke: her future husband. Not even kissing is allowed in this community before marriage. Weirdly borrowing abortion lingo, the doting fathers, or 'High Priests', claim to be protecting their daughters' 'choice'. What a tangle of hypocrisy, when in fact *any* worship of virginity is a denial of female sexuality and bad news for women.

20 The Equal Pay Act was passed in Britain in 1970, yet it is still unlikely that any woman now working in the UK will see pay equality in her lifetime. The pay gap for British women is currently twenty per cent below men.

21 The modest requirements of the Bechdel test: (1) A movie has to have at least two women in it, (2) who talk to each other, about (3) something besides a man (bechdeltest.com).

22 Despite seven women successfully suing the *New York Times* in 1974 for sex discrimination in hiring, pay, and promotion, the paper has never outgrown its male bias. In 2014 the paper fired its first female executive editor, Jill Abramson. Curiously enough, *Le Monde* fired *its* first female editor Natalie Nougayrède the same week. What unanimity! Female CEOs are more likely to be fired, and fired sooner, than their male counterparts (Edward Helmore, *Observer*, May 17, 2014): male bosses are given more time to settle in, while employers, colleagues, and junior staff are swift to grow impatient with female bosses. Female politicians are

Even Mary-Kay Wilmers defended her *London Review of Books'* lack of articles by and about women, on the grounds that men make more pitches and women have a lot of housework to be getting on with.[23]

~ Pause to scrub the stovetop. ~

---

treated with greater scorn too. The murderous venom directed at Hillary Clinton, Theresa May, Nicola Sturgeon, Angela Merkel, Diane Abbott, Caroline Lucas, Jill Stein, Elizabeth Warren, Kamala Harris, Kshama Sawant and Alexandra Ocasio-Cortez are examples of this intolerant attitude towards women who wield some power in the public sphere. But the harshest treatment of all has been reserved for Greta Thunberg, a *child* who dared to tell it like it is. The fact that she speaks out infuriates a lot of men. One attack came in the form of a cartoon depicting her being raped. Thunberg's unflinching response was: 'This shows we're winning.' (If only.)

23 In an interview conducted by *PN Review* (2001), Wilmers said: 'I think women find it difficult to do their jobs, look after their children, cook dinner and write pieces. They just can't get it all done. And men can. Because they have fewer, quite different responsibilities. And they're not so newly arrived in the country. They're not so frightened of asserting themselves. And they're not so anxious to please. They're going to write their pieces and to hell with the rest. And I don't think women think that way.' ('Why the LRB Should Stop Cooking Up Excuses Over Lack of Women Reviewers', *Guardian*, February 25, 2014.) As of 2015, eighty-two per cent of the articles in the *LRB* since its inception were by men (although it did also publish Mary Beard's lecture on the silencing of women, mentioned earlier). In *Three Guineas*, Woolf warns against such gender segregation, citing the enthusiasm that Hitler and Mussolini shared for the practice. Dictators thrive on division. So, ideally, men should perhaps review women's books and vice versa – if that is the only way to prevent women from being ghettoised. The *LRB*'s track record seems fairly progressive though, compared to the androcentric nonsense churned out by most Saturday newspaper supplements, in which all women seem able to do is eat noodles and model clothing. Most of the columnists, the gardening experts, chefs, travel advisors, car reviewers and other know-it-alls, are men! The self-aggrandisement of male chefs is particularly irksome – women cooked breakfast, lunch and dinner for thousands of years without any fandango. The worst thing about men taking over the cooking of fancy food in restaurants is that every dish now arrives covered in ejaculate, all drizzle, foam, and schmeers. Wait till male gardeners figure out how to make *plants* produce froth – just think of all the prizes, TV spots, and Chelsea Flower Show medals they'll hand themselves.

So, let's admit it. We've tried equality and it *doesn't work*. Equality within a society concocted *by and for* men? Phooey! What we need, what the victims of war and war crimes[24] need, what the terrorised need, what the isolated, and frequently annihilated, radioactive nuclear family needs, what all the tormented, neglected, broken, hunted, infected, injected, vivisected, near-extinct, factory-farmed, in fact *all animals*, need, what every living thing threatened by disease, disrespect, disheartenment, 'detainment', and disenfranchisement, needs, is *female supremacy*.

We can do this the easy way or the hard way.[25]

Veneration is the only *logical* response to the mammalian female. Motherhood is a necessity of survival, and I suspect its offshoot, matriarchy, was a blast. People had it good there for a couple of hundred thousand years, living in stable societies with a three-hour working day and plenty of leisure time. Free to think and act without fear, women invented agriculture, pottery, weaving, music, metallurgy, medicine, painting, sculpture, and astronomy.[26] Then men loused everything up,

---

24 Why *distinguish* between war and war crimes? They are the same thing. WWI veteran Harry Patch said war is 'nothing better than legalised mass murder' (*The Last Fighting Tommy*, 2008). For Thomas Bernhard, war was just further proof of male iniquity: 'War is the poetry of men, by which they seek to gain attention and relief throughout their lives... They [flee] from one misery to another, one misfortune to another, each one deeper and more inescapable than the last, and they always [make] sure of taking someone else with them' (*Gathering Evidence*, 1985).

25 See Valerie Solanas's *S.C.U.M. Manifesto* (1967) for a semi-jokey description of the hard way: S.C.U.M. stands for the Society for Cutting Up Men. But I myself advocate only peaceful methods of revolution. Violence is so *male*. The hell with it.

26 Elizabeth Gould Davis' *The First Sex* (Penguin, 1972) pieces prehistory together through a study of myth, anthropology, and archaeology, to find a predominantly matriarchal past that lasted tens of thousands of years. This, and Marija Gimbutas' archaeological work on widespread and highly creative prehistoric matriarchal cultures in Europe, give one hope that patriarchy was never inevitable, having lasted a fraction of the time that matriarchies persisted; and that there are better, fairer, and much more artistic ways to organise ourselves, i.e. with the focus on WOMEN.

driven by fear and envy (of women) and an unquenchable longing for organised sports.

~ Pause to darn a cheap sock. ~

Vengefully appropriating or negating all the progress women had made, men turned on nature and ecology, and instituted a bunch of lousy ideas: anti-female religions and taboos, hatred of the body, particularly female bodies, a paternalistic approach to medicine, and new pastimes like imperialism, slavery, witch hunts, war, rape, drug cartels, vampires, football, darts, and Monopoly. The Industrial Revolution was no picnic either – in the last few centuries, men have managed to ruin the environment for everyone, leaving us with toxic waste, climate havoc, smog, sweatshops, suicidal workers, traumatised pigs, chickens, elephants, and whales, crazed gunmen, conspiracy theories, and a zillion T-shirts that say things. Men have disastrously assumed the right to mess with the air, the water, the land, and our heads.

They are so *messy*, always wrecking things. They like to desecrate things for desecration's sake. They obliterate beavers so they can build their own dams! They shot dead the first grey wolf seen in Iowa for almost a hundred years, despite its being a 'protected' species (protected how?). They shoot lions and tigers, kick chickens.[27] Men denude the land. Men insist, INSIST, on killing everything and using up every last natural resource. War is the quickest way they've found to ruin the environment,[28] but they make peacetime pretty damaging too:

27 'Workers at a KFC and McDonald's supplier punch, kick and stamp on the heads of live poultry,' reported the *Daily Mirror* (August 12, 2016).
28 Warring is a classic male trait (noisily mimicked by the ridiculous male absorption in team sports). As Virginia Woolf writes in *Three Guineas*, directly addressing men:

do we really need cars and planes and air conditioning and six trillion throwaway pens and toothbrushes? Does every last thing have to be made out of plastic or concrete? Must the world be so UGLY? San Francisco Bay is still full of mercury from mining processes used during the Gold Rush, and will remain poisoned for the next ten thousand years.[29] The psychotic male addiction to nuclear power, concentration camps, waterboarding, fracking, lead, WMDs, surveillance, TV, computers, the internet, reversing-vehicle beeps, and bling, will finally destroy us all.

Why should we let those Bushes (Sr. and Jr.) get away with it? Or that warmonger Tony Blair? Why'd we let *Hitler* get away with it? Why should we let Jimmy Savile and Rolf Harris and Mel Gibson and Charlie Sheen and Ike Turner and Richard Nixon and Donald Trump get away with it, or Charles Manson, Fred West, Peter Sutcliffe, Thomas Hamilton, John Worboys, and Adam Lanza? Or Ronald Lee Haskell, who executed four children and their parents in their home in Texas, just to get back at his ex-wife. Or Stephen Paddock, the creep who shot sixty people from a hotel in Las Vegas. Not to mention IS and Boko Haram and the *Charlie Hebdo* slaughterers. Why should we let ANY of them get away with it? We can't. *Basta.*[30] And yes,

---

'Obviously there is for you some glory, some necessity, some satisfaction in fighting which [women] have never felt or enjoyed.' But she admits that Wilfred Owen did not share in this penchant. And then there's Harry Patch. And Thomas Bernhard. And all the men who refused to fight in the Vietnam War. And the Veterans for Peace who did fight but now declare: 'We, having dutifully served our nation, do hereby affirm *our greater responsibility* to serve the cause of world peace.' (My italics.) So, the male taste for war *can* apparently be overcome.

29 In fact, it's getting worse, not better! (Douglas Main, *Live Science*, October 29, 2013.)
30 I do, *sort* of, realise that *most* men are not directly, personally responsible for all the atrocities committed by other men; nor do women have an absolute monopoly on humanity and compassion. Women can be fucking mean! It's the kind of animal humans are. We're carnivorous, conflicted, spiteful (and not reacting well, I suspect,

I know, I know, women sometimes go along with some of this stuff. They shoot guns, they work for oil companies, they join extreme right-wing groups, they chit-chat in the Quiet Coach.[31] But that is no excuse for indulging *men* further! Never mind what women may or may not do — it's time for *men* to be mensches.[32]

In *Three Guineas* Virginia Woolf raises the possibility that patriarchy's based on 'unconscious sex-taboos'. But I think, if we're going to get fancy about it, what we're dealing with is more like mass hallucination. Among many other forms of wilful intoxication (are most adult men ever really sober?), men are drunk on self-delusion. Look at Trump: everything he says is the exact opposite of the truth. Merely by dint of their psychoses, their ridiculous conundrums (what pickles men get themselves into!), and their upper-body strength, men have forced women to engage with all sorts of surreal ideas about how life should be lived, from flirtations with nuclear warhead gaps to who gets to decide if women have babies, or how you make an omelette.[33] They have fashioned a whole theatre of the absurd, an extensive literature of alienation, and a great many cowboy movies.

But when do *women* get to dream? How about allowing *us* a

---

to our acute population density). But whatever the failings of women may be, this is no reason for men to be excused from the chore of making amends. The endgame we currently face was inflicted on us entirely by *patriarchy* and its unwillingness to live in harmony with nature — deforestation contributed to the Ebola outbreak, for example: 'Experts say the rising number of emerging viruses is largely the result of ecological destruction and wildlife trade… It doesn't have to be this way.' ('Hunting for "Disease X"', CNN, December 24, 2020.) Clearly, as a 'class' (Woolf's term), men have bungled things badly and *they should set them right*.

31 Still, ninety-eight per cent of mass shootings have been carried out by men.

32 (Or 'menschen'?) In *The Apartment* (directed by Billy Wilder, 1960), C. C. Baxter is urged by his doctor neighbour to give up his presumed playboy lifestyle (that has supposedly led to Fran Kubelik's suicide attempt) and behave like 'a mensch — a human being'. Baxter eventually takes the advice.

33 A word to the wise: very hot pan. There's nothing gentle about making an omelette.

few whims too once in a while? How about indulging women in the belief that we *look* okay, or that we're okay mothers and daughters, or that we have okay things to say or do? Women need time and space in which to develop our own particular brand of insouciance, our own hobbies, our own (pro-female) philosophies, our own sexuality,[34] our own *play*, goddammit!

> *~ A pause to contemplate a Handkerchief Tree*
> *in the Botanical Gardens. ~*

Once again, it's up to women to sort this out, I'm afraid. We shouldn't *have* to, we've all worked hard enough already for little if any recompense! But we will have to exert ourselves further, it seems.[35] So here's my *new* solution (since men wouldn't play the game and just hand over their money to women like I told them to): my advice is for women to go on strike, on a private, public, local, national, and international level.[36] Women make

---

34 The multiple orgasm is, after all, one of nature's triumphs. Why waste it? In a woman-centred society, there would be no further denial of the female orgasm.

35 Get things off to a merry start by painting easily erected corrections for street names – Solanas Street, Wollstonecraft Mews, Austen Avenue, etc. – a la artist Jackie Parry's feminised map of Glasgow, 'Women in the City' (2012); Sara Sheridan's book, *Where are the Women?* (2019), which tackles the whole of Scotland; and Rebecca Solnit's Revised New York subway map (*New Yorker*, October 11, 2016). Metaphysical acts of insubordination.

36 Barcelona has had Vaga de Totes feminist protest strikes, and there have been repeated strikes by women in Poland over new abortion restrictions: in October 2020, women put on a powerful mid-Covid strike, in protest against PiS party's draconian anti-abortion laws, the Catholic church, climate change, and patriarchy in general. Good posters, such as 'The government is not a pregnancy, it can be removed.' That's the kind of thing we need now, *globally*, from small, spontaneous gatherings, to bigger shindigs like the 2017 Women's March on Washington, V-Day, and the corresponding One Billion Rising demos initiated by V (Eve Ensler, author of *The Vagina Monologues*). The latter events are an annual public acknowledgement that one third of all women and girls alive today will be raped or beaten – one billion.

up the majority of the world's population so, united, we cannot fail to have an effect. And there will be jolly times later as we begin to enjoy the fruits of our efforts (see footnote 34).

There are three forms of strike I'd recommend: a housework strike, a labour strike, and a sex strike. I can't wait for the first two. While the ultimate object of all three of them is female supremacy, each strike would also focus on adjunct causes in women's interest: (1) environmental and animal justice; (2) peace and nuclear disarmament; and (3) you guessed it, female appropriation of wealth, property and power.[37] These issues are all bound together in the struggle to preserve nature, civilisation, and the better aspects of human culture.

~ Pause to help husband locate his manbag. ~

STRIKE ONE: NURTURE NATURE.

DESTRUCTION OF NATURE IS AN ATTACK ON WOMEN.

The housework strike will be held in protest against climate change and the destruction of the environment. Its slogan? 'How

---

The aim: 'We rise to show we are determined to create a new kind of consciousness – one where violence will be resisted until it is unthinkable.' It's a *celebration* of women, in fact, and its slogan is 'Strike, Rise, and Dance'.

37 When I first published this essay in *The Baffler* in 2015, I said the precise details of the three strikes were still negotiable and invited readers to help set up strikes, hone the bargaining points, and criticise or make amendments to the adjunct causes I propose – via the email address odalisquerevolution@gmail.com, which I'd just created for the purpose. Then I promptly forgot all about that email account, *for five years*, and missed an approving email from V, amongst others. Some organiser, huh? (I check it more often now.)

dare you?' – after Greta Thunberg's admirable 2019 outburst at the UN.[38] Human attitudes toward animals and the natural world are closely linked to male attitudes towards women: they spring from the same classist anti-nature, anti-life assumption that the world is there to be shaped, ravaged, and ruined by people (men), and all living things are there for the taking. (They want to ravage Mars next.) Animals, it has long been assumed, can be exploited, experimented on, and forced to yield their every atom in service to human greed. Ever since Christianity attested our superiority over other creatures, and scientists started up with their loose talk of 'tool-users' and 'higher' and 'lower' mammals, and philosophers chimed in with their capricious notions of instinct vs individuality, animals have been looked on as a commercial resource rather than as living beings in their own right, entitled to a place in the world. Prehistoric matriarchal cultures never conceived of working against nature in this illogical way – they left nature intact for *us* to destroy.

So, Strike One is a protest against patriarchy's rejection of nature, and the way our narcissistic homocentricism leads to the direct abuse of animals, and the indirect abuse of people. Current farming methods are not only cruel to animals but dangerous to humans, causing pollution, contamination, and superbugs.[39] Habitat assimilation and destruction are our legacy.

---

38 Thunberg delivered a searing speech at the United Nations' Climate Action Summit in New York: 'People are suffering. People are dying. Entire ecosystems are collapsing. We are in the beginning of a mass extinction. And all you can talk about is the money, and fairy tales of eternal economic growth. How dare you?' On a similar theme, Fran Lebowitz's advice to the young is to start searching for water, as 'apparently, we drank it all' ('Hall of Records', *Pretend It's a City*, directed by Martin Scorsese, 2021).
39 It's now thought that Covid-19 is unlikely to have begun with a pangolin in a Chinese wet market; it was probably transmitted from bats or farm animals. But

For the sake of the survival not just of the natural world but of human civilisation, women need to withhold their home- and family-oriented labour: stop mothering,[40] stop daughtering, stop wifeing. Stop cooking, stop cleaning, stop taking out the trash, stop making the beds and ordering the pizzas, stop shopping, stop lugging home bottles of booze for men to guzzle, stop gardening, stop ironing, stop washing your hair, stop putting on make-up (in fact, boycott the whole beauty cult[41]). Stop

---

the disruption of animal habitats, with resulting contact between species which formerly kept their distance from each other, is probably ultimately to blame. The emergence of bird flu, SARS, swine flu, variant CJD, and now Covid, seems related to the increasing interest in bushmeat, and farming malpractice. See Ravi Letzter in *Live Science* (May 28, 2020), and the *Meat Atlas* (Heinrich Böll Foundation/Friends of the Earth Europe, 2014), for evidence of the destructiveness of industrial livestock farming. Rachel Carson's outcry, *Silent Spring* (1962), remains a vital treatment of the subject. See also Nikolaus Geyrhalter's documentary, *Our Daily Bread* (2006), a quietly tragic examination of intensive farming. *Fishing* is now intensive too, causing unchecked pain, collateral death and damage, depletion of stocks, and waste, as well as incendiary disputes about international quotas. Whales, dolphins, and sharks are caught 'accidentally' in fishing nets, leading to *repeated trauma* and often death, even when attempts are made to free them. Seals, blamed for eating the fish, are summarily culled, or mangled in the rudders of boats. Meanwhile, the Great Barrier Reef has lost half its corals since 1995 (BBC News, October 14, 2020) and is unlikely to survive. Due to climate change, pollution, and acidification, the oceans are on track for *mass extinctions* this century (Carl Zimmer, *New York Times*, January 15, 2015). WHAT THE HELL IS WRONG WITH US? ARE WE ALL TOO BUSY GETTING LAID TO GET MAD?

40 This strike is not meant as an attack on motherhood. *Men* thrive on deriding women's bodies and reproductive power. This is why childcare, maternity services, abortion, family planning, schools, and parental access arrangements after divorce are so critical in any battle for equality. Laura Mulvey's film *Riddles of the Sphinx* (1977) movingly pinpoints the political implications of childcare provision. When women have control of their bodies and society within matriarchy, these practical matters will be resolved with ease. In the meantime, carry on shielding your children from danger, providing them with food, clothing, and shelter and helping them with their homework, even during the housework strike – since life, health, comfort, security, education, and freedom of movement are all principles we want to protect.

41 We are now totally obsessed with looks in the West. But the meagre delights of our enthrallment to beauty come at the cost of so much *misery*: anorexia, bulimia,

vacuuming and sterilising the cat litter tray and alphabetising the books and paying the bills. Stop making all those pots of tea and coffee for everybody and smelling the milk to see if it's gone off. Stop embroidering cushion covers. Stop doing all the things you do to try to make a nice home for your family. Stop taking care of things. Just stop it! (This won't be easy for most women. It goes against the grain, since women *invented* the home, in prehistory. Women invented *cosiness*. They needed to establish some domestic tranquillity, comfort and security, in which to raise children.)[42]

~ Another pause, this time to buy artichokes at the local corner shop. ~

OCD, suicide, the mercenary diet industry and plastic surgery, injuries from tumbling over in high heels, melanomas from sunbathing and tanning salons, the horrors of unaesthetic gymwear, and jokey vocab for aspects of bodies deemed physically deficient according to current mores (turkey neck, muffin top, cankles, bingo wings, spare tyres, love handles, hairanoia, etc.). People are so corrupted by the modern beauty fixation, they now have 'body dysmorphia', not just about their own but *other people's bodies*: we are troubled by *all* bodies and can see only the supposed faults. It's distracting, depressing, and a great waste of energy. There is no real *need* to assess people's appearance all the time. It's rude, it's abusive, it's dull, it's objectifying. It is thus part of a *spectrum of abuse* that ranges from anti-female biases at school and work, to their full-blown expression in rape and murder. Supreme beauty is a rarity, after all, an aberration. We don't all have to aspire to it. Our concepts of beauty are also based on class and race privilege (we're all aware of 'the skin of the rich'). Audre Lorde talked about 'the racist distortions of beauty', and the way 'gorgeous', even in the gay community, used to be decided by white male standards, 'that world that defined us as doubly nothing because we were black and because we were women.' (Speech at UCLA, early 1990s, https://youtu.be/OUXjoBVQkpw.) Therefore, in conjunction with Strike One, I would like to instigate a *one-year moratorium* on any mention of people's appearance. We can chat about other topics for a change. The beauteous would survive a slight lessening of attention and acclaim, and the rest of us could *relax*. After a year of such abstinence I bet we'll be cured of the habit, and be much better conversationalists.

42 For further elucidation of 'cosiness', see *Mimi*, ibid., pp. 24, 32—33, 37, 64, 66, 72, 82, 171, 195, 198—199, 223, 226, 230—231, 234, 273, 294. (Courtesy of the *Mimi* Index, kindly compiled by the writer Suzy Romer, odalisquerevolutionblog, 2014.)

You can put it all on hold for *a little while*, surely, in aid of animals and the natural world. And what a lot of *thinking* time you'll gain.

This strike will only be called off when governments agree to end animal cruelty, fracking, factory farming, and the intensive use of herbicides, pesticides, and chemical fertilisers. Also, pollution, cars, and dependence on oil and freight containerisation – one of the dirtiest practices ever invented. The money saved from all these shady enterprises can be reallocated to childcare provisions. Ten per cent of every man's net income will be devoted to animal welfare and the restoration of natural habitats and rainforests. Or he can remotely adopt a manatee or blue-footed booby. Six-pack plastic rings, in which turtles get tangled, will be banned. And every man must agree to clean the toilet weekly without being asked; and to confine the foaming, schmeering, and drizzling from now on to the boudoir.

STRIKE TWO: NO MORE WAR WORK.

BOMBS, WAR, CIVILIAN DEATH, NUCLEAR WASTE, AND OTHER FORMS OF MANMADE RADIATION ARE ALL ATTACKS ON WOMEN.

In contradiction of all the romanticised notions of women's contributions to war efforts that we've been asked to stomach lately – all those TV shows about selfless or bitchy WWI nurses, all the photographs of women slaving away in munitions factories, all those movies about the bored-to-tears girl patriots of Bletchley Park – war is no place for women. It's very unlikely that this form of mass homicide was ever women's favoured plan of action (though I admit Hitler had to be stopped some-how). People were apparently killing each other with arrows thirty thousand years ago, which is not nice, but outright group warfare only developed on a grand scale once metal weaponry was developed by Bronze Age societies, which were patriarchal.

War is not in women's interest: it is more likely to cur-tail women's freedoms, as well as distress, subdue, frighten, deprive, and annihilate women, through rape, the murder of offspring, and the degradation of animals and the environment. So, at the very least, women shouldn't have to *help* wars happen. They shouldn't have to fight wars themselves, or proudly wel-come home the injured and the dead. They shouldn't have to provide the world with new men and women to be killed and traumatised in combat.[43] War devalues birth: that is its primary function. War is the rejection, *demolition* of women.[44]

~ Short pause to check online for poorly paid part-time jobs. ~

This strike, Strike Two, involves withholding women's labour in the workforce.[45] But the intentions behind the labour strike are

---

43 This motive for refusing to bear children is mentioned in the two women's letters to the *Telegraph* in 1937, quoted by Woolf in *Three Guineas*.

44 Even military marching is bad for women. Female soldiers have been injured by the requirements of marching, which are always oriented to the length of the *male* leg. For further glimpses into such marching, including a chicken who's pretty good at it, see marchright.com. (And for the best *male* marching, see the bersaglieri of the Italian Army's infantry corps. They run while blowing trumpets.)

45 Of the three strikes I propose, I think the labour strike should be the easiest to pull off – because, after all, who wants to WORK? Why should women, any more than *bees*, participate in the Protestant work ethic devised by *men*? A Day Without A Woman was a labour strike staged in the US in 2017 in protest against Trump. If the necessity of women's labour must be proven in such an elementary way as this, then, so be it. Even a strike of a *day* – by all women everywhere – will bring things to a complete standstill. (Theme song: 'Union Maid', Woody Guthrie, 1940.)

to organise not just an objection to war but also to the threats to future life on earth posed by nuclear energy, nuclear waste, nuclear bombs, and nuclear fallout – and the suffering that they have already caused, through genocide, environmental contamination, and cancer clusters.[46] Men insist that these forces are manageable and necessary. They are not manageable and not necessary. A fifth of all environmental deterioration is caused by militarism. Some of the guys involved in creating the atom bomb had the grace to apologise for unleashing this cataclysmic weapon on us all, and ruining all hope for the future, merely to assuage their own scientific curiosity. But such apologies are of no value. Who in hell cares about Robert Oppenheimer's *conscience*, one of the tiniest things in the universe? Nuclear bombs should never ever have been produced.

Employers will soon 'come to the table' (such a nice domestic phrase!) and meet our terms – and think of the delicious sensation meanwhile of a day/week/month/year off. Overwork silences dissent and original thought and destroys physical, emotional and community health. That's what capitalists like so much about it. WoHeLo, short for Work–Health–Love, the motto (and greeting) of the youth group formerly known as the Campfire Girls (now just Camp Fire), may be a slightly better exhortation than 'eat–pray–love' but it makes no real sense, since most work is *anathema* to health and love. Anyway, women have already worked hard enough. For centuries! It's time they took things easy. This is why the Odalisque Revolution will entail much relaxation in cosy surroundings, eating bonbons and wearing harem pants. 46 The Hanford nuclear site in Washington State contains some of the most radioactive material in the world (fifty-six million gallons of it). Closed for the last thirty years, the containment and clean-up effort costs two billion dollars a year. So many people who live near the site get thyroid cancer that the now familiar throat scar caused by thyroidectomy surgery is known as the 'Hanford necklace'. See also *Hiroshima* by John Hersey (1946); John Adams' 2005 opera *Doctor Atomic*; Michael Frayn's play *Copenhagen* (1998); and Stanley Kubrick's film *Dr Strangelove* (1964), which offers a superbly ironic takedown of the hypocrisy and folly of war-mongering in the age of the atom bomb. In one scene, US forces fight *each other* beneath a billboard asserting their official ethos: PEACE IS OUR PROFESSION. You can't stifle American bullshit.

Women *told* men this,[47] but war is a way of silencing women –
through injury, exile, deracination, disease, starvation, disrespect, poverty, violation, bereavement, sexual frustration, grief,
and, to top it off, a tsunami of male punditry, speculation, and
decision-making. Twentieth-century warfare's innovation was
to direct itself *specifically* at women and children.[48] Militarists
claim a million compensatory motives, but as long as women
remain the targets and victims of war, warfare remains just one
more outlet for misogyny.

Even after *a million* Britons protested against the Iraq War,
Tony Blair went on lying his head off to Parliament and everyone
else, insisting the Iraq war was called for. He got away with it,
and has played his desired role in genocide. He's still running
around pontificating on any old thing. One of the demands of
Strike Two will be that Bush and Blair and their confederates
are tried by the Russell International War Crimes Tribunal, and
that, from now on, the only legitimate military body worldwide
will be a carefully monitored UN peace force.

A gentler aim of Strike Two is to give anyone who feels his
or her life has been blighted by war in any way, a year's paid

---

47 See Terre Nash's documentary *If You Love This Planet* (1982), in which the great
anti-nuclear activist Helen Caldicott challenges the official (male) acceptance of
nuclear energy and weaponry. Consider too the noble life's work of Sisters Ardeth
Platte and Carol Gilbert, in collaboration with the Plowshares movement.

48 Bombs and the suppression of women are passionate bedfellows. Sven Lindqvist's
A History of Bombing (1999) charts men's deep love of the bomb, and their willingness
to make civilians (women, children, and the elderly) its primary targets. Drone
strikes are a variation on this sport. And now we have Boko Haram's massacre
of 2,000 civilians in Baga, Nigeria in January 2015, the use of girls and boys as
suicide bombers, the abduction of schoolchildren, and their reliance on rape, forced
marriage, and slavery to achieve their ends. See Abdulwahab Abdulah and Uduma
Kalu in *Vanguard*, May 5, 2014, and Helon Habila's short personal account, *The Chibok
Girls: the Boko Haram Kidnappings and Islamic Militancy in Nigeria* (Penguin, 2017).

vacation in order to reflect and recuperate (people providing essential services, such as farming and medical care, might have to stagger their years off). This rehabilitation drive should include not only all military personnel, their families, and their victims, but anyone who's *paid their taxes* (so, count Trump out, sorry), since they too have incurred harm: it is traumatic to have your hard-earned money squandered on illegal wars.

~ Pause to sort through a pile of receipts for tax purposes. ~

There is the necessity of ending non-military uses of nuclear energy too. When exploiting atomic energy for 'peaceful' purposes of this kind, men seem prepared to take incredible risks with our lives and the lives of all future entities on earth. This alone is proof that men are unfit, as a sex, to rule. The deluge of nuclear mess they created may never be adequately contained.[49] Nuclear power stations fail horrifically, leaving us with Chernobyl in 1986 and Fukushima in 2011, both theoretically

---

49 Are we really depending on *men* to safely dispose of nuclear waste? What, are we CRAZY? These are people who have to be reminded to take the dog out. You have to beg them to change a poopy diaper. These are people who use every pot and pan and mixing machine in the house when they cook anything and leave the dirty dishes lying all around the kitchen after. 'They don't cover anything when they put it in the fridge,' Harriet the waitress remarks in *Sleepless in Seattle* (1993). 'Hot Particles' and 'buckyballs' from the meltdown at Fukushima will drift around the planet to *the end of time*. The Fukushima plant poured so much contaminated water into the sea, tuna on the West coast of America now have higher levels of radioactive contamination than ever before. (See Makiko Inoue and Mike Ives, *New York Times*, September 30, 2020, on the plan for compensation.) For the latest on nuclear waste containment strategies – strategies that probably won't ultimately work – see Michael Madsen's devastating documentary about Finland's radioactive waste repository, *Into Eternity* (2010). NB. *No* level of radiation is safe – yet, as far as I know, no government has abandoned the idea of nuclear power. Who gave men permission to risk life on earth for all eternity? Did we have a global referendum on this, I can't remember.

preventable. Where will the next mega-contamination incident occur? Hanford? Then there's the risk that vandals, terrorists, saboteurs or mischief-makers could sneak into nuclear power stations and make off with plutonium – this sort of scenario is never mentioned by politicians when they're foisting another bunch of reactors on us and boasting about how cheap and safe nuclear energy is. It's only cheap if *life* is.

This strike will end when all men quit their jobs in the military sector (female soldiers can remain, *if they must*, but only to work for the UN's peace force) and the government agrees to an immediate end to all peaceful *and* military uses of nuclear power. As punishment for belonging to the gender that thought this stuff up, men must also contribute means-tested contributions (ten per cent of their annual net income) to Women's Action for New Directions (WAND), the Campaign Against the Arms Trade (CAAT), Global Zero, Greenpeace, Friends of the Earth, Ribbon International, ICAN or CND. And good luck to us all.

STRIKE THREE: MONEY FOR SEX.

POVERTY IS AN ATTACK ON WOMEN.

As Woolf points out in *Three Guineas*, women have laboured in the home unpaid for thousands of years, while watching all the family money go on *men's* education, *men's* leisure pursuits, men's beer, men's cigars, and men's pizzas.[50] This debt

---

50 'The daughters of educated men received an unpaid-for education at the hands of poverty, chastity, derision and freedom from unreal loyalties... an unpaid-for education that fitted them for unpaid-for professions' (*Three Guineas*).

has now come due. The money must be reallocated to *women*, and until that is done, straight women should withhold themselves sexually from men.[51] *Men* go on sex strike all the time! They are always withholding sex and making excuses for their unpredictable genitalia, in order to keep women docile. Women knock themselves out trying to be attractive, and men still can't get it up. Well, two can play at that game. Now it's our turn! We mustn't be vindictive though. The pure-minded aim of our sex strike is simply to gain the assets, privileges, and power to which all women are entitled. Yes, I'm talking about *the money*. Since men wouldn't give it up voluntarily, they must be forced to hand it over in return for sex. They're always accusing us of being sluts anyway, so this equation should be easy to grasp: no money, no sex.[52]

The first known fictional try-out of this sexual blackmail strategy occurs in Aristophanes' *Lysistrata*. There, a female sexual resistance strategy is employed to bring the Peloponnesian war to an end.[53] Lysistrata enlists the help of both allied and enemy women, on the grounds that the war is bad for *all women*. They

51 It would be important to enlist the support of sex workers in this endeavour, since men (*currently*) have the means to buy their way out of sexual privation (something the cheerless incel brigade seems to have forgotten). Financial compensation will be offered to female sex workers, to sustain them through the furlough.

52 Lesbians need not participate in the sex strike. They can protest in other ways. Gay sex in both genders will be unaffected by the strike, or might even enjoy a surge in popularity. That is beyond our control. The purpose of the strike is *male* sexual privation, not female. Heterosexual women will have to handle this temporary hiatus as best they can. I don't agree with Andrea Dworkin, though, that feminism precludes heterosexuality. It's time for the fun to *begin*, not end! (Once all three strikes have succeeded.)

53 *Lysistrata*, by Aristophanes (411 BCE), in *Lysistrata and other Plays*, translated by Alan H. Sommerstein (2002). Spike Lee's fun and moving musical *Chi-Raq* (2015), transposing *Lysistrata* to the gun-filled streets of the South side of Chicago, bolsters the idea that sex can still be used as a major bargaining tool today.

hole up in the Acropolis together and it's really quite a successful sit-in. Some of the women do try to tiptoe off, offering feeble excuses like: 'the moths will be eating my sheepskin,' 'I turn out to be pregnant and have to go home to have the baby – I'll be back tomorrow,' and 'the owls [fellow inhabitants of the Acropolis] are keeping me up at night.' (I paraphrase.) But in the end, the plan works like a charm: the priapic menfolk are soon inspired to agree a peace deal, so they can rush the women back to bed.

Even with the sorry proliferation of porn, sex slaves, and sex arses (see footnote 6) – offering alternatives to men unwilling or unable to engage with female desire – a sex strike still seems a viable ploy with a proud history.[54] For even greater effect, we might try the showstopping power of vaginal display.[55] Such a

---

54 Chris Knight writes about sex strikes in his spectacular book on prehistory, *Blood Relations: Menstruation and the Origins of Culture* (Yale, 1991). Women held a sex strike in Nicaragua in the 1530s, as a protest against slavery, and Igbo women in Nigeria have often scared men with their sex strike power. More recently, the tactic was used in Liberia to protest against the vicious civil war (2003), in Naples in protest against dangerous, illicit fireworks on New Year's Eve (2008), in Kenya (2009), and in Ukraine (2010). The Strike of Crossed Legs worked in Pereira, Colombia (2006/2011), in protest against gang warfare: 'We want them to know that violence is not sexy.' Pereira's murder rate, at the time the highest in Colombia, dramatically declined as a result. In 2011, women in Barbacoas, Colombia successfully used a sex strike to ensure long-awaited road repairs were done. And it was utilised in the Philippines (2011), Belgium (2011 – *proposed* at least, by a socialist senator, if not implemented), Togo (2012), Sudan (2014), and Tokyo (2014), when women threatened not to sleep with any man who supported the corrupt governor Yōichi Masuzoe, who'd proclaimed that women should never hold top roles in government because they're nutty when they have a period (he was later ousted for his misuse of public funds, which he could not blame on menstruation). Femen too has sometimes advocated sex strikes. And a sex strike added an extra dimension to a protest against the Russian presence in Ukraine (2014), publicised with the slogan 'Don't Give It To A Russian'.
55 The vulva's mythic significance as the basis and origin of all human life makes vaginal display the perfect antidote to the male death-lust. In ancient history, women

strike would of course have to be carefully *policed*, because of men's dependence on violence as a means of comment and coercion. Not everyone's as sane and reasonable as Aristophanes' male characters (witness the violent and sexual threats launched at women who dare to speak out about anything).

Now, no shirking, sisters. No lame apologies and secret assignations! Remember, there will be *plenty* of sex (make-up sex!), once men have recognised their responsibilities as human beings, lovers, and *mensches*.

~ Pause to push through hordes of mamas and babies in a cafe. ~

We might also hope for a drop in the pregnancy rate as a result of the sex strike. Parenthood has many profound joys, and should have its rights too (maternity/paternity leave, etc.). It is a traditional and theoretically honourable part of adult life. But having a child doubles your carbon footprint. It's also harder and harder to get close to paintings in museums. A moratorium on childbirth might give women a chance to explore the freedom, leisure, self-containment, and privacy of childlessness. The missing tax revenue and pension contributions that a lower birth rate might cause could be replenished by opening the

---

resorted to vaginal display both as a fertility rite and as a form of protest. According to Catherine Blackledge, *Raising the Skirt*, women in Greek mythology used this method to subdue Bellerophon, who was threatening to flood the Xanthian plain. In addition, 'making derogatory remarks about female genitalia is punishable by vaginal display en masse... in [parts of] Africa'. In a rare acknowledgement of female sexuality, Sheela-na-gigs, those exaggerated ancient and mediaeval stone carvings of women pulling their vulvas wide open (surely a remnant of prehistoric mother-goddess cult symbols), were added to buildings to ward off evil and promote fertility. Femen activists not only use upper-body nudity to shame men, but sometimes go bottomless as well.

borders to more immigration. But this birth pause does not in any way discount the whole history and heroism of motherhood.

Some feminists complain that the concept of a female sex strike implies, dispiritingly, that women have no sexual needs of their own, and that sex is just a commodity that women supply for *men*. No. Nobody has any automatic right to sex. Withholding sex is simply one power women can wield, amongst others, in the service of a good cause. The sacrifice incurred by the sex strike will be borne by *both* sides, in aid of female emancipation. Once matriarchy is established, the needs, wishes, and capabilities of women will finally be given the attention they deserve. We'll have a ball.

The sex strike will only be called off once the majority of men permanently transfer the majority of their financial assets (on an ongoing basis) to one or more women of their choice, or contribute the same on an ongoing basis to a women's charity or non-profit banking organisation formed to issue women loans, such as the Grameen Bank in Bangladesh. Governments must also make all violence a crime, and tax men twice as much as women, the revenues raised to be earmarked for the enhancement of women's lives, in the form of safety, education, free menstruation materials,[56] childcare and reparations for slavery. In addition, schoolchildren must study prehistory in order to get an understanding of matriarchal cultures. So as to reinstate men's natural duty to serve female pleasure, biology courses and sex ed classes in school will work to revise our decayed approach

---

56 Scotland voted in November 2020 to become the first country in the world to provide free menstrual products to all who need them. But there is progress elsewhere too: Canada, Australia, India, Colombia, Malaysia, Nicaragua, Jamaica, Kenya, Nigeria, Uganda, Lebanon, Trinidad and Tobago, and a number of US states have stopped taxing period products.

to sex, with particular emphasis on the female orgasm and the abandonment of porn. Men must spend at least one day a week listening instead to what women have to say. And I wish they'd smile more – men's default facial expressions are too gruff. They frighten me.[57]

~ *Pause to caress husband's cheek.*[58] ~

If all else fails, we can always mobilise a pizza strike. That's *got* to work.

Would we settle for less than the demands outlined here, men might ask. But we *have*, we have, for thousands of years. It's terrible that Virginia Woolf had to settle for less.[59]

---

57 At a small Bloomsday celebration at the Irish consulate in Edinburgh on June 16, 2014, I noticed that all the men there were standing around *scowling*, while the women tried to be genial. This wasn't because the men were having a lousy time (the Guinness was really flowing), they're just LAZY. (What would Joyce have made of it?!) Men really need to acknowledge how threatening the male scowl is. They need to start learning how to adjust their faces into more frequent displays of beneficence. Is it fair for women to do all the giggling and smiling and buttering-up, forever trying to make everybody feel comfortable? Why *should* we, after what we've been through? It's MEN who make everybody uncomfortable, so it's they who should make more of an effort to be friendly. Sheesh, do we have to explain every little thing? Just as they can learn not to walk menacingly down a dark street behind a lone woman, they can also master the art of smiling.
58 Husband remarks encouragingly that, once the aims of all three strikes have been realised, capitalism will be kaput.
59 The Mea Culpa Declaration: 'I, the undersigned, confess to having, consciously or not, overtly or not, been part of a worldwide conspiracy that has constrained women's lives through centuries of violence, repression, distress, and discouragement. I recognise that this treatment of women has been a ploy in a power game – the result of male cowardice, stupidity, perversity, cunning, and corruption – and that the status of men has been artificially exalted by it.
I acknowledge that vast numbers of women have been unfairly treated throughout the era of male rule. I therefore apologise for any tyrannical behaviour of my own, and that of other men, and pledge to do my utmost to correct the

problem, and prevent such injuries, insults, and injustices from ever occurring again.

I apologise too for stubborn male resistance over centuries to women's ideas, thoughts, decisions, and remarks —in the home, at work, in business, in the arts, in education, and in government. In light of the loss of valuable female input over centuries, I now agree to abide by the decisions women make, without resorting to mindless criticisms and the usual reflex contradictions and derision, no matter how wacko or whimsical the ideas expressed by women may seem to me to be.

I renounce male power and privilege, on the grounds that they were unsportingly won, and I wish to relinquish all remaining economic, social, and political advantages I may have obtained, either as a mere consequence of being male, or because of my active participation (now regretted) in misogynist behaviour and acts of patriarchal terror, either overt or underground.

In aid of this, I have transferred, or will transfer and *continue* to transfer, my financial resources to a woman or women, *no strings attached*. By such means, I hope to see a societal shift and foster a more humane environment in which women and children are less likely to be mistreated or maligned. It is my hope that the handover of power and property to women will ultimately transform and benefit people, animals, and the natural world, as well as ensuring a future for thought, languages, nature, culture, and the arts.

I believe in the pleasure principle, and therefore renounce the male work ethic as an indecency imposed by men who wished to profit off the subjugation of others. I hereby renounce male privilege and assert the inalienable right of *all* creatures to life, liberty, and the pursuit of happiness.'

SIGN HERE: _____

73

A SPELL
OF PATRIARCHY

In the days before Covid, when thought ranged free and queuing wasn't lethal, I was standing in line at a cheese shop, contemplating our dependence throughout life on *milk*, mothers' milk (and all the other kinds, like cow, goat, sheep, buffalo, almond, oat and soya), when it occurred to me that the Hitchcock movie I'd just watched, *Spellbound*,[1] is really about sexual harassment. It's *not* about Gregory Peck's ridiculous psychological problems; it's really about *women's* problems – with men. It's a #MeToo movie from seventy-five years ago. Whether he meant it this way or not, Hitch was ahead of his time. Maybe his conscience was bothering him?

Notoriously keen on hiring blonde actresses, for personal and pragmatic reasons – blondes at the time were box office gold – Hitchcock was no feminist hero. He used (some would say abused) some of the most famous blondes around: Grace Kelly,

---

1   1945.

Carole Lombard, Eva Marie Saint, Tippi Hedren, Joan Fontaine, Doris Day, Janet Leigh, Kim Novak, and Ingrid Bergman. Oddly, he settled on Hedren for both *The Birds* and *Marnie*, an awkward actress at best, brittle and shaky. But still – a blonde. Yet, for all his Pygmalionic tendencies, and for a guy who spent so much time just trying to *scare* people, Hitchcock's portrayals of women can sometimes be surprisingly generous and sympathetic.

He also really knew how to make a movie, at least most of the time – his flop/gem ratio is pretty impressive. I had largely forgotten *Spellbound* when I saw it again, and enjoyed every minute. Though completely absurd, it's now joined my list of Hitchcock must-haves, along with *North by Northwest*, *The Lady Vanishes*, *Rear Window*, *Strangers on a Train*, *Mr & Mrs Smith*, and *The 39 Steps*. I can watch *The Birds*, too, even *Marnie*, once in a while, but they're pretty awful. And *Psycho* is just a joke – what a mess, with that mom and the rocking chair and all. The murder in the shower, a cheap stunt, frightened me every time when I was young, but you already know Janet Leigh is doomed as soon as you see her in her underwear. That amount of vulnerability is code for victim.

For discussion purposes, we could call Bergman and Peck by their fictional names in *Spellbound*, out of respect or something: Dr Petersen and Dr Edwardes. But at this stage of the game, who really thinks of them as anything but Ingrid Bergman and Gregory Peck? So, to Bergman. She plays a psychoanalyst, and she's not half bad at it. The job really seems to suit her. She could've helped even Hitchcock. She's not just well-trained and studious, she's bursting with snappy put-downs that help her thread her way through the forest of obnoxious men she's up against.

Hitchcock was such a sucker for proclamations about psychology, many priceless jewels of corniness are on display in his work. *Psycho* ends with one, just to make things feel even more ridiculous than they already did. *Spellbound* begins with one, and it's a classic of the genre, informing us earnestly that psychoanalysis 'treats the emotional problems of the sane'. The only trouble with this assertion in this movie is that most of the characters in *Spellbound* really are out of their minds. The shrinks are as wacky as the patients.

One principle of psychoanalysis is that what's buried deep in the unconscious will pop out in some way, no matter how well you try to repress it. It's a process of opening locked doors in the subconscious. Actual doors open for Ingrid Bergman in *Spellbound* – not *professionally*, natch, but in her head, when she starts to fall in love with Gregory Peck. To be fair, this was 1945, the bumpy start of psychoanalysis' heyday. Hollywood was full of shrinks (and locked doors, too, come to think of it). But the real craziness buried in *Spellbound* is not the libido, romantic love, mental collapse, nor the mysterious source of Peck's baffling complexes, but *misogyny*. The movie veers off from Peck's mental disorder to become an examination of everyday sexism: what it's like to be a woman tormented by men. For, wherever Bergman goes, she's under male scrutiny, if not direct attack.

On the surface, the story concentrates on Gregory Peck's mixed-up identity and amnesia and phobias and fainting spells and stuff, but you soon sense that Peck's psychological disintegration is by the by. The movie is told from *Bergman's* point of view, and what's really memorable about it are the difficulties *she* faces (Hitchcock was probably one of them). You can tell Peck doesn't matter much, by the way the three sensationalised crises of his life are handled so breezily. They turn out to be 'MacGuffins' (not a new fast-food breakfast item, but Hitchcock's word for the intentional distractions he liked inserting in his movies). What matters here is *Bergman*. Of course. I mean, you get Ingrid Bergman on screen, the movie's going to be about Bergman!

Here is a woman rising fast in a male-dominated profession. Dr Petersen is the Ruth Bader Ginsburg of psychoanalysis, a whizz-kid, and analytically sensitive up the wazoo. Hitchcock awards Bergman's character some genuine heroism as a career woman. She's so beautiful that her colleagues seem reconciled to having a female in their midst. But they don't *like* it, and they're constantly making gendered digs about her. They seem to have all the time in the world to mess her around. One pest likes to criticise her for her apparent asexuality. Because she rejects *him*, he accuses her of frigidity, that old salve to the male ego. He says touching her is like embracing a textbook, laddishly warns, 'Your lack of human and emotional experience is bad for you as a doctor. And fatal for you as a woman.' But Bergman's ready with the cutting riposte: 'I've heard that argument from numerous amorous psychiatrists who all wanted to make a better doctor of me.' Touché.

She seems to be the only professional in the whole institution. She *has* to be – her colleagues are all lazybones and chauvinists who tell her things like 'The mind of a woman in love is operating on the lowest level of the intellect,' and 'You're an excellent analyst, but rather a stupid woman.' Why don't you quit harassing her, you jerks? Just go straitjacket somebody or something. She's the best shrink in the place! It's pretty amazing Bergman ever gets a thing done, with all these malingerers hounding her. But she does, and she appears to be a genuinely good analyst: she takes on Peck of all people – a bundle of nerves, suffering from a bad case of impostor syndrome, amnesia, and PTSD, not to mention a crippling fear of whiteness and black stripes – and she 'cures' him.

Hitchcock's ideas on psychology are amusing throughout. They're highly physical – with him, it's never just about people's *thoughts*, there's always some violent dramatic experience at the heart of things, which has to be exposed. He equates neuroses with constipation and treatment is all about administering a good fig syrup of flashbacks. What's required, emetically, is for the patient to fully remember the trauma and expel it. So, to get well, Gregory Peck has to relive the three incidents that have cumulatively unhinged him – firstly, a childhood blunder, in which his brother got impaled on a fence after Peck accidentally pushed him off a wall; secondly, an injury during WWII, caused when he was an Air Force pilot and his plane was shot down; and finally, the quite recent sight of his psychiatrist skiing off a snowy peak to his death. (I don't know why anyone skis. Bergman herself has to ski later in the movie, very riskily, so as to stir memories in Peck. But she's Swedish, so she's good at it.)

Bergman's task is to figure all this out, and fast (before Peck ends up in prison), and she can do it too, but not without alienating every man she encounters – even Peck, though he's crazy about her. In their first encounter, she tries to draw a picture on a white tablecloth with the tines of her fork and Peck goes all woozy. We don't know why yet, except that the marks she makes are strikingly vulval in shape. Peck's aversion to the drawing adds a telling note of misogyny to his other quirks. Making things even more suggestive, he tries to rub the lines on the cloth out with a knife, the blunt blade urgently nudging the notional labia. The perfect start to a great romance!

Before she sorts Peck's pecker out, I mean his psyche, Bergman falls in love with him in a big way: the movie's full of kissing scenes. This development mixes interestingly with the therapeutic job at hand. One minute, she's wondering why the pinstripes on her bathrobe freak him out, the next they're kissing. One minute they're deftly evading the police at Penn Station, next they're necking again. And along the way, Peck's contempt for women bubbles up whenever Bergman pokes her nose too skilfully into what's bugging him. 'If there's anything I hate, it's a smug woman!' he snarls. She pooh-poohs this sort of remark as the inevitable annoyance an analyst rouses in the wary patient. She's undeterred, intent on being professional. But she's hurt. Falling in love is actually full of *pain*. This doesn't get mentioned enough.

～

Everywhere Bergman goes, sexual harassment follows. As Grace Kelly says in *Rear Window*, 'I'd say she's doing a woman's hardest job: juggling wolves.' *Spellbound* is the story of one woman up against a wall of male authority, from the outside world of male doctors and male cops to her troubled love object. Peck suddenly disappears from the psychiatric facility, fleeing the police. He only tells Bergman the name of the hotel in New York he's heading for. She rushes there, hoping to catch a glimpse of him in the lobby. An addled lech immediately hits on her, smoking his cigar right in her face and squeezing her into a corner of the couch. Peeved but perky, Bergman asks him, 'Do you mind not sitting on my lap in public?'

A hotel detective rescues her from this guy, and then deposits his own load of sexist preconceptions on Bergman. He somehow jumps to the conclusion that she's a sweet innocent teacher in search of her runaway husband. He's made the whole scenario up for himself. Bergman plays along with his fantasy simply to get hold of Peck's room number. Later, when the detective realises he's been had, he's affronted – having been charmed at first by her teacherly naïveté, he now feels slighted by her craftiness. Humiliated. Men are so touchy.

As many a #MeToo accuser has charged, merely by speaking to men, or working with them, or treating them, or loving them, women potentially provoke the most terrible retributions. There's even a hint of domestic violence in *Spellbound*. Early on, Peck threatens to 'biff' Bergman for prodding him with too many questions. And later, when they're staying at her old teacher's house, Peck seems sorely tempted to slit her throat. Why else is he so stirred by the sight of an open razor, why so drawn to stand menacingly over the sleeping Bergman, soft and helpless in the bed?

'He was dangerous,' her kindly mentor confirms the next day, having quietened Peck with a dose of bromide in his milk. Ah, yes, *milk*, that distinctly female secretion! White as snow, white, Snow White,[2] white, white... aaagh! Peck's not good with anything white, yet he drinks up his spiked milk like a good boy. What pops uncontrollably out of Hitchcock here is, on the one side, the mammalian female creating and nurturing life (also insightfully analysing people for free), and on the other, the male urge to kill somebody, *anybody*, for no good reason. These opposing forces battle for control of the love affair, and the movie, if not the whole society.

Psychoanalysis has often despaired of women. Detailing the faults of mothers has worn out the velvet of many an analytic couch. Freud expressed his own exasperation with women in

---

2 She too was overworked and underpaid.

the uncharitable question 'What do women want?' Well, maybe what women want is to *steal the show*, take the floor, regain centre stage, their rightful place in the world *and* in Hollywood films (they already have the upper hand in operas). Echoes of matriarchal prehistory lurk in the collective unconscious, and have a lasting appeal.

Who doesn't want Ingrid Bergman to be happy? We've seen her driven to distraction in nice outfits in so many movies. In Paris, all leggy in that gold dressing gown, just before the Germans invade and everything goes blooey – nothing like the dowdy pinstriped old-maid bathrobe Hitch lumbers her with in *Spellbound*, the vertical lines of which send Peck into a tizzy. We long for Bergman to relax and feel safe! Let's face it, we want her drinking champagne with Humphrey Bogart. Gregory Peck's just a little too complicated.

They work things out, of course. Peck is going to be an effective doctor again, with Bergman at his side. And the goons are gone: she's seen them all off. Patriarchy's only an idea after all, like an evil spell. We're not bound to it.

THIRD-RATE ZEROS

Now that the big fat loser of a president, that tremendously sick, terrible, nasty, lowly, truly pathetic, reckless, sad, weak, lazy, incompetent, third-rate, clueless, not smart, dumb as a rock, all talk, wacko, zero-chance lying liar, phoney, nut job, clown, fraud, con man, hypocrite, lightweight, poor loser, goofball, and low-life Donald Trump is gone (pending prosecution and ignominy), we need to start repairing the *neurological damage* Trump has done worldwide. It's amazing how quickly an undereducated, big-shot hooligan can make you forget there are such things as decency, decorum, honour, truth, kindness, politeness, humour, morality, intelligence, knowledge, justice, democracy, laws, a Constitution, even! And art.

Civilisation, in fact.

A good first step would be for everybody to stop belittling people the way Trump does. That includes attacks on Trump himself for *his* supposed bodily flaws. They are minor compared to his real crimes. People have often highlighted Trump's obesity, a cheap shot and indirectly offensive to millions of similarly afflicted Americans, obesity being something of a national sport. Trump's not alone in wolfing down the KFC and chocolate cake; and being fat is also not the worst vice in the world — unless anorexia's your thing. It's certainly not *Trump's* worst offence — not compared to raping, obstructing justice, killing hundreds of thousands during the corona-virus pandemic, inciting insurrection, and hurrying public executions in his final days in office while issuing pardons for fellow traitors.[1]

Trump opponents raised doubts about his *continence* too, suggesting various accidents and a reliance on 'diapers'. Rumours have circulated about his farting during public appearances (his lawyer Giuliani apparently does it too). But this strategy is problematic, since even contemptible, irresponsible, racist, sexist, fascist, tyrannical and gaseous assholes are still human. Trump has the right to an alimentary canal like everybody else. Criticise him — *please* — for sending immigrant children to concentration camps and losing track of their parents. Send him to jail for life for *that*. Deprive him of his golf bag even. But leave the creep's allegedly fallible anal sphincter out of it. That's playground stuff, caca and peepee. The emissions from his foul mouth leave the more lingering stink.

~~~

---

1 One of his final wretched acts in office was to push forward with the execution of Lisa Montgomery, a woman of dubious sanity and the first woman in America to be executed by the federal government in seventy years. This was the eleventh of the thirteen executions Trump rushed to complete during his final gory days in office (*New York Times*, January 13, 2021). Montgomery's lawyer said the execution of her client was not only a superspreader event but a 'vicious, unlawful and unnecessary exercise of authoritarian power'. An ex-classmate of Montgomery's *approved* though, claiming that 'it would definitely help with some closure'. Americans are hooked on closure. And see where it gets them.

Along with all his crassness, volatility, and tragic magnetism, Trump has exhausted us with his exaggerations, his rhetoric, his hyperbole, his suspicions, his attention-seeking, his pronouncements, his pronunciation, his grammar, typos, and tastelessness, his neediness, disrespect, lawlessness, madness, and outright lies. He has defeated us, defiled us, *crushed* us with gibberish – all those animosities of his and his sulks. The grievances, the mood swings, the meltdowns, the firings and hirings, the taunts and conspiracy theories. He has been proved wrong a million times – about the Central Park Five, whom he wanted to execute; about Obama's birthplace – but truth never gets in the way of a Trump moan. Without a shred, a *shred*, of evidence, he insisted that the painstaking efforts involved in the 2020 presidential election, conducted with amazing efficiency and heroism during a pandemic (the pandemic *his* policies exacerbated), was 'the most corrupt election (by far!) in the history of the USA'. Whenever Trump describes what's wrong with the world, he's always unconsciously describing himself, with some accuracy: if he'd said *he* was the most corrupt president (by far!) in the history of the USA, he'd be within range of the truth. If he just admitted that *he* is nasty, *he* third-rate, *he* the swamp that needs to be drained, the whole world could get a better night's sleep.

We will have to make an effort to regain our sanity, and a little modesty in our own use of language. Perhaps think twice before yelling 'You are the goddam stupidest person on the planet' and threatening the most gruesome forms of demise every time someone mentions avocados, Bernie Sanders, J-Lo, rain, memory foam, the Olympics, or, say, Canada. Enough already with the personal attacks, enough with the childish threats. We need a five-year ban on verbal abuse. Hold those adjectives! Here's an idea: replace them with *numbers*. That should lessen demand.

0 = Zero.
1 = Fat.
2 = Second-rate.
3 = Third-rate.
Etc., etc.
11 = Tremendous.
12 = Sad.
13 = Nasty.
14 = Lying.
15 = Dumb.
16 = Wacko.
17 = Clueless.
18 = Phoney.
19 = Goddam stupidest.

Trump, for instance, is a 15, 17, 3, 12, 13, stone-cold loser, 18, and the 19, 14, 16 0. See? Not very satisfying.

〜

Though becoming president may beat the many other inappropriate roles he's assigned himself in life, Trump also considers himself an indispensable judge in an ongoing notional beauty pageant taking place in his own head. The guy critiques every female body that comes his way, including his own daughters'.[2]

---

2 Amazingly, in the midst of his anarchistic campaign to block the outcome of the 2020 presidential election, Trump took time out, just after Christmas 2020, to worry about why 'nasty' Kamala Harris was allowed to be on the cover of *Vogue*, when the robotic Melania Trump had never graced the front of a magazine in the whole four years of her husband's presidency. Why, Trump railed, was Melania so neglected? Uh, maybe because Melania is merely an unremarkable *First Lady*, not the first woman of colour to become vice president? Could *that* be it? Besides which, Melania's sycophancy and baffling fashion statements make everybody vomit.

Instructions on female beauty are a generous extracurricular duty Trump has set himself, for the benefit of humanity. Many men do it, of course – openly or not, they're forever formulating opinions on women's looks and slotting us into position on a scale of 1 to 10.[3] Gay men seem equally busy establishing a consensus on male beauty traits. Immature and extremely insecure, men feel safer all lusting after the same object. Nostalgic men wallow in *memories* of perfect bodies, while men who live in the Now just stand around on street corners evaluating the passing throng, or embark on stalking missions. No one questions why beauty or the lack of it matters a damn.

Conventional beauty is a minor, accidental, and temporary achievement. Okay, it gets you modelling jobs and parts in movies, and occasionally stirs up a pang of envy, ruining a few friendship prospects. Sadly, our tendency to glorify physical perfection decides the fate of many supposedly less beauteous women. But people are more than just physical entities (*some* are, anyway). A lot of them have interesting insights or news items to offer. They also have plans, desires, meaning, lives, and rights. Reducing connections between people to the level of a beauty-based pillow fight diminishes both the judges and the judged. How much time in life and in literature has already been wasted on mean, irrelevant, and soon outdated notions of beauty? You know, *so what* if Cinderella was beautiful and her step-sisters weren't? Is this really *really* the key to an understanding of human capacity? Is it fair? Is it even interesting?

---

3 'Seen any good dicks lately?' the exasperated Texas Governor Ann Richards once asked, after listening to yet another man extol at length the exact virtues of some female acquaintance's body. (The columnist Molly Ivins liked to recount this remark.)

My mother thought it was rude to comment on people's appearance. I agree. Most of the attention we give people's looks is wholly unnecessary unless you're a police officer in search of a suspect. Physical descriptions of protagonists in novels likewise give me the creeps, or send me to sleep. Who the hell cares? *Dickens* can get away with it because he makes the whole business seem like harmless fun. And his plots feature so many characters, he *has* to hand the reader some way of remembering them all. Here he is on Uncle Pumblechook:

> A large hard-breathing middle-aged slow man, with a mouth like a fish, dull staring eyes, and sandy hair standing upright on his head, so that he looked as if he had just been all but choked, and had that moment come to.[4]

What could be better than that? Succinct and funny, the information is painlessly absorbed. Nobody would want to *be* Pumblechook, but we excuse it in him. Similarly, Marilynne Robinson playfully conveys one woman's chaotic personality through the way she looks, ending with a top-notch one-liner:

> She had lavender lips and orange hair, and arched eyebrows each drawn in a single brown line, a contest between practice and palsy which sometimes ended at her ear. She was an old woman, but she managed to look like a young woman with a ravaging disease.[5]

---

4 *Great Expectations* (1861).
5 *Housekeeping* (Farrar, Straus & Giroux, 1980).

But more straight-faced physical depictions can be ponderous, clumsy, insulting and inert. I struggle to scramble my way past all the big eyes and lips and cheekbones and nose angles and beauty spots and earlobes and hair colour and dress design and the svelte lines of a million pretty fictional heroines' figures that authors tirelessly line up for our amusement. We're rarely told about these people's fallen arches or faulty immune systems, their borborygmus or their questionable nose-blowing techniques – though these issues could be more pertinent to the way the person approaches life, and more entertaining, than the type of eyelashes they happen to be fluttering. Jane Austen never wasted much space on people's looks: all you need to know is one sister or other was generally considered the prettier. If that.[6]

Women bear the brunt of all this impertinent attention. Hermione Lee brings up the (large) size of Edith Wharton's breasts in her comprehensive biography of the writer – one scholarly intrusion too many?[7] It's usually *male novelists* who need to be forcibly restrained from breast-tracking. Some can't introduce a new female character without jumping to pinpoint, approvingly or not, exactly what her breasts are like – as if this were the pre-eminent issue in any woman's existence. The breasts of *unsexy* female characters are rarely mentioned, as if these lesser figures have been subjected to a wholesale double-mastectomy programme before the typing began. Such writers, intent on

6 In *Persuasion* (1818), she satirises Sir Walter's absorption in both his own beauty and the physical flaws of everyone else. 'We are not all born to be handsome,' Mrs Clay cautions helpfully. (Though, soon enough, Austen falls into a trap of her own making, dissing poor plump Mrs Musgrove for the incongruity of being fat and having deep emotions.)
7 Chatto & Windus (2007). How often do Henry James's biographers comment on his no doubt flabby tush?

their own lechery, become armchair, or desk chair, libertines: self-appointed arbiters of (imaginary) female flesh.

Pulling up another example almost at random, just because I read it recently, E. L. Doctorow, an American writer of historical fiction (praised incidentally by Barack Obama, and innocently recommended to me by my own publishers), annoyed me greatly in *The Waterworks*[8] by devoting much attention to his characters' physical attributes. If this is a delaying tactic, it works – it slows everything down to a moribund standstill. The whole book is murky throughout, but every now and then Doctorow rallies to nail someone's outward appearance with strange exactitude. A slave to the habit, he suddenly starts wrestling with the cleavage of the *less attractive* of his two main women characters: Miss Tisdale is a somewhat dowdy counterpart to the saintlike Mrs Pemberton, the requisite stunner (a fixture of much male fiction) who's adored by the narrator and eventually won by his rival in the course of this fitful, circuitous, and unsatisfying book. (I don't think that's a spoiler, since the book's spoiled anyway by all these descriptive passages!) By directing our eyes to the chest of the less hot character, Doctorow magnanimously flings her a little sex appeal, like a bone to a dog:

> Miss Tisdale was petite, but resolute, with a forthright, unaffected manner. Though she was *not a beauty*, she commanded one's attention with her high cheekbones [cheekbones again!] and fair skin and the eyes slightly slanted at the corners, and a melodious voice... She seemed to have no interest in the usual strategies of feminine presentation [tsk, tsk]. She wore

8 Penguin (1994).

a plain dark-gray dress, simply cut, with a white collar at the
neck. From the collar hung a cameo brooch that rode minute
distances, *like a small ship at sea*, as her bosom rose and fell.
Her brown hair was parted in the middle and held behind
the head with a clasp... *I found her quite fetching.* [my italics]

What is Doctorow getting at with the nautical stuff here, that
little ship on troubled waters? Who knows? Male thought is
so muddy. After delineating her modest charms, the narrator
fesses up to finding Miss Tisdale 'quite fetching'. Kind of him.
Without that crumb of forgiveness, Miss Tisdale's sturdy little
brooch might well have sunk without trace into the unfathomable depths of Victorian corsetry, in a perfect storm of aesthetic
and corporeal deficiency.

Doctorow's approach to Martin, the central *male* figure in
the novel, is comparatively lenient. In fact, he gives the guy a
godlike superiority:

He was a moody, distracted young fellow... He had light
grey eyes which spasmodically widened from the slightest
stimulus. His eyebrows would arch and then contract to a
frown, and he would seem for a moment to be looking not at
the world but into it. He suffered an intensity of awareness –
seeming to live at some level *so beyond you* that you felt your
own self fading in his presence, you felt your hollowness
and fraudulence as a person. [my italics again]

No mention of the teasing glow of Martin's trouser buttons,
twinkling like stars, under pressure from his jutting crotch.
Nothing like that. Is he even 'handsome'? We don't need to
know. Men don't have to be good-looking; they *do* the looking.

So, Martin can flash those light grey eyes of his at us all he wants to. His dignity remains intact. No little boats crawling all over *him*.

ᔕᔕ

In her book *Thinking about Women*, my mother Mary Ellmann analysed the sexist stereotypes male literary critics use when discussing women writers:

> Books by women are treated as though they themselves were women, and criticism embarks, at its happiest, upon an intellectual measuring of bust and hips.[9]

If Trump had been a literary critic, this is the kind he would've been. You can almost see him (were he able to *read*) grabbing women by the paperback and sneering at their periods.

My mother noted the way male critics like to identify flaws in women's writing that are curiously similar to the defects men often seem to find in women themselves, such as formlessness, passivity, materiality, and irrationality. Wow. When *men* are the most volatile people around! They steal our power then call us weak, steal our ideas then tell us we're not creative ('Where are all the female composers?' etc.). They stole the EARTH when we weren't watching. And then they dare to tell us we're naggers – when they're *tyrants*.

Nothing much has changed in the fifty years since she wrote her book (except that Norman Mailer has died). Men still equate 'soft body, soft mind', and there are still men who

---

9 Harcourt, Brace & World (1968).

fear that reading a book by a woman is beneath them, and might even deplete their masculinity. Masculinity is such a fragile substance – finite as helium, it's always draining away into the ether. Women like Melania Trump, or even Helen Gurley Brown (who liked to kneel at men's feet), devote themselves to suturing the male ego, but it's a thankless task. In return, men deride, deprive, and misinterpret us. And mansplain. Some system.

My mother said of male reviewers:

When the uterus-mind is seen as conservative or nutritive, it is praised. When it is seen as claustrophobic, it is blamed. By sexual correlation, all energy and enterprise is customarily assigned to male thought, and simple, accretive expectation to female thought. The one breaks through, the other broods. An immobility is attributed to the entire female constitution by analogy with the supposed immobility of the ovum. This imaginative vision of the ovum, like a pop art fried-egg-on-a-plate, is dependent of course upon a happy physiological vagueness. In actuality, each month the ovum undertakes an extraordinary expedition from the ovary through the Fallopian tubes to the uterus, an unseen equivalent of going down the Mississippi on a raft or over Niagara Falls in a barrel. Ordinarily too, the ovum travels singly, like Lewis *or* Clark, in the kind of existential loneliness which Norman Mailer usually admires. One might say that the activity of ova involves a daring and independence absent, in fact, from the activity of spermatozoa, which move in jostling masses, swarming out on signal like a crowd of commuters from the 5:15. The physiological contrast of apathy and enthusiasm might reasonably shift to one of individualism and conformity.

~

It will take time to flush away all the stereotypes generated by the Trump era and raise back up all the people he dissed: women, minorities, leftists, outcasts, the sexually and ethnically diverse,[10] the disabled and the poor. What better moment then to hand them the floor, be they chubby, nasty, big-eared, not smart, or a 10, in the overheated estimation of the ex-denigrator-in-chief? At the very least, they'll be a lot more coherent than our unmourned very stable genius.

---

10 This word is now highly suspect, usurped by capitalists. As Angela Davis said, 'Once the word "diversity" entered into the frame, it kind of colonised everything else. All we talk about now is diversity... difference that doesn't make a difference. It's *not* just about diversity, it's about *justice*' (from 'Audre Lorde: A Burst of Light Symposium', March 22, 2014 – https://youtu.be/EpYdfcvYPEQ).

93

CONSIDER PISTONS
AND PUMPS

We just can't leave the body alone, can we? We really think of little else. It's not just our obsession with looks. Nor our abundant revulsion towards bodily functions and what are generally agreed to be bodily defects, such as obesity, disability, and decrepitude. Never mind all that. What's so bad about *revulsion* anyway? It's a natural and rational state of mind.

No, let's consider the way that we approach just about *anything*, the way that almost everything we do or have or think or want relates to the body.[1] We are surrounded by things constructed to accommodate the human body: cities, cars, furniture, brooms, books, bookcases, hoovers, dishwashers, ovens, cutlery and crockery, pitchers and pictures, toilets and toilettes. Whole lorries travel from Holland full of flowers, just to please our senses (or *used to* before Brexit kicked in).

---

1 'I got my hair, got my head, Got my brains, got my ears...' (Nina Simone, 'Ain't Got No – I Got Life', *Nuff Said*, 1968).

Throughout human history, recipes and clothing fashions have swiftly crossed borders too. We organise ourselves around the body politic, bodies of evidence, bodies of water, government bodies, regulatory bodies, even celestial bodies. Body English! So much BODY stuff going on, it's funny we mostly talk about what's on our MINDS. But but the brain never stops tabulating what's happening in the body.

Linguistically, we refuse to be parted from bodily processes for a *second*. Everything is fucking this or fucking that, or it's shitty, nail-biting, vomitous, stomach-churning, toe-curling, piss-taking, back-breaking, nerve-racking, a pain in the neck, and fit for sore eyes.

We try to stand on our own two feet, put our best foot forward. We're footloose and fancy-free – until we put our foot in it. Meanwhile, our masters, with feet of clay, step on our toes all the time, and bring the down-at-heel to heel. They don't tiptoe around either. And the masses are all ears for their soundbites, until things go belly-up.

These and other coinages like 'eye-watering' or 'down in the mouth' or 'one foot in the grave' show that suffering is a great leveller. That these expressions are ungendered implies an unconscious but kindly craving for sexual equality, a recognition that being *human* may transcend being male or female. When you get right down to it, male and female bodies still have plenty of stuff in common.

But consider pistons and pumps. Shafts, cogs, funnels. 'Male' and 'female' plugs and sockets and computer wires. More than any other part of our anatomy, we equate almost everything with genitalia, and imitate genitalia in the things we make. Our machines are unashamedly coital, just one thing after another either sticking out of something or being thrust into it. And

95

buttons – how we love pressing buttons! It must be some dim collective memory of the G-spot. Every president has to have his or her finger on the Nuclear Button, when they're not buttonholing some underling about losing their shirts.

It's not just guns and missiles that are phallic. In *The Grapes of Wrath*,[2] Steinbeck turns metal farming equipment into something male and malevolent:

> Behind the harrows, the long seeders – twelve curbed iron penes erected in the foundry, orgasms set by gears, raping methodically, raping without passion. ... The land bore under iron, and under iron gradually died...

It's natural enough that we use anatomical analogies. Our thinking sprouts from the sensation of inhabiting a body: you start with yourself and move outward. This habit only gets dicey when the establishment declares one type of body superior to another. Having the *wrong* genitalia (female) currently means exclusion from clubs and other privileges such as respect, encouragement, leadership roles, cultural, economic, and political power, and many dull meetings. It entitles the bearer to *inclusion* in menial tasks, for which women, somehow deemed too frail to become business bigwigs or bullfighters or orchestra conductors, are assumed to have limitless stamina, talent, and patience: tasks involving physical mistreatment and onerous low-paid or unpaid labour. To these, women are expected to add sidelines in cake baking, bill paying, oven cleaning, and eyebrow threading.

----

2 Viking Press (1939). A surprisingly matriarchal novel. The theme of maternal power and heroism peaks in the final image of Rose of Sharon breastfeeding a starving man, reminiscent in its turn of Michelangelo's *Pietà* (which is also, arguably, matriarchal in essence).

The 'inferior' genitalia go publicly unremarked, while the 'superior' genitals are flattered with all kinds of expensive, official, civic homage and imitation (in the form of towers, turrets, plinths, monoliths, etc.). Since Roman times, the phallus has been especially beloved – while nothing about the womb is celebrated at all, except by Judy Chicago and the knitters of pussy hats. This is really rather strange, given that female anatomy has some pretty showstopping faculties (ovulation, menstruation, conception, gestation, parturition, lactation, and mammoth moping). Unless you're a seahorse or octopus, or were born by Caesarean, we all emerge from that juncture where two female limbs meet. The vagina is our red-carpet entrance to the living world. Out we come to seek and find (or not).

In his surrealist autobiographical movie *My Winnipeg*, Guy Maddin gives vulval symbolism a rare weight by repeatedly likening the fork, or Forks, where the Winnipeg's Red River merges with the Assiniboine, to the maternal groin, or 'lap'. At last, a bit of female anatomy hits the big time, symbolically. Rivers make good female emblems, since they flow and brim with life. The Forks is also an ancient meeting point for Indigenous peoples. Many cities besides Winnipeg have been similarly established at the confluence of rivers, for reasons perhaps both vulval and pragmatic. But womanly laps sneak their way into the human consciousness in other ways too, less geological, more literal and abstract: in architecture, in carpentry, in art and textiles; in fissures in stone or the clefts between the branches of trees.

For Robert Frost, forks made all the difference.

So, for a moment let's forget all the impotent phallic symbols so favoured by town planners. The Eiffel Tower can be looked at another way. If you look up its skirts, it becomes a cave, and

97

a monument to the *vagina*. With its legs outspread in a birthing squat, the Eiffel Tower displays its gaping carnal core to the tourists below. As nineteenth-century engineering's equivalent of a cancan girl, it's a flamboyant rival to Rome's Cloaca Maxima. The Eiffel Tower looks like it has girded its loins and expelled the whole of Paris.

Sure, men are cocky now, after all their cockeyed, cocka-mamie cock and bull. The dickheads think they alone have the balls to run the world. Wild ejaculations of respect for testi-cles spill willy-nilly across the globe. Which brings us to the crotch of the matter: people are rarely acclaimed for having the *breasts* to do something brave, it's always got to be *balls*, cojones – although the grandeur of the scrotal sac, in compari-son to breasts, seems highly debatable. In a misogynistic society, one could argue it takes balls to have breasts. As for the vulva, this is only used as a term of abuse. Trump threatened Mike Pence with being seen as a 'pussy' if Pence failed to (illegally) overturn the results of the 2020 election: 'You can either go down in history as a patriot, or you can go down in history as a pussy.'[3] Well, what else is new? They're both assholes.

Haven't we had enough seminal insights too? Men are always having those. They avidly disseminate their seminal ideas, in fact set such great store by anything seminal that they sometimes ascribe seminal achievements to women too. The obsession with *balls* persists, while all the fabulous, life-enhancing, life-generating wonderments of ovaries, Fallopian tubes, placentas, clitorises, labia, both minora *and* majora, are ignored. Where are the ululations for the uterus, the catchphrases of the snatch,

---

3 'Pence Reached His Limit With Trump. It Wasn't Pretty', *New York Times* (January 12, 2021).

the wit of the slit, in recognition of the crucially productive female groin, lap, funnel, box, spoon and fork? This really gets on my tits. But soon female germinations will be nursed to maturity, through a new fluidity of thought — if we could just egg on female supremacy a bit.

The ceaseless avoidance of vulval symbols is nuts. Let's return to the womb — you know you want to. It's time society was more womb-based. In honour of our new age of free tampons, we need to discharge a heavy flow of labial lingo and symbolism across the land, along with some hot flashes of vaginal ideology. As our emblem, the Statue of Liberty, with her multitudinous motherliness.[4] Mother Nature, Mother Hubbard, Mother Goose, mother love, mother vinegar, mother-of-pearl, the mother tongue of the motherland… The 'Mother of Exiles' was eulogised by Emma Lazarus, who awarded her an attitude very foreign to our bully-boy times:

> *Give me your tired, your poor,*
> *Your huddled masses yearning to breathe free,*
> *The wretched refuse of your teeming shore,*
> *Send these, the homeless, tempest-tost, to me,*
> *I lift my lamp beside the golden door!*

The gal has a lamp, because motherhood is an *enlightening force*. That's why, when your mother fades, darkness falls.

Motherhood has always been a moral force for good, and proof of women's importance in the world, whatever men might wish to believe. If most of human history was, as I suspect, matriarchal, human society was originally founded on

---

4 Built coincidentally with the help of Gustave Eiffel.

the exertions of the womb. Birth was a risky but honourable undertaking in prehistory, and women were cherished and respected, not just as potential mothers but *for their own sake*. What a revolutionary idea. Not repressed, not raped. *Respected*. Now women are paid less and violated more, and the female body has been ghettoised, strong-armed by machismo.

Time to put feminine curves back into the body politic. It's so flat without them! Pence, who calls his own *wife* 'Mother' (an Oedipal mix-up not to be encouraged), got all tangled up over womb contents a few years back when he was governor of Indiana, endorsing an abortion law so extreme that it required all foetal remains to be reported to the government and for-mally cremated or buried. Noting that their every discharge was now apparently of intense interest to Mike Pence, some women decided to keep him informed of every stage of their menstrual cycle. They heaped him with daily updates on flow, spotting, cramps; and included Trump, once Pence was chosen as his running mate in 2016. This uterine barrage only ended when Twitter suspended the @periodsforpence account. But briefly, the menstrual taboo, which requires women to keep totally shtum all their lives about their periods, and also about the lack of them (menopause), was demolished.

Well, it's a start. But we could get more mileage out of female naughty bits than that. We need city councils and cartographers to reclaim the matriarchal world order, inch by inch, with fem-inising place names. The hell with those little hamlets, Rump and Penice. We need: Womanhattan, Wombburrow, Wombledon, Breechbourne, Breastworthy, Tittsburg, Clitoropolis, Oviductia, Fallopidelphia, Loudmouth, Womenhoe, Uxoriousbridge, and the twin cities of Multiple and Orgasm. America already has the Carolinas, Louise-iana, Georgia, Virginia, and Mary-land.

Let's restore Petticoat Junction, and the adjacent Hooterville. In Britain, there's Maidenhead, Maidstone, Bournemouth, Eastbourne, Westbourne, Winterborne, Wombwell, Womenswold, Wigglesworth, Witchford, Titford, Thrushelton, Pity Me, Wendy, The Wash, and Crackpot. It's a start.

And we'll always have Lapland. Next stop, the Milky Way (breast is best). Now, I don't expect a standing *ova*-tion for this plan. Just let it gestate – it's pregnant with possibilities.

THE WOMAN
OF THE HOUSE

It's all so innocent: you live in a log cabin with the guy you love, snuggle up every night under your home-made patchwork quilts, churn butter, tend animals, bake bread, gather water, milk cows, sweep the floors, beat the rugs, black the stove, regularly refill mattresses with fresh straw, cook stuff, sew stuff, mend stuff, make mock apple pie out of green pumpkins, slap bears on the back (thinking they're cows), never ever forget to do the dishes, and somehow give birth, all alone, to any number of helpful children. That's the woman's point of view.

The man's? You perform powerfully outdoors: you hunt, you fish, you farm, you trade furs and news at the general store, and head home afterwards despite blizzards, buffalo wolves, bears, more bears, and tree stumps that *look* like bears in the dark. Your gun is slow, you think before you shoot, you examine unfamiliar migrating birds with interest, you help anybody you see in difficulty, and you can rustle up a little log cabin any old time. And a well to go with it! In the evenings, after a sturdy meal of bacon, lard, biscuits, and gravy, you either whittle a trinket shelf or take out your fiddle and sing.

A far cry from the state of the union today, in which the woman works full-time, worries constantly about calories, celebrities and cellulite, and routinely does ninety-eight per cent of the housework while the husband holds down *two* jobs or none at all and spends his leisure hours assessing porn. The kids go to school, where they are gradually indoctrinated into a society that cherishes men, money, and misinformation over the measliest little bundle of human rights.

All of this was in train when Laura Ingalls Wilder's family wandered the American plains in their covered wagon – they just didn't know it yet. They thought the further west you got, the freer you would be. Or Wilder's father did anyway. He had a bad case of wanderlust; his wife had more reservations about the pioneering life. Neither believed America, founded on usurp-ation, desperation, the forlorn ideals of misled emigrants, and the confused philanthropy of forefathers, had been stitched up from the start. But who helps you in a capitalist society when the locusts eat your crops, or fire destroys your homestead, or the bank calls in your loan? Kin, *if you're lucky*, and maybe your neighbours. Mostly, you're on your own – because everybody else is too busy and confused trying to *comply* with capitalism to think of outsmarting it. In *The Grapes of Wrath*, the inequities shine out clear as day. There's only so much anyone else can do for you, however compassionate they may be. If you help each other *too* much, it strikes of communism, a total no-no in the eyes of most Americans. This is a nation that eats propaganda for breakfast.

They should all have stayed in Europe! (Wilder's mother had Scottish ancestry, and her father English). Still, it's nice to assume, even wrongly, that things might go well. Charles Ingalls, depicted as 'Pa' in the *Little House* books, had a gift for keeping cheerful. When things were tough, he sang his 'trouble song' and got even happier. Here's the deal: you kill, you cook, you eat, you teach, you build, you repair things, you tend your livestock, you hitch up the team, you save lives when need be, and you do it all with a positive attitude or *you're all going to die*. This is one of the few situations in which optimism is not a sign of imbecility but a necessity. Or at any rate, it sure comes in handy. Cynicism can slow you down.

The Ingallses' impoverishment is at times severe, but they ride it out with impressive courage and good humour. One winter, Pa has to walk hundreds of miles, in worn-out boots and a thin coat, to find enough work to keep the family alive. On an earlier excursion, he's blown off course in a blizzard and has to hole up in a snow cave for three days, subsisting on the few pieces of Christmas candy he was bringing home to his girls. This is Depression literature, as was *The Grapes of Wrath*. When Wilder began publishing these childhood memoirs in the early thirties, Americans were in all kinds of trouble. They knew what she was talking about. And in the current fallout from Covid, Brexit, and a cascade of global financial crises, the Ingalls' hardships, economy measures, nomadism and other survival tactics sadly have a renewed relevance.

～

Her clued-up daughter, the writer and journalist Rose Wilder Lane, warned Wilder there was no market for children's fiction. But, in need of money, Laura pressed on and between 1932 and 1943 produced a big hit, her eight-volume series of autobiographical novels. Beginning with *Little House in the Big Woods*, set in Wisconsin, the books, based on Wilder's experiences as a child, were aimed at a young audience. They're adventure stories but also catalogue her absorption in nature and the domestic realm. They illustrate the female side of the Western Expansion, and follow a family triumphing against tremendous odds to retain a way of life that incorporated play, music, education, and kindness. Not a bad way to live, on the whole.

Yes, there are troubling blunders and omissions: the chapter on the minstrel play, for which Wilder's father wore blackface, is unbearable to read. It is now a chastening record of a tributary of racism that for some time people regarded as merely light-hearted pranks: dressing up as African Americans. And Wilder is not sympathetic enough toward Native Americans either. She's hardly cognisant of them. She isn't callous, exactly – leave that to Betty MacDonald in *The Egg and I* (1945). MacDonald never stops bad-mouthing in the bitterest of terms all the Indians she encountered during her own Western adventure (at the age of twenty, she married the first bloke that came along, and to her surprise he wanted to live on a farm). Macdonald speaks more highly of the local drunks! Wilder, on the contrary, had a humility and innate morality that saved her from outright bigotry. She even admits to some shame about the treaty betrayals, abuse, genocide and displacement of Native Americans that were taking place around her as a child.

She has a refreshingly pragmatic attitude to the idea of America too, that is never overly obsequious or smug – a respectable stance in a country that has now gone belly-up under the weight of self-styled patriots. Wilder could tell an ignoramus when she saw one. She was not unaware of Native Americans, nor intolerant of them, but had very little contact

with them. So, compared to MacDonald's obnoxious hostility, Wilder's occasional hesitancy on the subject seems fairly
mild for the times. A pity that in her first book, she myopically
claimed their little house in the Big Woods was far from *any
other people*, when in fact many Native Americans lived nearby.
She also treats her mother's distaste for Native Americans as
a legitimate point of view, though Wilder herself isn't sold on
it. Jack the faithful bulldog is: he was so antagonistic towards
Indigenous Americans that he became a liability. When the
family built a cabin – illegally – in Indian Territory, Jack had
to be tied up a lot so he wouldn't make trouble.

Wilder mentions in *By the Shores of Silver Lake* that *white* men
slaughtered all the wild buffalo (on which Native Americans
depended). So she's somewhat aware of the sins of colonialism,
and disapproves. In one of the later books, *These Happy Golden
Years* (1943), Laura (Wilder's authorial custom is to speak of
herself in the Third Person) and her future husband Almanzo
(or Manly, as she called him), a young farmer from De Smet,
ponder an old Indian mound they discover when out courting
in a horse buggy. These are clearly not the most racist people
around: they don't rush to *desecrate* the mound at least, as many
less enquiring people were always doing.

The takeover of the American continent is relatively recent,
conducted over the last five hundred years or so. But the *myth* of
America as a pristine and primordial land lingers in American
minds, especially during childhood. When out walking alone
as a kid in a Chicago suburb, I often imagined myself either as
a giant scaling mountains in a single bound (not sure where
I got that idea), or as a *pioneer* traipsing through the wilderness,
brave and free, in search of the right spot to build a cabin. The
latter fantasy was probably Wilder's fault, and may explain her

continued popularity. Who doesn't wish there was territory still left to explore, and land there for the taking? (Poor Mars.)

Laura Ingalls Wilder was not the problem; *Christopher Columbus* was, and reparations are not enough. The American 'experiment', now over, needs to dispose of itself in an equitable manner. Time to give the whole place back to the indigenous peoples and ex-slaves who suffered there the most, and see if *they* can fix it.

⌇

Now that people are ruthlessly scolded for failings in youthfulness, health, and wealth, Wilder's modest, non-judgmental and practical world view (reinforced by Garth Williams's illustrations from the 1950s) seems strikingly humane, even *socialist* at times. Despite the family's isolation, the *Little House* series becomes a tribute to community spirit. That is now an outmoded and radical notion in the United States, but America could not have come into being without collective effort. In *Little House on the Prairie*, Ma *overcomes* her antipathy to Native Americans enough to feed the Osages who own the land the Ingallses mistakenly occupy, and her hospitality is rewarded: the chief later saves them all from slaughter.

The Ingallses are especially charitable towards fellow settlers, tirelessly, even *tiresomely* so: I still don't get why Laura has to give her beloved rag doll to that spoiled neighbour kid, Anna Nelson (don't worry – Laura steals it back a few pages later). And there's the moment when, after slaving away all day and night for the church fund supper and never getting a morsel to eat herself, Ma seems to lose it for once and actually glares at Pa, who's babbling about how well the whole thing's gone.

But it's in *The Long Winter* that communal duty really triumphs. The inhabitants of De Smet, marooned for seven months by snow, and beyond the reach of the trains on which they depend for coal and food, have begun to starve. Every few days brings another ferocious three-day blizzard in which it's dangerous to leave the house at all. Two teenagers, Almanzo Wilder and Cap Garland, selflessly make a hazardous forty-mile round trip in search of some rumoured bushels of seed wheat on a stranger's claim. By chance, from seeing a wisp of smoke from his chimney, they manage to locate the guy in his dugout, bargain for the wheat, bag it up, and lug it arduously back to town just before the next deadly blizzard hits. The greedy capitalistic storekeeper then tries to sell this hard-won wheat for a profit to the desperate townsfolk. The customers get ornery, threatening to steal the wheat instead, until Pa persuades the storekeeper to think again. (Pa, Charles Ingalls, is often the hero in these stories – when it's not Laura herself.) *He* calls his solution to the problem 'justice', not socialism, but the storekeeper's mercantile mercilessness collapses under the power of Pa's argument, and everybody gets enough wheat to survive. It's really a very anti-American solution.

~~~

Both parents are strict at times. Pa (Charles) comes across as the more charismatic of the two. When excited about anything, it's to him that Laura goes. Ma (Caroline) is a little less welcoming. She's steady, orderly, perhaps shy (like her daughters), and usually compliant and subordinate. She has some influence, but only occasionally exercises it to stop Charles doing something reckless. Her restrained, somewhat pious personality is soft-ened for us by Pa's evident pleasure in her: their love sustains them and keeps the whole family alive. At one point, he climbs off the roof of the house he's building, just to hug Ma. He fre-quently praises her domestic know-how and 'Scottish' frugality, and her cooking drives him wild – 'Ma always could beat the nation cooking.' When their food runs low, he says the imprint of Ma's palm on the cornbread is all he needs. (Now all we have is palm oil, in everything! Acquired through child labour, while orangutans die.)

Wilder's world is full of work of the female hand. These stories aren't just about woods and prairies and creeks: they're about the *house* in the woods, the *dugout* by the creek. Wilderness is there, they believed, to be tamed by the American family, and this particular American family is almost wholly female. According to these recollections of Wilder's, pioneering was rarely a solo masculine activity. *Somebody* had to knit the socks, produce the babies, and make the codfish gravy to go with all the cod philosophy. It takes guts to cross the frozen Mississippi in a covered wagon, with your children huddled in the back. Ma even helped build the cabins, injuring her foot once in the process. And the spring cleaning is simply beyond belief.

Once settled somewhere, women imposed *home comforts* on the cabin, essential to survival. It's Caroline who figures out that they can grind wheat with the coffee mill during the long hard winter, to make the bread that is their only nourishment. It's she who brings literature into their lives too – Tennyson, no less – and insists the children go to school. There might well have been no *Little House* books without Ma's respect for education. She's also responsible for the braided rag rugs (which she teaches the girls how to make), the hair receivers (these things sound terrifying, but apparently they were much treasured objects in which to store lost hairs taken from a comb or brush, so as *eventually* to make, unbelievably, a pin-cushion or some other curio — it's a free country, I guess), their death-defying long underwear (itchy red flannel), all the cooking, pickling and preserving, and supervising the family's individual Saturday night baths (a big palaver). The domestic chore Laura hates most is sewing — she'd rather be outside helping Pa with the hay.

> Sewing made Laura feel like flying to pieces. She wanted to scream. The back of her neck ached and the thread twisted and knotted. She had to pick out almost as many stitches as she put in.

Nobody knows what feminism is any more, but it isn't just about equal pay and abortion rights. It's about appreciating female-ness for femaleness's sake. Wilder, who notably refused to say she would 'obey' Almanzo during their wedding ceremony (a conversation she inserted, for good measure, into one of her books), never elaborates on the source of her feminist bent, but it may stem from some awareness of her mother's strength. Wilder was much more rebellious herself, as seen in the fictional Laura's many moments of dissatisfaction and indignation, the sisterly rivalry (she admits she often wants to slap her older sister Mary), her physical courage (she saves her little sister from wolves and blizzards, endures a two-month stay with a knife-wielding madwoman, and was an enthusiastic rider of unbroken horses, bareback), her curiosity (while Mary stays indoors like a good girl, Laura's out playing in the snow, or peeking at men building a railroad), and the occasional naughty escapade (such as luring Nellie Oleson into a leech-infested pond). All in all, Laura's quite a bold role model for little girls.

～

Practically silent as a writer until her sixty-fifth year, apart from a poultry column in the local Missouri paper, Wilder suddenly delivered this touching account of settler life from a female perspective. Taking nineteenth-century individualism to include *herself*, Wilder daringly, and without apology, wrote about the daily lives of women and girls. Most of their activities are dutiful enough, of course. It was a restrictive world, in which bustles really mattered, lace had to be crocheted, and hoop skirts got stuck in doorways or invaded by kittens. At puberty, you put your hair up and lowered your hems and began to notice your family's stony broke. Wilder didn't rebel against any of that, but she did approach difficulties with an admirable sturdiness that belied her shyness.

She is at her best describing her *own* childhood as a frontier girl, but her second novel, a one-off, was about a boy: *Farmer Boy*. This tribute to her husband Manly (Almanzo Wilder) was based on his early life on his parents' thriving farm in Upper New York State. Though clearly an act of love, the book sometimes descends into envy. Wilder dwells exhaustively and pretty yearningly on the quite startling amount of food on offer in the New York Wilders' household. Pancakes, sausage cakes, golden buckwheat cakes, gravy, oatmeal, thick cream, maple syrup, fried potatoes, preserves, jams, jellies, doughnuts, spicy apple pie: that was breakfast. For snacks during the day, Manly got apples, doughnuts, cookies, popcorn, and watermelons. For supper: four large helpings of fried apples 'n' onions, roast beef and brown gravy, mashed potatoes, creamed onions, boiled turnips, 'countless slices of buttered bread with crab-apple jelly', and, for dessert, huckleberry pie, blueberry pudding, and a thick slice of birds' nest pudding covered with sweetened cream.

At Christmas things got even grander: roast goose and suckling pig, candied carrots, cream pie, mince pie, horehound candy, and fruit cake. But even an ordinary Sunday for Almanzo's family involved a three-chicken pie, beans, and 'fat pork' (bacon?), accompanied by pickled beets and rye 'n' injun bread, followed by pumpkin pie. Oh, and why not a piece of apple pie with cheese to go with that? This was all provided punctually by Manly's dexterous, hoop-skirted mama – while the Ingallses feasted on blackbirds, if they were lucky, and they were grateful for the occasional rabbit, pat of butter, or salt on their potatoes.

But wait a minute – how does she *do* it, Almanzo's mother? I find it hard enough to feed two people *once in a while* – how can there be all these mashed potatoes and doughnuts everywhere, when the woman has no servants and is usually to be found huddled upstairs over her loom, weaving huge bolts of woollen cloth for the suits she sews for her husband and numerous sons? Or else she's spinning, dyeing, knitting, patching, darning, churning her prize-winning butter, and making a year's worth of candles. She makes her own soap too! The only thing she *doesn't* do is card wool: it gets machine-carded in town. What a slugabed. Sheesh, lady, get real.

But the whole family works hard. When not partaking of dishes fit for a king, the nine-year-old Manly worked like a dog outdoors – weeding, baling, shocking, ploughing, planting, sowing, hoeing, harrowing, hauling, mauling, heaving whole logs around and chunks of ice, and breaking oxen and horses

all by himself. The Wilders were engaged in a constant frenzy
of back-breaking bounty and industry.

～

'Have to finish my mother's goddam juvenile,' wrote Laura's
daughter Rose, referring dismally to the latest children's fiction
manuscript Wilder had sent her. Rose Wilder Lane's substantial
role in the *Little House* editing process has unsettled some Laura
fans. A feminist and activist (first a communist, then an early
libertarian and very anti-FDR), Rose was a well-connected
writer who really got around: when she wasn't babysitting
for her friends Sinclair Lewis and Dorothy Thompson, she
was travelling the world, adopting Albanian kids, or taking
off on road trips around America with John Patric or Zora
Neale Hurston. She wrote freewheeling biographies of Charlie
Chaplin, Jack London, and Cher Ami, the heroic WWI homing
pigeon (Chaplin sued; Jack London's widow objected vehe-
mently; Cher Ami made no comment). Lane also produced a few
(adult) novels of frontier life, borrowing a lot of her mother's
material: grasshoppers, debt, wolves, etc. *Let the Hurricane Roar*
(1933), published the same year as Wilder's *Farmer Boy*, is a
novella full of struggle and cataclysm that, in the absence of
the heartfelt quality of her mother's 'juveniles', smells of the
lamp. Lane lacks her mother's connection to the lived pioneer
experience. Still, her books sold so well that her fame wasn't
surpassed by Wilder's until some time later.

Wilder didn't envy her daughter's literary career at all, from
what she gleaned of it during visits. She once commented in a
letter to Manly, 'the more I see of how Rose works the better
satisfied I am to raise chickens.' But after financial disasters

hit the whole family, partly due to Rose's bad investment ideas, she encouraged her mother to get writing, which was the only way Rose knew how to make money. Lane's biographer William Holtz has implied that Lane proceeded to turn her mother's mud into gold.[1] But *Wilder's* biographer John E. Miller vetoes this interpretation of things.[2] His view is that Lane's contribution to the *Little House* series was less rewriting or ghostwriting, as Lane herself called it (she did ghost for Herbert Hoover), as thorough line edits, questions, coaching, prodding, pressurising, squeezing, and some light censorship. Plus a lot of bossy advice. So, more typing and griping than magical transformation. Miller convincingly establishes Wilder's dominant role in a working arrangement that was always fraught, with many disagreements on content that Wilder usually won: she was a toughie.

Writing is a process of loosening up, unravelling what has been balled up tight, an abandonment of silence and abbreviation. Lane helped draw her mother out, but may never have fully grasped what her mother went on to accomplish. Knowing something, though, about the children's book market, when she could Lane steered Wilder away from venturing into dark subjects, including illness and death. Wilder snuck some hardships past her, though. She refused to leave out her older sister Mary's blindness, for one, claiming that this event changed everything for the family and had to be there. She was right: the books would have less life to them without that tragedy and the fluctuating relationship between Laura and Mary.

Lane didn't manage to remove every *peculiarity* in her mother's writing either. Wilder's technical descriptions – of

---

1 *The Ghost in the Little House* (University of Missouri Press, 1993).
2 *Becoming Laura Ingalls Wilder* (University of Missouri Press, 1998).

how to construct bobsleds, railways, whatnots, extremely complicated Victorian dresses, or grow a giant milk-fed pumpkin – can be very hard to follow. Undaunted, she often interrupts the progress of the story to explain, say, how Pa made a door-latch (I guess, just in case you're ever lost in the wilderness yourself). It's a bit like getting a bookcase from IKEA:

> First he hewed a short, thick piece of oak. From one side of this, in the middle, he cut a wide, deep notch. He pegged this stick to the inside of the door, up and down near the edge. He put the notched side against the door, so that the notch made a little slot. Then he hewed and whittled a longer, smaller stick...

Uh huh? 'Up and down near the edge', you say? Right. Wilder's also got quite a bad little comma habit, and uses the word 'little' a little too much. If Lane was hoping for a more sophisticated literary style from her mother, she lost that battle from the start. The writing remains flawed, limited, and often very plain. But it has its charm.

~~

Maybe Wilder just needed more practice. The writing grows up with its readers. The early books are a bit thin but by the time she produced *On the Banks of Plum Creek*, Wilder was getting into her stride, with more emotional depth, more drama, better character development, and a wistful attention to landscape – cattle out of control, flooding creeks, locusts, sunsets, that sort of thing. As customary in survival stories, there is a steady supply of ill fortune: Mary's blindness, the harsh winter (the true horrors of which *were* softened to placate Lane and the publisher), the family's occasionally acute penury, and their efforts to overcome it. But there are also genuine delights: music, singing, sleighing, rolling down an irresistible haystack, getting a fur cape for Christmas, and the poignant moment when they're sitting around the campfire on their trek west, fearing Jack the bulldog has drowned in a flooding river. But he *turns up*, creeping cautiously towards them in the dark.[3] Big relief for the reader.

The older Laura gets, the more she emerges as a fully conscious being, both naughty and inventive – qualities that come in handy when she exacts her leech revenge on her nemesis Nellie. Her impatience with churchgoing, too, is frankly put:

> Laura thought [the preacher] would never stop talking. She looked through the open windows at butterflies going where they pleased. She watched the grasses blowing in the wind... She looked at her blue hair ribbons. She looked at each of her finger nails and admired how the fingers of her hands would fit together... like the corner of a log house... Her legs ached from dangling still.

Religion is torture, but hardly anybody in America will admit it! Wilder stuck ostensibly with conventional Christianity, but late in life admitted her *joie de vivre* really came from a naturalist, even pagan, bent:

> I can still plainly see the grass and the trees and the path winding ahead, flecked with sunshine and shadow and the

---

3 Jack's death scene later on was all made up. His actual end is unknown – they gave him away. Jack, Jack! Poor racist dog.

beautiful gold-hearted daisies scattered all along the way. I am beginning to learn that it is the sweet, simple things of life which are the real ones after all.[4]

Throughout the books, memories of such things are meaningful to her and lush, and it's in these pastoral recollections of the outdoor world that Wilder's at her most elegiac. But who are these descriptions for? Surely not *kids*. They assume more feeling for meadows, birds, and flowers than I think most urban children ever had. As a child, I skipped them. Now I like them. Maybe she just wrote these passages for *herself*, to record and revisit sensations that mattered to her.

Another crucial element in the books is Laura's fondness for her father, who can converse with birds on the violin:

> Phoebe-birds called sadly from the woods down by the creek... Softly Pa's fiddle sang in the starlight... The large, bright stars hung down from the sky. Lower and lower they came, quivering with music... The night was full of music, and Laura was sure that part of it came from the great, bright stars swinging so low above the prairie.

Yes, her frequent mention of stars can get aggravating – especially now that we can't see any at all. (I couldn't even see the recent conjunction of Jupiter and Saturn. Bah.) But on a *prairie*, stars count for something.

The whole family likes a joke. When the government forces them to move on at one stage, like Steinbeck's Joads, leaving the house they'd effortfully built with their own bare hands (all

---

4 From the *Missouri Ruralist*, 1917 (quoted in Miller, *Becoming Laura Ingalls Wilder*).

except for the precious store-bought glass windows), Pa claims they're actually taking away more than they'd brought with them.

'I don't know what,' Ma replies.

'Why, there's the mule!' Pa says. The horse he'd spent their last few pennies on had unexpectedly given birth to a mule. But they've got something else as well, something equally stubborn: the girl in the back of the wagon, taking it all in.

THE LOST ART OF
STAYING PUT

Not that long ago, air travel was a badge of distinction. The jet set prided itself on the habit, and Sinatra sang 'Come Fly With Me' to encourage them further. Mile-high sex on a plane was de rigueur and considered only slightly less point-scoring than surviving a hijack. People actually used to dress up to take a plane (*before* getting naked in the lavatories). Pan Am claimed '*The travail has been taken out of travel*'. For some, the excitement still lingers. One blogger, in the rarefied world of airline fandom, flew himself and his wife from Houston to Frankfurt, just to try out United's new Business Class perks. 'This flight was also special,' he enthused, 'because my wife... would become a United Million Miler. I can think of worse ways to celebrate.' I can't.

You'd think the joy of flying a million miles on a plane would be over by now for most people, especially since the advent of Covid (long plane rides being just about the most perfect way to catch and carry it[1]). But apparently people still miss flying. During the early days of Covid, some diehard would-be travellers visited Taiwan's locked-down airport just to experience the sheer thrill of going through Security and wandering the departure lounge: fake checking-in, fake passport control, fake luggage screening, fake duty-free shopping, fake airplane, fake flight attendants. People signed up for this! They didn't fly *anywhere*. Incredibly, these fanatics were really missing the whole airport experience.[2]

Nostalgia for trains, yes, I can understand that, but airplanes? Modern flying is about as stimulating as filling out tax forms, and Covid makes it crummier yet. A global pandemic could reasonably be an opportunity to reconsider the whole crazy business of zooming about the globe like this, but instead loads of people are itching to jump on board again as soon as it's allowed, and egging others on to do the same. Less for the pleasure of flying perhaps, or even of vacationing, than that of exciting the customary envy in friends and colleagues by temporarily depositing one's pallid frame on a foreign beach. In the midst of the pandemic, the *Sunday Telegraph* urged people to 'hop around the Pacific... wander with reindeer in Russia... take the kids to Tajikistan... track big cats in Mongolia... connect with nature in Australia... [and] spend the summer hols in Namibia'.[3] Uh no, don't, please don't.

---

1 'In 2019, the HHS [Dept. of Health and Human Services] conducted Crimson Contagion, a simulation examining the government's ability to contain a pandemic... The scenario envisioned an international group of tourists visiting China who become infected with a novel influenza and spread it worldwide' (Lawrence Wright, 'The Plague Year', *New Yorker*, December 28, 2020).

2 Aditya Singh hung out in Chicago's O'Hare airport for three months, apparently for fear of Covid. You've got to really like airports to do that. ('Man lived inside O'Hare for 3 months before detection...', *Chicago Tribune*, January 17, 2021.)

3 December 27, 2021. What'll the newspapers *do* if people stop booking these needless trips? All that ad revenue down the drain! No. Commerce outweighs Covid and the climate crisis.

Travel is now such a habit, people just can't imagine life without these regular culture-shocking transplantations. They risk death, disease, penury, language barriers, and bedbugs (who wants BEDBUGS?), not exactly to 'find themselves', but to find themselves in a new time zone. Do they think it's actually *time travel*? The famous, and not so famous, often *die* just getting someplace they believe they have to go: Carrie Fisher, Glenn Miller, Helen E. Hokinson, James Dean, Buddy Holly, Bessie Smith, Albert Camus... These sobering examples seem to deter no one. And then there's Robert Frost, for ever debating that tricky dilemma in the woods:

> *I took the one less travelled by,*
> *And that has made all the difference.*

How about taking *neither* road, bub? Ever thought of *that*?

～

Everybody's mindlessly weight-watching and whale-watching these days, in individual acts of migration that echo and often accentuate their addiction to individualised transport, the car. But, as the Covid lockdowns have proven, we don't absolutely have to drive everywhere, we don't each have to own a car.

When I first came to Britain in the 70s, not everyone had a car. A significant number of middle-class men never learnt to drive, preferring to be driven around by others. I drove a few of those guys around myself. Mistake. But now people act like owning a car is a wholly justifiable necessity, just something adults do. They object to fatal motorway crashes only when they cause *traffic jams*. Nobody seems to notice what a terrific waste of *time* it is to drive yourself about in a tin can. They never question having to spend a tenth of their lives in furious, anxious, high-alert situations, negotiating their own individual, cumbersome, smelly, expensive, lethal death box-on-wheels round everyone else's individual, cumbersome, smelly, expensive, lethal death box-on-wheels. The parking, the licensing, insuring, and tax-discing, the servicing, washing, polishing, and valeting, the vandalism, car theft, and carjacking, the skids, the crashes, the scratches, the close calls, the roadkill, road rage, the AA, the RACs, fluctuating petrol prices, three-point turns, black ice, bird shit on the windscreen, the embarrassment of not knowing how to check the oil or fix a flat tyre, the scary purchase of the car in the first place, and (worst of all) the snoozefest of having to read a *car manual*. How do they endure all this zooming and blinking and passing and honking and emergency braking and power steering and satnav, and the buzzing, the buzzing!

The noise of motorways has by now ruined many a rural idyll. Yet, as Covid has proven, most drivers don't really need to commute to work at all, nor see every friend or enemy in person all the time. We have Zoom, and Zoom backgrounds, and Zoom cat filters, for that. We have BOOKS too. Books on travel — these could save you a trip. You don't *have* to see the seven wonders of the world, you know, nor visit geographically distant family members. Even if, oddly, you *want* to see them, you can in fact survive without each other (which is why you live so far apart in the first place). No need to fly around the globe to attend football matches either — cardboard fans can do that for you now (one could argue the fans were cardboard *before*, along with their robotic excitement). So, why all this dumb transporting of our vulnerable bodies from place to place, at the expense of our nerves, our sanity, our health, our time, our bank balances, and the environment? New York's champion and wit Fran Lebowitz, who claims she has a carbon *fingerprint*, not footprint, only travels for work. For pleasure, she stays at home.

> As far as wanting to go places, I can't believe people do it for fun. When I'm in airports and I see that there are people going on vacations, I think, how horrible could your life be? Like, how bad is your regular life that you think: you know what would be fun? Let's get the kids, go to the airport... with these thousands of pieces of luggage, stand in these lines, be yelled at by a bunch of morons, leave late, be squished all together – and this is better than their actual life?[4]

*

Airlines ought to have Jerk of the Year awards, and not just for the passengers but for their own employees. These days, you need a bulletproof vest just to deal with the cabin crew. It's awful that United's planes proved attractive to jihadists – 9/11 was the most sorrowful tragedy to hit America since Vietnam and as a result of it, United's staff must still be under constant strain. But so are the passengers! *They're* tired of terrorism too, of having to queue to take their shoes and belts off, of cramming shampoo into 100ml bottles, of forgetting their small change in the Security trays and having their favourite nail scissors confiscated – only to be met essentially by bouncers once they reach the plane, uniformed despots who ban ten-year-olds for wearing 'inappropriate attire' ('form-fitting' Spandex leggings)

---

4 'Metropolitan Transit', *Pretend It's a City* (directed by Martin Scorsese, 2021).

and bully a mother of twins for bringing a pushchair aboard.[5] Airlines now actively hate on their passengers. If they can't bump you off the manifest just by yelling at you, next thing you know you're bodily kicked out of the plane. On a Hawaii to LA flight, Delta recruited airport police to threaten a couple with jail and the *confiscation of their children*, merely for refusing to give up a seat they'd booked and paid for.

Airports and airlines seem very exacting about how passengers behave. They make you wander miles of shops, starve you, bore you, intoxicate you, hassle you, despise you, and then pillory you for your resultant 'air rage'. More and more passengers do threaten to shoot everybody or leave the plane mid-flight. Some complain about sitting next to fat people, or start eating their own mobile phones as a form of protest. In disaster movies, pilots wrestle with the yoke, trying to get full throttle – now they just throttle the yokels.[6]

United has a particularly high rate of animal deaths.[7] United allegedly killed Simon, one of the largest rabbits in the world. Poor Simon. And it was a United flight attendant who forced a woman to put her ten-month-old puppy in the overhead locker, where it smothered to death during the flight.[8] Pups and rabbits

5 'After Barring Girls For Leggings…' (*New York Times*, March 26, 2017); 'American Airlines Suspends Flight Attendant After Altercation Over Stroller' (*New York Times*, April 22, 2017).
6 Airlines never stop squawking about Covid travel restrictions ('UK aviation sector need urgent support, industry leaders say', *Guardian*, January 16, 2021). What crybabies, after they helped spread it everywhere in the first place!
7 'In 2017, United had the highest number of animal deaths of any US carrier… with 18 animals killed and 13 injured in transport. Six animal deaths in total were reported from the other 16 carriers…' (*Guardian*, March 14, 2018).
8 'United Airlines "saddened" by death of giant rabbit after transatlantic flight' (*Guardian*, April 26, 2017); and 'Dog Dies after United Airlines Attendant Forces It into Overhead Bin' (*Independent*, March 13, 2018).

go quietly belly-up, Spandex-clad teenyboppers sob and slip back into obscurity, taking their improper contours with them. But the sight, in 2017, of the tactics used against Dr Dao on a United Chicago to Louisville flight, provoked lasting outrage. The airline had apparently overbooked the flight, as they frequently do. A legitimate ticket holder, with patients to see the next day, Dao declined requests to give up his seat. As a result, he was eventually dragged by force, bleeding, half-conscious and half-naked, off of the plane, in front of all the other passengers. He was left with a broken nose, a concussion, and two lost teeth.

Originally from Vietnam, Dao said the experience was more horrifying than the fall of Saigon. United's CEO, who defined his staff's violent approach as 're-accommodating' people,[9] and unconvincingly described Dao as 'disruptive and belligerent', had to perform some pretty tricky manoeuvres to steer the airline out of its self-inflicted PR nosedive. But even he couldn't censor all the new slogans:

> *United: putting the hospital back into hospitality.*
> *Fly the unfriendly skies.*
> *Red eye and black eye flights available.*
> *Board as a doctor, leave as a patient.*
> *If we can't seat you, we beat you.*

Dao's plight resonated because it encapsulates the now customary destruction of human dignity and the will to live, otherwise

---

9 'I apologise for having to re-accommodate these customers' (https://hub.united.com/response-united-express-3411-2353955749.html; https://eu.courier-journal.com/story/news/2017/04/11/male-hs-teacher-aboard-united-flight-didnt-need-happen/100319308/; and 'United's Apologies: A Timeline', *New York Times*, April 14, 2017).

known as air travel in the twenty-first century. Next time they ask if there's a doctor on the plane, will anyone reply?[10]

But okay, let's say you aren't machine-gunned, beheaded or hacked to pieces with a machete on your way to so-called Security. Let's say you survive the invasive (radioactive?) full-body scan, as well as the obligatory two-to-three-hour Duty-Free dwalm in the departure area. Let's go crazy and suppose you make it to your seat on the plane without being publicly shamed or socked in the jaw, either by airline staff or the people sitting near you. Your reward is that you now must *fly*.

During the cramped, airless, comfortless journey that follows (for which more and more wondrously you have to *pay*), amid air contaminated by engine oil and the pesticides used in fumigating the plane, a martyr to the airline's idea of water, alcohol, snacks, and movies, you will also be at risk of congestion, constipation, nausea, dizziness, headaches, hypoxia, jet lag, deep vein thrombosis, solar flares, fleas, pandemics, colds, flu, flatulence, and whooping cough. No one ever seems to voluntarily delay a flight because of illness, even Covid-19 — that would be cowardly. No, they tramp on board in service to their microbes, and cough, sniff, and exude contaminants all over you for hours on end. You can catch Ebola or TB in the time it takes you to untangle your gratis audio set.

I'm not saying your seat is small, but if it were a haystack, you'd find the needle. While the business-class swells chow down

---

10 Flight attendants somewhat redeemed themselves in January 2021 by urging their union to establish No Fly lists banning Trump's supporters from homeward-bound planes after they'd staged the coup at the Capitol. ('Flight Attendants Call for Pro-Trump Rioters to be Added to the No Fly List', *Revolt*, January 11, 2021.) That was heroic, and the surprise this move caused amongst the insurrectionists was pretty gratifying.

on their business-class lunches in their business-class lounges at the airport, and, once on board, guzzle their business-class suppers, encased in their big-assed business-class thrones, making big-ass business-class deals and getting business-class grease from their business-class filets mignons all over the business-class upholstery, the *Economy* passengers' food, if it ever arrives, is a throwback to TV dinners of the 1960s. Or maybe they *are* TV dinners from the 1960s? I once ordered the kosher meal, just to see if it was any more palatable. The stewardess unceremoniously (and, I thought, rather antisemitically) flung a solid block of ice labelled 'KOSHER' on to my tray table. Inside it you could dimly see some kishkes. It might have thawed by the time we reached Patagonia, but I wasn't going to Patagonia.

⌇

I have no objection here to purposeful uses of travel, of course, as in the case of emergency workers, international election monitors, refugees, or political, economic, or environmental migrants. Seeking a safe haven is a human right and unavoidable amid war, injustice, and climate change. It's also beneficial to the host society: as Fran Lebowitz said when discussing New York City, 'Immigrants make the culture and tourists ruin it.'[11] So, though travel's no picnic, let the nomads, grape harvesters, sheep shearers, job seekers, asylum seekers, detainees, gypsies, adventurers, artists, earthquake sniffer dogs, and St Bernards with their little casks of brandy go wherever they need to go. My beef is with frivolous travel of the selfish kind, the act of

11 'Who's Afraid of Fran Lebowitz?', All About Women Festival, March 6, 2018 (Sydney Opera House Talks and Ideas Archive).

inflicting yourself, uninvited, on other cultures, this constant movement to and fro of the chronically rich, with their taster menus of destinations to which they're attracted purely due to their own lack of direction, humility, and self-knowledge.

In winter, weather forecasters often warn people to avoid anything but essential travel. The trouble is, whenever anybody hears this, they seem to leap *immediately* into their cars and get caught in snowstorms. Maybe it was the same paradoxical impulse that led the Prime Minister's senior advisor Dominic Cummings, at the start of England's first lockdown in April 2020, to drive his whole family (some of them, including Cummings, already displaying Covid symptoms) from London to County Durham, including an educational side trip to Barnard Castle. His excuse for the latter jaunt was that he needed to test his eyesight. There seems vast disparity in determining what 'essential travel' is.

Is *any* travel really essential though? I understand that *some* travel is a necessary evil. Hoover salesmen and drug dealers have to keep on the move. Ditto estate agents, reporters, imams. It's *leisure* travel, the time-filling, culture-sampling, cuisine-dissing, planet-defiling, water-guzzling invasions of the overprivileged that I really abhor, and that unthinking, knee-jerk rush to the computer to book cheap flights every January (we barely even notice we're doing it any more!) because without a gad-about in Guadalajara, a dubious spree in Dubai, or the chance to go berserk (over pea soup) in Zeebrugge, people apparently lose all standing in society. We could just stay home and listen to Scarlatti but no, people are bombarded with bucket lists of faraway things they *must* accomplish, and they fall for it! Lambing in Maine, prancing through Croatian lavender fields, pottering round the Pyramids, personally inspecting the coral reefs and rainforests before they are no more (thanks to all the people who flew out to see them), riding on a donkey, a dromedary, a double-decker, trotting through Central Park in an anachronistic open carriage (who *does* that?). A hot dog here, couscous there, sashimi up, tortellini down, *Figaro su*, *Figaro giu*, always seeking some remnant – any will do – of uniqueness and authenticity in a world the human race is racing to destroy. *Figaro, Figaro, Figaro!*

We're such saps. We've been fed a great big bunch of flimsy reasons to travel, by evil geniuses determined to use up all the oil and gas as fast as possible so as to coerce us into adopting 'cheap' nuclear power, a craven idea that will torment and baffle future generations for thousands of years to come (if there *are* any future generations). Do we ever stop to think about all this motion, this *commotion*, this agitation and all of its attendant aggravation? Far from it. We gullibly galumph across the earth at our masters' bidding and get ourselves into all kinds of scrapes. We get lost, we get robbed, we get raped, we get fleeced, we get flummoxed, we get misdirected, mistranslated, and misunderstood, we get hot, we get cold, we get sick, we get nervous, we get confused. We get delayed interminably in airports. We unwisely hang off cliffs or drown in waterfalls, all for the sake of a selfie. We struggle with unfamiliar phones, plumbing, and foreign currency, and collect bottles of limoncello or artichoke brandy, just so we can hold our heads up high when we finally limp home sick, broke, exhausted and bewildered.

Aviation accounts for 3.5% of global warming.[12] The effects of cement production are far worse, I'm told. Yes, okay, there's too much cement. But 3.5% is not nothing. And cement is

---

12 Hannah Ritchie, 'Climate Change and Flying' (ourworldindata.org, Oct. 22, 2020).

probably more lastingly useful to people than the obligatory Mediterranean swim, New Zealand cider tasting, or yet another Thanksgiving with the aged p's. But we continue to prioritise human mobility and interaction over all other considerations, even despite the current plague. Meanwhile, the Great Barrier Reef dies for us. It's lost half its corals in the last twenty-five years and is eighty per cent bleached already, cooked alive.

Birds are allowed to migrate without too much human interference and their flights don't cause global warming. Officially though, only *people* are now free to dart all over the place. We let passengers with Covid cross borders all the time, but the Australian government got all worked up about the arrival in Melbourne of a racing pigeon who seemed 'foreign'. Joe the Pigeon (named by the man who first spotted him) was considered a potential biohazard because he might have been carrying an American pigeon disease. Joe was therefore in imminent danger of being euthanised or deported. But later it was decided he was Australian after all.[13] It's *people* who should undergo this sort of rigmarole – not euthanised perhaps, but banned from travel.

Animals bear the brunt of our allegiance to travel, and not just in the effects of global warming on wildlife. We now inflict travel on animals themselves, from the meat industry's horrific live animal transport operation to the way day-old chicks and exotic pets are mailed around the world. Then there are the doomed personal encounters with animals when on holiday. Ever tried to save a stray cat or a mistreated dog in some foreign country? It's not easy – they don't have passports. No, your trip is much more likely to *damage* a local animal. A young sniffer

13 'Fake US leg band gets pigeon a reprieve…' (Associated Press, January 15, 2021).

dog was shot dead at Auckland airport in New Zealand in 2017, just for capering around loose at the airport and delaying a few flights. He wasn't even on the tarmac, but in some outer perimeter area. Birds, being a danger to airplane engines, are routinely shot or poisoned in the vicinity of airports. All for 'your travelling comfort'. This is what you unwittingly commit to when boarding a plane, the possibility that animals will be executed in honour of your pointless itinerary – and not just the ones they make into 'selected medallions of beef'.

Donkeys get the worst of it, but they're getting wise to us. According to Olga Tokarczuk, Jordanian donkeys now baulk at having to carry American tourists around. They don't want to be ridden by Americans, Americans are too obese.

> The donkey is an intelligent animal, it can evaluate weight right away, and it will often start to get upset just seeing them come off their tour bus, all overheated, big sweat stains on their shirts, and those trousers they wear that only reach their knees.[14]

In Santorini, waves of Americans pour off cruise ships in hopes of finding a horse or donkey to take them up the hill. Many animals have been injured coping with this onslaught.[15] No wonder donkeys start to bray and buck when they see Americans closing in on them. (Don't we all?) One of the better things about Covid has been the thought of Paris *free* of American tourists: their weirdly compulsive descent on that city has been briefly halted.

---

14 *Flights* (tr. Jennifer Croft, Fitzcarraldo Editions, 2017, p. 125).
15 'Tourists urged to avoid riding donkeys up Santorini's steep steps' (*Guardian*, April 2, 2019).

There are Americans who will not visit anywhere in Europe that doesn't have a Holiday Inn. There are Americans who spend their whole time in England disputing the British pronunciation of Birmingham. There are Americans who refuse to enter Ely Cathedral on the grounds that Britain has not yet sufficiently recognised America's part in winning the Second World War. (Actually, America had a lot of help.) And there are American children who can detect insurmountable differences between Scottish McDonald's and New Jersey McDonald's. There is an American blind spot to other cultures that really gets in the way of their deriving any discernible benefit from travel. *So why go?* Be content to stay in Birmingham, Michigan, gobbling your Happy Meals.

Americans scour Bulgaria for a whisky sour. They freak out if their credit cards don't work, or the plumbing's weak, the bandwidth too narrow. They fall in the lousy limey hotel shower, break some bone, and to their utter disbelief get X-rayed and bandaged at the hospital for free. (Yes, it's called socialism.) Everywhere they go, they assume and *insist* that everything is or should be done the American way; otherwise it's weird. They assume everybody knows English – if they don't, they're weird. Everything *amazes* them, everything comes as a great big shock. You mean this was built before the *American Revolution*? Gee. You mean I have to put some of these crazy coins into this *slot* and then the bus will take me where I want to go? Weird. And, having almost single-handedly caused global warming, the way Americans freak out about rain seems rather overplayed.

The Accidental Tourist,[16] the most biting of Anne Tyler's customarily timid and meandering novels, hits the nail on the head regarding the insistence of many American travellers on

---

16 Knopf (1985).

remaining completely unaffected by the places they visit. 'Other travellers hoped to discover distinctive local wines; Macon's readers searched for pasteurized and homogenized milk.' Trump's a good example of this type of tourist, taking his own steak and golf clubs with him everywhere he goes. He takes his whole dull family too! Or the ones he acknowledges as family.

⌇

In the seemingly endless American TV series *Away*, a recent Covid binge-watch from Netflix,[17] five supposedly multinational astronauts (the Commander's American, the other four are foreign but *act* American) head off for Mars together in what must be the worst-made space rocket of all time. Something is always going wrong with that ship! But there's really very little about space travel or astronomy or even about Mars in the show. Instead, the drama is entirely taken up with crying and trembling, the exchange of potent glances amongst the crew, and messages of love with people on earth – people whom, let's face it, the crew has just *determinedly* left behind. But boy do they love and love and LOVE them. It's exhausting. The humourless commander (Hilary Swank) is an emotional wreck throughout the trip. I wouldn't let her drive a little red wagon. Yet here she is, steering her own space capsule towards Mars along with her four homesick minions, each of them an anxious, emaciated pin cushion of platitudes.

Their bodies are spontaneously *decomposing* before their eyes because of weightlessness, there's a big water shortage due to the ship's lousy plumbing, and there's the constant danger of death

17 Created by Andrew Hinderaker and aired in 2020.

from all those pesky unforeseen consequences that tend to crop up when one's a million miles from home (and oxygen). But still, like American travellers everywhere, they all remain absolutely unchanged and untouched by anything that happens to them. Even a year-long trip into outer space leaves them cold. What *is* the point of Americans going anywhere? Especially Mars, of all places — that's a lot of love miles, and an expensive traipse through the solar system, so far from hot dogs and the Super Bowl, while again and again and AGAIN, they phone and email and record declarations of devotion for their boring families in case they die. How they cry. (Wasting water!) Someone in the script department failed to heed Frank Capra's advice, that it's the *audience* who should cry, not the actors.

∽

Travel is colonialism. Travel is WAR. Religion travels fast, as does ideology. Tourists, missionaries and our roving billionaires pretend they mean well but they don't. They haven't come to help, they've come to take advantage. The Romans really got around too. You'd think taking hot then tepid then cold baths, eating dormice with fellow aristos in Rome, and running around on pretty mosaic floors to the chimes of your tintinnabuli, with the occasional outing to Pompeii for an orgy, would be enough for anyone. But no, Roman generals were always on the move, subduing, crucifying, enslaving and decimating people, paying centurions in salt, importing wheat, papyrus, grapes and gossip, and building walls to make Rome great again. The trouble is, when you're away from home too much, things go to pot and, if you're not careful, you come back to find it's not only your colosseum that's cracking but your whole civilisation.

The movement of people and ideas, grandly called globalisation and exemplified by the Columbian exchange,[18] is not just an innocent sharing of cultures and silk trading. Columbus, along with his overt sadism, managed inadvertently to transport to the 'New World' worms, rats, smallpox, chickenpox, typhus, scarlet fever, leprosy, malaria, whooping cough, gonorrhoea, TB, and the bubonic plague. He picked up potatoes, tobacco, and syphilis on his way out. A real import-export kind of guy, he unified the world with mutual catastrophes. Thanks a bunch. Since then, international interaction has led to industrial horror, wars, slave labour, the spread of kudzu and Dutch elm disease, pandemics, a regrettable cultural homogeneity and oceans full of plastic. The pretence that going global might spread wealth and strengthen ties has proven hard to buttress, with trade wars and people starving just outside the five-star resort precincts to which wealthy travellers dumbly flock.

All anyone gets out of this passing acquaintance with foreign lands is a crushing conformism, an expensive revitalisation of arrogance, and the obtusest form of worldliness, wherein they blindly experience the same banalities the world over: the same slang, same pop music, same video games, same crummy hotel decor, same fast food, same views of Notre Dame, same big wheels, same terrorist atrocities, same jogging trails. Travel *kills* as much knowledge, taste, and culture as it purportedly spreads. The compulsion for sameness has an insidious effect: languages, costume, dialects, and accents start to die out as soon as the Coke and jeans and T-shirts arrive. To ensure uniformity and reduce the chance that the traveller will actually experience something new, major cities now offer exactly the same chain

---

18 Alfred W. Crosby, Jr., *The Columbian Exchange* (Greenwood, 1972).

hotels, restaurants, and designer stores – ideal receptacles for morons on the move. But if Prada, Superdry, and H&M are *everywhere*, what's the point of city-hopping shopping?

Cuisines travel invisibly between countries, and English cooking was radically improved by French influences (even in the midst of the Napoleonic wars), and later by Indian flavours and recipes. It's arguable that the shameless British takeover of India is all that's made it possible for today's British foodies to *survive* (chicken tikka masala is now the UK's national dish). But is it really necessary for rivalrous *marmaladers* to circumnavigate the planet, flying all the way from Australia to Lake Windermere to show off their marmalade at a marmalade festival? Marmalade. Yes, it's hard to make a good one. But must we burn the last of the fossil fuels just to prove it can be done in *Australia*? (Which I still doubt.) Funny kind of conserve-ation that is, and a world away from Elizabeth Bennet's hopes for her planned trip to the Lakes:

> Oh! What hours of transport we shall spend! And when we *do* return, it shall not be like other travellers, without being able to give one accurate idea of anything. We *will* know where we have gone – we *will* recollect what we have seen. Lakes, mountains, and rivers, shall not be jumbled together in our imaginations; nor, when we attempt to describe any particular scene, will we begin quarrelling about its relative situation. Let *our* first effusions be less insupportable than those of the generality of travellers.[19]

---

19 *Pride and Prejudice* (1813). As it turns out, she goes to Derbyshire instead and spends most of the trip thinking about Darcy.

Woody Allen's best work is long past,[20] but his film-making in his dotage slid even further downhill once he started setting his bottom-drawer scenarios in Destination Cities. Most European capitals now exist merely as theme parks for this kind of cinematic abuse (Jason Bourne leaves them in *ruins*), along with their function as bachelorette party, beer binge, and corny lover hotspots. Prague, Dublin, London, and Barcelona have been drained of meaning and individuality, and are now completely interchangeable.

Edinburgh, where I live, used to be a fine old mirthless town, grim, austere, dirty, and dignified. Twenty-first-century marketers have turned it into a fairground. Whenever possible, the city's few green spaces get trashed by amusement arcades, glühwein, vomit, festivals, fringe festivals, markets, fringe markets, outdoor exhibitions and exhibitionists, coffee bars, beer tents, merry-go-rounds, tat stalls and ice-skating rinks. The pavements are falling to pieces, the parks and trees are in a state of collapse, the trash is never collected, and the lockdown puppy poop is never scooped. The homeless used to die on the streets while the Edinburgh International Festival conducted its annual month-long experiment in overpopulation and over-pricing. The fireworks displays alone used to be relentless, *daily* in August. Occasionally there were wee calls from residents for *silent* fireworks, but their requests couldn't be heard over the din.

This historic city, once home to the Scottish Enlightenment, has been intentionally emptied of thought and refilled with fake fun. Edinburgh has reinvented itself by obliterating its own

---

20 As the Martians tell him in *Stardust Memories* (1980), 'We like your movies, particularly the early, funny ones.'

inventiveness. Writers get short shrift: Burns, Boswell, Henry Cockburn, David Hume, James Hogg, Walter Scott, Robert Louis Stevenson, Conan Doyle, Muriel Spark, and even Irvine Welsh wouldn't know the place. All we've got now is J. K. Rowling and Alexander McCall Smith, the Betty Boop and Mickey Mouse of Scottish letters.

~

But you simply must see the Taj Mahal, pussycat, or Machu Picchu, or Outer Mongolia, before you *peg out*, we're told again and again and *again*. All exotic places *must* be trampled. *Immediately*. It torments people to think of leaving a single foreign banquette unwarmed. Just mention the Galapagos or the Faroe Islands and watch them jump – because they've got to get there before everyone else. Before it's *ruined*. The seagrass meadows of the oceans are disappearing at the rate of *two football fields an hour* just so people can boast about having bothered a turtle in some unfortunate clime.

The truth is you *don't* personally have to survey every square inch on earth, no matter what your so-called friends tell you or what you read in all that newspaper and magazine travel porn. After all, the only really interesting thing about travel is seeing new flora and fauna, and we've killed off most of that. What is more important in the end than listening to Bach or reading Dickens? *Humankind should be your business*, not this hypnotic holidaying. Locusts are big adherents of bucket lists too; they too strive to get out and about before they die.

But no, we must endorse every work break, school break, birthday, death, divorce, bicycle accident, cancer remission, basketball game and gender reveal party with a long, hazardous flight or drive to somewhere or other. There are a million family occasions that require your presence (we act like we still live in villages and the bris or grindingly dull graduation ceremony is only a block away!), a million new reasons to travel are manufactured every moment. Grief, joy, honour, guilt, humility, curiosity, habit, tradition – all can be met by a remote pageant, banquet, fair, hot tub orgy, or jamboree.

Courses for this, courses for that. You can, you *must*, attend a week of weaving, and probably weeping, in Wales; a five-day workshop making doll's-house furniture in Cumbria; a backgammon cruise through the Norwegian fjords; courses in hillwalking, pottery, juggling, watercolour, yoga, I Ching, karate, quinoa cookery, or the arrangement of spit curls, in a compound situated anywhere from Padstow to Phuket. How does a crash course in straw-hat manufacture, drystane walling or Orkney laddering grab you? Or why not discover lost tribes in the Amazon, then lose them again; or learn sock-knitting in the Arran Isles, croissant-twirling in Dieppe, asparagus farming, wildflower and mushroom differentiation, or even scything. Yes, there are classes in scything. What they need is a creative *writhing* course.

You can do a restaurant crawl through sub-Saharan Africa, or put a poor old pony through its paces all over Iceland. Almost simultaneously, if you must. Tired of London and Londoners? You can solve this by flying all the way to Montana on an unsuccessful 'man-hunt' and write an article about it for the *Spectator*, turning innocent strangers into props for your fantasy life. Sex and travel often merge this way: it's not called a 'drive' for nothing. Many travellers hope a change of latitude will cure their sexual lassitude. Can't they just put on a French accent and *pretend*? No. Passion requires the sacrifice of fossil fuel.

The more blatant sex tourists, the ones with nothing to declare but their criminality, incessantly cross the globe, sharing their diseases and disillusionment with the young and desperate of other countries. The Grand Tours of Europe — nicely encapsulated by Laurence Sterne, who liked to be 'incontestably in France'[21] — were open excuses for debauchery. Sterne may well be the *only* novelist who should ever have been allowed to travel. Apart from Joyce and Wilde, that is — it's essential for Irish writers to leave Ireland.

Gun shows, pedigree cockapoo summits, koan contests, horse races, guru reunions, nirvana attempts, stag shooting, Bayreuth pilgrimages, and gangster get-togethers where they plot assassinations, offload stolen jewellery, and swap nuclear materials, are further great reasons to travel. Spark up your plastic surgery experience by getting it done in Mexico, Moscow, Bulgaria, Beijing. Lipo on the lido! Visit chateaux, Chartres, shacks, shepherd huts; wineries, cattle farms, tobacco plantations, roller coasters, and wildlife refuges. Gaze on every sort of bull torture. Climb various famous groups of mountain peaks. Tour Cézanne's studio. (If you'd turned up when he was *alive* he'd have killed you.)

How about a nice artist residency? All artists now have to travel. They'd probably rather be paid to stay home, where they're already set up with a studio, assistants, and paint-bomb machines. But no, the whole world's watching and it's hard to resist the pressure, the prizes, the prestige. You're nothing as an artist these days unless you've spent a month in New Mexico, the Arctic, Trinidad, Tibet, and Sumatra, and regularly attend the Venice Biennale. People forget that reality is *wherever you*

---

21 *A Sentimental Journey through France and Italy* (1768).

are. It's what you're thinking about that matters, but nobody cares about that. Anyway, everybody's thoughts are so scattered now – because of the jet lag.

People travel for business. Until Covid struck, academics *never* sat still – they were constantly in the air overhead, deconstructing something. Rewarded by financial bonuses and promotions for business trips and abstruse conferences, and ordered not to return without some impact and relevance, people learn to crave these junkets and to crow about how many they've been on. Their underlying assumption is that travel is irrefutably fun, worthwhile, and enviable – a status symbol – when really all that's happened is that these poor wretches (more sheep than locusts, and therefore to be pitied) have left their work and their lives behind in order to spend twenty-eight hours in the air and in airports feeling disoriented, twelve hours drinking in a variety of unsanitary places, an hour or two at a dull meeting or under-attended talk, and a few hours playing hooky in unfamiliar surroundings and getting laid by a drunk and equally lonely business colleague, assistant professor, or total stranger. The possibility of sexual shenanigans, such as they are, is the big draw.

〰

Eco-tourism is a nebulous concept, whereby the deteriorating environment is further warmed and eroded so that people who think they really *understand* nature can go enjoy its last gasps by surfing it, scuba-diving it, or climbing, caressing, and collecting it. The world's tiniest begonia, newly discovered in Peru, is now at risk of being *squished* by a million amateur botanists stampeding up the hill in a frenzy to mark it off their score sheets. Nature would be much obliged actually if we would just LEAVE IT ALONE.[22]

There's a multitude of alternative health tourism too, ashrams, hot springs and sulphur spas, meditation camps with ley lines to lie on, curative meccas to heal you in some short-lived way. You know what? Making debilitated people feel duty-bound to go to Lourdes, Baden-Baden, the Grand Canyon, the Dead Sea, or the Swiss Alps for the sake of their health is one hell of a despicable idea.

Alternatively, for those who have it all and want *less*, there are staycations, essentially stagnations, where you still spend a lot of money on yourself but stay within a few hundred miles of home patting yourself on the back for 'saving the planet'.[23] Or how about a *starvation* vacation, where you go all the way to Bavaria for a toxins purge, releasing *more* toxins into the atmosphere in your wake for the *rest of us* to purge, in a self-perpetuating contamination cycle. It's a capitalist's dream come true: pollute the whole world by detoxifying *yourself*.

'Groundhog holidays' are for unadventurous vacation-*repeaters* who want to return to the same dump in, say, Cancun, or Majorca, or the Black Sea, *anywhere*, even Denver, year after year. Well, you part-own some hideous condo so you've got to go at least once a year to make sure all the ashtrays are just where you left them. People really do this, and kick up a fuss if the other fifty families they time-share with have moved a chair!

---

22 As soon as humans desert a place, 'feral eco-systems' emerge, no-man zones much appreciated by wildlife. See Cal Flyn, *Islands of Abandonment* (William Collins, 2021). Kim Stanley Robinson recommends leaving *half* the earth free of humans (*Guardian*, March 20, 2018).

23 The *planet* will survive actually, whatever we do. But *we* won't. *We'll* be extinct. And what a shameful mess we'll leave behind. Dinosaurs and giant sharks lasted millions of years, and left the place as they found it.

These scaredy-cats are a world away from the daredevil traveller, the climbers and hotheads and perilous sports advocates. Skiers fly thousands of miles just to put themselves in traction. Arctic aficionados, jungle johnnies, rhino poachers: the idea is to test yourself and return home euphoric for having survived — *if* you do. One minute you're in Texas, the next you're up Everest in a blizzard, on a trip that set you back $100,000. They can't help it, risk-taking is addictive. There are so many mountaineers trying to 'summit' on Everest right now, they really ought to install a funicular. In the movie *Everest*,[24] a whole group of semi-experienced climbers gets caught on some narrow ledges without gloves or even a sleeping bag. It's hard to believe, and harder to watch. (What I hate most is the way they all pretend to be interested in Nepal.)

Maybe the real purpose of travel is to scare yourself. First, on the plane (or other speeding vehicle), and later, at your sunstroke-ridden, malaria-swamped, typhoon-prone, elephant-stampeded destination. It's all an experiment in alienation, a stranger danger endurance test. People really can't decide between the horror of staying at home and that of dying in transit. They replace their natural fear of travel with *fear travel*, travel designed to scare you a bit. What is a trip to Vegas for after all but to *frighten* yourself by excessive drinking, whoring, and gambling? The birds do it, the bees do it, the holier-than-thou jihadists do it, and everybody likes Tom Jones.

〜

---

24 Directed by Baltasar Kormákur (2015).

You don't *have* to poo and pee and copulate and take snapshots of well-known landmarks in every country on earth, you know? It's not the law. But the PRIDE travel engenders is beyond belief. Smugness is a guaranteed travel bonus: they hand it out during take-off and landing.

I go [someplace], therefore I can gloat.

We booked, we bustled, we boasted.

Maybe people got sick of Marco Polo's reminiscences too, and of Vasco da Gama's, and greeted Amerigo Vespucci's cocktail party chat with heavy sighs and glares – 'Guy's been to Rio twice and never shuts up!' But at least travel then involved some genuine challenges. Now there's very little to be proud of – if you have the dough, you can get pretty much any place you want, and fast. So, what's with all the triumphalism? 'We've been to China,' they coo, or (the lesser claim), 'We haven't been to China *yet* but we're going to go.' China's old hat! Everybody's been to China now, even vegetarians (who always complain about the food – so why not stay home and eat your *own* damn bean sprouts?). Once they've done China, they have to top that with something even more exotic – Guatemala, Micronesia, the moon. Okay, go if you must, but don't come back.

And they're so bossy, these modern-day explorers, especially if you travel together. Having been somewhere once for a *week*, they're bursting with superior knowledge of the place. They alone now know how to find the lesser-known museums, or what to order in Marseille (bouillabaisse) or Oaxaca (a tamal). They tramp you all over Moscow without pausing for a pepper vodka. They know every hidden lily pond in Lagos or Lisbon, and where to find a dentist, from Clapham to Cape Town, but they don't know when to go fly a kite and jump in the lake.

The reckless needlessness of most travel is never touched upon by these eager beavers. Instead, we're all just automatically supposed to join the exodus, at the risk of stability, sanity, and solvency. The illogicality of this push to be on the move is nicely touched on by Padgett Powell in *You & Me*, when two sedentary characters consider taking a supposedly desirable trip from Florida to some desert – a plan which actually fills them both with dread. None the less, they try to convince themselves to go.

> Our tiny growing familiarity alone, as we sit there or walk around parched and frightened, will convince us we now know more than we did before the onset of the fear and the disgust, and we will feel better about the desert.
>
> Veterans of an hour in the desert, we will like it, a little bit.[25]

*

Even charitable or political-action tourism can fall flat. It was great, for instance, that women marched on Washington to protest during Trump's inauguration in 2017. Brava! But it would have been even better if they'd *walked* all the way instead of flying. And once they got there, why not *stay*? If only they'd camped out on the White House lawn until their wishes were met. Until the guy gave up the presidency in shame. But of course he has no shame.

---

25 Echo Press (2012).

However heartfelt the expedition is, the means almost always defeats the ends. Apart from those kind ophthalmologists who fly around Africa or Haiti fixing cataracts (hoorah!), and maybe a few UN or Peace Corps employees here and there (hard to verify), it's time to reconsider most forms of supposedly altruistic travel. You might do more good in the world if you quit with the wanderlust and sent the cash you save to somebody who hasn't *got* any disposable income. The *New York Times'* educational trips for high school students, in the company of *Times* journalists, cost $5,000. On one such Student Journey to Peru, the kids were apparently 'taught' racism and disdain for the concept of white privilege.[26] *The Nation* offers similarly priced trips to Cuba for adults, as if there were something extra responsible about gadding about in a country America tried to boycott out of existence. These olive-branch tourists would presumably never dream of sacrificing five thousand bucks each to *help* Cuba or Peru directly.

Another popular destination for the conscience-stricken is the European concentration-camp circuit. Great day out for all the family![27] The Nazis put fossil fuels to previously unimaginable uses, and you too can deplete what remains of our irreplaceable energy supply by transporting yourself – voluntarily! – to Auschwitz to gawp at the gas chambers in a Hawaiian shirt.

The biggest travellers, the wealthy and mobile twenty per cent, are causing the most environmental damage. As Bob Hughes observed in his book about the ways in which technological liberation has liberated *nobody*, bikes and even horses

26 'Star NY Times Reporter Accused of Using "N-Word"…' (*The Daily Beast*, January 28, 2021.)

27 Sergei Loznitsa has covered this new type of voyeuristic jaunt in his movie *Austerlitz* (2016).

are not only cleaner forms of transport but *quicker* too, if you calculate the actual time and energy invested.[28] Airlines claim that their ever-bigger aircraft are more egalitarian and environmentally friendly, but they never add in the costs of enlarging runways, building the planes, and hiring enough Security goons to flatten all the passengers – I mean, protect passenger safety. There's nothing admirable about getting on an Airbus.

～

As for the VIRUS, what *it* likes are cars, restaurants, airports, globalism, poverty, superspreader get-togethers, close contact, coughing, panting, yelling, and a catastrophically diminished environment. Covid *loves* to travel and it really gets around. It thrives on apathy – ours and that of our lethargic and asinine leaders. Let's thwart it, beef up what the virus *hates*: community, quiet, carefulness, consideration, stasis, solitude. Clean air. Masks. Morality. Conservation, the common good, individual commitment to a single locale. And *staying put*. We fight it with *these* while we wait for the vaccine, whaddya say?

The UK's Covid lockdown in the spring of 2020 did have one heartening effect: an almost instantaneous burst of wildlife. Birds sang more – for once, they could hear each other. Plants seemed to grow more vigorously, with better air and no one outside to trim or trample them. Weeds blossomed boisterously. Streets were calm and quiet. For a little while in Edinburgh, we were spared the sight and sound of cars in motion, and even of tourists clanking their wheeled suitcases over the cobblestones.

---

28 *The Bleeding Edge: Why Technology Turns Toxic in an Unequal World* (New Internationalist, 2018).

Dolphins have been spotted in Venice. In Hong Kong, within a week of the cancellation of the usual two hundred express ferries to Macau, native dolphins returned in great numbers. They played in the water, and apparently had lots of sex. Dolphins really know how to live — if only we'd let them.

There is beauty in less activity, less financial transaction, less mayhem, less hurry, less frenzy, less movement.

Individuals are *not* responsible for global warming, it's true. Corporations are largely to blame. But irresponsible individuals don't help! Maybe what we need is an intervention: just put travel addicts on a low-mileage diet, or make them go cold turkey. If they need ongoing support, they can join Carboniferous Anonymous (CA), a twelve-step programme I just made up for people stuck on burning up all the fossil fuels.

It will be hard to stick to your resolve at first, especially when you see your friends scoring their usual peregrination points. You may even be shunned for not putting yourself through several long-haul flights a year, not catching the usual half a dozen colds, and not knowing the best coastal bus route in Honolulu (No. 55). Don't listen to them. Sticks and stones will break your bones, but travel buffs will never hurt you. Throw out your cholera pills. Recycle all those little plastic toiletry containers. And try having sex with people who live nearby.

BRAS:
A LIFE SENTENCE

It's like always meeting under a PYLON. The bra is the omni-present structure of the twentieth century and now the twenty-first. Every woman you know, love, hate, help, vex, need, revile, misconstrue, and repudiate is probably wearing one, has worn one, and will continue to wear one every day of her life. Aunts, mothers, grandmas, teachers, doctors, estate agents, travel agents, theatrical agents, secret agents, dental psychiatrists, friends, sisters, daughters, and nieces are all enduring this unmentioned bondage, post-puberty, and we just accept it! They live and DIE in bras. Stifling cups and biting straps and niggly hooks and rotting elastic and silly little bows and frills and embroidered flowers or polka dots. Women have come and gone, fledged in love and hope and doomed to desolation, all whilst wearing bras. Their upper torsos have been twisted, tainted, squeezed, and adulterated by these garments, which rarely make them happy.

MEN HAVE MANAGED TO EROTICISE BRAS, BUT THEY DON'T HAVE TO WEAR THEM.

Apparently the smooth back of the human female must never be seen; it can only appear in public, roped in, with seams criss-crossing it, and bulges along the seams, that are now more familiar than a real breast, unleashed. We are so offended by the rocking and rolling of breasts when loose, so ignorant of their natural substance and behaviour, we have reached the delusional state of thinking it unnecessary and *outlandish* that breasts should ever wobble at all. Their gelatinous quality will not do. In its place, we get engineering feats that are more like BRIDGES than breasts. Are we trying to get to the other side?

CHILDREN MUST WONDER IF BREASTS WOULD *FALL OFF* IF THEY WEREN'T FASTENED ON BY BRAS.

Women survive WARS, or don't, wearing bras. They cook thousands of meals wearing bras. They have arguments, go to movies and restaurants, go to the DOGS, wearing bras. They even manage to BREASTFEED wearing bras. They drive, they run, they dance, they trip, they fall... some even try to sleep, wearing bras. They collect prizes, pensions, the kids, the groceries, and the service wash, wearing bras (and have to wash the damn things back home *by hand*). They're badgered by authorities and family members, beaten by bad men, given parking tickets, and disallowed child custody, wearing bras. They're kept so busy doing all that stuff, they don't have time to OBJECT to bras. Ideally, they'd be offered *tax-free handouts* annually, in compensation for this sartorial torment. Instead, all they get are strong shoulders, from toting their breasts in bra baskets all their lives. Only during the politically advanced sixties and seventies – and in 2020, as a vegging-out by-product of Covid lockdowns – have there been some poignant efforts at bra-avoidance.

MARILYN MONROE NEVER TOOK HER BRA OFF.

Considering the physical responsiveness, sensitivity, and the erogenous tissue of what it encloses, the bra is pointedly anti-sensual. It pulls, it pierces, it pinches; it exerts a death grip all day. It causes rashes, chafing, irritation (both mental and physical), and lasting striations on the skin. And form follows function: the bigger the breasts, the uglier the bra. Apart from the lace (if you're *lucky*), most bras are made of very weird materials, unbecomingly combined. Policing the breasts is the main requirement. The topographical complexity of the territory and elaborate design standards also ensure that bras can never be home-made, so manufacturers can change whatever they want for these straitjackets. Compared to the authoritarianism of these compulsory fabric containers, breasts begin to seem primitive, rudimentary, RUDE, idle, anarchic, whimsical and unschooled. Unstrictured structures, ripe for rebellion, breasts are dubious, naughty, irrelevant, optional, a subject of debate, practically ILLEGAL. Breasts are *detainees* – tracked, branded, interrogated, maligned, discouraged, and 'supported'. No other body part suffers from this level of scrutiny and distrust.

THE STRAPS CAN BE SNAPPED BY
GOOFBALLS
TO ADD STING TO RIDICULE

Breasts have clearly seen their day. Shabby and outmoded, their future is bleak. With the help of implants, they've even started to EXPLODE. This makes wearing a bra yet more vital, as protection for others in the vicinity. Mayhem might ensue if breasts were ever released from their prisons, so there they stay, serving life sentences, and our compliance is chilling.

MORNING
ROUTINE GIRLS

How convenient for capitalism that the self morphed so easily
into the cell phone. The doomed and the dying use selfie sticks
to record their every car accident and tiger encounter. The
Web is awash with self-promotion, from glossy offerings like
Comedians in Cars Getting Coffee (in which Jerry Seinfeld and
fellow comedians go eat chicken and waffles together, and
advertise cars on the side) and *Freunde von Freunden* (where
arty careerist Europeans show off their carefully curated homes,
offices, products, and dogs), to many other types of veiled
bragging: terrorist training camp highlights; Christians trying
to sell Rapture, and alt-right groups the 'Storm'; countless
photographic compilations of thumbtacks, thimbles, antique
weaponry, corkscrews, or Daily Carry; glitzy and glitchless performances of niche culinary tasks; tame discussions of periods
and tampons; and giggly videos of boys trying on bras. The
web is for lonely, needy, greedy show-offs and the people who
love them.

Among those most suckered by the new technology of self-absorption are the most unhappy people on the planet: prepubescent and teenage girls. Young women rightly live in terror of the society in which they find themselves, understandably aspiring to reach adulthood *without* getting raped, shot, manhandled, murdered, trolled, or publicly discredited. It's ambitious of them. Huddling strategically behind their screens, *computer* screens, these girls have invented a new kind of purdah. From the safety of undisclosed locations (usually upper-middle-class American homes), they participate in their chosen amazeballs genre, a bottomless pit of boredom and twaddle: the cinematic low point known as the Morning Routine video.

These videos are short, quasi-home-made autobiographical films that record in a certain amount of intimate detail these girls' sheltered existences ('Just woke up!'). The final products are uploaded on to YouTube and elsewhere for the edification of an insular, supposedly all-girl audience (though anyone can tune in – anyone who can *bear* to, that is). The self-appointed and well-defended girl-stars welcome other (lesser) girls into their bedrooms (but only in the virtual sense), and in return get summarily liked or hated. (Let the bitching begin.) Each video thus functions as a daily workout for the barefaced, bug-eyed, belief-beggaring, bullshitting self – for both author and audience. If not exactly works of art, they are masterpieces of narcissism.

Product endorsement is the sinister inspiration behind much of what these girls inflict on one another. Alternately self-aggrandising and self-deprecating, affectedly awkward and sometimes flirty, these girls *seem* to want to be your pal, but it's the attention of multimillion-dollar cosmetics companies they really crave. Starbucks probably wins the Ubiquitous Product Placement award here though – hardly a single Morning Routine girl fails to demonstrate an allegiance to the incomprehensibly popular coffee brand. Even half-drunk pumpkin spice lattes from *yesterday* are worth tenderly recording on the bedside table, as proof of sophistication. Or the girl descends to the kitchen to concoct, barista-style, some sort of drink made out of Starbucks creams, syrups, and milk alternatives, from a stash of matching logoed canisters.

Another category of the Morning Routine video world is the Shopping Haul, rhyming conveniently with shopping mall. In these broadcasts, a dimpled teenybopper sits chummily on the floor of her bedroom, displaying bags of recently purchased clothing and her encyclopaedic knowledge of everything on offer (and Special Offer) at chain stores. She may emphasise that all this awesome stuff is like really really cheap, but is anyone fooled by this pose of frugality? Anyway, everything in this all-girl land is super-duper cute. Crazy-cute! And I mean *everything*. In a baking video, two cute girls make cute cupcakes out of cute ice-cream cones — all cute as can be. But how mercilessly would they diss any girl they knew who dreamed of eating one. Because anorexia's cute too.

MEN SHOULD BE FORCED TO WATCH THIS STUFF, TO SEE WHAT THEY'VE DONE TO WOMEN.

The slicker the whole shebang gets, the more effort the girls put into making things look humble. For atmosphere, the make-up tutorials feature deceptively amateurish product shots, with cutely shaky close-ups of every lip gloss, shampoo, perfume and itty-bitty container of wrinkle cream. Yes, wrinkle cream for twelve-year-olds.

To me, the make-up sessions seem *endless*, crazy-bad, with the juvenile mentor spending twenty minutes at a time basting her face like a Thanksgiving turkey. If you skip ahead ten minutes, she's still at it! Or she's straightening or curling her hair with an electric hot brush, a business that often seems to take about an *hour*, while the ditzy monologue goes on. These people are indefatigable, and clearly lead the most leisured lives on the planet. Ever been in such a rush you forgot to brush your hair or apply lipstick, deodorant, nail polish, jewellery? These girls never do, and by example they pressure other girls to spend hours and hours of *their* young lives too on this self-conscious prettifying. They even pretend it's fun, smiling non-stop while they administer the gunk. They seem to get a particular kick out of trying to hide their acne. It's all very upbeat, anyway.

Then there are the more serious sisterly advice talks, when they tell their viewers that friendship is a 'two-way thing', unhappiness a 'waste of time', water necessary, and that bees, yeah! 'bees make the world keep going'. In solipsistic Q & As, the funette answers 'questions' from viewers, such as what's your favourite item of make-up, or your OOTD (outfit of the day), or the craziest thing you ever did. In Mom Tags, another recurring strand of the genre, it's the *mother* who's quizzed on the craziest thing the girl ever did. There are also whole videos of hairdos, supposedly created in response to viewer demand. Hard to believe. Or, now and then, a ten-minute video on What's in My Purse. Here, the depressing contents of the poor chump's hand-bag (the contents of handbags are always depressing, because there's never enough MONEY in there) are dumped on the floor, so that she can mull over yeah! the mind-numbing purpose of each object. Why not dump out what's in the *bin* instead? Let's see the roaches, honey, the needles, the prophylactics... But drugs and sex have nothing to do with this particular web world. These are rich, pretty, artfully self-censoring princesses – *nuns* of a sort, showing off their habits.

The most unnerving thing about these videos is how *alone* the girl is. Despite the hazy form of a mom or sibling standing in the background sometimes, it seems highly likely the video girl was incubated and hatched in her bedroom by remote control, without human intervention. And there she continues her solitary reign. The bedroom is always surprisingly neat, the walls white or lilac, with the emphasis on the bed (always a double), her throne and pedestal. Lying there in stylish sleepwear, surrounded by scented candles and electronic devices, the girl studies herself on all available screens. The TV, laptop, smartphone, and mirror (or 'meer', as they all pronounce it) become interchangeable. The house beyond, occasionally glimpsed, is brand new, ostentatious, cleansed, and minimalist, with a comically well-stocked fridge. The girl appears to be in sole command of this empire, or wills herself to be. No sign at all of the retinue of servants either, who must actually keep the household afloat. Outside sits a BMW she claims is hers.

But what does she need a car for? Especially during a pandemic. Many of these self-chronicling shut-ins were already homeschooled *before* the lockdowns. They happily admit they hardly ever leave the house. 'I don't have anywhere crazy to go.' Their idea of an expedition is to sit on the *balcony*, where they complain that people in the outside world make noise, noise which interferes with the all-consuming video project and soon forces the girl to retreat indoors.

Little Kaspar Hausers, their only abiding interest is in looking, sounding, and, yeah! acting cool — so as to receive thumbs ups on their vlogs from people they will never meet. They are dolls come to life: they move their limbs, chatter, and change their clothes a lot. Their bodies are smooth, their skin blemish-free (almost). Other lonely, less cosmetically privileged girls are

157

allowed to benefit from this shamanic performance. They can learn, for instance, how to carry on an endless soliloquy while applying the daily dolly mask that ensures they will prematurely age and require multitudinous ameliorating skin preparations for life. *Vita brevis, Noxzema longa.*

These girls have all mastered the Valley Girl accent and manner, even if their home valleys actually lie in Minnesota or Pennsylvania or, for all we know, Transylvania. It's always Christmas in July for them! Their conformism is totally standardised. But distress abounds, and not just in the denim cut-offs. Most of these young women are fearful and cranky, however serene their foreheads may be. They have been manipulated, they know it, and their revenge comes in handing on to fellow sad sacks an intimidating set of criteria for being acceptable. They're like all the girls you hated at school, and their airbrushed pretence of happiness is one of the most exasperating things about them. They rightly stare at themselves in the meer, wondering who's the unfairest of them all.

Why aren't these girls out saving whales, planting trees, building railroads, dismantling Guantanamo, dating people, or just reading a book? They do half-listen to *audiobooks* sometimes, books adapted for recent Hollywood offerings. But they're so 'crazy busy': they're pretend New Yorkers, hurriedly 'grabbing' a coffee, a bottle of water, their boots, and their car keys before they're 'good to go'. They live in envelopes of arid, pseudo-cosmopolitan nonchalance. They have fenced themselves off from our collective impending annihilation and, yeah! banished any hint of it from their speech, their looks, their demeanours and their boudoirs. Negativity has no place here (all the negative vloggers must have been burnt at the stake) and the prissiness is beyond belief.

The Morning Routine video issues from their YouTube *channel* (the hosts dwell on this word as if they believe they own whole TV networks) and sometimes begins with an intro, in which the kid flings her arms around a lot and wags her head alarmingly from side to side to make sure you know she's not just cute but full of irony. Then the 'routine' blasts off. The convention is that, as the filming begins, she's still asleep in bed — wearing a bra under her cutesome top, though, and crazy-comfy 'sweats' (sweatpants) perhaps. Her phone buzzes a wake-up call, she drowsily silences it, and then proceeds to spend a good amount of time lying in various angular poses on the bed, texting people and, yeah! checking social media. A memo of the mid-teen midriff. Sometimes a purse-dog or bunny rabbit joins her, to be cuddled (bunnies are big in this world, though the bunny itself must be small). Then, abruptly forgetting all about the squiffy pet, our hostess stumbles into her own private en suite bathroom.

No one excretes, of course, in this fairyland. Instead, at the sight of yet another meer, the girl starts dancing excitedly to her favourite music. And soon she's trotting, still in her PJs, through the echoing mansion to the fridge, which handily houses another video camera so that we can see her, yeah! exact facial expression as she decides what to eat. Her breakfast — yogurt, granola, fruit, and Starbucks — hints again at constipation. Then we're back upstairs to watch the exhausting make-up routine. It's, you know, I mean, yeah! it's like the worst sleepover you ever attended. Absolutely drained of mirth or interest. To liven things up a bit, she may take a shower, since she has at least four soapy liquid products to delightedly present. In the shower, Morning Routine girls wear *bikinis*: again, the whiff of the nunnery. Perhaps they fear some unfortunate sexual awakening might cause the collapse of this Eden in which everything's cute *except* boys.

Who watches this stuff? It's no great comfort that, for every Humbert Humbert who may be spying on Morning Routine videos to see budding adolescent girls acting kooky for the camera, there are probably dozens, if not hundreds, of faithful female contemporaries online, soaking up the atmos, thrilled to be spoken to nicely by *anyone*, even by a girl born to annoy.

Artificiality is a given, as is all the lying. It's like a cash-conscious *Clueless* – though these girls are backed by a certain level of wealth. Despite the pretence of artlessness and autonomy, most of the videos obviously get a lot of technical help. Since, the more energetic the camera angles, editing, lighting, and colours, the more hotel-like the domicile, and the more savage the dermabrasion, the happier the sponsors will be. Which is super-crazy-great.

You should see all the jars of brushes and eyebrow pencils, the array of eyeshadows and eyeshadow primers and eyeshadow concealers, the eyeliners and eyelash curlers and earlobe enhancers; the lipsticks, the lip exfoliators, the lip-slimers and lip-swellers; the cold cream, the foundation, the ointments, the unguents; the mists and sprays and monsoon mud packs; the scissors, the tweezers, the Dead Sea nail balm; the sponges and cotton balls and foam pads and pad foams and, yeah! all the hair-knuckle-undering machines! It's enough to satisfy an army of make-up artists on a Busby Berkeley picture. The shelving alone deserves an Oscar, with all the little totalitarian drawers of very well-organised stuff. With such pigments and such priorities, these kids should be painting the Sistine Chapel! Instead, Morning Routine art is ephemeral and all wiped away twelve hours later by the Night-time Routine.

There's a confessional element to these before-and-after cosmetic transformations: these girls are admitting to their fascinated viewers that channelling Barbie takes work. Even if yeah! you're like the prettiest girl in town already and just can't help it. To show that they're *human*, they often include a blooper reel at the end, and throughout the ordeal that is their lives, the girls are upbeat – because unhappiness is like such a waste of time. They lead eventless, nourishmentless, friendless, freedomless, and odourless lives – apart from all the fumes from the promotional sprays and scents and toners with which they hourly asphyxiate themselves. 'I get so many compliments on this perfume. Not that that's *why* we should ever do things. But it's *nice!*'

They are spatially-challenged cheerleaders, with blusher brushes for pom-poms, purse-pups as mascots, and the bedroom their field of dreams. Some of these home-based advertisers are under sixteen, incidentally, making them child labourers. Exploited by cosmetics firms, they in turn exploit their hoodwinked viewers, flaunting their sponsorships and luring the unwary toward their deranged music videos as well, which they also want to sell. Vulnerable to thumbs downs from across the globe on account of their asses (fat!) and eyebrows (thick!), their resolutely pally personas are perfect avatars of capitalism. The phenomenon isn't new. As Shirley Jackson put it in the fifties:

From the time my daughter gets up in the morning to brush her hair the same number of times that Carole up the street is brushing *her* hair to the time she turns off her radio at night after listening to the same program that Cheryl three blocks away is listening to, her life is controlled, possessed, by a shifting set of laws... The side of the street she walks on, the shoes she wears to walk on it, the socks, the skirt, the pocket-book... even the jacket and the haircut are rigidly prescribed.[1]

But those baby-boom popularity-seekers were spared the extra barbed wire of social media. Will our pampered twenty-first-century slave girls ever break free? Their YouTube, Instagram, Keek, and Vine experiments *could* turn into real girl power, yeah! if these ostriches could only find time for activism, between the waxing and waning of their daily beauty regimens. A little light political posturing might spark up those monologues too, and brighten the bleak days of their dotage – unless they just become online Miss Havishams, documenting their disintegration, with the Mourning Routine.

Come on, dump the face powder, gals. *This* is the stuff of girl dreams:

To turn somersaults naked, outdoors,
your cunt in the air.
To wallow in baths of whipped cream
and maraschino cherries.
To ride a galloping stallion bareback along a beach.
To understand the phases of the moon and Dog Star.
To be free as a mermaid adrift in the sea.
To run into a bullring and befriend the bull.
To discover something very very important.
To speak the language of goats and hoop snakes.
To be unique.
To fly.
To hide a pet mouse in your mouth and scare people.

---

1 *Let Me Tell You* (Penguin, 2015).

SING THE UNELECTRIC!

(In Praise of Buttons, Bikes, and Jam)

Once there was a world without power: without power stations, power surges, or power suits. A world in which, okay, people ruined their eyesight reading and sewing stuff in the dark. They also had the occasional accident on the stairs. Indoor plumbing still had a way to go too. But at least genes and gonads weren't permanently damaged by man-made radiation leaks, and light pollution from earth didn't keep the whole cosmos awake. They were spared so much, our ancestors: struggling with Teasmades and twin-tubs, microwaving cakes, and becoming self-taught computer technicians. They had it all – freedom, individuality, culture. They even had time to think. And then electricity was tapped, Henry Ford ruined civilisation with the private car, and Steve Jobs forced an Apple on us all.

A few years ago, I went to an exhibition at the Ashmolean Museum in Oxford of nineteenth-century Japanese silk embroidery. Probably not the best tapestries ever. They seem to represent an odd, slightly cheesy, cul-de-sac in the history of decorative arts, and are characterised by brightly coloured stitches crammed together against a black background of silk or velvet. They were mostly made for export, to please a taste for the oriental in England, America, and elsewhere. A lot of these tapestries are *frightful* pictorially, just idealised scenes in which excesses of silk and gold thread conjoin to produce lifeless souvenirs of hillside temples or tigers. One triptych screen of a life-size embroidered peacock offered the closest approximation of peacock feathers I've ever seen – but it was *not* a real peacock. It was a needless exercise in imitation.

Padded silk is an art form, it turns out, and an endearing one sometimes. One folding screen featured tiny labourers, village characters, and fancy ladies, all meticulously rendered in silk-padded bas-relief. Every detail of their garments was hyperreal, and the effect was stupendous. Maybe you have to sew a few thousand vulgar panels to come up with one good one. But even at their most grotesque, these silken offerings still had a dignity and verve that most printed images and photography lack. They exist, they *coexist* with us, they age, they breathe; they were very cleverly, painstakingly, put together by hand, *many* hands (mostly male hands, apparently), years ago. How much life had to be lived just to get the thing done! *Human time* was invested in these peculiar productions. And no electricity was involved.

The same goes for many denigrated handicrafts (usually the work of women): the elaborate and time-consuming culinary traditions of India, France, and Mexico, tapestry weaving, needlepoint, knitting, lace-making, basketry, batik, macramé, rug-braiding, knitting, crochet, gilding, quilting, or the long-lost art of dough pictures, whereby you stick thin layers of white dough on a dark background to make a bas-relief picture of Victorian milkmaids lugging water or making butter (maybe it was a way of using up leftover pastry). And all the other crafts with which people kept idle hands busy, like beadwork, coiled paper pictures, silhouette-cutting, stencilling, all those goofy foil and sequined pictures made from kits, soap sculpting, and gluing spray-painted macaroni on to the top of a cigar box.

Where are signs of the hand now? Within the alienating realm of digital technology and industrialisation, we're not just losing sight of what art is, but what the human hand can do. It's capable of a lot more than just texting, gliding a mouse around or separating Velcro. As James Joyce said about 'the hand that wrote *Ulysses*', 'It did lots of other things too.'[1] Hands are appendages of major importance! We wouldn't last a minute without them. Nobody would catch you when you're born, or affix you to the nipple, or change your nappy, or embrace and caress you. No matter how much we like machines, consumerism, and remaining motionlessness at the altar of Netflix, the human hand is our biggest love.

Not to see anything made by hand is a kind of death, a deprivation closely aligned to the prospect of never being touched again. Shaking each other's hand in greeting is an acknowledgement of the significance of hands. People have missed this during the era of Covid. Poking elbows at each other just isn't the same. Handbags are an extension of the hand. Thatcher was naked without her handbag.

～

I'm tired of electricity, coal, gas, petrol, and especially nuclear power. I now only like the kind of energy that plants and animals

---

1 Richard Ellmann, *James Joyce* (Oxford University Press, 1959).

naturally expend going about their daily business. Electricity is a kind of ethereal rapist, interfering with everyone. It's a form of abuse. And I'm not talking electric shocks, just the devious way electricity insinuates itself into your house, into your life – and money drains out of the bank. We're not given any choice in the matter. We even read our electricity bills by electric light.

Not having electricity has long been a stigma, a sign of either poverty or incompetence. Most of us are convinced we *must have it* – as a result, hydroelectric companies throw people *out* of their homes in order to build more dams. It's amazing they get away with it. Electrification has taken the place of education, health, and financial benefits, as the one thing governments must provide – before developing countries get their mitts on it.

It's grown on me gradually, like a turtle shell, that I hate electricity. (Turtles are well-protected against electric eels.) It gives me a buzz to think about unelectric things. I get this warm, private, halogen-free glow. And I've begun almost unconsciously to search the world for anything that doesn't require electricity. I appreciate wrinkles in clothing now, because they imply an electric iron lying fallow somewhere. Dust bunnies under beds attest a dormant hoover. My attitude is not really a moral position, nor a hygienic or political one, though there are ample ways of defending it morally, hygienically, and politically. It's not merely melancholic either, derived from nostalgia and worry over the environment – though I do think my distaste originated the moment I learnt, as a child, that Lake Erie was officially dead, flooded with so many toxins from factories on its shore that no fish or plants could live in it any more. I wanted to get back to nature. This developed into a disdain for fashion, new buildings, the space programme, tree surgery, polyester, pharmaceutical companies, men with short hair, witch-burning, and the Industrial Revolution.

But I've recently observed in myself an acute disgust with all things pulsing, humming, and zapping, too, an awkward handicap in the modern world. I have an increased respect for simple stuff that doesn't move without help, stuff that just sits there, stuff that doesn't require the aid of power stations to animate or validate it. These artefacts may have *started* life in factories, through various uses of fossil fuel, but they've since rebelled against such parentage to claim a quieter, independent existence. Such noble and obliging things as keys, buttons (a *kind* of key: they open and shut your clothes for you), bidets, bathtubs, bicycles, butter, bells, belts, Band-Aids, balloons, blankets, books, beards, pens, paper, pisspots, pottery, poodles and parrots, shoes, sheds, sleds, skis, skates, wind-up clocks, musical instruments, hand tools, water taps, toilets, (non-electric) typewriters, (non-electric) toothbrushes (non-electric) tennis rackets, tulips in a glass of water, tables, chairs (who would want an *electric chair* – outside of Florida?), candles, matches, cupboards, clothing, Kleenex, corkscrews, cigarettes, needles and cotton thread, doorknobs, doors, hinges, drills, hammers, nails, screws, pliers, saws, see-saws, scales, sliding scales, corkscrews, home-made jams, and padded silk panels.

The wooden shutters in my bedroom, which keep out the light and the cold, were created before power tools, and can only be repositioned with human help. No external force, no artificial, doomed, or dwindling power source, is involved. And they work! They've lasted for two centuries. The duvet works too, without electricity, as do the drawers, shelves, floorboards, and rug. So, too, the pictures on the wall. My husband runs on his own steam too, especially when he's steamed about something.

We can even open and close our bedroom door without enlisting the services of the National Grid.

I admit there is also an old laptop in our bedroom. Such things jar. Plus, several environmentally unfriendly lamps – though not as many of them as a friend of mine would advise. She always says I have too few lamps, but I think she has too *many*. She lights up her home like an operating room, and would be wholly unsupportive of my aversion to electricity if I ever dared mention it to her.

I haven't yet reached so extreme a position on electricity that I have to retreat to the desert or up a tree. My electricity tolerance fluctuates. On a plane, I'm resigned to being saturated in electricity (including the risky proposition of flying through electrical storms). I more or less tolerate the little reading light and the fake fan overhead. The suck-you-uppo toilets, the blazing TV screens. The drinks trolley at least is hand-powered – such restraint! But, once at home again, I flee all these hateable things for stable, non-vibrating, non-blasting, non-grating, non-sapping, unexplosive and unelectric entities: fruit bowl, wine, plants, candlestick, husband, playing cards, baths, hot-water bottles, sellotape, pencils, scissors, paper, stone.

Why do we find computer screens so compelling? We can't stop looking at their glittering, glowing, jewel-like colours. They're the new stained glass. Perhaps we half-mistake them for *picture windows*, and feel an instinctive need to check them constantly for visitors, marauders, and weather changes. But computer screens *aren't* windows – they're prison bars! This subjection to a life of digital confinement is repeated by the billion, worldwide. You leave your office jail cell for your handy home prison, with your smartphone to shackle you like an electric tag on the journeys in between. And the 'cloud' now uses more electricity than *whole countries*.

Fantasies of electricitylessness: to live in a steading some-where, equipped with a reliable well, vegetable patch, fireplace, wood-stoked Aga. Not a microwave or pressure cooker in sight. White wine chills in a gurgling spring just outside the door. Life would be all porridge and padded silk, a chicken or two pecking each other outside, and musical instruments, which we'd play to warm ourselves up. I would miss the ready supply of music recitals now provided instantly by YouTube or CDs. And washing clothes by hand would be a chore. Many household devices are addictive – cooker, kettle, fridge, freezer, toaster, dishwasher… But they take up so much space. It's time they all merged into one servile machine that would hoover things, dust things, toast and boil things, broadcast your favourite music non-stop, and cook up a stew too, through sheer friction while it's doing the housework. An iPlod.

But it would have to be silent. I can't stand the *noise* gener-ated by these contraptions of ours. Industrial noises have driven people crazy since the beginning of mass production. Workers were deafened by nineteenth-century cotton mills. Now the noise has penetrated the domestic scene. I'd do anything not to have to hear an extractor fan ever again, or a washing machine on spin cycle, or *our shower*, which has begun to squeal at certain temperatures. Noise is a feature of our age. Why *manually* rake leaves, allowing your neighbours to sleep late, when you can frazzle everybody with a leaf blower? Why sweep the streets with brooms when you can send out an ineffectual little mechanical pavement sweeper with twirling brushes, suds squirters, and a cutesy name? In an alienating electronic voice, it wends its troubled way blindly down the street, leaving a little trail of water and dog shit wherever it goes. Sooty the Street Cleaner repetitively declares 'Attention. Take care. Pavement cleaning in progress' – from afar, it sounds like 'Buzz off buster, buzz off buster, buzz off buster...'

I recognise I'm fighting a losing battle – going up the down escalator – since everything is becoming more and *more* electric, not less. I am too! I watch too many movies and don't read enough books. And I used to write on an old typewriter. Typewriters, for your information, are twentieth-century machines that automatically printed what you wrote, without being asked, and never lost your work because you've forgot to 'save'. They didn't catch viruses, they didn't bother you with questions, questions, questions, and updates, and glitches, and reboots, and they cost almost nothing to run. Mine had very small type, which I particularly like. But here I am now, like everybody else, tapping out a Word document on a computer, staring at my individual light panel, with Pieter Wispelwey playing Bach's suites for solo cello to me on the same machine. Oh hell. I'm just another volt dolt. And most of my mail is email now. Physical letters, which were usually much better written than emails, are practically extinct. Posties risk Covid merely to deliver junk mail now.

What'll happen when every good, plain, manually operated mechanism is replaced with an electronic one? When your battery-powered lipstick whizzes uncontrollably across your face and your shoes lace themselves? (Too tight!) We're already being offered electric toilets, and electronic airline check-in and electronic key cards in hotels and universities. Maps have been outmoded by satnav, books by Kindle, Nook, Kobo and Audible, and the phone has been supplanted by Zoom, WhatsApp, Snapchat and Skype. Poker, solitaire, Scrabble, crossword puzzles, jigsaw puzzles, recipes, newspapers, shopping, and gambling have all been abducted into online existences.

You can't even have a baby any more without using vast amounts of electricity, though our ancestors somehow managed without, and most animals still do. We go from battery-operated sex toys to ultrasound scans to electric breast pumps and baby monitors. These are followed by baby computer games, baby TV shows, and baby food blenders. We wallow in dependence on electricity. As if there were never power cuts! Hospitals and factories all have to have back-up generators. After 2012's Hallowe'en hurricane, people in New York apartment buildings couldn't use the *elevators* or *toilets*. They had no water supply because city-wide power cuts meant the electric pumps were on the blink. It's no joke walking up fifteen flights with your dog and your groceries. The food in people's fridges and freezers rotted, and dialysis had to be rationed.

The more dependent we get on electricity, the more we're at the mercy of the energy providers. We have given up any illusions of self-sufficiency or manual dexterity to become electricity-purchasing units. Humans now exist only to establish more and more outlets for electricity and to make ever-increasing demands on it. Our entire culture is in hock to electricity. It doesn't serve us, we serve it. The pathos!

~~~

It would be wonderfully calm and quiet in our steading, and so *private*. No computers. When you're on a computer, a million advertisers, hackers, malware gremlins, and the FBI are always staring over your shoulder. Electronics are high-anxiety, high-maintenance novelties. The cost alone — everybody has to invest thousands of pounds in new IT equipment every few years, just to get their emails! (Computer enthusiasts *exult* in these equipment updates, like car fanatics obsessing over new car designs.) With all these machines clanking away for us, our increased immobility further disables us. We *try* to control our expanding bellies with walking machines and electric toning belts, and obliterate facial hair with electric shavers and electrolysis. Meanwhile, what little is left of the handmade or do-it-yourself continues to be obliterated in favour of the distant and virtual, a far less charitable commodity.

Bathed in artificial light, we're really back in the Dark Ages. No trace will be left of our culture soon besides climate change, millions of Nigella Lawson mixing bowls, the Gutenberg project (*maybe*), and the heaps of radioactive waste. I'd rather *walk* to London than take a train fuelled by nuclear energy. There's no feasible or responsible plan for dealing with nuclear waste and nuclear accidents. We have permanently ruined the environment in honour of electricity, in honour of Fukushima and Chernobyl. We're like kids with their new toys: we want stuff that requires electricity and we want it *now*. Entranced by the virtual, we've lost contact with the earth. We're impetuously, mesmerically, floating off into cyberspace. Insects will be pleased.

And the world was once so verdant! It was there to be loved. Despite the ravages of religion, war, tyranny, massacres, patriarchy and suspect Cornish pasties, there was at least some guilt-free joy in the natural world. Look at Tobias Smollett, writing about Glasgow.[2] Think of it, *Glasgow*.

---

2 *The Expedition of Humphry Clinker* (1771).

Glasgow... is one of the prettiest towns in Europe... From
Glasgow we travelled along the Clyde, which is a delightful
stream... Here is no want of groves, and meadows, and
cornfields...

Groves? Streams? But things were still beautiful then, just a
few hundred years ago – before the industrialists backed us all
away from nature with our hands held over our heads. 'Nothing
to see here.' I know there was no whooping cough vaccine. But
there was a whopping amount of clarity, not just in the air and
the water but in people's *minds*. Now we go to war over unsus-
tainable forms of energy. Our romance with fossil fuels has
peaked in absurdity.

Skateboards are electrified now, but skis are still human-
powered. Rafts require nothing but a handheld paddle. Or you
can just sit on one and let the current take you where it will.
Sailboats only need a sail (and a good sailor). And there's always
the bicycle, the pedalled kind. Suspended on your little seat,
with the wind in your hair (or helmet). A bike proceeds at a
human pace (usually), and you can park one anywhere, unlike
a car, which is just a two-tonne metal box and killing machine,
ravenous and needy. Maybe we should use up all the remaining
electricity to manufacture *bikes*, and then just *turn it off*.

Know what works fine without electricity? Night-time. We
all endure a nightly electricity fast without harm (unless you're
dependent on an electric blanket, electric alarm clock, a night
light, or an iron lung). You can sleep right through these low-
tech periods of darkness, or get up and enjoy the quiet.

Another unelectric thing is people. And animals. They're
not electric *yet*, anyway – make the most of them now, before
they're all replaced with robots.

This world is too expensive, too ugly, too heartless, too hand-less to bear! Where's art, where's kindness and comfort? Where are the simple, amiable, graspable products of our labour? All I'm saying is that when the primordial shit hits the electric fan and all current sources of energy are gone, *I* will have books, pencils, paper, index cards, a hole puncher, candles, matches, needles and thread, soap, socks, sweaters, long johns, a working loo (I *hope*), quite an assortment of ink stamps, some paintings I really like, old photos, a plain old manual toothbrush, a type-writer, and a wind-up torch. What'll you have?

AH, MEN

Every now and then people bafflingly try to depict the late Doris Day as some sort of feminist trailblazer or iconoclast. Doris Day was one of the corniest cream cakes ever produced by male self-love: not just the goofy girl next door but the goody-goody *bore* next door who put up with anything her nutso 1950s neighbours, and Rock Hudson, asked of her. By playing frisky nitwits, she was seamlessly sucked into the misogynistic vortex at the centre of our punitive culture. Like Monroe, Garland, Goldilocks, Medea, Medusa, Salome, Lady Macbeth, and Shirley Temple, Doris Day materialised from deep in the collective male psyche to become just another gal to kick around. It's depressing.

'Ah, men,' as Bette Davis would say.[1] I'm sorry to have to mention this, but men don't like women much. They subtly let us know this from time to time, through rape, murder, public stonings, porn, prostitution, female circumcision, anti-abortion laws, the pay gap, constant scoldings (online and in person), and sulking when you win at Scrabble. Though forever in the wrong,

---

1 *All About Eve* (directed by Joseph L. Mankiewicz, 1950).

men are not gracious in defeat. Hence the geyser of fury they exude. Ciudad Juárez in Mexico is now famed for its femicide rate. Congrats. As a beleaguered Honduran woman recently told the *New York Times*, 'Just because you are a woman you feel hatred. Like someone is always trying to kill you.'[2]

Why do men let us live at all? It must really go against the grain to see us still trotting about, after all their efforts to defeat us. Are they just *humouring* us while they farm us for our vaginas?

Of course there are men I love, men I admire, I admit it, and a fair number I put up with. Hell, I put up with them all! We *all* do. But that doesn't mean they're good for humanity. It's *women* we need in charge of things: they're much less emotional, and far more likely to have their priorities right, such as life, liberty, and the pursuit of happiness. Also, as Fran Lebowitz has said, they rarely rape their employees.[3]

Women have a lot of latent power. Think of all the stuff we do – paint, teach, write, sing, dance, compose, medicate, self-medicate, vote, quit, quilt, invent, invest, divest, divorce, ponder, squander, and produce young. We go to the gym, to the moon, to the dogs, to the morgue. It's a multitasking nightmare! We even dare call ourselves 'Dr' if we happen to have a PhD, despite being belittled for it – in Jill Biden's case, by an irritated male columnist in the *Wall Street Journal* who patronisingly redubbed the new First Lady 'kiddo'.[4]

UXORIOUSNESS SHOULD HAVE BEEN THEIR BUSINESS.

Instead, men still use marriage as a stick to beat us with. A

2 'Someone Is Always Trying to Kill You' (*New York Times*, April 5, 2019).
3 'Who's Afraid of Fran Lebowitz?', All About Women Festival, March 6, 2018 (Sydney Opera House Talks and Ideas Archive).
4 Joseph Epstein, 'Is There a Doctor in the White House?...' (*Wall Street Journal*, December 11 2020).

woman's marketable charms have merely broadened to include her financial assets as well as her ass. Doris Day did her best sixty years ago to help forge the path of obedience, in her usual role as the single career girl in search of a husband to complete her (after mildly competing with her). In a male world, women juggle home life and working life. Men just go to work.

Women are also made to seem responsible for everything that happens in a marriage. People are always blaming wives for fattening their husbands up, for instance. But what if it's the other way around? What if it's *men* who make *women* fat, with their customary insistence on three meals a day? Some women are frightened off living with men because of all the eating involved. They write to agony columns about it! There are all those 'hangry' grumps too, on the 5:2 diet, who make Mondays unbearable for everyone in their vicinity. People don't talk enough about the metabolic strains on marriages.[5] Men make you cold, get you fat, then ditch you for somebody warmer and thinner, and act all innocent about it.

～

Amazingly, men are still deciding if we'll *do*, in the flame-choked, tsunami-soddened, silicon-breasted, carcinogen-ripened world they created for us, this great big radioactive cowpat of Growth and Progress and Pointlessness they've deposited everywhere.

Body-shaming is on the increase. Thanks to the ubiquity of porn, young women are now expected to produce a whole new

---

5 Differences of opinion on the ideal temperature of the home is another example of metabolic discord. Men often object to the thermostat being turned up, and prefer to see female life partners shiver.

level of nubility. It's not just putting a 'face' on that has reached a horrific level of professionalism. There's now the designer vagina. A global effort is underway to stamp *out* female genital mutilation, yet women in the West lust after elective labial surgery. Can you *get* any more dutiful than believing all vulvas have to be the same, even if achieving this uniformity involves excruciating pain? You can't even SEE the damn thing (the entire trade in pared-down pudenda is reliant on the male gaze). Add to this the customary scored-out pubic triangle: reduced by shaving and waxing to a narrow landing strip, the trimmed vulva is today's must-have signal of subservience. Is it for fear men will *miss* the vagina completely and head off with their joysticks into the stratosphere?

In guilty mimicry of female hair removal, *men* have started shaving themselves from top to bottom too! Everyone has to be hairless, just in case they're called upon to perform in a porn movie at any moment. You have to be expert in sex toys too, the Kama Sutra, S & M, bondage, striptease and pole-dancing. Sexuality is now Olympian in its competitiveness.

The obsession with bodily eligibility is a great distraction (along with *The Crown*, *Bridgerton*, the *actual* Olympics, and other forms of bread and circuses), from the real calamities of our times: racism, sexism, and climate change. Instead of confronting men about all these lousy ideas of theirs, women engage in a lifelong beauty competition, expensively daubing the face and fighting the flab while men distinguish themselves through acts of aggression and beefing about what's in the fridge.

Yet it's women who apologise and apologise! Our whole posture, our whole mode of being, is apologetic – when we have nothing to apologise *for*. Women's crimes come nowhere near what men have done. Who invented genocide, totalitarianism, whaling, rugby, and snuff movies? Or those medieval skimming-ton parades in which women deemed argumentative 'shrews' were dragged through the village, followed by a ducking? Who invented the goddam atomic bomb?

MEN HAVE RUINED LIFE ON EARTH.

How do patches of cellulite, unthreaded eyebrows, the occasional burnt pound cake, sharp word, or crying jag compare to *that*? After *men* get through with us all, only a few viruses will survive – viruses, prions, buckyballs and carrier bags.

Men delight in unauthorised violence, but glory in *legalised* murder too, protecting pugnacity with an official stamp. How eagerly they cosy up to armies, warfare, war movies, military history, or any kind of uniform – they love to be drenched in camo or battleship grey. Give them a big grim death-promoting system they can glom onto, a male hierarchy that provides them with goals, loyalty, doom, destruction, epaulettes, good opportunities for rape, a general miasma of testosterone, a guaranteed pass on domesticity, and a stage for showy acts of heroism, and they're happy as clams. They can't even write about *beer* without bringing war into it:

> Thanks for choosing to spend the next few minutes with this special homicidally hoppy ale. Savour the moment as the raging hop character engages the Imperial Qualities of the Malt Foundation in mortal combat on the battlefield of your palate![6]

Talk about killing yourself with drink. It almost makes you mourn the lost art of duelling. One good thing about duels was

---

6 From a bottle of Lagunitas IPA.

that a single confrontation could potentially rid the world of two idiots.

~~~

The other thing men like is *crime*. Crime's had a good long innings during patriarchy. We've had crooks, hoodlums, knaves, rogues, renegades, seducers, agents provocateurs, insurrectionists, pirates, scamps, scoundrels, scaramouches, scallywags scapegraces, quacksalvers, mountebanks, rapscallions, charlatans, backsliders, black sheep, and bad eggs. We've bred fraudsters, felons, forgers, royal families, chisellers, cheaters, con artists, traitors, impostors, wage thieves, identity thieves, bike thieves, horse thieves, dog thieves, cat burglars. Grave robbers, pickpockets, shoplifters, slum landlords, shoddy builders, parole violators, bail jumpers, human traffickers, racketeers, snitches, squealers, superspreaders, and card sharks. Our lives have been blighted by hedge fund managers, embezzlers, pyramid and Ponzi schemers, perfidious perjurers, scammers, slanderers, libellers, stock brokers, insurance brokers, money launderers, insider traders, offshore bankers, lobbyists, monopolists, tax evaders, bribe takers, poisoners, and plagiarists. Libertines, adulterers, liars, fakers, fakirs, truants, malingerers, gold-diggers, lounge lizards, practical jokers, time and motion men, industrial spies and saboteurs, wastrels, vandals, smugglers. Flashers, stalkers, drink spikers, stickup men, kidnappers, pornographers, assassins, unelected despots, whisky waterers, collection box nickers, washing-line marauders, and photo-doctorers. Hijackers, human rights abusers, Holocaust deniers, drunk drivers, bootleggers, lynch mobs, public enemies, manslaughterers, cut-throats, hit-and-runners, chainsaw

massacrers, bombers, spree-shooters, polluters, the crimi-
nally negligent, ricin mailers, shite hairdressers, Nazis, Tories,
Republicans, Brexiteers, and book borrowers.

We obviously get some kind of kick out of transgression.
Our mythology, folklore, balladry, historical records, and the
annals of aristocracy rely almost entirely on the noteworthy
actions of chancers, barbarians, and piss-takers. Sin and guilt,
strange satellites of crime, have provided lucrative territory
for religions too. There are elephants who storm villages, and
macaques who seize people's smartphones to use as ransom at
the Uluwatu temple in Bali.[7] But, of all animals, humans seem
to make the best criminals. Do kangaroos court mayhem, plot
insurrection, seethe with egotism, vanity, and resentment, and
exult in deception and vengeance? Rarely. But with humans, as
Trump and his cronies have proven, one traitorous tax-avoiding
genocidal dumb-as-shit jerkball at the helm is never enough.
It seems we want whole stacks of them.

Only in such a brutalised society could a sci-fi horror action
drama like *The Terminator* become enshrined as family fare.[8]
Right at the beginning, Arnold Schwarzenegger tears somebody's heart out with his bare hands – on camera – and then goes
on to shoot a gun-seller and an innocent woman in the face, at
close range. (Why is it always the *face*?) The woman is executed
merely because she shares the same name as the Terminator's
intended victim. I forget why the gun-seller's obliterated. That's
as far as I got – there's only so much nonsense a person can
stand – but I gather it's a bloodbath: the IMDb estimates the

---

7 'Study finds macaques go for tourists' electronics and wallets over empty bags
and then maximise their profit' (*Guardian*, January 14, 2021).
8 Directed by James Cameron (1984).

death count at thirty-nine and, perhaps in deference to our love affair with crime, most of them are cops. I think the police should be *defunded*, but that's taking it too far.

Or how about the seemingly civilised movie *American Beauty*? What appears at first to be a gentle domestic satire ends inevitably in a shooting. Well, this is America, after all. What you get here is not so much suburbia personified as suburbia puréed. As if the only way to shut all these caricatures up – the homophobic ex-army dad, the bummed-out teenagers, the acquisitive and secretly lascivious mom, the underappreciated onanistic husband – is to shuffle them all into a crime scene. What if *It's a Wonderful Life* ended with someone shooting Jimmy Stewart in the head? Movies used to have a little tact. Now, the answer to all plot points is to blow somebody's brains out. It's Hollywood's *raison d'être*: bullet envy.

And then there's crime *writing*. Writing genre fiction of any kind is a cop-out. (Would it *kill* those people to write something fresh and new? Something honest and original? Something beautiful even?) But, of all the genres, from horror, sci-fi, cli-fi, po-mo, and chick lit, to travel, sex-and-shopping, speculative, supernatural, fantasy, historical, adventure, thrillers, war stuff, spy stuff, mob stuff, monsters, UFOs, etc., etc., nothing sinks lower in celebration of human lousiness than crime fiction. And it's usually such bad writing too! So lazy, so hackneyed, so awkward and mechanical – it *has* to be, to convey the stupid story and attendant clues. There's little room for organic flow. The plots are prone to sagging. Yet I once got into trouble merely for suggesting crime novels are 'overrated'. I didn't say they shouldn't exist, I didn't say nobody should read them, I didn't say their authors should be arrested for crimes against humanity – though it's tempting. All I said was, in response to a question about which book I felt was overrated: 'All crime fiction, I don't care who it's by.'[9] The backlash was startling. In tones familiar to anyone who reads Twitter or delves into the Comments section beneath online articles (never go below the line!), one disappointed *Guardian* reader called me ignorant, another said I was an asshole, and one wrote me right off: 'I was done with Lucy Ellmann when she was shitty about crime novels.'

Crime writers took it especially bad, and those people are *scary*. They know how to murder you every which way from Sunday! But I wasn't trying to burn their crummy books: censorship is even worse than the vice of writing godawful fiction. I just get tired of hearing crime fiction writers and crime fiction readers contend that these nasty ghastly novels are not only genuinely literary (they're not) but also some kind of validation of right over wrong, or a vital way of pinpointing and rooting out our darker tendencies. As if they're trying to *help* us in some way, striving to warn and educate us! I don't buy it. Nothing is being identified or conquered here. Nothing's being solved either. Nothing generous is being offered. All that's happening is that a lot of characters' eyeballs are being plucked out (and very remuneratively so for the writers). We are back in Ancient Rome: a murder mystery allows us the schadenfreudian fun of watching other people get mutilated. And in the case of crime fiction, that's usually women. Some readers evidently require such gruesome fairy tales nightly, so as to go on living in an unsafe, male-oriented world. Maybe solving one isolated mystery is simpler than facing how messed-up the whole bloody system is. Death struggles and near-death throes may even

9 'Books that made me', *Guardian* (August 16, 2019).

give ghoulish types a pleasurable adrenaline rush. Or, more legitimately, they may act as memento mori, an impetus to wise up. Or perhaps they spur in some the will to live. They quell mine. So, read your penny dreadfuls if you must, but have the taste not to mention it.

Accused of inexpertise on the subject, I proudly accept the slur. But I've read enough of the genre to form an opinion. Chandler rises above the rest – he's worth it for the wordplay. Highsmith's no stylist, she's repetitive and tedious and dreary. *But* she's rightly more interested in psychology than crime, which somehow makes her books ideal for an arduous plane trip. Agatha Christie's atrocious, only suitable for people with colds. And old Sherlock Holmes is barely a notch above Poirot and Miss Marple. What hacks these writers are.

On first reading it long ago, I did enjoy *The Moving Toyshop* by Edmund Crispin for some long-forgotten reason.[10] I think I approved of the way it scooted quickly past the crime to get on with the sleuthing. Looking at it again now, I find I've totally forgotten everything about it (another telling feature of most crime writing), including the runaway carousel scene at the end that Hitchcock stole for *Strangers on a Train*.[11] Here's what irks me about crime novelists: they can't even be bothered to think up something plausible, despite the ready supply of *actual* crimes in the world to study. And they're so reliant on coincidence, it's embarrassing. Is it likely that a man, off on a spur-of-the-moment trip from London to Oxford, would remember to bring a torch and a gun? A poet yet, named Cadogan. Did everyone own a gun in 1946? Maybe. Things were still unsettled

---

10 Gollancz (1946).
11 1951.

after the war perhaps. But still, make an effort, Crispin. Keep it real.

The murder plot is elaborately and shamelessly fanciful. Cadogan himself described it as 'strictly meaningless'! Crispin's memory of the layout of Oxford, though often pertinent to the story, often seems askew. And the baddies keep repetitively knocking people out with some sort of death grip on the neck – a technique I don't think it's very wise to spread around. (NB. I could never be a detective. Crispin's Gervase Fen is always springing up to use the phone! He's the most willing telephoner you ever saw. It would take me *weeks* to make even *one* of those phone calls, and by then the case would've gone cold.[12])

Mild times. Current fads in crime writing and Nordic noir seem to be all about gritty forensic enquiries into human horridness. Okay, enquire away. But don't pretend it's art, jewel-like in its finesse or complexity; nor that you're performing some kind of public service. Crime writers are in it for the money and their only job is to envelop a corrupted public in more and more examples of human depravity. Why would anyone research and write this guff *except* for money? So, sell out if you must, but there's no call for pride here. Gerald Ratner had the guts to admit his jewellery was crap.

What people don't object to enough about crime fiction is its maintenance of the misogynistic status quo. Just as war

---

12 In the book's favour, Crispin's asides can be nicely humorous, and I like the way his characters fall into literary chit-chat in the midst of trouble: the friendly lorry driver is a Lawrence fan, the Chief Constable has a *Measure for Measure* obsession. (Which suggests most people would prefer to think about something else, *anything* other than crime.) But Crispin's snotty about the murder victim's 'spinsterhood', a character flaw deduced on Cadogan's first sight of the corpse (with the aid of that handy torch): 'the flatness of her breasts suggested that she was unmarried.' Wow. So, there's the real crime: being flat-chested and single. Get a hold of yourself, man.

movies, even anti-war movies, inescapably glorify war, crime fiction romanticises the hell out of crime, no matter how many female detectives you proffer, nor how many sexist outrages they manage to sort out. You're still reinforcing an interest in patriarchal behaviour patterns that damage women. Our fixation on fictional criminality might seem innocent enough if there weren't such an obvious parallel between the invented visions, on paper, of women being sliced up and silenced, and the concurrent enactments in real life.

Quite clearly a lot of men still feel they have a right to decide if women live or die, fictionally or not. For some time now, Karen Ingala Smith has been compiling the Counting Dead Women project, a list of women murdered by men in the UK (there were about a hundred in 2020). But I agree with my friend Eloise Millar[13] that Ingala Smith should start *another* list: Counting Fictional Murdered Women. There must be MILLIONS by now, and almost as many murder methods, along with all their associated cults and copycat killers like the much-beloved Black Dahlia mystery, the Manson family, Jack the Ripper and all the rest of them, these tragedies multiplied beyond trace for our entertainment.

Refusing to read crime novels is a feminist act. But what about all those *female* crime writers, you cry, and their hordes of bloodthirsty female fans who turn up in droves at crime fiction festivals, avid for the next serial psycho dismemberer to hit the shelves? This is simply one of patriarchy's many perverse effects on the female mind. Women have been subjected to several thousand years of disenfranchisement and abuse. So, like any other colonised population, they're full of self-hatred.

---

13 Co-founder of the great Galley Beggar Press.

They have now picked up a habit of punishing themselves with lashings of imaginary violence – just as we routinely frighten our children with horrific bedtime stories.

Women may also read crime fiction for practical tips on self-defence: feeling vulnerable and demoralised, and well aware of male animosity towards them, female crime addicts prepare themselves for disaster by studying the territory and the criminal mindset, while also rehearsing fight or flight moves. Their brutish predilection for gore suggests the need for therapeutic repair work, not censure. Give women a peaceful, nurturing environment, give them a little self-respect and a sense of safety, give them *hope* that they are not in imminent danger of being garroted, trapped in a dungeon, or dissected at any moment, and they may no longer fixate on these terrifying tales of death and woe.

But why do MEN read this stuff? And write it? What do *they* get out of crime fiction except the chance to gloat over their own petrified paternalism and misanthropy? They cherish it like their prosthetic sex arse equipment. They want it because it does them no good at all, but it does violate women. The truth is, men don't need to know more about crime, they need to know *less*, they need to *unlearn* what they already know, the mess they invented. They need re-education and rehabilitation. They need a firm hand. They need to *discard* maledom, not burst their brains expanding on it and profiting off it.

How about working on the unsolved crimes of *environmental devastation* instead, or the chicanery of depriving people of healthcare, the petty larceny of monarchs, or the hoax of trying to resurrect Doris Day every decade or so?

TAKE THE
MONEY, HONEY[1]

The simplest proof that patriarchy's based on a load of lies, all lies – and that men are stinkers – is the way servants were treated just a century ago. In Britain, while the upper classes swanned about pretending, nauseatingly, that women were frail, helpless vessels incapable of serious thought or deed (there'd have been a lot less swooning if they'd just loosened up those corsets), the skivvies, 'slaveys', or aptly named 'maids of all work', toiled sixteen hours a day with hardly an afternoon off, emptying slops and lugging pails of water up and down flights of stairs, tending a million hearth fires, washing floors, and cooking, shopping, and ironing, all while being reprimanded, slandered, harried, underfed, and routinely molested by their 'masters'. If rebellious, they were quickly torpedoed from the household: those impossible people, the well-respected writers

---

1 As Audre Lorde said, 'The power you waste is being used against us' (https://youtu.be/OUXjoBVQkpw).

Thomas and Jane Carlyle, kicked one of their maids out for giving birth (very quietly too) in a china closet. Such abuse was essentially a legal form of slavery: servants were kept in unhealthy conditions and paid a pittance (or *less*, due to breakages and other supposed deficiencies), while they ministered to the status quo.

Despite men's much-applauded upper-body strength, somehow it's *women* who are still the main skivvies today, performing as maids of all works, or sometimes as presidential press secretaries. Behind every man who helps with the housework, there's a tired woman following him around *thanking* him for helping with the housework. Male domination hasn't gone away, it's simply hidden itself behind a pretence of equality and a rather too convenient blurring of the gender divide. This game is still in play and thrives, like Trump and his buddies, on the power of IDIOCY.

A guy in England beat up his wife on their wedding night. But he had a reason: she'd asked him to help her take off her wedding dress.[2] I guess foreplay's a thing of the past. Imagine if she'd asked him to take out the trash!

Look, haven't we all had just about enough of men's idea of a good time? Drones, beheadings, *The Bullingdon Club*? Factory farming? Polluting every available body of water – and then *charging* you for a bottle of drinking water! Soon they'll be charging us for AIR too, the air they've filled with petrol fumes, stone dust, cow burps, asbestos, and nanoparticles, as well as smoke from all their stupid factories, stupid cigars and stupid barbecues.

---

2 'Bride beaten by new husband... because he couldn't get her dress off' (*Daily Mirror*, February 16, 2015).

Them and their goddam Industrial Revolution – which, when I was at school, was spoken of with such reverence! Agriculture and tree-clearance started to upset ecology long ago, but heavy industry has ruined the ozone layer, so that now we have record droughts and floods and hurricanes and blizzards in places that used to be habitable, and walruses have nowhere to lay their heavy heads. All to enable a few bellicose bully boys to make a mint. 'Make a buck, make a buck. Even in Brooklyn it's the same,' as Alfred says in *Miracle on 34ᵗʰ Street*.[3]

The pesticides, the herbicides, the murder–suicides! Institutional racism and sexism. Freemasonry. Online backgammon. School shootings. Diablo chicken wings. Breweries, microbreweries, whoppers and sliders, nanobytes and gigabytes and terabytes – men like anything that's either really big or really small. I wonder why.

And all the penile neckties. They never tire of them. Men are so *repetitive*! Them and their neon trainers and football scarves and football shirts and football hooliganism and baseball caps and baseball games and baseball mitts and baseball cards and other baseball memorabilia. Their dissertations on Spider-Man comics. Their lust for every sort of nonsense, for exclusive clubs and secret handshakes, for embezzlement and tax breaks and presidential pardons and golden showers and the unpardonable electric chair...

These pursuits come in tandem with their wilful, ruinous indifference to the enormities they have perpetrated on women's lives: through domination, violation, and the objectification of women's bodies, including their scorn for menstruation, gestation, parturition, and lactation, all that yucky female stuff

---

3 Directed by George Seaton (1947).

that is, incidentally, essential to mammalian survival (which Spider-Man isn't). What would become of us all if *men* had to breastfeed? When there's so much pinball to be played and gun barrels to be oiled, so many noteworthy trains coming and going and pints of beer waiting to be drunk? Babies would starve.

The sausages, so many SAUSAGES! Along with sausage-shaped pens, bullet trains, guns, missiles, space rockets, sky-scrapers, columns, plinths, obelisks, and towers. They have littered the globe with phallic symbols and equestrian statues, hedge funds, gold futures, sub-prime mortgages, and obstruc-tions of justice. Also, Mafia rings, cement feet, arms deals, urban blight, suburban sprawl, crack cocaine, misleading election fraud allegations, and those horrible khaki-coloured fisher-man's vests they wear, the ones with all the pockets. Not to mention all their damn *fetishes*: for steak, coins, stamps, guns, fishing tackle, cricket, racing, Moleskine notebooks, tool-kits, gadgetry, potato chips, birds, butterflies, Nasa, the soiled undies of schoolgirls, antiquarian memorabilia, exclusive brands of shaving cream, electronics, more electronics, high heels, rubber gear, leather gear, cars, motorbikes, unbelievably expensive hi-fi set-ups, apps, abs, six-packs, tobacco, boastful fables of derring-do, quantum theory, golf, lad mags, Mahler, Wagner, and Bob Dylan (they never shut up about *him*).

We're dying over here, man! We're snoring in the aisles and you don't even notice. I'm particularly tired of having to listen to them all play the guitar.

Them and their capitalism and their corporations and con-niptions and philosophical convictions, their nihilism, their defeatism, their elitism, their egotism, their optimism – inex-plicably conjoined with their love of apocalypse – and all the other huge fatal male cop-outs, all the *crummy ideas* we've had

191

to stomach for the last five thousand years, while men barely even acknowledged that women EXIST.

They have proven themselves *apocalyptically* unfit to govern. Women would do a better job with their hands tied behind their backs (which, of course, they often are).

Why *do* women work for men? Not only that, but now we twerk for them too! Look at us, traipsing abjectly around our polluted earth, planning the supper! Always trying so hard to be *nice*. Having to *beg* for a few measly reproductive rights, a break in the wife-beatings, or just a little help with the dishes. Poking our pink parasols up at glass ceilings, tap, tap, tap... It's so demeaning – especially when you're twerking at the same time.

Women now bring home the bacon and *cook* it too. And men praise us for our *autonomy* – which leaves them free to watch their requisite ten hours of porn a day, decide on gender quotas, and pollute rivers.

But why *should* women work, why should we pay for *any-thing*, when we've been robbed blind for centuries? And I do mean blind. And yet there are women in this world who refuse alimony, preferring a 'clean' break. An attempt at resentment mitigation? Please. This is no way to behave!

Let's just forget equality, okay? It's dopey, it's insane! EQUALITY DOESN'T WORK.

It's a half-measure. This is an emergency – we've got to think big. To end sexism, racism, violence against women, worldwide bombing campaigns, and avert the coming ecological catastrophe, women need to get their hands on the reins, and fast. In fact, forget the reins, just grab the cash.

Sadly, in the current mercenary scheme of things, power rests on wealth and property, and is therefore mostly in male hands. Land ownership is an offensive idea but, if the world must be owned by anyone, let it be women.[4] Once in charge of things, women can institute a system of *common* ownership, with everything shared amongst women and animals. (Men can have a beer allowance.)

Men need to pay us what we're owed. Not just money. We're owed orgasms, we're owed world peace. I know, I know, I sound like Miss America when I start talking about peace. Hey, they owe us for *that* too, all those beauty contests we've had to sit through! And John Wayne movies. Men owe us for all the lip-smacking, wolf-whistling, catcalling, ass-pinching, crone-bashing, gun-slinging, cotton-picking gas-guzzling that's ever gone on.

And as for orgasms, the problem with men is, they think sex is for *them*. Let's get this straight once and for all:

SEX IS FOR WOMEN.

Throughout nature, it's *female* pleasure that counts, reproductively speaking. The female multiple orgasm tops any humdrum climax a penis can achieve. Sorry, guys, that's just the way it is. Life isn't always fair.

Men got everything about sex topsy-turvy. They invented monogamy and homophobia because they suffer so terribly from jealousy. But it's *men* who should be monogamous; women should be freewheeling. It's a shame to waste all that orgasmic capacity.

Men should pay us back for their belittlement of women. (It would take an eternity.) *Pay* us for their vulgarising of sex; for prostitution; for the invention of the phone, the camera, the gun, the car, the airplane, the internet, TV, nuclear power, liposuction, and tanning salons. *Pay* for the puny percentage

---

4 'If you put money in the hands of women, they can do magic.' UN women's representative Comfort Lamptey, speaking about Margaret C. Snyder's life's work (*New York Times* obituary, February 5, 2021).

of rape convictions. *Pay* for the cyclones and forest fires, *pay* for the poisoned water. *Pay* for the world wars, *pay* for toxic waste. *Pay* for atom bombs and chlorine gas and all the Nobels they awarded themselves for creating them. *Pay* for the gas chambers while they're at it, and animal extinctions, child soldier indoctrination, and the desecration of ecosystems. *Pay* for Hitler, Mao, Columbus, King Tut, Genghis Khan, Trump, Giuliani, the Proud Boys, and the Ku Klux Klan. Why not, why shouldn't they pay and *pay*?

They can pay for the pay gap too.

Once women control all the money, we can start reversing the fatal destructiveness of men. During this transition period, by the way, we won't need any male carping. Men are always so *critical*, jeez. A three-year ban on the male voice in public would be a big help: women will need time to think about how to *fix* this mess.

Any man in possession of a moral conscience should instantly recognise the logic and justice of these ameliorative measures and start forking out. NOW.

But it's not enough for well-meaning men to offer women their money. Women have got to *take* the money, and without shame. Why even show gratitude? *It's our bloody money.* We and our female ancestors earned it − the hard way.

So take the money, honey. And let's have no neg-head downer shit about being a kept woman or something. That sort of consideration is a luxury of the past. This is no time for self-doubt, self-abnegation or charity. No time to go Dutch on dinner either, or share the mortgage repayments. The world's going to hell in a handbasket, and something's got to be done about it! (Somebody do something about that 'handbasket' expression too.) The time has come for all good women to peacefully plunder. Yanking cash out of male hands is a humanitarian act. It's your new job, it's your right... and it's our only hope.

TAKE THE MONEY HONEY.

Don't sing for your supper, sing for *yourself*, as Bizet's Carmen would say – okay, bad example, since Carmen gets killed by her idiotically jealous boyfriend. Ah, men. They love to have the last word, even in operas. Listen to Helen Humes instead, with her astute 'Million Dollar Secret'.[5] (In essence? Find a rich man and make sure his will's made out to you.)

We will of course have to battle against some pretty powerful mind games. We've been bullied for centuries into believing there's something terrible about being branded a whore, slut, floozy, or gold-digger. What a clever male trick *that* was, when whores had it right all along! Not in terms of contorting your sexuality or risking your life to please men, no, but in terms of TAKING THE MONEY.

Why are we still trying to figure this out? *Men* can't handle money! Look what they do with it: Harley-Davidsons, Doc Martens, vintage steam train rides, the stock market, Lolita islands, big-game hunting, and the cultivation of giant vegetables. Men are *crazy*. They're always calling *us* crazy, but men are completely off the beam. They must have lost the plot some time ago. You can tell by all the tornado-chasing.

Now, there may be a tricky interval there, during the female-oriented redistribution of wealth, when newly enriched and empowered women will be bombarded by lounge lizards, murderers, rapists, thieves... So what else is new?

Just be strong, sisters. Never mind the names they'll call us, their pathetic pleas and hard-luck stories, the physical and

---

5 Modern (1950).

emotional blackmail, the sure-thing investment opportunities, and all the other forms of backlash that will inevitably ensue once men realise they're broke. Just be brave and take the moolah.

It is only a matter of waiting it out. Once worldwide matriarchy is firmly established, women will at last be adequately safeguarded against male petulance. (Just being safeguarded against male *decor* decisions would be progress.)

So, TAKE THE MONEY HONEY, and take it proudly. You've nothing to lose but your chains and your poverty and your crappy job and your crap pension and your unheard voice and your unpaid domestic labour and your painful stilettos and your time-consuming beauty treatments, and about a million trillion mother-in-law jokes.

Just TAKE THE MONEY. It's not prostitution, it's your civic duty. Your *skivvy* duty. Take it for Carmen's sake, take it for all the opera divas who died in poverty, take it for the maids of all work, take it for all the women violated and unavenged, take it for the seven brides of seven brothers and that woman still stuck in her wedding dress. Take it for the powerless and penniless – so that someday you can empower them.

Take it for your *mother*, take it for your *daughter*. Come on. Just take it. Take the money and run! Take men for a ride, take them to the cleaners! Take the house, take the kids, take the cake!

And for godsake take the Pill while you're at it, or something equivalent. Let's face it, motherhood is for the birds. If it weren't for hormones, instinct, propaganda, peer pressure, tax cuts, faulty contraceptives, and an idle hankering to reread old children's books, nobody would ever procreate.[6]

---

6 As Audre Lorde wrote, 'Only within a patriarchal structure is maternity the only social power open to women' (*The Master's Tools Will Never Dismantle the Master's House*, Penguin, 2017).

SOURCES

Things Are Against Us
Previously unpublished.

The Underground Bunker
First published in the *Irish Times*, July 8, 2019, under the title 'Did we really massacre Indians, enslave Africans and poison rivers for this hellhole?'.

Trapped Family Fingers
First published in *The Globe & Mail*, October 12, 2019, under the title 'It's a mad, mad, mad, mad country'.

Three Strikes
First published in *The Baffler*, March 2015.

A Spell of Patriarchy
First published in the *New York Times*, December 26, 2019, under the title 'Patriarchy Is Just a Spell'.

Third-Rate Zeros
Previously unpublished.

Consider Pistons and Pumps
First published in *The Baffler*, September 5, 2016, under the title 'Womb Up, America!'.

The Woman of the House
First published in *The Guardian*, December 28, 2012, under the title 'The Little House books as feminist classics'.

The Lost Art of Staying Put
First published in *The Baffler*, December 2017.

Bras: a Life Sentence
First published in *Deliberately Thirsty*, ed. Sean Bradley, Argyll Publishing, August 2000.

Morning Routine Girls
First published in *The Baffler*, October 2015, under the title 'Distressed Cut-Offs: The morning angst'.

Sing the Unelectric
First published in *Aeon Magazine*, January 24, 2013, under the title 'Sing the Body Unelectric'.

Ah, Men
Previously unpublished.

Take the Money Honey
First published in *The Evergreen: A New Season in the North*, Volume IV, ed. Lucy Ellmann, The Word Bank, 2019; based on a talk given at the Poisson Rouge, New York, March 18, 2015.

〜

Many thanks to commissioning editors Mark Medley, Martin Doyle, Valerie Cortes, Chris Lehmann, John Summers, Peter Catapano, Justine Jordan, Sean Bradley, and Marina Benjamin. It's nice to be asked.

ABOUT THE AUTHOR

Here's the THING: Lucy Ellmann is extremely shy. She's so awkward and self-conscious that meeting strangers, or almost anyone, exhausts her. She's lousy at remembering names. She cannot add or subtract. She hates having appointments in her diary and prefers to wear the same outfit every day. She's a fretful iconoclast, much prone to anger. She's also distrustful, lazy and easily hurt. She is not a team player. She prefers interrupting people to organising them, and cries if she doesn't get her way. She fears she's neglected everybody she knows, and vice versa – not to mention people she doesn't know. She can't stand protocol, committees, business hours, ceremonial occasions, public performances and filling out forms. And she never wants to be carried through a crowd on a palanquin. Otherwise, the world's her oyster!

She has written seven novels, including *Sweet Desserts* (Guardian Fiction Prize, 1988), *Dot in the Universe*, *Mimi* and *Ducks, Newburyport* (Goldsmiths Prize, James Tait Black Memorial Prize, 2019), and an illustrated book for adults, called *Tom the Obscure*. Born in the USA, she now lives in Scotland. This is her first book of essays.

NB. If this book results in one extra multiple orgasm some-where, aided by a repentant man who's finally seen where his true responsibilities lie, my work here is done. The hills should be alive with the sounds of ecstasy.

GALLEY BEGGAR PRESS

We hope that you've enjoyed *Things Are Against Us*. If you would like to find out more about Lucy, along with some of her fellow authors, head to www.galleybeggar.co.uk.

There, you will also find information about our subscription scheme, 'Galley Buddies', which is there to ensure we can continue to put out ambitious and unusual books like *Things Are Against Us*.

Subscribers to Galley Beggar Press:

· Receive limited black cover editions of our future titles (printed in a one-time run of 500).

· Have their names included in a special acknowledgement section at the back of our books.

· Are sent regular updates and invitations to our book launches, talks and other events.

· Enjoy a 20% discount code for the purchase of any of our backlist (as well as for general use throughout our online shop).

Galley Beggar Press would like to thank the following individuals, without the generous support of whom our books would not be possible:

Tonia Collett
Gordon Collins
Gerard Connors
Helene Conrady
Joe Cooney
Kenneth Cooper
Sarah Corbett
Paul Corry
Andy Corsham
Mary Costello
Sally Cott
Nick Coupe
Andrew Cowan
Diarmuid Cowan
Felicity Cowie
Isabelle Coy-Dibley
Matthew Craig
Nick Craske
Anne Craven
Emma Crawford
Anne-Marie Creamer
Alan Crilly
Joanna Crispin
Ian Critchley
Brenda Croskery
James Cross
Kate Crowcroft
Miles Crowley
Stephen Cuckney
Damian Cummings
Stephen Cummins
Andrew Cupples
HC
Emma Curtis Lake
Chris Cusack
Siddharth Dalal
Elisa Damiani
Rachel Darling
Rupert Dastur
Claudia Daventry
Mark Davidson
Harriet Davies
Jessica Davies
Julie Davies
Linda Davies
Nickey Davies
Paul Davies
Alice Davis
Joshua Davis
Toby Day
Robin Deitch
Rebecca Demaree
Stanislaus Dempsey
Paul Dettmann

Turner Docherty
William Dobson
Dennis Donathan
Kirsty Doole
Kelly Doonan
Oliver Dorostkar
David Douce
Janet Dowling
Kelly Downey
Jamie Downs
Guy Dryburgh-Smith
Ian Dudley
Fiona Duffy
Florian Duijsens
Anthony Duncan
Antony Dunford
Stanka Easton
David Edwards
Nicola Edwards
Lance Ehrman
Jonathan Elkon
Ben Ellison
Ian Ellison
Thomas Ellmer
Stefan Erhardt
Alice Erskine
Fiona Erskine
Simeon Esper
Paul Ewen
Adam Fales
Monique Fare
Sarah Farley
Lori Feathers
Gerard Feehily
Jeremy Felt
Timothy Fenech
Vitcoria Fendall
Michael Fenton
Charles Fernyhough
Edward J. Field
Paul Fielder
Joy Finlayson
Elizabeth Finn
Catriona Firth
Becky Fisher
Fitzcarraldo Editions
Holly Fitzgerald
Eleanor Fitzsimons
Alexander Fleming
Grace Fletcher-Hackwood
Hayley Flockhart
Nicholas Flower
Patrick Foley
James Fourniere

Ceriel Fousert
Richard Fradgley
Pauline France
Matthew Francis
Frank Francisconi
Emily Fraser
Annette Freeman
Emma French
Ruth Frendo
Melissa Fu
Graham Fulcher
Paul Fulcher
Lew Furber
Stephen Furlong
Michael Furness
Brid Gallagher
Timothy Gallimore
Marc Galvin
Annabel Gaskell
Honor Gavin
Michael Geisser
Phil Gibby
Alison Gibson
Nolan Geoghegan
Neil George
Andy Godber
James Goddard
Stephanie Golding
Elizabeth Goldman
Morgan Golf-French
Matthew Goodman
Sakura Gooneratne
Sara Gore
Nikheel Gorolay
Cathy Goudie
Simon Goudie
Emily Grabham
Paul Greaves
Louise Greenberg
Chris Gribble
Judith Griffith
Neil Griffiths
Ben Griffiths
Vicki Grimshaw
Sam Guglani
Robbie Guillory
Dave Gunning
David Gunning
Andrew Gummerson
Rhys Gwyther
Ian Hagues
Daniel Hahn
Alice Halliday
Peter Halliwell

Karen Hamilton
Emma Hammond
Paul Handley
Rachel Handley
Kirsteen Hardie
Hal Harding-Jones
Vanessa Harris
Jill Harrison
Alice Harvey
Becky Harvey
Shelley Hastings
Simon Hawkesworth
Sarah Hawthorn
Patricia Hayes
David Hebblethwaite
Richard Hemmings
Padraig J. Heneghan
Stu Hennigan
Penelope Hewett Brown
Felix Hewison-Carter
Martin Hickman
Alexander Highfield
Jennifer Hill
Molly Hill
Susan Hill
Daniel Hillman
Rod Hines
Ned Hirst
Alex Hitch
Marcus Hobson
Peter Hodgkinson
Camilla Hoel
Aisling Holling
Tim Hopkins
Shane Horgan
Rashad Hosein
William Hsieh
Hugh Hudson
Anna Jean Hughes
Emily Hughes
Gavin Hughes
Richard Hughes
Robert Hughes
Andy Hunt
Kim-ling Humphrey
Louise Hussey
LJ Hutchins
Simone Hutchinson
Simon Issatt
Joseph Jackson
Paul Jackson
Jane Jakeman
Hayley James
Gareth Jelley

Kavita A. Jindal
Alice Jolly
George Johnson
Jane Johnson
Bevan Jones
Emma Jones
Jupiter Jones
Kerry-Louise Jones
Rebecca Jones
Amy Jordison
Anna Jordison
Diana Jordison
Atul Joshi
Claire Jost
Benjamin Judge
Gary Kaill
Darren Kane
Laura Kaye
Thomas Kealy
Andrew Kelly
Michael Ketchum
Peter Kettle
Jeffrey Kichen
Vijay Khurana
Jacqueline Knott
Amy Koheealiee
Teddy Kristiansen
Elisabeth Kumar
Gage LaFleur
Philip Lane
Domonique Lane-
    Osherov
I Lang
Kathy Lanzarotti
Jackie Law
Jo Lawrence
Sue Lawson
Rick Le Coyte
Carley Lee
Liz and Pete Lee
Darren Lerigo
Joyce Lillie Robinson
Yin Lim
Rebecca Lake
Rachel Lalchan
Eric Langley
Catherine Latsis
Elizabeth Leach
Ferdia Lennon
Joanne Leonard
Chiara Levorato
Mark Lewis
Elizabeth Leyland
Christian Livermore

Jesse Loncraine
Katie Long
Nick Lord Lancaster
Isaac Lowe
Lele Lucas
Sean Lusk
Simona Lyons
Marc Lyth
Jean Mackay
Wendy and Dave MacKay
Victoria MacKenzie
Tom MacLean
Andrea Macleod
Duncan Mackie
Brendan Madden
Joseph Maffey
Anne Maguire
Eleanor Maier
Johnny Mains
Philip Makatrewicz
Anil Malhotra
Tom Mandall
Joshua Mandel
Matthew Mansell
Emily Marchant
Chiara Margiotta
John Marr
Natalie Marshall
Paul Marshall
Iain Martin
Amanda Mason
Rosalind May
Philip Maynard
Stephen Maynard
Sally Mayor
Sara McCallum
Amy McCauley
Paul McCombs
Ella McCrystle
Fabia McDougall
Kieran McGrath
Sheila McIntosh
Alan McIntyre
Gerald McWilliams
Victor Meadowcraft
Jason Merrells
Andy Merrills
Tina Meyer
Ali Millar
Jacob Millard
Michael Millington
Phillipa Mills
Sally Minogue
Fiona Mitchell

Lotte Mitchell Reford
Ian Mond
Fiona Mongredien
Sue Mongredien
Alexander Monker
Alex Moore
Clare Moore
Gary Moore
Michelle Moorhouse
Rachael de Moravia
Nigel J. Morgan
Carlos Eduardo Morreo
Jackie Morris
Julie Morris
Patrick Morris
Clive Morrison
Donald Morrison
Roger Morrison
David Musgrave
Electra Nanou
Polly Nash
Zosha Nash
Linda Nathan
Tim Neighbour
Amanda Nicholls
Catherine Nicholson
Sophia Nixon
Mariah de Nor
Calum Novak-Mitchell
Anna Nsubuga
Georgina Nugent-Folan
Arif Nurmohamed
James O'Brien
Liam and Wendy
    O'Connor
Rodney O'Connor
Richard Offer
Seb Ohsan-Berthelsen
Janet Oliver
Alec Olsen
Laura Oosterbeek
Sheila O'Reilly
Valerie O'Riordan
Liz O'Sullivan
Jack Oxford
Jenny Owen
Steven Palter
Dave Parry
Gary Partington
Debra Patek
Nicholas Paton Philip
Ian Patterson
Nigel Paulson
Stephen Pearsall

Alexa Pearson
Rebecca Peer
Jonathan Perks
Connor Perrie
Tom Perrin
Tony Pettigrew
Dan Phillips
Jennifer Pink
Robert Pisani
Ben Plouviez
Louise Pointer
Erin Polmear
James Pomar
Jonathan Pool
Giacomo Pope
Christopher Potter
Ailsa Power
Trine Prescott
Lesley Preston
David Primost
David Prince
Victoria Proctor
Jill Propst
Samuel Pryce
James Puddephatt
Joyce Pugh
Alan Pulverness
Sarah Pybus
Richard Pye
Alex Pykett
Lisa Quattromini
Leng Leng Quek
Shiva Rahbaran
Sim Ralph
Polly Randall
Jane Rawson
Euan Reed
Dawn Rees
Padraig Reidy
Emma Reitano
Barbara Renel
Vasco Resende
Amy Reynolds
Gaynor Reynolds
Annie Rhodes
Alison Riley
Thea Marie Rishovd
Laura Roach
Chris Roberts
Stephen Roberts
Rocky and Kat
Liz Roe
Brian Ronan
Angela Rose

Kalina Rose
Wendy Ross
Nathan Rowley
Martin Rowsell
Beverly Rudy
Giles Ruffer
Libby Ruffle
Tomilyn Rupert
Tim Russ
Rebeka Russell
Naben Ruthnum
John Rutter
Tobias Ryan
Amanda Saint
Floriane Sajdak
Alison Sakai
Michael Saler
Himanshu Kamal Saliya
Robert Sanderson
Valentina Santolini
Lior Sayada
Liam Scallon
Amy Scarrott
Linde Schaafsma
Robert Scheffel
Jordan Schlipf
Benedict Schofield
Florian Schroiff
Jan Schoones
Ros Schwartz
Nicola Scott
Stephen Robert Scott
James Scudamore
Miss Scullion
Darren Seeley
Kelly Selby-Jones
Elie Sharp
Samuel Sharps
Richard Sheehan
Nicola Shepherd
Emma Shore
Larry Sides
Deborah Siddoway
Kate Simpson
Yvonne Singh
Ann Slack
Jay Slayton-Joslin
Ben Smith
Chris Smith
Connor Smith
Hazel Smith
Ian Smith
Kieron Smith
Nicola Smith

Shannon Smith
Tom Smyth
Lisa Solley
Louise Soraya Black
Arabella Spencer
Karmen Spiljak
Sarah Spitz
Hannah Spruce
Chiara Spruijt
Connor Stait
Karl Stange
Daniel Staniforth
Cathryn Steele
Gillian Stern
Stewart Stevens
Mark Stevenson
Tabatha Stirling
Dagmara Stoic
Justina Stonyte
Anne Storr
Colette Storrow
Elizabeth Stott
Jochen Stremmel
Julia Stringwell
Andrew Stuart
Zara Stubbs
Daryl Sullivan
Jesse Surridge
Drashti Sutariya
Juliet Sutcliffe
Helen Swain
Helen Symington
Ewan Tant
Sarah Tapp
Justine Taylor
Peter Talor
Moray Teale
Alan Teder
Gill Thackray
Vivienne Thackray
Natalia Theodoridou
Cennin Thomas

Sue Thomas
Susannah Thompson
Caroline Thomson
Graham Thornelow
Sam Thorp
Nan Tilghman
Matthew Tilt
Amie Tolson
Margaret Tongue
James Torrence
Kate Triggs
Steve Tuffnell
Devin Tupper
Nick Turner
Harriet Tyce
Eleanor Updegraff
Raminta Uselyte
Esther Van Buul
Bart Van Overmeire
Nicole Vanderbilt
David Varley
Francesca Veneziano
Irene Verdiesen
Essi Viding
Boris Vidovic
Bea Vincent
Meg Vincent
Gabriel Vogt
Stephen Waderman
Julia Wait
Chris Walker
Phoebe Walker
Stephen Walker
Ben Waller
MJ Wallis
Sinead Walsh
Steve Walsh
David Ward
Jerry Ward
Kate Ward
Peter Ward
Rachael Wardell

Guy Ware
Emma Warnock
Ellie Warren
Stephanie Wasek
Daniel Waterfield
Sarah Webb
Lucy Webster
Adam Welch
Clemency Wells
Nathan Wescott
Karl Ruben Weseth
Jo West-Moore
Mark Wharton
Tom Whatmore
Wendy Whidden
Robert White
Indra Wignall
Kyra Wilder
Claire Willerton
G Williams
Sam Williams
Sharon Williams
Courtney Williamson
Sarah Wiltshire
Kyle Winkler
Bianca Winter
Lucie Winter
Sheena Winter
Simon Winter
Astrid Maria Wissenburg
Stephen Witkowski
Jonathan Wood
Nathan Wood
Paul Woodgate
Emma Woolerton
Christine Wyse
Ben Yeoh
Ian Young
Juliano Zaffino
Sylvie Zannier
Rupert Ziziros
Carsten Zwaaneveld

Cheap Shots, Ambushes, and Other Lessons

Marc "Animal" MacYoung

Cheap Shots, Ambushes, and Other Lessons

A Down and Dirty Book on Streetfighting and Survival

PALADIN PRESS
BOULDER, COLORADO

Also by Animal MacYoung:

Barroom Brawling
Down but Not Out (video)
Fists, Wits, and a Wicked Right
Floor Fighting
Knives, Knife Fighting, and Related Hassles
Pool Cues, Beer Bottles, & Baseball Bats
A Professional's Guide to Ending Violence Quickly
Safe in the City (with Chris Pfouts)
Safe in the Street (video)
Street E&E
Surviving a Street Knife Fight (video)
Taking It to the Street
Violence, Blunders, and Fractured Jaws
Winning a Street Knife Fight (with Richard Dobson) (video)

Cheap Shots, Ambushes, and Other Lessons:
A Down and Dirty Book on Streetfighting and Survival
by Marc "Animal" Mac Young

Copyright © 1992 by Marc "Animal" Mac Young
ISBN 10: 0-87364-496-4
ISBN 13: 978- 0-87364-496-4
Printed in the United States of America

Published by Paladin Press, a division of
Paladin Enterprises, Inc.
Gunbarrel Tech Center
7077 Winchester Circle
Boulder, Colorado 80301 USA
+1.303.443.7250

Direct inquiries and/or orders to the above address.

PALADIN, PALADIN PRESS, and the "horse head" design
are trademarks belonging to Paladin Enterprises and
registered in United States Patent and Trademark Office.

Visit our Web site at www.paladin-press.com

Dedication

This book is dedicated to my lady, Tracy David, who, aside from just putting up with me, has helped me leave the place where this information is necessary.

About the Author

Marc "Animal" MacYoung is somewhat of a living legend in certain circles of California (a state known for producing weirdos). His attitude of "Life is what you make of it" has led to the observation that "he could have fun in a paper bag." The downside of that is that he has made more than a few enemies with his antics. That, and his propensity for not staying put, has landed him in more than a few fights. He is reputed to be currently roaming the greater L.A. area. While he claims to have "settled down," his idea of what this constitutes would give Attila the Hun a stroke. His hobbies include beer, embarrassing his girlfriend in public, and just being a pest in general.

Contents

Preface

Precedence is no excuse for failure.

Carol Cureton

We were sitting around drinking beer and laughing about some guy who'd gotten his finger chopped off in a fight. Since his finger lying in the dirt was a direct result of a "dumb" move on his part, we weren't inclined to be sympathetic. In fact, we were closer to asphyxiation we were laughing so hard. There was a girl next to me who was obviously getting upset at our apparent callousness.

She looked at me and said, "That's terrible! Why are you laughing?"

In a moment of gut-wrenching, sobering truth, I said to her, "Because it hurts so much."

I wrote this book in order to convey to you facts, theories, and philosophies I have spent nearly two-thirds of my life learning. It took me seventeen years of scrapes, jams, combat, blood, mud, grease, and beer to learn all this. The rules of thumb that I will be telling you about aren't hypothetical, unless you call getting kicked in the nuts hypothetical. I don't. It's happened to me too often to call it anything less than painful. More often than not, my descriptions were much more colorful.

I will be telling you these things in a rather unorthodox manner. It happens to be the manner that I communicate best in.

I grew up in the streets; my language and especially my attitudes reflect this fact. I make no apologies for either. Grammar is something else, but that's my editor's problem.

I say things in this book that will offend certain people. Whether it is from content or language, my response is the same: tough. What I'm speaking of here are some raw realities about self-defense, combat, and survival. It is my intention to teach you things, things that have saved my life more than once. (I do mean that. I'm not a theoretical fighter; my combat experience comes from getting bashed upside the head in barroom brawls, and from bullets whizzing past.) This is, in one sense (a very big sense) a practical guide to survival. If some fancy martial artist gets his ego hurt by my comments, fine. If he disregards the concepts because of his pride, I will feel no pity when he is blindsided by a beer bottle and summarily stomped.

In case you're wondering about my name; yes, it is Animal. I've carried that name for ten years now. People are always asking me how I got the name. I now have a pat answer, which is true: "By doing all the stupid and dangerous things one usually does to get that name." That's how.

Acknowledgments

Live and learn, or you don't live long.

Michael "Creature"

Some people have asked me what it is that makes me qualified to write this book. These people are often distraught when I tell them that my major qualification is that I'm still breathing. They somehow don't think that means anything. The number of my friends, enemies, and acquaintances of whom that can no longer be said should be an indication that it is an extremely *good* qualification.

In one sense, there are no qualifications for a streetfighter except the ability to survive. I have known far too many people who achieved their black belts and then got taken out by a sucker punch. They aren't fighters; they're dancers. The only qualification is that you avoided the beer bottle swung at you.

For you sticklers for details, I have formal training in five "recognized" fighting forms. These, with teachers, are: Wing Chun kung fu, under Sifu Hawkins Cheung; Shao-lin kung fu, under Sifu Alex Holub, student of Di Sifu Ark Wong; tai-chi chuan, under Steven Barnes; shotokan karate, under some schmuck instructor who almost got me killed; and sabre technique, under Theodore Katzoff, Master at Arms, Salle Gascon.

This is my formal training by "qualified" teachers. The first two, I should point out, are excellent teachers—I owe them a

xiii

lot. Steve is no slouch either. My "unqualified" teachers are the many friends who I have fought side by side with. They are my real teachers: the former SEALs, Green Berets, Airborne Rangers, Vietnam vets, bikers, brawlers, bouncers, gang members, assassins, mercenaries, Indians, Blacks, Whites, Mexicans, Orientals, and all other "warriors" I have known. These are my "brothers," who I have fought beside, bled with, laughed and cried with. We have lived and died together. We have taught each other intentionally and unintentionally.

These are my qualifications for writing this book, and the following are some of my brothers, teachers, and friends:

Tom Collins, Green Beret, who taught me short men can walk tall.

Oberon, who opened the door to the cosmos.

Allan Kahn, Airborne Ranger. Damn, that was fun!

Larry Kahn, the "Tupperware Kid," my good friend and partner.

David "Doc" Marks. In the dark, from behind, and at a distance.

Doug "The Mighty" Ipock, who helped me back from hell.

Michael "Creature," who taught me love is a warrior's greatest gift.

Dr. Michael Hyson, who, by teaching, I remembered.

Conn MacLir, a good man. May his path be easier.

Major John Donovan, Green Beret. Thanks for the advice and encouragement.

David B. (you're still hot, bro') and Frank Gasperik, two righteous "oldtimers" turned editors. Thanks for the input and help.

John Savage, my sword brother.

Paul Mohney, the gentle giant and dear friend.

Clan MacColin, who opened their hearts and arms (and liquor cabinets) to me.

Sifu Dr. Alex Holub, a blend between ALF and "The Terminator."

L.H.C. Security force. They took their worst problem and gave me responsibility.

Silas Andrews, brains not brawn all the way.

Quinton Klink, 82nd Airborne. I'll see you in hell before I see you in Utah again.

"Indian Mike," a stout friend and a hell of a guy.

Sidney Hableman, who taught me always to think of options.

Carol Cureton, who taught me to think five steps ahead, minimum.

Donna Jo Wade, ex-cop and a damn good person.

Rick Foss, who taught me to expect the unexpected.

Matthew Cross, the Sword Demon.

Dave Taggart, Sam, Trini, and Mark Fabian—a beer lifted in toast, a tear shed in remembrance, and a candle lit in respect. Their deaths still hurt. Dear friends and comrades, I miss them.

Katie Tigar, from whom I learned how deeply I could love.

My brother, Chris "Kaos." Let's not do that again, okay?

Gary Gunn. I didn't know about what he did until after he had taught me.

Richard Jones, whose death taught me this isn't a game.

Terry Rourk, a trained killer who was always gentle to me.

Peter, a sword brother and biker.

Arthur Payne, who taught me to go for blood in a fight.

My mother, from whom I learned not to take shit from anybody!

And most of all, my stepfather, Richard Nelson, FBI ret., who showed me it is possible to be bigger than I ever dreamed.

Introduction

This is the use of memory: For liberation—not less of love but expanding of love beyond desire, and so liberation from the future as well as the past.

T.S. Eliot
"Little Gidding" III,
The Four Quartets

To live through an impossible situation, you don't need the reflexes of a grand prix driver, the muscles of Hercules, or the mind of an Einstein. You simply need to know what to do.
Anthony Greenback

You hold in your hand a rather unique book. It is not a how-to book on fighting. Nor is it a book on *quack hop sock* (the dancing duck form that was founded in 1978 by Grand Master ABC). There are so many of those, if I only used one copy of each, I could stuff a blue whale.

What you could call it is a guide to the tools you will need to learn self-defense. Let's expand the analogy of tools. You can go out to a store and buy a book on how to do any home repair. This is great, yet you will encounter no end of difficulty if you don't know how to use the tools you'll need to do this repair. Sound familiar? The other thing is, those manuals don't tell you what to do if it doesn't work. (I think my next endeavor

1

will be writing a manual on home repair; I get just as infuriated with the crap they teach there as I do with what's taught as self-defense.) Instead, I will teach what I think is necessary to be able to truly defend yourself.

This isn't an abstract theory book on strategy or a "how-to-fight" book. There's too much of my own blood spattered on the street for me to write that sort of garbage. It's not that sort of book for one simple reason—it's more. It consists of things that I have seen and noticed over the years, things which I pass on to you in the hope you won't have to bleed to learn them, as I did.

You may wonder about some of the things I mention. What, for instance, do "world models" have to do with self-defense? A "thunderin' herd," as a friend of mine would say. Self-defense is a state of awareness. It isn't being able to break boards or make funny-sounding squeals while spinning. Most people are badly misinformed about this subject. They think that self-defense is being able to boot someone in the head. I think self-defense starts long before that. General Ulysses S. Grant (later President Grant) once posted cavalry guards on the outskirts of his camp. One of his aides asked why he did so, since any attack would surely blast through such a thin line of defense. His response is the best example of this book's intention: "They buy us time. That way we don't wake up with the bastards in our tents." *That's self-defense!*

You may, at first, have a bit of trouble with the way this book is organized. That's because I'm trying to communicate something different to you. We've been taught, for some screwy reason, that in order to teach something (or learn it), it has to be presented in a linear form. "If A, then B. If B, then C. Therefore A equals C." That may look pretty on paper, but it's total garbage when brought to bear here. What I will be trying to communicate is a *global* system, not linear. The difference is that a global system is not what is called "binary." That means, unlike a linear system (which is very logical), there is more than yes/no as an answer. In a global system, there are "Maybe" and "Sometimes" and "It depends" as answers, as well as yes/no. That means, when I speak of something, it also depends on other factors that can't be contained in a single line of thought. One fact is altered, changed, or totally voided by others at any given point. In other words, global thinking is what you do every single day of your life; you just don't know that you do it.

By writing this book, I will try to help you build a global image regarding self-defense. What that means is that it will sometimes sound like I've just run out to left field from where I was originally. I assure you this is not the case. What I'm trying to do is establish the skeleton structure for another aspect of self-defense that relates to the whole. It might help to imagine you're building a giant space station out in the weightlessness of space (if you saw the movie *Star Wars,* a "Death Star" will do as an image). There will be times when it looks like we were working on the core, and I suddenly ran off and set up a flag pole, then another. It will make no sense—until you realize that I'm setting up the pylons for the next level.

Once you get the hang of global thinking, it becomes easy. The solutions for problems will begin to evolve into self-evident answers without much work on your part. I will help you get into the swing of global thinking. There won't be anything in this book that you have to have a Ph.D. to understand, so sit back and relax. If it's your style, crack open a beer while you read it. The idea here is to get the information across in a way that you can easily understand, not sticking to what is proper writing form. I'll explain something, then later I'll explain it again in a different way. Sooner or later, I'll find a way to communicate to you what I'm trying to say.

What I hope to do with this book is broaden your horizons. There is a world of magic and wonder out there, waiting for aware adventurers who can take care of themselves. I personally have seen and done things some people wouldn't believe. I have done what most people just fantasize about, all because I had the knowledge contained in this book with me (that, and a serious case of chutzpah). *Self-defense isn't fighting, it is awareness.* The rest is just details.

People with martial arts training are always asking me what "style" I am. I tell them "PIBU." Now, most people with just a little training take me seriously. Those with more training look at me like I'm out of my mind. You see, PIBU is an ancient combat form from the Honkitonkbar Province of Socal. At least that's where I learned it. I've met other practitioners from as far away as England and the Philippines. For those of you who haven't caught on, PIBU stands for Pitcher of Beer. (Actually, it's a specific type of beer, but if I put it in print, the beer company might get bent out of shape. Hell hath no fury like a megacorporation scorned.) In regard to PIBU, either me and the other guy are going to sit down and drink it together, or I'm gonna brain the fucker with it. This is not some special technique that will never fail. There is no such animal. Every move has a counter, and every fight is different. *If you go into a fight full of assumptions and relying on a "never-fail" move, you're going to get creamed.*

You are going to learn what goes on prior to, during, and after a fight. I can't tell you every specific trick and cheap shot that you will encounter. There are thousands that I know of, yet that doesn't even scratch the surface of possibilities. What you will be told about are the key points these things have in common. You will also learn what some things *mean.*

It might help to use a bit of imagery here. If you were sitting in a camp in the jungle, and you saw a flash of orange and black stripes in the bushes, you'd know to get up a tree *immediately*! There are people, however, who wouldn't recognize that what was just seen was a tiger. In fact, they might laugh at you sitting in the tree. If that tiger was just passing through, well, you'd feel silly. If, however, that tiger stopped off for dinner, it's laughing boy's problem. You had the insight and knowledge to recognize what was going on, and you got out of the way. That is what I will try to teach you.

What I'm trying to say is that I will try to help you build a foundation. All the tools in the world won't do you a whit of good if you don't use them. Self-defense is not a machine. It is not something that you can put in the closet and ignore until you need it. It is not a series of moves that you can intellectually learn and then use when the need arises. Self-defense is a dynamic, organic system that must be nurtured and grown within yourself. Self-defense, in order to be anything close to effective, must be as ingrained as driving your car.

It is up to you to practice whatever form of self-defense you choose to learn. *The philosophy, without the training, is wasted—just as is the training without the philosophy.* Watch TV while practicing your blocks. If you're doing your laundry, practice accuracy of your blows by poking your fingers into the eyes of the photo of the lost dog that's posted on the board. Play handball, or try juggling, to improve your eye-hand coordination. Walk along railroad tracks or on top of brick walls to learn balance. *In short, do anything! Your greatest weapons are your awareness and the reactions that become instinctive tools of your awareness.* The thing is that unless you exercise them in daily life, they won't operate efficiently in a self-defense situation. I may look like a complete fool when I hit the dirt when a car backfires near me, but I've never been shot at in a dojo. I have been shot at in the street. It is no time for heroics when lead is flying. If you have no one to protect, get out of danger. The reason most people get hurt is that they react incorrectly in a crisis. They stop to look: they try to run when they should fight, or they fight when they should be doing the "flight" bit.

This is why I feel most "self-defense" courses are complete garbage, and that same attitude applies to most schools of the martial arts. They teach you just enough to get you killed in a real fight. What they teach you is the moves, not the spirit or the awareness that will save you in actual combat. However, this book assumes that you are now studying, or have studied and are now practicing, some form of self-defense. I do not now, nor will I ever, claim to have a monopoly on truth about fighting (*nobody* does). Everything here is just another tool that you can use to help you survive. It is up to you to practice and train yourself in the use of them.

You may feel that some things will not apply to you. Fine, put them in the closet. Maybe they will never be needed. If something doesn't fit the way you look at the world, disregard it. There is no law that says you must take this book *en todo*. It's more like vitamin C: you take what you need and piss out the rest.

Fighting is a greatly overrated profession. Now that I am older and (ha ha) wiser, I say that if I have to throw a punch, I've made a mistake. Why? If I am aware of the factors around me and how my actions affect them, I can maneuver them, and myself, in such a way that I will not have to crush someone's ribs. If I have to cream someone, that means I wasn't aware of all the factors around me and/or I didn't control them correctly.

In this book, I refer to "fighting" and "combat" as different things. They are. A fight is a sociological function, in which there are rules and limits. Combat is a free-for-all, where victory is awarded to the survivor. There are no rules; in combat, you do what you have to do to win. These things are as different as night and day. If you can't differentiate between them, you can land in a heap of trouble. I will try to give you the information necessary to tell the difference. Most situations are not combat; they are fights, and therefore less intense. So relax about it. Calmly and rationally knowing that something is dangerous makes it not as dangerous. By the end of this book, I hope you will understand.

The Foundation

We have met the enemy and he is us.

Pogo

What is it that makes a good fighter? Is it a wanting to hurt your fellow human being? (Nope.) Is it being "tough"? (Nope.) Is it being fast enough to hit someone first? (Unh-uh.) Is it the ominous black leather jacket and punch glove? (If that were the case, michael jackson would be rambo—lower case letters intentional.)

As odd as it may seem, most of what makes a good fighter is *attitude*. Now we all know that if attitude were all it took, we'd all be famous. So, somehow, it depends on having the *right* attitude. Now what the hell is the "right" attitude? Contrary to popular belief, it's not the hunched-over surliness that one sees on street corners in certain sections of town. If fact, most of those "toughs" you could stomp right now, with no training whatsoever, if you had the right attitude.

> **stomp** (verb)\often attributed to sound of boots on ribs\ 1. to beat up severely 2. to incapacitate by applying boots to portions of downed adversary's anatomy 3. to be beaten up severely. **stomped, to get stomped, stomping.** See: ass kicking*

*Humor will play a large part in this book. It is important to be able to laugh at this whole thing in order to put it in proper perspective.

By attitude I mean, in a bigger sense, spirit. What makes a mother defending her young ones the most lethal killing machine on the face of the earth? What makes your cute and cuddly kitty such an effective organism when it comes to removing other creatures from this plane of existence? You can say instinct, but what is that? What does instinct do that our conscious mind does not? And while we're at it, why *doesn't* our conscious mind do that?

I'd like to take this opportunity to let you think about it (actually, I gotta go to the bathroom).

In this case, the bulk of the instinct question can be answered by simply saying that *it allows an organism to operate toward a goal without conflicting emotions interfering.* In other words, every ounce of energy is directed toward the accomplishment of the task.

The stories of mothers lifting entire cars off their children, or the Green Beret found unconscious with eighty-three enemy bodies strewn about him, give you some idea of what human potential is. These are examples of attitude (spirit) being allowed to move toward a directed goal, uncomplicated by other emotions. Size, strength, sex, reflexes, experience, or anything else doesn't matter when you can tap into this.

We all have the capabilities to do this. But, all too often, we have been trained not to use this ability. Here, I am going to state an assumption: most of us were not taught by our elders in a manner that was beneficial for us in the long run. Rather, we were taught in a way that was convenient for our elders. It's not a case of evil intentions on the part of our teachers; it is instead a case of simple laziness.

I'm someone who has had more than a few people try to remove me from this world, yet what scared me the most in my life was something I once heard in a restaurant. I was listening to the conversation of the family next to me. The eldest child was telling his parents about a story he had read. The story was the *Tortoise and the Hare*. In the middle of the story, the kid's mother interrupted him and asked briskly, "What's the moral of that story?" The kid sat there thinking frantically, trying to remember what the moral of the story was. His mother supplied her own version. "The moral of that story," she loudly proclaimed, "is don't be smart! That rabbit was smart and that's how come he lost!"

Now you can rationalize that what she meant was "don't be a smart ass." That way, the only thing that should happen to her is that someone should drag her into an alley and put a bullet through her head. If you don't feel so benign to allow for what she meant, she should be beaten before being shot. The sheer immensity of the crime that she was committing against that kid's spirit (to say nothing of his intelligence) boggles the imagination. Think about it for a moment: if you were going to beat someone down in a way that would keep them from challenging you, you couldn't find a better way than what that woman said.

Even though that was an isolated incident, it was obvious that it was an isolated incident in a much larger pattern. What that woman was doing was not only condemning the child to a life of stupidity and ignorance, she was removing any chance that kid had of ever fighting his way out of it. Now, if you think about it, you will find similar situations, if less extreme, in your own history.

The woman's goal seemed to be, "Don't teach the kid to challenge our assumptions (especially, if they're wrong or contradictory); instead, teach the child to roll over and be submissive." How many of you remember when you were bullied into something by your parents, not because they were right, but because they were in a stronger position? ("It's right because I say it is.") The implied threat is that something terrible will happen if you stand up for yourself.

This is an attitude that far too many people carry with them into their adult lives. They allow this awe of terrible repercussions to lock them into a life of misery, terror, and impotence. In other words, the main emotional barrier that we must overcome is fear—the gut-wrenching terror that a small child develops when bullied that controls him into adulthood. As an adult, you've had time to rationalize this fear into other forms, just as immobilizing and frightening. This is how insidious fear is—fear of punishment, fear that something will be taken away from us if we stand up for ourselves, fear of getting hurt, etc. For some "solid rational" reason or other, we allow unpleasant things to continue. When these reasons are examined, they can usually be boiled down to one thing: Fear.

If you allow fear to rule your life, it is no one's fault but your own. People live their entire lives in fear, thinking that the price is too high to do anything about it. Yet they never realize that the price they pay in the end—the price of their self-respect—is far beyond anything they might have paid before. If that is gone from a person, anything can be done to him or her.

During World War II, millions of people died in concentration camps like dogs. Yet the reason we tell Polack jokes is that the Polish Hussars, a corps versed in honor and tradition, decided to die honorably instead of waiting for death in the trenches. They taped dynamite onto their sabres and charged the advancing German tanks. Those who survived the charge stuck their swords into the tank treads, blowing themselves up and disabling the tank. We "Oooh" and "Aww" over the atrocities that were allowed to happen in the camps, yet we tell jokes about people who decided to take some of the bastards with them. It is your choice to allow yourself to be a victim. If you live your life in fear, *you* open the gates of hell, nobody else.

Now, lest I go on about fear too much, know that there are other emotions that can, and do, cloud a person's spirit. These, too, must be overcome before one can become good at self-defense, though they are pale ghosts next to fear. (On the other hand, after slaying a dragon, wrasslin' alligators doesn't look like too big of a thing. It doesn't mean it isn't a sizable job by itself, it just isn't as big as others.)

The critical voice is that little voice inside your head (if not your voice, then someone else's) that tells you what a fuckup you are. If, by some miracle, you have escaped the critical voice, understand that it is a big motivating factor in others. It is the same voice that whispers into your ear that you aren't worth anything, and anything that you do bearing a resemblance to independent thought is going to fail, and that you are always wrong. This is the critical voice that controls most people. If you're normal, it's within you, as well. The only problem is, *it's wrong!* It is your enemy as long as it has control over your life. This aspect of yourself has to be brought into line in order for you to proceed.

It is impossible to teach true self-defense to someone without them first overcoming fear and the critical voice. True self-defense is an awareness that can't be switched on instantaneously. It is automatic, in the sense that it is *always* switched on. Your spirit should automatically rise to defeat your opposition when it has been transgressed. You have your limits and your rights, and nobody has the right to be there unless you give them permission. You are the ruler of yourself, and right or wrong, these are the things that you hold sacred. You would rather die than see them defaced.

That's why most martial artists are nothing more than dancers. They have the moves but not the determination. Any determined streetfighter will make a gelatinous mass of any black belt who crosses him. The streetfighter knows what a busted nose is about, and frankly he doesn't give a shit. If a broken nose is the price he must pay for victory, so be it. The school-trained black belt doesn't have that sort of commitment. He's playing for points, not fighting for his life. Because he doesn't have that direction of spirit, he will lose. The woman who would rather die in the process of killing (not hurting, but killing) the son of a bitch trying to rape her will, in all probability, never be raped. No rapist in the world is going to risk life and limb on someone like that; the price is just too high. This is the attitude that is necessary in order to truly be able to defend yourself. This is what self-defense actually is. The rest is just moves.

A large part of the training in the book will be teaching you how to turn on and off certain aspects of yourself—namely, those parts that keep you helpless and submissive. At first you may find it difficult, because it goes against your training since childhood. In fact, you are your own worst enemy at this stage—you've been taught not to be this effective. It was the responsibility of the people who taught you to make you weak. It's your responsibility if you keep that weakness. (The difference between trained and tamed is that when an animal is trained, it reacts to certain cues, but when those cues are not present, it reverts to its natural state. Tamed, however, means that the "Master's Voice" is always present, affecting behavior.)

You are a human being; you have the ability to think and change. If you don't like something about yourself, it is up to you to do something about it. It is possible, you can do it. Yet, you may find yourself "rationally" deciding to quit practicing, or you may find yourself freezing at a critical moment, thereby sustaining injury. These are manifestations of your previous training trying to reassert itself. It believes that it is correct in its assumptions of the world. Any attempt to give you control will be met with resistance. Awareness of this problem will give you the advantage you need to achieve the personal freedom necessary to become effective at self-defense.

Before we go on, I want to restress a fact that I mentioned earlier. There are differences between what I call "combat" and "fighting." *Fighting is not combat!* A fight can be many things, and occasionally it can escalate into combat, but it isn't initially. Combat and fighting call for radically different mind-sets. Often, a fight is used to settle disputes and to establish dominance. Combat has no rules. It is a fight to the death or the crippling of your opponent. Combat is for extreme situations only, like someone trying to mug or kill you. Even if you only cripple your opponent, the spirit has to be the same as if you were going to kill him. The mind-set is a ferocious disregard for personal injury. Don't tell me that you can't get to this mind-set. When a mother is protecting her young, she's in that mind-set. Any time that you're so ticked off that you don't care, you're in that state. Hell yes, you can do it! So, now that we have an idea about where we are headed mentally, we can get into some specifics of self-defense.

Range

---

*Don't yield to impotence! It is unnatural in you! Banish this
petty weakness from your heart. Rise to the fight Arjuna!*

Bhagavad Gita
2nd teaching

There are basically three ranges of hand-to-hand combat.
These ranges each have their strengths, limits, applications,
techniques, advantages, and disadvantages inherent within
them. While your chosen range will depend on personal choice,
and what fits your physical and psychological makeup the best,
it is important to understand the basic underlying techniques
in each range and how they operate.

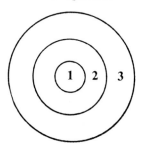

Here is a diagram of the three basic ranges. In the center we
have range #1. This is "wrestling," or extremely close fighting.
Range #2 is somewhat apart—this is primarily short punches
and the like. This range is usually preferred by shorter people,

and it is often called "infighting." Range #3 is "distance fighting." It is the area of long punches and kicks. This is usually the preferred area for taller people with long arms and legs.

Most people make the mistake of relying too heavily on the area that they are comfortable with. A distance fighter will make dogmeat out of an infighter in an open space, where he can move about and keep the infighter at a distance. However, in a crowded, cluttered bar or in a tight space (i.e., between cars at a stoplight), the distance fighter should leave an address where they can ship his body. Both of them are in trouble if a wrestler muckles onto them, whereas if the wrestler can't grab onto them, guess who's in trouble? In other words, you may prefer a certain form of fighting, but you can't predict what you're going to run into out there. Therefore, you must be capable in all three ranges, in case you end up in a situation that is not advantageous to your preferred range. Important safety tip: different formal martial art styles can dwell overmuch on certain ranges.

Let's look at distance fighting first. Basically, a distance fighter will want to keep you at a distance. This you should not let him do. A good distance fighter has a great many nasty, extremely painful blows that can be delivered from all the way out there. Blows from this point have lots of time to pick up momentum. Figure about two to four feet is average distance fighter range. Yes, four feet. He can close that to kicking distance real quick. The disadvantage of this range, however, is that these blows, relatively speaking, are slow. They take time to get up to speed. The other disadvantage is that they often need "mucho" room. Your best defense against a distance fighter is not to stay in his range. Whether that means backing out or closing is up to you. The other thing is to get into an area where he doesn't have room to move, which limits his options of possible moves.

An infighter operates about one to two and a half feet away. This doesn't mean that he can't hit as hard as a distance fighter. Infighters use their body weight much more efficiently and more quickly. I've seen guys blown off their feet by punches that were

Distance fighting.

delivered from damn near nose-to-nose positions. Infighting is faster and subtler than distance fighting, as well. Setups and traps can be nothing more than a rotation of the wrist in a certain way. The other thing is that infighters are pure trouble in confined areas, sort of like a cornered badger. Don't think that being bigger than a person in a tight area is going to let you overpower him more easily. Infighters *like* areas where they can turn larger size into a disadvantage.

The disadvantage to this range is that if someone can keep an infighter at bay (e.g., a distance fighter not letting him come any closer than three feet), an infighter is nearly helpless. If you are a distance fighter, keep him away from you! Move, backpedal, whatever. Just don't let him inside your guard. The other way out is to close with him. Most infighters can't deliver an effective blow from closer than six inches. Glue your body to his. If he pulls back to strike, follow him. Hit him on the way in, but follow him.

Infighting.

A good wrestler will nail anybody to the wall that he can lay his hands on. Street wrestling is different than competition. A street wrestler will maim you when he grabs. It's like fighting an octopus who has giant crab pincers with cat claws attached to the end of its tentacles. The strong points of street wrestling are the hands and locking techniques. The hands of a wrestler will clamp on to a soft spot of your anatomy and proceed to try to remove it. Gouging, pinching, ripping, jabbing, bone-breaking, joint dislocation, and biting are real common. This isn't competition wrestling for a pin; it is closer to the old Greco-Roman wrestling, where they carried out the loser. All sorts of nasty things can be done at this range by the strength of the hands alone. Getting your eye gouged out, for instance, can really louse up your day. Obviously, the weakness of this range is that the wrestler has to catch you. It's up to you to prevent it.

Wrestling.

Mobility

If you can't be grateful for what you've received, be grateful for what you've escaped.

Quote on a box of tea.

Mobility is your best defense. Or to quote: "What's the best way to block? Don't get hit." Too much of this "toe-to-toe" shit is bad for the brain. John Wayne be damned; duck! It isn't written in any rule book that you have to stand there and either take a punch or block it. You can dodge. There are no penalty points for backpedaling. This may sound stupidly obvious, but you'd be amazed...circle, linear escape, up, down, sideways... it doesn't matter, just get out of the way! There are many ways to accomplish this:

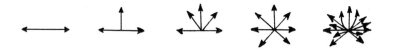

You get the idea.

Practice scuttling around, bobbing and weaving, twisting and tumbling; do anything until you learn how to dodge. Tumbling and rolling is real important. Don't worry about form; learn how to tumble and pop back up onto your feet. This will teach you to roll out of danger if you're knocked down. By the time your opponent has chased you down, you're on your feet again. Now if your sensei tells you that it's not necessary to practice falling because it will never happen, *he's lying!* You can never guarantee what's going to happen in a fight!

Another good thing to do is practice blocks while back-pedaling. My old karate sensei didn't teach this, God knows why. Realistically, you will have to retreat now and then. Start at one end of the room and have someone chase you, throwing blows as fast as he can. Practice skipping to the side while blocking. Don't just stand there and take it!

The first thing to learn is to get out of the way. Once you have that down, there is another step. You can get out of the way of danger and position yourself in such a way as to return the favor to the chump. In other words, why just dodge when you can dodge and at the same time place yourself somewhere convenient to turn his kidneys into guacamole? In one sense, it's like the game of pool. A good pool player will not only make a shot, he will add control to the ball's ballistics so it either puts him in a good position for another shot, or he will manipulate the ball in such a way that it will leave his opponent without a clear shot. The same technique can be applied to self-defense: you can either step in to deliver a punch, or you can step aside in such a way that it is impossible for your opponent to deliver an effective second punch. Mobility, therefore, is both an active and passive aspect of self-defense.

Balance

Awww! De poor puddy tat faw down an go boom!
                                                    Tweety Bird

Balance is to mobility as orgasm is to sex. Mobility is great, but balance is the finishing touch. If someone is off balance, it is incredibly easy to get some other force to finish him off, namely gravity. Think of the ease of it. With just a slight push or pull in the right spot, your opponent will be sucking asphalt. Wow, and you didn't even work up a sweat.

On the other hand, it is an unfortunate truth that the same can be applied to you. Balance consists of keeping your center of gravity in the proper place (especially during motion), namely low. With women, since their center of gravity is near their hips, it is rather convenient. Men, on the other hand, have a much higher center of gravity; this makes them easier to knock over. They have to squat a bit more. Since all forms should be done with the knees bent and the center of gravity lowered, this won't cause any problems, will it? (If you believe that...)

Most people's muscles aren't exercised in the way that makes this bent-leg bit comfortable, so it is up to you to exercise your horse stance (or whatever) until your legs are strong enough. Do your laundry or watch TV in your stance. This is real important, because it will seriously affect your balance. Balance, as you will see, is one of the most critical aspects of physical combat. It is also one of the most neglected. One thing to watch when you're practicing is the tendency to float up by straightening your legs, which means that your center of gravity is off. This can lead to cement chewing, so a certain amount of caution is advised. Since there are many forms of combat that rely on you being off balance and using that against you (start with judo, aikido, tai chi and work your way back), you can see the advantages of keeping your balance.

Poor balance and proper balance.

A ball is a perfect example of the kinetic balance that you need. It moves around, can even get knocked around, but its center of gravity doesn't change. While it may seem easier to keep your balance while stationary, it is actually easier to keep your balance while in motion. This is because you can move out of the way. If pushed, retreat. If pulled, come forward. If you are stationary, you have to absorb the force of the blow. The difference is that, if you are in balance, your ability to give the gift that keeps on giving (i.e., a fat lip) is greatly enhanced. Most people never understand this blend, and this is, in all probability, one of their major weaknesses (read: one of your best chances to save your ass).

Mobility and balance are the foundation of the physical moves of self-defense. Keep on ragging your teacher about them. Don't let him blow it off. Practice developing your mobility and balance until you have it right. When you have mastered these aspects, you are now the proud possessor of a choice— passive or active self-defense. If you have mobility and balance down pat, the odds of the average thug being able to harm you are equivalent to the proverbial snowball in warm climates. That is passive self-defense. Active self-defense means you have the option of turning his face into pudding.

Blocking

When the opponent attempts to execute a move, frustrate it from the onset. Make whatever the opponent was trying to accomplish of no use...

> Miyamoto Musashi
> *Book of Five Rings*

The main objective of a block is to keep from getting hit. In other words, the motto "Fuck the art, get the job done" is especially applicable here.

There are many different types of blocks. Some work against certain moves, while others don't. (Incidentally, there are certain moves which cannot be blocked. By blocked, I mean the energy stopped by equal or greater force. Any attempt to block these particular moves will result in the notification of the next of kin. Don't worry, Buckwheat, they are easy to spot once you know how.) Often, it is a compromise between speed and efficiency. Somewhere along the line, a fairy tale creeped into the story, saying "You can't block and dodge at the same time." The proper retort has something to do with bovine feces. In a pinch, a block that, by itself, would not stop a certain blow will do just fine when combined with the fine art of backpedaling.

In order to choose the correct block, you must be able to identify what sort of blow is being thrown at you. Since there are basically only four types of blows (explained later), this is not as difficult as it may seem.

The thing about blocks is that their main design is to stop a blow. "Sounds good to me!" you may say, and rightly so. But did you know that a block can also be applied in a manner that can only be described as "passive aggressive"? A block can be done in such a way that it maims the person who is striking more than the person blocking. The technique consists of extending the most bony protuberance available to you at the moment to the most tender section of the person's strike. An elbow to the muscle on the inside of the arm is far from comfortable. The really neat thing about this trick is that it bruises, and hence slows, the muscles of the striker. This does, of course, require a bit of accuracy on your part; but since you're practicing already, it won't be that hard, will it?

Another technique that is a definite benefit to your continued survival is a block that is used to "blow" your opponent's limb out of effective range. These are called slap blocks. With the proper physics, you can cause your opponent's strike to rebound so violently that it effectively removes that limb from the fight for a few seconds. Now that doesn't sound like much until you realize that we are talking operating systems that measure survival in fractions of a second—small fucking fractions. A quarter of a second can mean the difference between life and death in this business. There are slap block techniques that are used against certain types of blows that will do the job. Yet, if used against other types of blows, they will only deflect them a little bit, possibly not enough to save your ass.

There are other types of blocks. Sticking blocks are sort of like hitting wet clay, only the clay sticks to you and hangs on, adding weight and slowing you down. Until you run across them, they're hard to explain. It's like having someone riding your arm down to leave you open. The ancient Picts (Scots) used a similar technique; they'd throw a spear intentionally into some guy's shield, and then jump onto the spear. The Pict's weight would drag the guy's shield-arm down. Then *blamo!* This explains why the Scots were the only people to hold off the Romans. In fact, the only legion in Roman history to *disappear* was lost in Scotland. Put that in your pipe and smoke it.

Blocks are many and varied. There are effective types of blocks against every type of blow that you will encounter. Here is where you will encounter the truth of the saying, *for every move, there is a countermove.* The problem is dependent on finding the correct one, whether it is a full-force block, an absorption technique, a whip block, or plain and simple back-pedaling—and each of these is dependent on doing it in time.

Most martial arts, I am sorry to say, spend far less time on these aspects than they should. Mobility, balance, and blocking are what can passively save you a trip to the hospital. These are the foundation that the physical manifestations of self-defense are based on, so you should practice these the most. These principles, when mastered, are what will protect you. Most people don't want to take the time to learn this—they think the only way is to strike. This is not true, and by giving

Front and side views of a whip block.

in to people's desires to become instant Bruce Lees, most martial art teachers are doing something akin to building a pyramid upside down. These people are, for the most part, off balance, improperly grounded, self-defeatingly flashy, and stone cold sloppy. The art of striking can end the confrontation quickly, but if your opponent cannot touch you, he cannot harm you. By not being able to be harmed, you are in control of the situation. In simple words, you are safe.

You may have noticed that I didn't go into detail on different blocks. What I'm trying to teach here is a little bit of theory, to be backed up by a lot of practice on your part. I could try to tell you details, but you'll remember them better if you learn them on the mat or in an alley. I can't explain an effective block to you in writing, but when you do it, you'll know.

What I can do is tell you where certain types of blocks work and don't work, so when you know the actions of blows and blocks, you won't go trying to use a light block against a heavy blow.

Front and side views of a full block.

Full blocks are used against heavier blows—those where much of the body's weight has been committed (the infamous "Nighty Nite Bunny Rabbits"). Full blocks, however, are slow, and therefore should not be used against faster blows.

Lighter blocks are effective against blows where less body weight is committed (Rattlers). They can sometimes be too slow to stop a fast blow with no body weight (Setups), and other times not strong enough to stop a heavy blow.

Front and side views of a lighter block.

Slap blocks are especially effective against fast Setup blows and many Rattlers. They are very quick, but they won't really stop a heavy blow.

Front and side views of a slap block.

Counters

When crossing swords with an opponent, regardless of what the opponent does, know in advance the design of the opponent. When the opponent tries to strike, he will be stopped at the very onset of his attempt.

Miyamoto Musashi
Book of Five Rings

A counter is a mutt, and like most mutts it's a damn good critter. It's not as pretty or as well-bred as a full-breed, but it can be ten times as effective. Now you're probably going, "what the hell is he going on about my kitchen counter like that for?" I'm not; the counter that I'm talking about is a different thing altogether. The counter that I speak of is a blend between a block and a punch.

"Say what?" you say. Like I said, it's a mutt. There is a thing called a counterpunch in boxing. When most people throw a punch, they leave themselves open on the side from whence the blow came. So by punching at the same time and on the same side, but on the inside, you can knock his punching arm aside and deliver your own blow. Most good boxers are counterpunchers. Mike Tyson has got some hellacious counterpunching techniques.

Counters are faster than blocks. In some cases, though, you need to block, because a counter doesn't have the "oomph" that a block does. As a sort of model, a block will connect at a 90 degree angle, while a counter will come in at about 45 degrees and ricochet off toward your opponent's tender spots.

Now here is where we get into physics. Not the book-type where you have to compute to the nth degree a trajectory consisting of a thousand million miles. We are talking about field physics here. What is it going to take to keep from getting hit? Deflection of your opponent's blow is, in reality, just as efficient as stopping it. The bottom line is that you didn't get hit. The thing is, somehow we got the idea that to be safe from it we must stop it. That simply ain't so. A blow that misses you by an inch is just as ineffective as a blow that missed by a foot. If it misses you, that's just as good as stopping it. Savvy? Deflecting a blow takes less energy than stopping it, which means it's faster.

Countering a punch.

Countering a kick.

Remember, a counter is a deflection of your opponent's punch while your punch is on its way. It's sorta like a little detour. You have to find which way the energy of the blow is going and manipulate it. If you don't manipulate it just right, it won't do any good. Yet, if you kick back at the right moment, you can break an untrained fighter's foot, so maybe I'm not entirely right. Anyway, the other thing about counters is that they are object lessons on why you still must guard yourself while striking. Tighten your guard when you attack. It takes less time to deflect an attack and counterstrike than it does to get your guard back to where it should have been in the first place. As usual, object lessons are painful.

Blows

If you are going to hunt tigers, you must learn all you can about them. How they hunt, sleep, make love, everything. If you don't, you're not hunting, you're just walking in the woods.
The liberal rendition of a quote I sort of remember.

Okay, we've finally got to the "chop socky" part (that's what they call those kung fu flicks where the lips don't match what's being said). There are literally thousands of different types of blows. There are more ways to cream your fellow human being than you can imagine. As odd as it may seem, most of these can be put into four categories. These are: Setups; Rattlers; Maimers; and Nighty Nite Bunny Rabbits.

Now these names aren't exactly common in usage. In fact, more often you'll hear names like, "The swooping monkey gathering pearls of wisdom in the sunset with a westerly wind blowing," which is the English translation of "Konichi ebooboo watchamakallit hiyoundai." While my list isn't an exact guide, it will get you aquainted with the bulk of what is out there. So leave us to explore the wonderfully varied world of attacks. (God, that sounds like a "Wild Kingdom" lead in—"Here's Jim dealing with a Maimer...")

Setups

The first type of blow is what I call a Setup. In one sense, it's nothing more than a feint that can and will connect. Its main purpose, however, is not to really connect; it is instead to lure you into opening your guard so something with a little more clout can be delivered. Setups come in and get out fast. They aren't really effective except to unnerve you and/or lead you into making a mistake. For the most part, very little body weight is committed to these kinds of blows; rather, they rely on speed alone. The other tricky side of these is that they scare you into thinking that your opponent is faster than you. When you're scared, you tighten up, which, among other things, means you slow down. In other words, you begin to make mistakes. So these blows are both psychological and insidious in nature.

Setup.

Setups are especially vulnerable to counters and whip blocks. The *main* thing to remember about them *is that they are a setup!!* In case you haven't noticed, there was a certain amount of emphasis on that last sentence. Their objective is to get *you* to make a mistake. Now, before we get going too far, let's look at something of major import: mistakes. We all make them—they happen, shit happens, etc. If you get uptight about making mistakes, you will get double-clutched by your own emotions. Remember conflicting emotions clouding the spirit? If you're worried about making a mistake, you've just committed the biggest mistake possible. So he lands a stinging slap on your head—so what? If you get mad, or go chasing after that little will o' wisp, or allow yourself to get scared, you're going to leave yourself open and get something a whole fucking lot worse. If it annoys you getting slapped, set a trap: leave an opening and counterpunch the chump. Let *him* get uptight 'cause he got clipped. You stay cool.

Now, since you know that Setup blows are a trap, you, not he, has the option. There are two ways out of a trap. One is not to walk into it. The other is a little less known, and that is to blast through it. The best analogy that I can come up with is, when a dog is trying to bite you, ram your fist down its throat. This disturbs the dog's concentration somewhat. In fact, Rover usually becomes more interested in trying to keep from choking than biting you.

Now you know what not to do when these blows are used against you. Slap blocks, by the way, are the most effective way to prevent getting stung by these. The next logical step is for you to know how to do these blows. Since you know that they are setups, you can apply them accordingly, i.e., you snake one in while coiling up with another, more devastating blow. The chump takes the bait and leaves a hole in his defenses. With what you got waiting in the wings, you show him the error of his ways. Simple, eh?

Rattler

The next type of blow is a Rattler. It has more personality than a Setup. In other words, it's a heavier blow. It hurts when it kisses you. It's slower than a Setup and faster than a Nighty

Nite Bunny Rabbit. Its main purpose is to cause damage; not enough to put you away by itself, but cumulative. Five Rattlers can equal one N.N.B.R. This blow won't knock you out, but it can bust your nose, cause deep bruising, rattle your brains (hence the name), etc.

There are many variations on this sort of blow. For the most part, Rattlers consist of your opponent committing a certain amount of his body weight. This is the major technicality that differentiates them from Setups. The thing to watch out for is that there are people out there who can, with their arms alone, throw a Rattler. It's a weird combo of a whip and tightening up at the last second. If you get hit hard by a blow that shouldn't have had that much clout, it may be just a fluke or that the guy knows how to throw a Rattler. If it turns out to be the latter,

Rattler.

go for the arms. Don't block, strike. The target isn't his body, it's his arms. It calls for some practice, but that's what you're doing anyway. Even if you're good, these guys are a real pain in the ass. If you're inexperienced, it could be stomping time for you unless you stop them real quick.

Rattlers form the bulk of blows that you will encounter. They are designed to damage you. In their own way, they are a Setup. They are designed to hurt you and slow you down enough so the slowest and yet most lethal type of blow can be delivered safely: the infamous "Nighty Nite Bunny Rabbit."

Rattlers should be blocked, countered, dodged, or whatever. The idea is to minimize the damage that they will do. If one gets through your defenses, roll with it. Mobility is to be used here. Do your best not to take the full effect of these blows. There is a technique called "shedding" that is especially useful against these blows. If the blow is thrown at the center of your face, you shift to the left or the right; then, as the blow lands, you sort of shed it off by rolling to the side. Oriental styles have this equivalent.

Imagine a string that runs through the top of your head, goes through your body, and comes out between your genitals and anus. You spin around on that string. On whatever side you are pushed, you spin with the force. If a Rattler gets through your defenses, you must be on that string and roll with the blow. You strike on the left side of the string and I roll towards my right. Simple, eh? This is part of the balance that was discussed earlier. Now, since you're aware of counterpunching, you can use the energy that this nice person gave you to boomerang it back at him. You push my left, I hit you with my right, and vice versa. It is important to remember not to take the full abuse these mothers put out. Neither you nor I have a red "S" on our chests, so don't do it.

The reason that these blows are slower than Setups is that they have more body weight behind them. By the same criteria, they are faster than N.N.B.R. blows because they don't have *all* your body weight in them. The most important thing to remember about throwing a Rattler is *you must be in balance!*

If something goes wrong and you aren't in balance, you are in some deep kim chee. Let's look at some of the possibilities. You miss (i.e., he dodges); you can either fall on your face or you can get hit several times, because you're flapping your arms to keep from falling on your face instead of blocking. He blocks and knocks you further off balance. Again, you get hit several times while trying to keep from kissing asphalt. It was a trap— that hole in his defenses was left there intentionally. Because you're off balance, you can't backpedal out of the way of seven Rattlers and two Nighty Nite Bunny Rabbits he had waiting for you. You go to the hospital and end up with casts and your jaw wired for six weeks.

Now, lest you think I'm an alarmist, I have to say, without boasting, that I can kill someone in less than ten seconds. If they don't die right there, they will in the next few hours unless an emergency room is reached. But that, for the most part, can only happen to someone that I can blow off balance, even for just a moment. If I can't get through their defenses and knock them off balance, I won't have time to put them away without putting myself in serious jeopardy. You dig? If I can hurt them badly enough to get them to choke, that means they weren't in balance to roll with my punches. Either way, balance and mobility play major parts in the scenario.

A key that somehow gets left out of most of the training techniques that I've encountered is this: if you are in control of yourself, no one can touch you. More often than not, we defeat ourselves with things like overcommitment. The other chump just adds the extra incentive. The same can be said for him, of course. If you're in balance and mobile, you can defeat damn near anybody who isn't.

Maimers

Here we find a unique critter. Unlike the three other types of blows, Maimers are mostly done with the hands. You will notice that I've spoken of *types* of blows, not specific punches or kicks. That's because the other three can be either. Maimers are almost exclusively done with the hands. They come pretty much from the Shao-lin styles, but they can come from anywhere. For the most part, you won't encounter Maimers because they take too long to perfect. In fact, most people don't even know they exist, and boy are they sorry when they find out about them. They are undoubtedly the most vicious form of strike, and are definitely not for the squeamish.

A Maimer is a type of strike that is a punch only by definition. Unlike a punch, it does its damage *after* it arrives—a punch does its damage *while* arriving. Sound too subtle to differentiate? Let me put it to you this way. A punch to the face is just that, a fist hitting your face. A Maimer not only gets the hand to your face, it rips your ear off your head once it's there. I am not joking.

Maimers cause serious damage, either externally or internally. They can rip off portions of your anatomy, or they can cause deep, specific strains and/or ruptures. In a sense, the hands become claws for ripping and crushing. A Maimer to the arm will drive the fingers into muscle, then with a jerking motion it will rip the ligaments. Throwing a Maimer to the genitals will leave you, literally, with his pecker in your pocket.

Maimers can be used against your opponent's body or his extremities. The same force that would rip a man's testicles off will, when applied to his hand, shatter every bone in it. Not break, but shatter the bones.

The techniques vary, but the defense remains constant—*keep the fuck away from their hands! Don't let a trained maimer grab you.* If, God forbid, one does, go with his attacks. The jerks are short and sharp; don't fight them. If anything, you might be able to rush him. If you survive the first jerk, and he still has his right hand on you, his right side is open. Use it, because it's your only chance. If you can break free, run. When fighting one of these people, there is no way anyone who isn't seriously trained can come away without massive damage. They are dangerous.

You must get past your squeamishness about this form of fighting. It is a matter of knowing exactly what you are doing when you do it. Nonetheless, you will coolly and efficiently proceed with it. In a battle for your survival, there are no rules. Victory is awarded to whoever is still breathing when it's over. Crushing someone's thorax sounds terrible, until you realize you are only doing it to him first. You have Maimers at your disposal; it is your choice whether or not to use them. A mugger doesn't have that ability; you do.

As you may have noticed, we have been slowly moving toward more serious aspects of fighting. The truth is, as much as I joke about it, there are some serious assumptions underlying this business, and a major part of it is that you must take responsibility for your fighting abilities. That means you must realize that in your hands is the ability to hurt and maim people for life. If you don't misuse it (i.e., I'm pissed and I'm going to go beat someone up), you can become accustomed to it to the point of being able to see humor in it. It's odd, but part of what makes taking responsibility for your abilities bearable is being able to laugh at it.

There is a certain black humor about a coyote that, instead of going out and hunting, tries to steal a wolverine's kill. The term "dumbfuck" is a great adjective for situations like that. Since most people have no desire to take this training and go out and misuse it, the only ones who, like the coyote, will discover that they have picked the wrong targets are the ones who deserve what they get. The mugger who feels that it is easier to rob than work; the bully who wants to take his anger at the world out on someone smaller and weaker than himself; the rapist who wants to vent his anger at women by degrading them—these are the people it is really hard to feel sorry for when they pick the wrong target.

Here are only a few of the various Maimer hand positions:

Dragon.

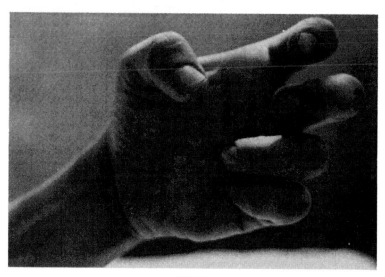

Eagle.

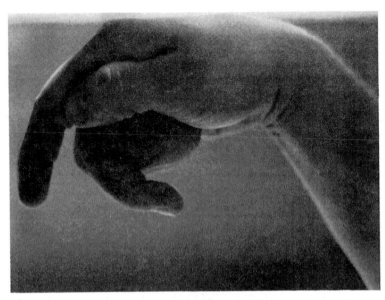

Mantis.

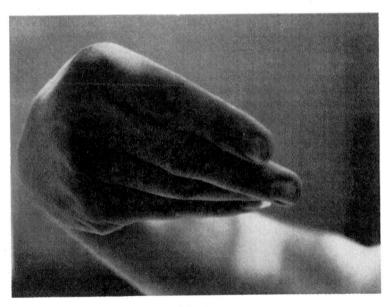

Monkey.

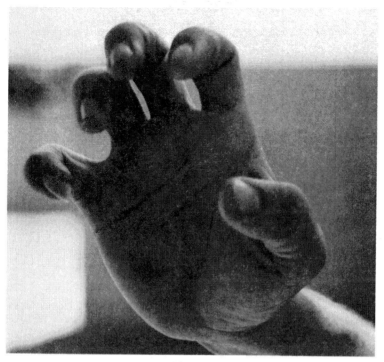

Tiger.

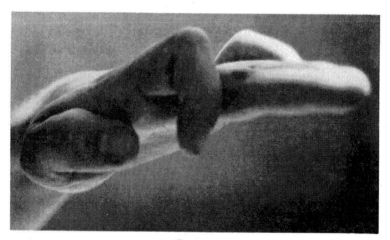

Snake.

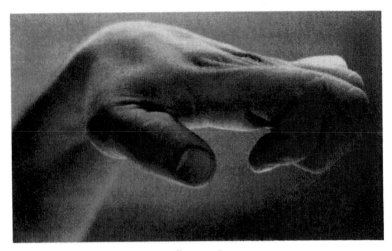

Leopard.

Nighty Nite Bunny Rabbit

Now we come to the finishing touch, so to speak. The Nighty Nite Bunny Rabbit is any blow that puts your opponent out of commission. It ends the conflict by putting the sucker down for the count. It either knocks him out or hurts him so badly he can't (or seriously doesn't want to) continue. My brother "Kaos" coined this phrase from a Bugs Bunny cartoon. I liked it so much I started using it. And, as the Immortal Bard once said, "The rest is history."

The Nighty Nite is the slowest of all blows. That is because it has all of your body weight behind it. Take your weight and figure it's going, oh, let's say sixty miles an hour. Now let's figure it's all localized in an area of...homina homina...six square inches. Intellectual types can figure mass × velocity = impact psi. Me, I'll just figure the blow would hurt like hell and in all probability do some major damage. Therefore, it would behoove me to be nowhere near that sucker's destination.

The other three types of blows all can be countered or slap blocked out of the way. Not these babies. They need either a full-on block or out-and-out ducking (see *backpedaling*). Since they are the slowest of all attacks, they are usually reserved for somewhere near the end of the fight (if they land, it is the very end of the fight). They are not to be used when your opponent is fresh, aware, unhurt or expecting it. Because they are so slow, they leave you wide open for a counterstrike.

Now, there are certain types of N.N.B.R. blows that the only thing you can do is dodge. I know of three: The taekwon do stick kick, the Shao-lin kung fu elephant punch, and the same style's crane kick. If you try to block these moves, you will either be blown into the next state or go down until you hit bedrock. I'm sure that there are other blows that fall into this category, and, except for the crane kick (which looks a lot like a front snap kick, but with some subtle differences—enough to be recognizable by the paranoid), they are easily recognizable. They start somewhere out in Kansas and leave the attacker seemingly wide open. So, like a stampede of buffalo, you can see it coming from way the hell out there. And, like the stampede, the only thing you can do is get out of the way once it has steam.

Nighty Nite Bunny Rabbit.

The bulk of Nighty Nite blows aren't as bad as the three I have mentioned. That's sort of like saying, "a brown bear isn't as bad as a Kodiak." It's true, but don't let that fool you. They can both mess you up pretty good. Whereas the real bad Nighty Nite blows start in Kansas, the bulk of them seem only to come from Nevada (using Pacific coast fighting time). Either way, it's a good time to remember how to dodge.

The other big weakness of N.N.B.R.s (other than the fact that U.S. Mail is faster) is that most people are off balance when they deliver them. Since we all know what happens to bad boys and girls when they're off balance, I don't have to waste time repeating myself.

Here's a rule of thumb about N.N.B.R.s. Remember, it isn't a law—there are a thunderin' herd of exceptions. For the most part, you can tell where the power blows will come from by noting which way the guy squares off against you. If he leads with his left foot, the odds are (but not always) that the power blows will come from his right side. So watch how someone squares off and, if possible, try to keep out of the sector where the power blow will come from. That means if he squares off facing you with his left foot forward, try to keep to his left side. If you wander towards his right, you've just walked into danger. The reverse goes for you: you want him in the area of highest danger.

This may sound strange, but you are now more consciously aware of the basic types of blows than most "toughs." They may have an instinctive grasp of these things, but if they haven't put two and two together, you still have the edge. If you see someone winding up to start a N.N.B.R., you can convince them not to by donating two Rattlers to their reality. You can also avoid having the same gift given to you by being aware of the timing of a fight. Don't try certain moves while he's still intact enough to counter.

What I have told you about here are types of blows. The particular fighting style you study will obviously affect what forms these will take. Remember, these blows do exist out there. If you don't learn them from the style you study, do independent study. You don't know which style your opponent knows. Each style has its own strengths and limits. Being aware of this is your greatest survival tool. If you know that there is something out there, and your style doesn't cover it, go out and find something that will.

Punches

Violence is the first option, and the last choice, of the competent.

Frank Gasperik

Now, we finally get down to specifics. Instead of general "blows" (which can be punches, kicks, elbows, or whatever), let's talk about punches. Naw, let's be more general than that. Strikes with the hand, that's better.

A punch consists of balling your fist and striking straight in (or with enough of an arc to be called a hook) toward your opponent. Now, while there are about three hundred or so variations of what most people call a punch, that is nothing more than a drop in the bucket of the many different hand techniques out there. The hardest (and, with the proper angle, strongest) part of your hand is your palm. Surprised? These days I hardly ever strike with my knuckles. In fact, I can think of at least a hundred strike forms that never use a standard balled fist (that's not even including elbow shots). So you can begin to see the possibilities.

I'm sure at this point, somewhere along the line, a little voice has said, "Oh my God, I can't possibly learn all of this! It's far too complicated! At least a thousand hand blows! I'll never learn to defend against them all!" *Can that voice!* It's your "rational" voice that has kept you down all this time! That little sucker is already starting to try to keep you in line. You don't need to learn three thousand eight hundred and fifty-two blocks. Learn twenty good blocks and five counters and perfect them. Add in mobility and balance, then damn near nothing—and I do mean nothing—is going to be able to touch you.

Okay, enough psychological evaluations: let's get back to hand strikes. Well, maybe back to "blows" for a general rule, then back to hand strikes. The general rule, which is actually a law, is *get out as fast as you got in!* An effective technique you will learn is called "trapping." Oddly enough, it consists of trapping some portion of your opponent's anatomy long enough for you to pummel the shit out of him. If someone is great at getting in fast but lousy at retreating at the same speed (don't laugh, it happens out there), he is a prime candidate for a trapping technique. I will gladly exchange the receipt of one Rattler for the golden opportunity of delivering six of the same. Diminishing returns my ass! The sucker is mine!

Getting out as fast as you got in is another aspect of something called "overcommitment." Overcommitment usually consists of three parts: one, failing to observe the in/out rule; two, being out of balance when you start a move, so you can't get back to a guard position in time if something goes wrong; and three, when starting a move and something doesn't work right, you continue with that move anyway. Any one of these can get you killed. Overcommitment means that, for whatever reason, you can't defend yourself after a move goes wrong.

Now back to hand strikes (this time for sure!). You now know about balance, grounding, in and out, blocking, counterpunching, and the four types of blows. Great, that takes care of most problems you will encounter with blows...except one.

It's not really a biggie, if you think a broken arm isn't that big. I do, so I stress this little fact: *Never, ever, lock your elbow!* When you strike, no matter what form, your elbow should be bent slightly. It complicates things slightly, but then so does a broken elbow. You can disregard this idea, but I'll laugh when I see you in a cast. (I'm less prone to laugh when I see people in a casket, but if you fell for this one, I might make an exception.) With the elbow locked, it is incredibly easy to trap the arm, and then with the proper motion snap the elbow. I have used this technique to end fights. It works, no lie. And after training, you will be able to do it, too.

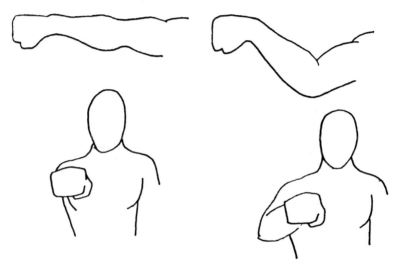

This is inviting a broken arm.   **This is much harder to break.**

Kicks

Oh fuck!

   The last words of a guy before my kick
got through his defenses and sent him to the
hospital with blood clots in his balls.

Remember the TV show "Kung Fu"? We used to love
watching ol' Quinine Chai Candy Cane (as we used to call him)
fall over after he kicked. He did it a lot. He'd do a tiger tail
sweep and corkscrew into the dirt. He'd do a spinning heel kick,
followed immediately by two bunny hops. It was real cute.

The reason I tell you this is because most kicks look real
good, but they should be filed in either the fantasy department
or busted down to the same time zone as the Nighty Nite Bunny
Rabbit blows (when your opponent is so hurt or tired that he
can't respond in time to hurt you badly). The other thing is,
try not to turn your back on your opponent during a fight.
There are times when you have to eat this rule raw (like when
you're running like a bat out of hell). For the most part, though,
if you like your kidneys you'll try to keep this in mind. These
are good rules of thumb, but they're not laws. That's next.

The only real law I have ever discovered about kicks is
incredibly easy to understand, and if you're into self preserva-
tion, it ain't too hard to follow. It is simply this: *In actual
combat, don't kick above waist level!!* That's easy, isn't it?

You may be wondering why I have such a strong feeling

toward that rule. This is serious. I have spent nearly two-thirds of my life, seventeen years, learning how to maim and mutilate my fellow human beings. This also means I have spent a considerable portion of my life getting mauled and mutilated myself (no observations as to overall intelligence if you please). This book is the culmination of those things that I have learned physically, mentally, and strategy-wise.

If there is one thing I have learned, it is that those peachy keeno boot-to-the-head moves are, bar none, the best way there is to get your nuts ripped off and stuffed into your mouth.

I lie to you not on this one. I used to really be into shotokan karate kicks. Man, I was bad. I had those Bruce Lee kicks and squeals down pat. Then, during a fight, I did a spinning heel kick to this guy's head. Unfortunately, he did a front snap kick at the same time. The resulting explosion in my balls left me on the floor for five minutes. Verified reports indicate that I was lifted at least three inches off the ground by that kick. I am here to tell you, children, I was in pain. I couldn't move. He managed to sink in a few boots to the ribs (see *stomp*) before my friends pulled him off.

The problem was that the move that had almost ruined my sex life was a move my sensei had taught us and had advocated as extremely effective. That was my first experience with the potentially lethal difference between dojo fighting and actual combat. What I had learned in class had failed miserably in the real world. So, being somewhat of a bright boy, I went out into the streets to discover what worked and what didn't. Oh boy, ever heard the old joke, "Everything you know is wrong"? I had learned a thundering herd of fancy moves that were about as effective as a fart in a tornado. Well, rather than being overly upset, I began to learn. The thing that became immediately obvious to me was that most experienced fighters knew this little tidbit about kicking above the waist, while it was the martial artists who hadn't quite caught on. Did the little lights go on in my head? You betcha!

It is my fervent hope that you can learn from my mistake on this matter rather than go out and have to learn it on your

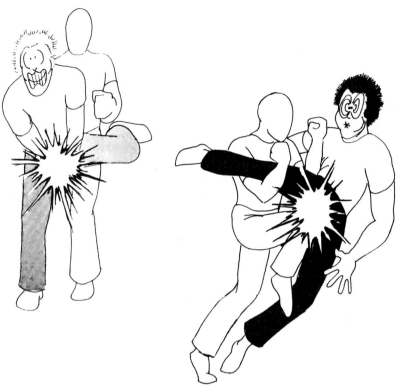

Why you never turn your back on an opponent or kick above the waist.

own. If you do, your future generations can write me letters of thanks for my part in ensuring their existence. If you insist on checking this particular maxim out for yourself, well, the gene pool needed a little chlorine anyway.

Now that we have that out of the way, we can move on to another neato thing. What if you encounter someone who kicks high? Well, let's start with the fact that most kicks above the waist are off balance (hint hint, nudge, nudge, wink wink, say no more, say no more). The other thing is, if you know some maiming techniques, you will soon have three things to practice your juggling with.

Grounding

Ewe ma' ha' grounning' ewe no ha' grounning, punch no goo!
Sifu

Grounding is another nebulous theory that confuses many people. Until they encounter it in reality, it sounds sort of ethereal and misty. After they get hit so hard that it feels like their nose is sticking out of the back of their skull, it begins to make more sense.

What grounding is, basically, is using leverage and shock absorbers in a fight. It can be used either offensively or defensively. Let's first be offensive.

Guys, have you ever seen a really cute girl that you were thinking about making a move on, only to discover that she had a real protective older brother? You know the sort—one eye, steel teeth, wears platform shoes so his knuckles don't drag on the ground, etc. Well, guess what? Balance is the little cutie and grounding is the ape of a simian. . .er. . .sibling. Grounding is using the earth as a pushboard. When your center of gravity is hurled forward by pushing off old terra firma, you can get some serious clout behind your blows.

A grounded blow puts all of your weight into the blow without losing your balance. A grounded blow consists of a wide base and directed energy. Different styles teach grounded blows differently, so I can't give you an all-encompassing statement about them. What I can do is give you an image.

Imagine a semi-truck with a full load going eighty miles an hour. Now imagine what it would do to someone who got in its way. That is a grounded blow. The reason it is so strong is because it pushes off the earth in a forward motion. The mother has clout because when it hits, it is still pushing off the ground. It's driving forward.

Okay, let's change the scenario a bit. Same thing, but in outer space. (For you purists: same mass, same velocity, construct form, etc.) First of all, the truck loses its weight, not its mass. That means it's still going to hurt when it hits. The most important factor, however, is that it's not being pushed along by the earth when it hits. That means it is floating. You can roll with it. Other pressure applied at different angles can, and will, deflect its course. It's still coming at you, but if it's not connected to anything, it's easier to stop.

A major factor in grounding is balance. If you are in balance, you can effectively drive your center of gravity forward. If not, most of your blows will be like the truck in space. Most people don't know how to balance or ground; that's why most people don't hit very well. When you move, don't *throw* your center of balance forward; you will end up all over the place, waiting for the rest of your weight to catch up. If you *drive* your center of balance forward, the impact of the blow will go—and stop—where you want it to.

Often, when people hit, the fist will land and then try to push your body backwards to a point behind you. This is because of two different reasons. The first is that most people don't know that an effective punch should stop about two inches into target: the entire force of the blow should be deployed somewhere inside of your opponent's body. The end of the strike is where the power will be delivered. The difference between that and the way most people strike is that most blows are targeted, sometimes as much as six inches, *behind* the target. That means, in actuality, the blow is interrupted before it can pick up full steam.

The second reason goes like this. Often a blow is thrown in

a manner which is utterly ass-backwards. The hand starts to move first, then the arm, then the shoulder, then comes the torso; finally the extremely off-center center of balance gets to a lurching start. To top it off, there isn't any muscle tension connecting everything. This is about as efficient as a Chihuahua tied to a dog sled. It can run like hell and maybe budge the sled, but it is the little thing trying to move the big thing. Using that as the formula, that means the fist is trying to lead the center of gravity instead of the other way around. It's like getting hit by a bug when you're riding a motorcycle—it stings but it doesn't hurt. But when the center of gravity is in place and the blow is balanced and grounded, it's like getting hit by a truck. The hub (center of gravity) is only moving at five miles per hour, but that big rock at the end of the yardarm (fist) is doing fifty.

Defensive grounding is much harder to explain. It is taking the energy of your opponent's blow and absorbing it, yet passing it into the ground. It isn't "taking a punch" in the normal sense. It's more like bouncing something off armor.

I first encountered defensive grounding when I met up with an old streetfighter who, amused by my bluster of how good I was in the martial arts, suggested that we go out back and spar. Let me tell you, children, I threw everything that I had at the guy and he just batted it away. Well, rather than go down in total defeat, I decided to throw my "Sure-Fire, Never-Fail, Gets 'Em Everytime Blow." (Remember what I have been preaching about betting on these things?) Ah hah! The infamous spinning heel kick to the back of the knees!

I tell you, Bruce Lee would have been proud of me. I first cocked my left shoulder back while thrusting my right shoulder forward. Then, with my arms twirling like one of those little gyros you get out of cereal boxes, I began the killer spin. I even put in the terrifying "Kiai!" (sounding like a pig passing a kidney stone).

For those of you who haven't caught on yet, it didn't work. In fact, the whole move was more than just a dismal failure. It was something that I had never before encountered: he grounded the blow. Ignore, if you will, the fact that the guy had time to have a cup of coffee and read the paper before the blow even got close. I broadcasted the move so badly, he had time to walk to the store to get the newspaper that he was going to read. He also had time to make the coffee. The thing about it was, the blow was done right. I admit I was a little off balance, but not much. I was mostly striking from my hips; there was a little energy bleed, but again, not much.

He moved his hand and let the blow land...and I stuck.

Yes, there I was, wondering what the hell had happened. My foot was extended to where it had made contact. I had, up to that point, felt blows land and blast through people. I had even felt them bounce off people before. However, I had never felt a blow be so totally absorbed. It was like hitting a blob of wet clay. I froze. I looked at him in total shock. Then he beat the snot out of me. I went on to become one of his pupils.

I really wish I could explain it to you better. Somehow I picked up how to do this trick, but to this day I can't explain how. It's something I can now do after years of practice, almost instinctively, but explaining it is a little more tricky. My Sifu drilled me for three months on walking and grounding. Nothing else. Finally, one day when we were practicing, he body-checked me. I felt the impact and then transferred it into the ground. I didn't budge, and his energy went elsewhere. Find someone who can explain it to you; then perfect it.

Linear and Nonlinear Forms

Where did that come from?
A quote heard coming from the practice floor.

In the West (that's Western world, not California), we're prone to think along linear lines. Straight to our goal, beat a path to his door, etc. I like linear fighters. They're easy to beat. They like to charge, and like a ram with its head down, they can't see much. "Well looky here, that ram's a chargin'. I thin' I jes step out the way." That and sucker punching the critter when it goes by usually keep things easy.

A pussycat is a damn good example of nonlinear attacks. Which of the four sets of claws and/or teeth are going to take a hunk out of you? And from which direction? It is important to realize that circling can be just as effective as a straight blow that lands, primarily because people, as a rule, don't think circular.

Look at your arm. Now look around the room. Anyone there? If not, good. If yes, do they get weirded out easy? If yes, go into the bathroom or something. Now, back to your arm. Spin your wrist with your hand open. See how much area that covers? Do it again, but this time with the fist closed. Now, keeping your wrist still, spin your elbow. A lot more room covered, eh? Now spin your shoulder.

These are called pivot points. They are designed to allow you

63

to move in ways other than linear. You must learn to look at each section as a member of a team of specialists. Not a football team—more along the line of a fire team. Six Rambos instead of just one. They all rely on each other to get the job done. While each can stand alone it its own area, as a combo they are spectacular.

Each has its own special form. The situation dictates which one is used. The shoulder is the mover; its job is to get you into the city. The elbow is for getting you into the neighborhood. The wrist is to get you to the address. If you really want to get specific, the fingers will get you into a room. Now if you're going to use an atomic bomb, the city is an exact enough location. If you're going to use a conventional bomb, the neighborhood is good enough. If you're going to use a grenade, the address is fine. If you're going to use an assassin, you'll need the room number. Get the idea?

Now let's get more exact than that general analogy. While there are many exceptions (mostly having to do with when blows are blocked), there is a generalization to be made here. Distance fighting consists of shoulder and elbow, while infighting relies heavily on elbow and wrist technique, with some backup from the shoulder. Wrestling has elbow, wrist, and fingers as major factors.

Many distance styles rely on straight lines, with some circular attacks: roundhouse kicks and the like. At this distance, going around takes a little longer and therefore leaves you open longer. Don't think this means you're safe from circular attacks while fighting out there. Most Nighty Nite Bunny Rabbit blows come from this range. A taekwon do stick kick comes circling around from the back at this range. An elephant punch comes crushing down from above when you're about three feet away. A crane strike can knock your brains into another state, yet it looks like it's going to take out the spectators, it's so circular. But most attacks at this range are pretty much straightforward.

Incidentally, if it seems that I'm saying one thing, and then saying something else that totally invalidates it, you're missing the point. There are no laws that will guarantee what is going to happen in a fight. There are no guaranteed never-fail moves, blocks, strategies, or anything. Anyone who tells you differently is a liar. They may be lying to put you at ease, or because they don't know any better, but they are still lying. There are variables that cannot be controlled, so what will work in one situation won't work in another. You have to be aware of this. Smart-asses may say, "What about a .45?" My answer is simple: "A .45 won't save you from a knife in a dark alley if it's still in its holster." Nobody is immune to a blindshot. If you're not paying attention, it can and will happen. This is a raw truth that most people don't want to accept.

There ain't no guarantees in combat. Things change; factors are different; what worked once may not work again. A distance fighter who has fought three other linear distance fighters is going to get hurt when he encounters someone who fights in circles. What I am teaching you is rules of thumb—rules that are true most of the time, yet can be affected by certain factors and totally voided by others. If you begin to think of these rules as immutable laws, that there are no exceptions, you will get blindsided by reality. Duncan Idaho, the swordmaster in *Dune* says, "Only expect what happens in a fight." I couldn't agree with the man more.

If you're overconfident about something working, you will not react fast enough when it doesn't. I know of three excellent examples of this. The first was the time I saw a guy break a pool cue over another guy's head, a supposed surefire move in any brawl. Well, it wasn't. The recipient of the blow snapped the heavy end of the cue, shook his head once, and grabbed the cue-wielder. The guy who had swung was immobilized with shock; it hadn't worked. Actually, he was only immobilized for a moment; the next, he was flying over the pool table. The second example was when my friend knifed the guy who shot him. Yes, with a bullet hole in him, he moved in and gave the punk an emergency appendectomy. (I'm not going to say who my friend was, because minions of the law, while agreeing with the context of the action, feel compelled to arrest people for that sort of behavior.) The third and final example was when a "black belt" made the mistake of kicking me in the balls while I was trying to negotiate peace between him and someone else. His expression was priceless when he saw my reaction. Rather than the expected crumpling up and crying, I looked at him in cold fury and calmly handed my radio off to someone. The rest is history.

These are actual examples of what happens when someone relies on a "never-fail" trick. Remember, there are no rules in a real fight for survival. Awareness of this and of what is happening around you is your best weapon. It could save your butt.

Anyway, back to linear and nonlinear techniques. Most infighting is done in circular forms. Uppercuts, hooks, and elbow shots are common. Also, I learned from hard experience that there is a thing called a crescent kick.

I was all over my sparring partner, Cean. I had breached his defenses and was too close for him to use his distance techniques. Suddenly out of left field, his foot took me across the face and blew me out of the fight. He had snaked in a crescent kick. I had been watching for a low kick, not a boot to the head. There is a certain shift of the shoulders that accompanies the kick. Once you've learned to spot it, the never-above-the-waist rule comes into play. So when you're infighting, most of the moves will be short, sharp arcs.

Infighting also consists of twisting. Wrestling is where most of twisting is done, but you will encounter it in infighting, as well. What I mean is this: you block a move, yet with a slight twist of the forearm or wrist, your opponent is again in a position to strike, often using the force of your own block to quicken his blow. The bar none best counter for many of these moves consists of getting to this person's elbow. Wing Chun taught me a technique called "sticky hands," and it is the best training technique I have encountered for infighting. It consists of two people standing toe-to-toe with their forearms touching; you then begin a dance of shift, counter, attempt to shift into a striking position, counter to that shift, counter to that counter, etc. What it does is teach you to sense what your opponent is going to do. If you have any part of your body connected to the inside of his elbow, with a shift of pressure you can prevent an effective strike by him.

While we're on this subject of predicting your opponent's next move (if you see it coming, you can either block or dodge at your leisure), there is something you should know. Damn near nothing comes out of nowhere. A kick is usually announced by a shifting of weight. A punch from most people will be broadcast by a shift in the shoulder. The term "broadcast" is sort of a general slang term which simply means the person broadcasts his intention to move from certain parts of the body. If you're distance fighting, watch your opponent's navel area if he is in balance (read: very good). If he's not, the shoulders are a good bet. If you are fighting someone without a lot of training, the shoulders will tell you what's about to happen. If, however, your opponent has training, an unfocused attention to his navel is very important.

Back to nonlinear attacks. As already mentioned, infighting is seriously nonlinear, but wrestling is about as linear as a snake. In fact, if, during your practice with infighting and wrestling, you try to imagine your arms as snakes slithering around the opposition, it could greatly enhance your learning speed.

I mean, hell, if your opponent is pushing here, move there and snake one in on him. It's irritating to fight someone who isn't there except to hit you. But then again, as we all know, it's better to give than to receive.

Hard and Soft

Legend has it that Richard the Lionhearted once hacked an anvil in half to show the Saracen leader, Saladin, how powerful the European broadsword was. Saladin then took a silk scarf and threw it in the air. When the scarf fell upon his sword, it was sliced in half.

In the previous section, I mentioned that it is irritating to fight someone who isn't there. Shadowboxing aside (sorry, Corwin), it is a serious aspect of a fight. Oriental fighting styles can be broken down into two categories: hard and soft. I'd rather fight a good hard stylist than a good soft stylist—I'd win more with the hard stylist. The problem with soft styles is that they take a long time to be effective. This might have something to do with what is used to defeat your opponent, namely your self-control and balance. The gentle circles of tai-chi are incredibly beautiful, but I always like blending art and practicality. I hit them first.

Soft stylists are in control of themselves, and therefore can control you. It doesn't matter that you're able to break boards with your bare hands; they can dodge it. What's worse is, somehow you end up being knocked over without them attacking. It's real embarrassing, to say nothing of painful.

Hard stylists are more prone to beat you into the ground. In the beginning, they are much more effective than soft stylists.

If they can lay hands on those elusive "softies," they can usually seriously "torque their Wa."

For brawling, the hard styles are the best. For spiritual maturity and growth, the soft styles are magnificent. For true self-defense, a blend of the two is what you need (with a hunk of out-and-out sneakiness thrown in).

Hard styles can be called, well, a little "aggressive"—if ripping body parts off people while causing internal hemorrhaging can be considered a little aggressive. Therein lies their greatest strength and weakness, all rolled into one. You can charge into shit, with both eyes open, and still get stomped. The soft styles rely on a more gentle approach, like taking an aggressor's energy and leading it headfirst into a wall, your head being the leading edge of all aggression. The problem is, these styles rely a little too much on you falling down nicely. I loved the first time I kidney punched a tai-chi person as I was falling (he'd knocked me off balance). Not only that, I muckled on to him and took him down with me. It was the sock to the ol' pee buckets that threw him off balance enough for us to both hit the ground.

In case you hadn't guessed, I advocate a blend of hard and soft styles. It's real annoying to fight someone who whirlwinds in with blows, and then you have to chase all over hell and back trying to hit him. It's also tiring, which is something you can use to your advantage.

When I tell you about mobility and balance, I am preaching soft style. When I tell you how to deliver blows, that's hard style. If you discover that someone is off balance and falling over (with a little help, like stepping on his foot while he's advancing) and you hit him three times on the way down, that's both. Judo, aikido, jujitsu, etc., all work better if you've stunned the chump with a Rattler beforehand. For some reason, he's more prone to be cooperative when you do this. Little things, like knives, are less likely to show up in your kidney if you do this.

By the way, there is something I feel you should know about some of those near-wrestling forms of self-defense: watch out for knives. A good knife fighter will give you an arm, and while you're going for it. . . nuff said. A good number of those styles' moves involve both hands on the arm being used to throw the opponent, leaving you wide open for a blade to snake in. That's why I advocate distracting someone before trying to throw them.

Now some of you will want to run out and ask your sensei about this. Remember, as he shows you why "Chuckeeyuyonee-headee" is so good and what I'm saying is impertinent trash, he isn't the one dealing with a mugger hyped on adrenalin. I have met very few instructors of any style who could withstand a full-bore lethal attack by a member of our Special Forces with combat experience. In fact, most martial artists I have met have only been in one or two fights, and most of those were pre-training. So my attitude is: "don't tell me something is going to work unless you've been there, sucker."

I can give you a very good example. I'm not exactly a slouch when it comes to a knife, but I was hanging out with a long-since retired Airborne Ranger when we began to talk "shop." I said that this Chinese knife technique has always given me trouble; it's really a mother to get through. He claimed it wasn't and we squared off. Mind you, I'm a twenty-year-old fighting buck at the time, with nearly ten years of training under my belt. He's a fat, balding, snaggle-toothed, old Jewish fart. No problem, right? You got it. That man crossed up my defenses and slid the practice knife into a kill spot so fast, I swear I hardly saw him move. I would bet on him in a dark alley, beer belly and all, against 90 percent of all the senseis I have ever met. And I've met a lot. So again I stress there is no surefire technique that will work every time. In the final draw, your best defense is always your own awareness of what is going on.

Trapping, etc.

The trick isn't to walk into the Dragon's mouth; any idiot can do that. The trick is to walk out again.

A D&D maxim.

I can hear the groans of "more?" Yeah, more. The thing about this book is that it takes seventeen years and tries to condense it to about two hundred pages. That is one hell of a lot of information covered in a short space. To that end, I suggest you read this book several times over a space of time. What will work best is: you read this book, then go out and practice for a month, keeping the attitudes expressed here in mind as your goal. This will allow your body (unconsciously) to absorb some of what I'm saying. The experience you will gain on the practice floor will also give you a bigger context to absorb more of what I am saying here. Then read this book again, and many parts will fall into place. The old "Is that what he meant?!" will come into play. If you read this book three or four times over a year of practicing, you can add incredible amounts of useful information to your system.

Crossing, hooking, and binding are the children of trapping, so we will deal with them as one big happy family. They are designed to put your opponent into an unfavorable position while you wreak havoc on his frail little body. In other words, he shouldn't be able to do anything but try to escape, if it's done right.

The main thing to remember with these techniques is that they work best on hard stylists. People who lock their elbows and rely on strength and force are extremely susceptible to these suckers. People who are fluid and relaxed with their pivot points are much less likely to be caught so flat-footed. Look at the illustration below. If you try to use your arm as a club, you'll fall prey to these techniques. If you use your arm as a snake, they won't be as effective because you can slither out of them. If you picture a snake that can pull back slightly, turn, and strike at what is trying to trap it, you get a very good idea of what is going on.

If you think of what would happen if you had to pull back straight with the bar, you see the effectiveness of these. Going back straight causes friction and lack of leverage, making the whole process slow. If the person is trying to escape using this technique, it will slow him down and keep him from striking, while you're firing on him wildly.

Crossing is a form that can be summarized as forcing your opponent's arm across his body in such a way that it blocks his other arm. You dodge his blow and grab his elbow (the back this time), then step forward. If you use the force of your moving body instead of the strength of your arm, it is damn near an irresistible force. The normal reaction that people have is trying to push back. This is the last thing you should do; it causes a stalling of energy, and any time that happens it is bad. Actually, if he does it, it is good. If you do it, it is bad. If you feel someone trying to bind you, backpedal or spin off his force. *Just don't let it happen to you!*

While your opponent is crossed up, you can come in over or under his arm with blows. This technique also works with kicks; if you catch his leg and lift, you can flip him on his head.

Crossing.

Be careful about what direction you do this in; a good fighter can sometimes take your energy and twist it into a kick. He may have been thrown on his head, but you've just received a boot in the teeth. This is usually something that will cause you to be a little slow in pressing your advantage. This catching a kick and dumping an opponent is extremely common, especially against people who don't get out with a kick as fast as they went in. Remember this and it won't happen to you. Being able to do it to an opponent is a damn good thing to know how to do.

You need to remember that this move is a trap that many people fall into. It's one of the first things a streetfighter will do against a formally trained martial artist. This is because most martial artists don't expect this move. They aren't trained to deal with it. Therefore, they kick high and get out slow; all the bad moves regarding kicking that can lead to trapping.

There are two ways to survive a trap: don't walk into it or blow your way through. Most traps are designed expecting the person to try and fight back out of it after they realize it's a trap. Shark's teeth are a prime example of this design. They are slanted back into the mouth, so trying to pull away inflicts more damage. Yet if you were to look at the situation in a rational manner, you'd see things differently. Namely, "Well, my arm is already in there, so if I rip out its gills, it'll die and I can get away with just a maimed arm instead of dying." So, regardless of what your first reaction is, usually the best way out of a trap is, "Damn the torpedoes! Full speed ahead!"

The trick of flipping you on your head is only good if you land on your head. If you are flipped, you can add in a little extra energy and kick his teeth in while flipping further than he expected: namely, landing in a crouch on your hands and feet if you're good enough, or just rolling if you're not that good (by the way, I fall into the latter category, too). That kick and not landing as hard as he wanted have given you a chance to get to safety.

So crossing is a trap that most people fall into because they try to fight the trap and not the person behind the trap. You can do unto others, but don't let it happen to you. If you feel your limb being crossed up, get out of there! If your opponent succeeds in crossing you, you can't strike back effectively.

Binding is another Chinese brother. (Remember the old story about the five Chinese brothers, each who had a special ability? The emperor had ordered one's death. Each time that an attempt was made to execute the condemned one, another brother would go in his place. Their special skills made them unkillable by any form of execution.) Binding is like crossing. Instead of shoving your opponent's limb into his own way, binding makes his limbs curl up and stay there, helpless. Crossing usually is done by locking your opponent's elbow in the open position and jamming his upper arm or thigh against his body. Binding consists of making the limb collapse and then locking it in place. Binding strikes are done on the inside of the joint while external force is being applied to a point further out: a blow to the inside of the elbow while the forearm is being pressed by a blocking advance. With a shot to the back of the knee, gravity does the moving; you just land on him to make sure he doesn't get up. Binding strikes are in between Rattlers and Setups; they have the speed of Setups, yet they carry some of the clout that Rattlers have. If they don't have both, they will neither get in fast enough nor have anywhere near the power to shake your opponent's energy. It is that shaking of his power and your *in balance* advance that will cause him to fold up. (Did I just stress something there or what?)

Defending against binding is the same as for crossing. Backpedal or spin from it while leaving a trail of blows in the kisser for anyone following. If you get caught in one, fire off a few. Since it depends on the situation, I can't tell you to fire on the binder or the bind. It's up to you to decide at the moment which would be more effective.

Trapping simply means holding the sucker while you hit him. Now if this means grabbing on to him with your hands, do it. *Trapping does not mean wrestling!* It is used in wrestling, but it isn't wrestling. Trapping can mean anything from intentionally stepping on someone's foot while attacking, to keep-

Binding.

ing them off balance for one second longer, to catching a blow
and stuffing that limb in your armpit and holding it there while
you clobber the rube. You can use your hands, elbows, armpits, teeth, or even the back of your knee to put the sucker where
you want him. I say back of the knee because once, in a fight,
I took a kick there and the guy didn't get out fast enough. The
move had worked—I was falling down. But somehow my knee
got tangled up with his leg. He had a choice: either drop with
me or get a broken leg. Once I realized what was happening,
I muckled on tighter and he fell in a rather unwieldy position.
I sort of sat there on his legs grinning for a second before I
scrambled up his legs and all over him.

I couldn't recreate that move again if I tried. It was just an
example of how the unexpected can happen in a fight. The kick
was his idea of a surefire, guaranteed move. It got him beat

Trapping a punch.

Trapping a kick.

up because he wasn't prepared for the unexpected. It is also a very good example of trapping. He was being controlled by a powerful force that he couldn't control. The fact that it was my ass taking an unexpected fall is entirely beside the point.

Locking is any form of joint immobilization. Human joints work certain ways and don't work in others. (Oh, the choruses of "No Shit, Sherlock" that I hear.) If you try to take them past a certain point, they will break. You can keep someone where you want them, usually convincing them that to move will snap their wrist. Since there are three or four styles that teach locking, I won't go into it much, except to tell you how to get out of most of them.

If you feel your joint heading towards a lock, *get it out of there!* Since most locks are done on the wrist and elbow, punch. A short, sharp, snakelike strike can sometimes set up the necessary factors to break their grip. If they have your wrist, a short, fast, unexpected shove/strike can shift their grip to your forearm. This could be all you need to twist out of their grip. If you can't get away, grab the son of a bitch by something (preferably tender) and shove! Take him down with you! They're supposed to be in balance; let's see how well they stay in balance with you hanging, kicking, and screaming at the end of their arm. Twisting and kicking as you go can seriously affect their attempts to land on you (biting at moments like this is also pretty effective).

Joint locks are often mistaken for judo by the masses. While there are differences, they're not significant enough to change what I'm about to say. Any judo-like technique should be dealt with like you would a maimer blow—don't let them get their hands on you. If they do, wrestle them. Put them on the ground with you, where balance doesn't mean shit. Judo mostly teaches joint locks and throws. You use eye-gouging and biting to win in this situation. So, your best choices are keeping away from them with mobility, or grappling to maim.

Hooking is a form of locking. In one sense it's like jamming a stick into spokes of a wheel. In another, it can be best described as that long cane that comes out from offstage to quickly yank someone out of the public view. Hooking can be used in either distance or infighting. Hold out your arm and imagine the hooker putting his arm against it, his bent elbow near your wrist while his forearm lays over yours. His wrist is bent so that his hand is on the other side of your arm, where your elbow is. This is the perfect position to teach lessons on leverage, since your arm is now in a position to be controlled.

In this position, a variety of motions will have varied effects, especially if you try to fight it (like hard stylists are prone to do). Most of what will happen is simple leverage. Ten pounds of sudden kinetic pressure at the end of your arm will become more than your shoulder can bear and it will usually end up giving way. If the hooker's arm is suddenly straightened (with a whiplike snap), your arm will be blown out of fighting range. If the hooking arm were to do a circling motion, the end-effect would be like a sling. Your shoulder would pivot and your hand would be chucked out into space. That same lever can twist around and cause your elbow to lock. Then in comes some other

Hooking.

blow and—snapola!—broken arm or dislocated shoulder. Finally, this technique is extremely good for stalling your opponent's energy long enough for a grip shift and a yank. Guess who, if they're off balance, gets concrete poisoning? The other possibility, if you're not off balance, is they can drag you into a serious beating.

In case you hadn't noticed, hooking is sort of an effective technique. You learn how to do it and hope your opponent doesn't know it that well. If you are unfortunate enough to encounter hooking in an altercation, go snake-armed. When that hook lands, spin away before it can set. If he pulls you, you step forward with a Rattler or three to show him the error of his ways.

Another version of hooking.

Strategy

Arjuna, action is far inferior to the discipline of understanding so seek refuge in understanding—pitiful are men drawn by the fruits of action.

Bhagavad Gita
2nd teaching

Brer Bear was always a favorite of mine. "Les jes bash 'im on de head." Instead, Brer Fox had to be slick and throw "dat Rabbit" into the brier patch. Yet Brer Bear's attitude isn't exactly correct for a great many situations, like trying to keep from getting jumped.

> **Jump** (verb)\often attributed to action while coming out of bushes\ 1. to ambush 2. to be ambushed 3. the act of several persons cornering one person preparatory to the act of stomping. 4. the aforementioned act happening or having happened. **jumped, get jumped, got jumped.** See: bushwhacking, stomping, etc.

Strategy has been extolled by a whole mess of people. Many of these people made important names for themselves by sounding awfully boring about a real interesting subject. I assume that most of your experience with strategy consists of getting your ass whipped in chess. Well, don't feel bad; that's sort of related to what I'm talking about, as astrophysics is to balancing your checkbook.

Let's check out for a moment your ideas about strategy. If it's anything like most people's, it's sort of hazy and indistinct— some weird form of magic that little wacko guys who are always scratching their armpits go around muttering about.

Well, not exactly. Strategy is the active blending of several key elements. To effectively defend yourself, you will need to build an understanding of strategy.

Most people, for some reason, confuse tactics with strategy. There is a marked difference. Walking is a form of movement, but movement isn't confined to walking. Tactics are the immediate manifestations of strategy. Strategy is the overview; tactics are what you do in the immediate situation.

Try looking at things in relation to one another, and see how they affect each other. What would happen if this were done? How will it affect that over there? This is the basis for strategy. It is not a normal way of thinking for most people, and to get there you might have to change some thinking forms. Here are some things to consider when developing strategy for self-defense.

Knowledge

Most problems resolve themselves into self-evident solutions if you have enough information that is reliable, and if you can eliminate emotion from the evaluation of it.

Mel Tappan

When you have a pretty good grasp of certain facts, you have knowledge.

If, for instance, you know that a certain neighborhood is a bad neck of the woods, you can arrange not to have to go there. After reading this book, you'll have a good grasp of what's involved in setups for muggings. That's knowledge.

You know certain techniques of self-defense. There are other techniques out there which you have never encountered before.

Some people have moves you might not have encountered before. That's knowledge of what you *don't* know. When it's explained that way, it makes some sense, doesn't it?

Let's say you're an infighter. What sort of terrain is advantageous to that technique? Disadvantageous? (Ain't it fun to make up words?) Distance fighting—the same questions.

The thing is, most people think of knowledge as damn near a static concept. Maybe it grows slowly, step by step, after years of practice and training. Yet you always have to listen to those experts who know more than you. Now, doesn't this shit sound like something we've encountered before? Those of you who said "critical voice," pat yourself on the back and look proud.

That's right, that little @#%$*&(*&@$#$#@{}|{%$#!!!! voice has come into play one more time. This time it's trying to keep you thinking that you know less than you do. One of the incredible things to me is how much time really intelligent people (not those schmucks in the shiny-bright ivory tower, i.e., academia) spend thinking that they don't know anything. I'm talking about *practical* knowledge here. If you were to sit down and stop looking at what you don't know and instead look at what you do know, you'd be amazed.

The point that I'm trying to make here can be exemplified by a little story. I was trying to fix my car, which had an electrical problem that I couldn't track down. I was getting more and more furious with the problem and my own lack of knowledge in electricity and electrical systems. Then my mother walked out of the house (at the time I was living in an apartment and had no area to work on my car except at her house) and noticed I was distressed (my swearing like a sailor might have tipped her off). When I explained my frustration to her, she looked at me and said, "Why are you so upset with what you don't know? Look at how much you do know." It was then that I realized how much I *did* know about cars. Hell, I'd nearly rebuilt my engine on the side of the road not a year before. That was no small feat. So, what I'm saying here is that, all too often, we get so caught up in the emotions of "not knowing" and how hard it is to know something that we shoot ourselves in our foot.

A good portion of knowledge is simply being confident about what you do know. If you have knowledge, nobody can ever take it away from you. It's yours. Nothing can change that fact. If you're not sure about it, go out and recheck it. Shit, even if you *are* sure about it, go recheck it. Knowledge isn't a stationary thing. Another aspect of knowledge, though, is how you put things together. That is called *thinking*. Thinking is something that we will discuss in a bit.

Knowledge is a data bank, a giant computer that you have in your head. If you learn how to tap into it, you can save your ass in a jam. The thing that fouls up most people is that they hang on too tightly to little details. There are ten thousand little details floating around that don't mean anything at times when there are two that do mean something. If you know that many muggings consist of pincer moves, details regarding that are important. The smudge on the sidewalk, the fact that the building is dirty, and the garbage cans set out for collection are not as important to self-defense as the fact that two unsavory characters have moved into a position that would be advantageous to them if they were up to no good. The part of this that is knowledge is knowing what constitutes an "advantageous" position.

You have knowledge of the factors that make up an advantageous position, referred to by professional tacticians, in their exact strategic terminology, as a "fucked situation." Knowledge of situations you don't want to be in will prevent you from accidently falling into them. So, in simple language, you know both where you want to be and where you don't want to be.

Something you should know is that there are things called "shortcuts." For some pissant reason, 99 percent of the people who formally teach self-defense don't teach shortcuts. For those of us who are old enough to remember "old math" instead of "new math," I'm going to quote a famous mathematician/ entertainer: "Getting the right answer isn't as important as understanding the formula." Hey, guess what, kids! In self-defense, it's the right answer that counts! If you can find shortcuts to find the right answer, *do 'em!* There's enough stuff to know without cluttering up your head with extra garbage.

An extremely good example of shortcuts is when Dr. Leakey (yes, him of missing link fame) was a student of "Father" Huxley. Huxley, after all his anthropological and biological training, set two skulls down in front of Leakey—one tiger, one lion—and asked, "Which is which?" Leakey said to the effect, "I dunno." Huxley said to the effect, "After months of study and research, you can't tell by looking?" Leakey said, "Nope, I'd have to go out and measure, weigh, etc." At this point, Huxley reached forward with his finger and pushed the tiger skull; it rocked. He pushed the lion skull; it didn't. "The way to tell," he said, "is tiger skulls rock, lion skulls don't." Bingo! That's what I mean by shortcuts!

Man, if you want to spend months studying a subject, finding every plodding, meticulous, detail-oriented process, go ahead; just know that there are shortcuts. What will help you find them is to know that it is the people in the "field," not the lab or schoolroom, who know and use these techniques. Learn to look for the real shortcuts, not the imagined ones.

George Edison's Old Grandma Rode A Pig Home Yesterday. Sounds silly doesn't it? I learned that over twenty years ago. And to this day, I have never misspelled "Geography" again. Welcome to mnemonics and learning aids. Let me tell you something that'll piss you off. The way that you were taught is one of the biggest "Keep up with the Jones'" fuckups that ever came down the pike. It seems that in the 18th or 19th century, there was this little musical genius. This kid was so smart with music that he could play entire concertos from memory. Oh fuck—that meant everybody had to start using just their memory. You see, up to that point, people wisely used learning aids and mnemonics all the time. The trick was that they'd use something that would remind them of something else. Ever heard some music, smelled something, or saw something that reminded you of something/someone else? Heya, heya, heya—that's what mnemonics are! These things really make learning easier.

If you have bad memories of trying to learn things as a child,

what you probably have is bad memories of rote memoriza-
tion. Remember your times tables? Shit, I don't. What I do
remember is sitting there trying to "memorize" the damn things.
If they hadn't been trying to compare me with some snot-nosed
musical punk, they might have been able to give me the tools
that would have made it easier. Well, I'm now pointing out to
you people that there is an easy way to learn; you don't have
to grind your brains into mush trying to keep up with some
brat who's been dead nearly two hundred years. Knowing that
there are shortcuts—and mnemonics are a shortcut—will make
your life and learning much easier.

Knowledge isn't just having facts at hand. In one sense, it
is knowing how things are interrelated. You should know how
"something" you know affects "something" else. In this meaning, knowledge isn't just having facts; it's being able to apply
them to a dynamic global model. How do each of these facts
interact? What aspects of a subject does a fact cover? And what
doesn't it cover? Can some of these facts be grouped together
in actual categories? This is knowledge.

Thinking

*System theory looks at the world in terms of the interrelated-
ness of all phenomena, and in this framework an integrated
whole whose properties cannot be reduced to those of its parts
is called a system.*

Fritjof Capra
The Tao of Physics

I realized too late that there were a few elements I had
overlooked. I only had time to swear, close my eyes, and begin
to roll out of the way. That's when the fireball engulfed me.
I laid there for a moment, wondering what had been blown
off. I cracked my eye open and checked; after a moment, I
opened my other eye. Much to my surprise, to say nothing of
happiness, everything was right where nature had put it. My
beard was a little crinkly and scorched, but that was it.

What I have just told you is a classical case of not thinking, in the sense of strategy. I knew every damn factor that had led up to that explosion with the water heater, and yet I hadn't put them all together in my head to realize what would happen. Instead I put them together in reality and almost blew my ass up.

The problem is that most people have never been taught to think. They've been yelled at for not thinking; but those doing the yelling haven't taught them how one achieves this glorious state of intellect. This situation might be explained by the small fact that those doing the yelling don't have a very good grasp of the subject themselves.

We in America have a great school system. Looking back at the way I was taught (in California, at least), it's a wonder that I can put together a rational thought, much less write it down. They tried to teach me specifics about Generalities, and generalities about Specifics. What the fuck?

In other words, they wanted to teach me how to exactly formulate to the minute how long it would take to travel 360 miles at exactly 55 mph (with only the faintest nod to reality of adding in one twenty minute stop). About seven or so hours wasn't good enough for the instructors. They also wanted to teach me the formula for metal fatigue when I was trying to get a goddamn screw loose. "I don't care about metal fatigue! I wanna know how to get this #%@*($@&! screw loose so I can fix this thing! If metal fatigue comes into play, I'll replace the screw!" (As you can tell, I was really impressed by what was being passed off for school.)

What you end up with by these techniques of teaching is a division of people. You either get theoretical jockeys, who can tell you the oscillation factor of an electron when put into a electromagnetic field of so many giga hertz off the top of their head, but who can't be trusted with a burnt-out match. The other option is someone who can build a house blindfolded, but can't figure out which is the better bargain at the supermarket.

The problem stems from an imbalance of theory and practical application. I think too many people get overloaded as kids in regard to exact theory. You don't really have to know the equations to figure gas to air ratio conducive to explosive potential. You do need to know, that there is such a thing as gas explosions, so if you smell gas you don't go looking for the leak with a match.

What I'm trying to say is you need to have theory in one hand and practicality in the other. Too much attention to either is a dead end street. If you are too busy chasing the exact details of theory and you overlook the practical, it will rear up and slap you in the face. If you are too wrapped up in the practical here-and-now, the theoretical results of that action will cream you three steps down the line.

What has happened, though, is most people are afraid of the other side of the fence. They got slapped so many times with not having "the right answer" that they avoid it altogether. Hey folks, this is the real world! Seven or so hours is an acceptable answer! If someone wants the exact answer, tell them to go look it up! It's there if you want it, but seven or so hours is perfectly acceptable!

There are two terms that my engineer friends have taught me that I'd like to share with you. The first is S.W.A.G., which stands for "scientific wild-ass guess." In other words, it consists of "I know these factors; I don't know these. Knowing I don't know some factors, I am still going to make a guess. I'm not married to the decision, I'm just heading toward the answer. Along the path I may discover other factors which will entirely change my direction. Thus I'm going to keep my eyes open for new information that may help me get there." These are guys who put rockets and huge machines into space, beginning with guesses they *later* substantiate!

The other term is a "wicked problem." A wicked problem is a problem where there is no right or wrong answer. There are several answers; some may be better than others. Example: How can we get to San Francisco? Answers: airplane, bus, car, motorcycle, train; if you're into it, walk. All are right answers! There is no wrong answer to a wicked problem. The only reason people think of them as "wicked" problems is that they want a single yes/no, right/wrong answer. General George Patton is alleged to have said, "If you tell the men to be at a certain place at a certain time, but you don't tell them how to get there, you will be amazed at what they come up with to get there."

What I'm trying to point out here is that in most cases, general theory is good enough when blended with on-the-spot practicality. All you need to do is put them together. You know that sound causes things to vibrate; to hell with the exact equations. What that means practically is, don't put something light that you don't want broken on top of a stereo speaker that will be turned up. You need a light source to look into your gas tank. Gas fumes are extremely flammable. That means any form of flame is out. That's all thinking is!

Knowledge is having the data in your gourd. Thinking is putting together the facts in a way that is helpful to you. It's imagining what will happen when you put two things together; not what you want to happen, or hope will happen, but what will happen.

To this end, there are things that you can do to help yourself. Ever heard the old cliché "from the other guy's shoes"? (Okay, so that's not it exactly.) Try to look at things from other perspectives. Instead of looking at the gas tank from the standpoint of light, stop for a minute and look at it from the standpoint of explosions. Remember that gas is flammable, so try to figure out how to blow it up. The fastest means being a match immediately rules a match out as a way to light the inside. That's looking at it from another perspective.

Another way to help yourself think is to imagine what could possibly go wrong. Not long ago, I watched as a pair of girls were rescued from snowbound mountains in Arizona. They had been there five days and were nearly dead. Their car had broken down. Now, with a little visualization, they could have been a whole lot better off. What if you're going into a deserted area that is snowbound? Point A has people and Point B has people; it's just that all the space in between doesn't. Hey, take a CB radio! A small hand-held runs about $30. That's one way to do it. C.Y.A.—Cover Your Ass. If you think of what can go wrong and figure options from there, you can save yourself a heap of grief. If something does go wrong, you have something else you can do.

I always make it a habit to have in my car food for a week, a sleeping bag, camping gear, three days worth of clothes (including a nice outfit in case I want to go out to dinner), a CB, tools, and spare car parts. This habit started out in the country, but I kept it going in the city. The given reason was that I never knew when I would get stuck out in the sticks. The fact that I boogied out there a lot made it a viable reason. The actuality of it was, though, that I lived an eclectic lifestyle and never knew when I'd get home. I'd show up once a week or so, give my roommates money for the bills, and head out again. Nowadays I live with my girlfriend and have mellowed out, but the kit is still there. The thing is, I always have other options available if something goes wrong.

There were a few times that I ended up sleeping in my car, comfortably I might add, because I couldn't find a gas station open at 3 a.m. Smug people will say, plan ahead and that won't happen. I say, I try, but it's sometimes impossible to plan for all the variables, like getting your gas siphoned. City life somehow seems to make people forget that things go wrong, and that the best way out of it is relying on yourself. After that, you end up bailing other people out. Get a pickup with a tow hitch and you'll see what I mean.

Guess what, kiddies! It's story time again. That's right, I'm about to bore you with another long-winded yarn about my wicked youth. (This is great. I have an "ex" who used to get ticked off when I told "war stories." Now I can tell all these stories under the guise of teaching without getting in trouble. Since I'm a natural storyteller, you can see part of the reason why she's an "ex.")

I grew up in an area where gangs, while not exactly ruling the streets, were a serious factor to contend with if you wanted to grow up. Well, I had the misfortune to cross one of these charming little glee clubs. It was over something trivial; I slept with one of "their" women, or outmaneuvered one of them in a drug deal that he was intending to rip me off in, something like that. Or maybe it was that they tried to kill me and I ripped one of their members' testicles off with a Maimer. I really don't remember, but whatever it was, it was enough to get them slightly pissed at me. Slightly pissed in Venice, California back then meant you were heading toward dead. The thing about it was, while I never really expected to make it past twenty-one, I was only eighteen at the time and not quite ready to go. (Hell, I'd only just recently lost my virginity, and I wasn't about to miss any more of that action.)

So, here was the problem: my hormones were not about to let me get killed off yet, but at the same time, I was on the hit list of a fringe group of the worst collection of white trash in Venice. (Recently, I saw one of the guys get hauled up for stabbing a city councilwoman. Charming people, just the sort you want to invite over to meet mother.) The bad point was that there were more of them than there were of me. The good point was, I had my training from such charming people as ex-streetfighters and former Green Berets. That meant only one thing: one on one, they were mine. A collective "them" against me was not kosher by my standards; they thought it would be perfect.

What ensued was undoubtedly one of the most fucked periods of my life. For six months we played cat and mouse. They tried to catch me alone, while I tried to catch individual gang members alone. It was my job never to be put in a situation where I was alone without escape routes, without my friends, or out of easy access to a major authority figure. It was their problem never to let me catch any one of them alone and out of sight of someone who could save their ass.

This is where I learned to think. Every move I made might have ended up being a mistake that could have cost me my life. What I want you to do is pretend you're in the shoes of an eighteen-year-old—me. (No! Not young, horny, and cocky.) You are in the game of cat and mouse where you have to think about the possible effects of every move and position that you take.

For a week, pretend that you are being pursued by amateurs (but *a lot* of amateurs). How would you set it up where they wouldn't be able to try anything in public? Witnesses are bad. If they identify them (or you), it is over. Therefore, you must maneuver your opponents into making mistakes (like speeding past a parked cop car), and make sure that, when you aren't setting them up, you are protected. Figure how you would take someone out alone, without guns. (This, I must admit, was before the L.A. gangs went totally chickenshit. We had drive-by shootings, but they were not against innocent civilians. By the way, that's how come this went on so long; both sides wanted to get the gratification of doing the other side damage with their hands. Well, maybe a knife or two thrown in. It's much more personal that way.) Guns will not teach you how to think. In time, after you get proficient at doing this without projectiles, then move up to guns if you want. It is important, though, for you to be able to think correctly long before you even consider picking up a gun.

This drill will teach you how to think about several different aspects of a situation: offense, active defense, situational possibilities, maneuvering, and, most of all, how to apply specific tactics to general strategy.

I am alive today because I learned these things while under fire. This drill will prevent you from having such an imminent test as I did. The thing about the drill is it teaches you to think in several veins at once. What is there? What is not there? How can this be used: if not now, when? Who has the advantage now? Is this a safe place? If so, why? If not, why not? Where are the exits? The entrances? Where can I place myself to see without being seen? This is serious thinking. If you can master it you will have what all the experts that I have ever known have.

Awareness

The fabric of life is woven from many subtle threads. The threads beneath the surface may not be perceptible, but they hold the fabric together.

Jewish proverb

Awareness is a critter that is sort of hard to pin down. A whole lot has been written about this particular subject. A lot of people pay it lip service, but very little practical application of awareness is taught. Well, what is it? Is it knowledge? Feelings? Emotions? Thinking? What?

The answer is yes, all of those and much more. If I were to give a definition of awareness, it would be: The understanding of what is actually happening in your environment, both within yourself and outside, and how they affect each the other.

I could write a book on the subject of "world models" alone. I will sum it up by saying that people have these little things in their heads called world views. These "views" affect how they see and interact with the real world around them. Sound confusing? It doesn't have to be.

Let's have an example and some hairsplitting for a moment. Something happens, and three people see the same event. Yet their reactions to it all differ. In fact, their reactions differ so much that they all describe the same event entirely differently. Why?

What we have seen is an example of actuality vs. reality. The "actuality" is the fact that an event happened. The effects that it had on the observers are entirely dependent on their "reality." Sound subtle? It is.

A person's view of the world is dependent on their "model" of it—that means what they consider to be reality. Since the world is really too big to take in at once, we make pictures of what we think the world is: sort of like a map of an area. Problems arise, though, when people think that the map *is* the area, rather than a representation of the area. (Now you may be wondering what this has to do with self-defense, fighting, and strategy. The answer is, a lot.) Fucking with somone's model, or accidentally treading on some portion of it, can and will get you killed!

Self-defense is much, much more than being able to fight. If you don't think so, go out and just learn Jeet Kune Do. I'll see you at your funeral. Self-defense is constantly blending many different aspects of life. It is the art of continuous kinetic balance. It is understanding your fellow human being as well as you understand yourself. It is knowing how your opponent thinks and weighing possibilities in your head. It is understanding that your opponent doesn't think he's a bad guy in his own eyes, and neither do you. If that's the case, why are you fighting each other? You say, "because he attacked me." Are you accepting the responsibility that you might have done something to irritate this person? You may have made a major faux pas in the world model that he operates in. Bad news, kids; ignorance is no excuse as far as most people are concerned. Are you aware of his model? Do you know what the outcome of your actions would be.

Let me give you an example. You may think that the Hell's Angels are a group of repressed homosexuals with inferiority complexes, who try to compensate with massive phallic symbols. You may also be under the delusion that individually they are cowards. (Great. Stupid and wrong, but great. By the way, could you leave me your stereo?) Let's say that you get into an altercation with one. It was an honest mistake; you didn't see his bike and you ran it over. He's furious, but since you know how to fight you aren't about to be intimidated. Since you are sure this hoodlum scum is nothing more than a repressed homosexual, cowardly bully, you're not afraid to fight him. But you aren't aware of one small factor: the Angels' world model is that if you fight one Angel, you fight them all. This is a case of your lack of actual knowledge, while relying on your assumed reality, putting you in the hospital for three weeks. Stompings are that bad. By clinging to your world model to the exclusion of actuality (i.e., other world models), you've gotten yourself stomped. *You were righteous, but you weren't right.*

Awareness is knowing that there are other world models existing right next to you, and that these models are neither right nor wrong; they simply are there. If you know that reality is dependent on who's experiencing it, you are more capable of seeing the actuality of the situation.

How are your actions affecting the other guy's model? Right or wrong is entirely academic when that guy swings at you. Does his model include blindshots? Is he actually not interested in fighting, but your actions are threatening him? Does he feel that he has no option but to fight? Is he looking for a fight? Do you know the actuality of his model, or are you just assuming?

The most common mistake that is made about other people's models is using your own "ruler" to measure it. By this I mean that many people assume that the same significance is attached to a certain event in other models as in their own. Nothing could be farther from the truth. If the same significance was attached, it would be the same model. Often, identity is intermingled with the model. Someone isn't a person, and then a Marine. They are, first and foremost, *a Marine!* If the person who you are dealing with has the sort of model that his identity is involved with, you could be making a tactical error by assuming that he will view things in the same light as you do.

As an example: I once got a guy out of a jam with a local pimp. It wasn't over a hooker, in case you're wondering. It was, however, in front of several that belonged to the pimp. Anyway, I had pulled the guy out of it and we went into work (we worked together). He couldn't understand what was going on, and said something to the effect of, "I don't care if he is a pimp! How he makes his money is his own business!" I had to explain to him that being a pimp wasn't a nine to five job like ours was. It was a lifestyle, and things like backing down from some guy over such a minor thing as a fight can seriously undermine that lifestyle. If the word got out that the pimp had backed down from some nobody, that meant that he was weakening and contenders could take a shot at him. My co-worker just sort of shook his head; he didn't believe that it was different than a nine-to-five. (I just worked with the guy, okay? I don't take responsibility for his intelligence.) He was attaching the same significance to being a pimp as he did to his own job.

You may see no problem about backing down, but if someone else has an operating model that does have that problem, it could get hairy. Offending someone's "honor" can be lethal in certain circles. You don't think you did anything wrong, but he thinks you slighted his honor in front of witnesses. If nobody was there, he could blow it off, but not in front of witnesses. That is what can and does happen out there, so be aware of where you step.

Now those are examples of how models are expressed externally. What's going on internally? Why did what just happened irritate you? What assumptions that you had just got stomped on? Was the affront intentional or purely accidental? "Accidental" being defined as not knowing what someone else's model is and unintentionally stepping on sore spots. Are you just tired and cranky? These are all part of being aware. I was once about to put some guy through a wall when I saw a look of confusion cross his face. Instead of hitting, I stopped and asked, "Hey did you mean. . .?" The guy looked shocked and said no. He meant it, too. I had been getting bent over something I attached significance to and he didn't.

This part of awareness is a personal thing. There is no way that its full application can be taught. It is something that is organic within you. You can get ideas and tools from all over, but in the end it is you who will have to do the work of increasing your awareness of other people's models. There is no one answer that works for this. It is the biggest wicked problem that you will ever encounter. No single system will work on everyone, nor will any single system work completely.

There is another aspect of awareness—what things mean or could mean. Since you are now so busy watching other people's models, you will begin to see patterns in behavior. You can begin to spot what is normal for a situation and what is abnormal. If you have a rough idea of what is involved in a mugging (if you have questions, go to a cop bar and strike up a conversation), you can begin to spot key ingredients. For example, if someone steps out of the shadows on a dark, deserted street, looks at you, and then slips back into the shadows, you know something is amiss.

This aspect of awareness is what will save your butt when you begin to use it in the face of crime. The average American citizen needs to be kicked in the crotch before they notice something out of their model. The "bad guys" know this and rely on it heavily. Most people don't look past the end of their nose. You've seen bushes before, so instead of paying attention to them, you slip back into thinking about your boss yelling at you earlier in the day. Except, in these bushes that you didn't pay any attention to, is a mugger. Surprise, you're caught flat-footed. If all you had done was added another step to your thinking, you might have been saved. That little step would go like this...

"Bushes. Anything out of the ordinary about them?"

Even a cursory scan might have turned something up. Like...

"Bushes. Anything out of the ordinary about them? Hmmm...Just the crouching shadow with eyes...Okay...Gee, Mr. Melton shouldn't have sa...*Holy shit!!!*"

By recognizing what was going to happen and/or that something was out of the ordinary a few seconds before shit happens, you can save your life. It doesn't sound anywhere as easy as it is. You just need to add that little step. Begin by playing a game in your neighborhood. Look at a house and try to notice things that you haven't before. Like the cat sitting on the porch, or "Did they really put that tacky little jockey statue there?" Try to notice things about people around you. Try simple things at first, like clothes (God, are there some ugly rags being worn, I warn you in advance), or the size of your favorite erogenous zone on other people. After a while, it will become fun. The most important thing is that you will begin to become more aware of what is going on around you. Like looks of interest from members of the opposite sex. That one came as a complete surprise to me, but I'm not complaining.

Timing

What's that bit about knowin' when to walk away and when to run?

My friend, to me, moments before we attempted to break the land speed record for retreats.

Timing is a little more involved than simply getting to class on time. In order to get the most out of timing, you need to have a grasp of the other concepts we've gone over. With good timing, you can call someone a "fucker" and they'll laugh. If you say that to them in the same tones with bad timing, you'll get stomped. What's the difference?

Well, it has something to do with the fact that the world isn't a static place. It is always changing. The Oriental concept of yin and yang represents change. It isn't stationary; it's always revolving and moving. Like your balance, timing is a kinetic thing. Because of this, something that is appropriate one time won't be so later, or sooner.

In combat, timing is two different things. One is the pattern (beat, meter; whatever term you understand) that a person uses. Most people have a pattern, and it can be used to your advantage. Timing, in combat, is also knowing when to use something or not to as the case may be. This is very important.

Let's look at the first definition of timing. Let's say that you spar with someone over a period of time. You will eventually come to know how this person moves. It is an awareness of his body signals, or his patterns. By a pattern, I mean you can set your clock by the fact that he always jabs three times. In fact, he might even have a rhythm—"one. . .two-three." That's his timing. You can relax with it. You know all about it. The only problem is, one day he goes "one. . .two-three-four." You've fallen into his pattern so well, the fourth blow just walks right in. Ouch. With practice, however, you will learn how to use it to your advantage and your partner's disadvantage.

The second type of timing is a little more difficult to explain. It consists of knowing what will have the most effect when delivered at the proper time. A Nighty Nite Bunny Rabbit punch thrown at the very beginning of a fight has little chance of landing if your opponent is fresh. On the other hand, if your opponent is so trashed that he can't react fast enough, a Setup punch is a waste of time.

Have you ever been in a tug of war and your opponent suddenly lets go? As long as you both were pulling with equal force, you stayed in balance, but when the equalizing force was removed, you took a nosedive. Timing consists of knowing when to push, when to pull; when not to do anything, when to do something; when to resist, when not to.

With a proper sense of timing, you can, in a sense, get in a pushing match, slowly move over to the cliff, and then step aside. If you meet no resistance, you can keep your balance by not pushing too hard. Most people don't realize this, go charging forward, and end up flying off the cliff.

Timing, therefore, is knowing that, in the end, you can get things accomplished by doing something, or in other cases by doing nothing. Timing is also a case of knowing *when* to do something. If you were to pull at a rock on a mountain side during winter, nothing might happen due to the ice binding everything together. But if you were to pull that same rock in the spring, when everything is soaked by the melting snow, you might get an avalanche; in the summer, a rock slide. Timing consists of balancing factors that are always changing, and applying action (or inaction) at the optimum moment for the greatest results.

There's a great game to teach timing. Take two blocks—one foot square by, say, three inches high—and about twenty feet of rope. Set the blocks about three feet apart and divvy up the rope so it's equal. Now you get on one block and have someone else get on the other. The object of the game is to get your opponent to fall off the block or lose the rope. It's a tug of war with brains, not brawn. If they pull too hard, let go; they fall. If they don't pull hard enough, you either drag the rope out of their hands or pull them off the block. Try it; it's a hoot, and you learn about timing.

Luck

Allah loves fools and children, and I ain't a child no more. That leaves only one option.

Animal, aka me

Years ago I knew a man by the name of "Lucky." He really did deserve that name, too. Someone had decided to remove him from existence via two or three goons with machine guns. Well, Lucky had just settled down on the toilet and lit a joint when they began to blast through his front door. This was not a professional job; they blew his hotel room away and didn't check to see if they'd got him. With his pants around his knees, he flattened himself against the wall and had his sawed-off shotgun pointing to the entry way. Well, they beat feet, and he was left to clean up. All of the bullets missed him and utterly sloughed his room. What pissed him off the most was he got evicted for that incident. This is luck.

Luck is exactly what it is. It's dumb luck that a two-by-four just happens to be there when you're confronted by two punks. Who are we to complain? It's sheer chance that the mugger kicked a piece of garbage while he was sneaking up behind you. Look a gift horse in the mouth—who me? For good or bad, you have to play the cards dealt to you. Don't even think of disregarding the X factor. The best laid plans of mice and men, etc. If you accept that luck is the wild card in the game, you won't ever get fat and lazy.

As a matter of fact, the card bit is a good analogy. You can't control what is dealt to you, but you can sure as hell try to improve it. Knowing the odds, knowing what to throw away, what to keep, etc.; all of these things can improve luck. If you know what you're doing, you can walk away a winner. So luck, in a sense, is something that you do have some control over. In fact, a large part of luck really has to do with timing as much as anything else. That means you know when to use the little things that life suddenly gives you. I once heard a great definition of luck: *Laboring Under Correct Knowledge.* Keep your eyes open on this one, because real luck doesn't come in big waves; it sort of trickles in. If you know how to use that constant trickle, you can do real well. So now that you accept that luck is a serious factor in self-defense, we can get into the next step.

Improvisation

"I looked at all of them and knew I was outflanked, out-fucked, and outgunned."
"So whatcha do?"
"I went over to the edge of the porch and took a piss."
"You what?"
"Yep, and when I turned around I had my .45 and my dick pointing at them."

A conversation with my stepdad.

There is no such thing as a designer fight. If you can improve your odds by adding a beer bottle to your arsenal, do it. Improvisation has come up with some of the best life-saving tricks that I can remember. Anything can be used to your advantage. Let me tell you, I didn't believe this until I had it used against me. I now laugh about the time that I got the snot beat out of me by a hair brush; I didn't then. Then there was the time I threw a punch and it was caught in a pot. These things do happen. Improvisation teaches you to use what is there, while hoping something better comes along, like a cop. Yet, as we all know, cops aren't able to be everywhere at once, so you may just have to wing it on your own. That's okay. That's why I wrote this book; you can do it.

Improvisation consists of three things: situation, tools, and location. There might be more, but you can make them up as you go along.

Situation is who is involved, why they are involved, and is it good or bad if they are involved or not? Let's say you are about to get into a jam. Nothing actually has happened yet, it's just some guy giving you the hard eye. Well, lo and behold, who should walk in except a group of your acquaintances. Oh boy, one or two of them are real knuckle draggers too. Go talk to them, be friendly, buy the first round, or whatever. This is improvisation. You see your friend about to get into it. Suddenly you are very drunk; you stagger up to them and slur to your friend that you need his help. You're about to be sick and need to be helped outside. The opposing tough guy has a choice; he could buy it, or he can think it's a scam and run the risk of getting puked on. I don't care how tough you are, getting barfed on is really uncool. (By the way, that is a real good way to get through a crowd. Bug your eyes, look pale, and tell people you are going to be sick. Moses didn't get such a fast parting as you will.)

Doing something out of the ordinary is another one of your best defenses. Go apeshit on the dude. Start screaming incoherently about his mother's poor taste in herbivores for sexual partners. Drool, bug your eyes, start quoting scriptures liberally laced with profanity while ripping off your clothes. Scream that he has turned into a tarantula. *Anything!* Just so long as he thinks you're nuts.

I have something that I picked up a long time ago. All of my life I have been around animals (the four-footed type). After watching critters for a while, I realized that they had a great way of communication when they didn't want another being near them. They growl. I discovered cats understand when you communicate to them in this form. English sucks. One growl, however, can say: if they try to snap that piece of chicken off your plate while you get up to get the pepper, you will rip their whiskers off one at a time. This they understand.

I began to growl more and more often. Something annoys me, and if a sentence would take too long, I growl. Great way to get someone to suddenly remember that they have to go shampoo the cat. The thing about this is, it isn't a bluff. When I do it, I mean it. In order for it to work you must mean it, too.

What I am saying is that out-of-the-ordinary behavior is spooky to most people. If you start bleeding, wipe some of the blood on your hand and lick it off. Then, with a maniacal smile, look at whoever just hurt you and advance. They'll get the message—it's time to go.

I have a friend who was about to get jumped in a bathroom. He turned and pissed on one of the guys. While the guy was looking at his shoe in shock, my friend hit him and then blasted through the rest. That's improvisation.

An important part of situational improvisation is the goals of your opponent(s). If they are going to jump you, for money or whatever, they don't want attention. Do something that will allow you to get into an area of attention before you make a stand. Run into a crowd of people screaming "Fire," then spin around to face your attackers. You'll have an audience, which is exactly what your attackers don't want.

If, however, someone is really gunning for you and is bound, bit, and determined to fuck you up, having an audience may not be in your best interest. If it is in an area where brawling is the norm, then it's different rules all together; an audience will cheer, drink beer, and enjoy the show. If there aren't any witnesses, it's just your word against his. He claims that you busted his knees and then bashed him repeatedly with a trash can. You claim that en route to do a heinous deed, he was running down the alley and he tripped into a trash can. The multiple bruises happened while he was trying to get up; he is a bit of a klutz. No lie, I have seen official reports written this way (shit, I've written a few like that). So knowing what is going on plays a very important part when improvising.

By the way, here is an important point. I have met more than one bucket of scum in this world. These people are real sneaky in one way: they will do all kinds of illegal, harassing shit to you, but the moment you retaliate in kind, they go screaming to the police. Your car was trashed and your house windows broken. You go seeking revenge, and they have you thrown into jail for assault. The trick? They have witnesses around them all the time. You now have a demolished car, broken windows, and a bust to contend with. This is a real trap, so if you go "fuck 'em up" in front of witnesses, they have you. If you're even seen in the area by someone else before they got busted up, your ass can be in a sling. The dark alley, with a lead pipe, with your car (or a rented one) several blocks away is *sometimes,* I am sorry to say, the best way. Knowing this, you can avoid that particular trap.

Meanwhile, back to improvisation. Tools are anything you

have available at the moment. Whether it is a beer bottle, a pool ball, or rolling over a car to buy some time, it doesn't matter. Effective use of what is there can spell the difference between a hospital trip or not. (For you; who gives a rat's ass about him?) Start picking up things and looking at them as possible weapons. How would you use a rolled-up newspaper? A guitar case? A guitar? (*El ka-bong!*) A pencil? A chair? A rake or a broom? A telephone? A man's tie? All of these I've found uses for.

The fighting style which this book is about, PIBU, proves what I'm saying. Even if you miss with the pitcher, have you ever had beer splashed in your eyes? It's not nice. (Incidently, the art of PIBU was dealt a serious blow when they started using plastic pitchers, but as always, we, the hard core practitioners, will get by.)

By the way, don't discount throwing things. A very good friend of mine used to travel with a carnival. Among the members was a guy who would always pick a fight with a local in the "town" bar. Dumb man, but he'd always get anyone else with him involved. After a while, my friend would see the shit on the way and walk over to the pool table, put a quarter in, and get a rack of balls. From then on, anyone coming near him during the altercation would get a pool ball in the chest. Not something easily ignored, in case you're wondering. Also, when you are in a situation that is beginning to look bad, it is best to *casually* get over to where the pool table is. Darts aren't too bad for that department, either.

Proper location is another example of using what is around to aid in your cause (surviving). If you are a distance fighter and you realize things are beginning to look bad, check your locale. Are you in an area where distance fighting won't be that effective? If that is the case, what style does the guy squaring off against you look to be? Is he a distance fighter, too? Or is he an infighter? If he is a distance fighter, is he in a better position than you? Do you have a wall or a table blocking you in one direction. Is it on his strong or weak side? (In other words, can he, with his stronger right side, keep you pinned against the wall to his left? Your stronger right side has a wall stopping it, while your weaker left side has to deal with whatever he's throwing. Incidently, this was a common design in castle stairs. Attackers would have the wall blocking their sword arm, while defenders had a full swing area.)

More questions: Is there more than one of them? This includes fighting one guy who has friends. While he may have started it, if he begins to lose too badly, his friends might feel compelled to help him out. If so, are you in a place where you can be circled around and struck from behind? Remember the world model you may be facing. To a streetfighter, the Marquis of Queensberry is some fruit on Broadway. There are no gentlemen in a brawl, and that is why they are so dangerous. The first and only rule is survival.

This is also why so many formally trained black belts go down in a fight. They're used to being on the mat, where movement is unrestricted and they don't have to worry about tripping over trash cans. In an alley, you do. Aikido is a great style in the wide open, yet it relies on dodging blows. If you put a wall to one side so an aikido stylist can't duck that way, it really fouls up his chances. The same can be said for most formal styles. Unless you spar in a hallway, if you're caught in one you won't really know what to do. This is a major weakness in most of the teaching of self-defense. Therefore, I advise practicing in unconventional situations to teach you what to do if you can't do a certain move. Hell, one of the best fencing "brawls" I was ever in was up and down a cramped stairway. (We used to spar about three steps shy of mutilation. That way when you went into a fight, you were really ready to kick ass. That's why I advise free-for-all sparring in self-defense training.)

If you're an infighter or wrestler, is there area for him to retreat if he's a distance fighter? Is there somewhere that you can tuck yourself into? Do you have a retreat? Where are his friends? Can you put something big between them and you? What can he hit his head on that will hurt the most when you drag him off balance? Can he be crowded more? If he is an infighter, would it behoove you to get out into space? If he is a wrestler, the answer is, hell yes, don't get trapped. If he's another infighter, then the answer is, it depends.

Location can mean up and down, as well. If you live in an area of fire escapes or hills with stairs, higher ground can seriously help you out. Fighting upward usually leaves people a little twitchy, and off balance, and we all know what that means. One person can hold off many if he can wedge himself into a spot where only one attacker at a time can get to him. Narrow hallways, doorways, stairs, between parked cars, etc., can all be used for this purpose. Look around your house and see what areas would be best for what range.

There is no law that says a fight has to stay put. If it starts in a bad location for you, hit him two or three times and boogie to where you have the advantage. If he's dumb enough to follow, that's his problem.

All of this and more is improvisation. I regale (or bore, depending on how you look at it) people for hours with tales about me and my friends winging it out of terrible situations. It is the improvisational parts where most of the humor comes from. The sheer genius of mankind for getting out of scrapes is incredible. Use it as often as you use awareness; after a while you will begin to see what is funny about it. It wasn't funny at the moment, but let me tell you about the time I was kidnapped by pygmies in Abu-Dhabi...

Summing up strategy

The world thus appears as a complicated tissue of events in which connections of different kinds alternate, overlap, or combine and thereby determine the texture of the whole.
                                        Werner Heisenberg
                                        Physics and Philosophy

What I have just spent considerable time doing is teaching you about what I feel is necessary to have a foundation for strategy. In the bibliography, there are listed several excellent books on the subject. I can't give you a detailed description in such short space, but I can give you the foundation on which to build. Understand the basics of knowledge, thinking, awareness, luck, and improvisation—from there on you have the ability to continue along these lines. Understanding these factors, and how they will affect both your strategy and tactics, is what will help you on your way with the least amount of problems. Go out and talk with people, and read, for these are your best sources of information.

It is a real world out there, with real limits and practicalities. The theories and philosophies you have must reflect these practicalities. Things that you have always accepted as real will be proven wrong as you re-examine them. Limits that you have always believed in will fall away. Beliefs that have kept you chained to certain behavior patterns will be proven false. A bolt of lightning didn't fry me for masturbating, like they said it would (the hair on my palms comes from something else). Your world will expand with your awareness. Things that you always thought normal will be proven different. Things will become humorous that never were before.

With this new outlook, I must also tell you, will come confusion. Your world model has already been enlarged just by reading this book. If you go out and practice, safe little lies which you lived by will be exposed. You will see glories of life and horrors of it, too. And not just the terrorization that you see on the newscasts. So what; helpless people were gunned down in a fast food restaurant by one wacko with a machine gun. I have heard that the same thing happened in another western state, except that the "crazed machine gunner" was shot by about three people who happened to be in the restaurant at the time. When he opened up, they just pulled their guns and plugged him. Yet the news media didn't even mention that example of people saying "Fuck you" to the chaos that can engulf us. But, boy, did they get some miles out of the "helpless" people bit, and the terrified public ate it up.

You will begin to see the suffering of people simply because they don't know any better—the dumb suffering that being taught to be helpless induces. I cannot help you with this, except to tell you it is out there and you somehow must find some bigger system to cope with it. You must add to your world model until it is encompassed. "You learn to live with what you can't rise above" is one way of looking at it. But I am always looking for the best shot to win. In this case, winning is putting an end to it. The way I have chosen to slowly win against chaos is to teach. You must find your own way. Good luck.

Anger, Bullies, and Berserkers

I'm gonna gouge out your eye and skull fuck you to death!
A biker on biker's corner, Hollywood,
moments before trying to accomplish same.

I don't know if you, reading this right now, are a man, woman, adult, or kid. Nor do I know what your particular situation is. You may be a woman afraid of being attacked and raped. You may be an office worker afraid of being mugged. Or, for all I know, you may be a kid in high school who is getting chased by "bad dudes." I've dealt with these kinds of people and more in my teaching. While what is going to be said in this chapter may not, as you see it, be applicable to your situation, I assure you it is in a general sense. The specifics are different from case to case, but most of the general rules of thumb are applicable to you now, or will be somewhere down the line.

Anger is self-control's greatest enemy. In conflict, true self-control will beat anger nine times out of ten. Yet most people are afraid of roaring anger. Somene who gets into a red-faced yelling fit will intimidate most people into giving in to his tantrum. So, he thinks it works. Let's look at this shit.

It may seem rather odd, but this is the best example of "Nothing fails like success." It's true, I assure you. These people have realized they can get away with this sort of juvenile bullshit.

If they yell and scream long enough, most people will give in to them. This is usually due to the fact that most people don't like scenes.

The thing is, nobody likes to get bullied. "Step light on old toes. Until you've been beside a man, you don't know who he knows." (Thank you, Bob Seger.) If you bully someone, you've made an enemy who will set you up the first chance he gets. So the bully gets his way in the short term. He also gets someone who slides one in between his ribs the first time the bully isn't looking. These shiv-sliders are what is called "passive aggressive." The bully doesn't want to understand that what went wrong was revenge for his bad behavior. So he roars again, thinking that that will cure the person of doing things other than the bully's way. "And the widening gyre..." This is one form of success failing. The other is much more dangerous.

There are people out there (few, thank God) who are "quiet mad." I happen to be one, so I know from whence I speak. It took me years to mellow out from the vile temper I had. Mentioned above were two types of anger: aggressive (the bully) and passive aggressive (the revenge seeker). They are the types you meet most often. The third type will rip your head off if you're not careful.

Quiet anger people try very hard to reach compromises. Most, not all, are rather easy going and mellow. They are, for the most part, very calm and rational. Yet when they get pissed off, they go quiet. The eyes narrow and the jaw clenches. These subtle signs are often overlooked by aggressive anger types. This lack of awareness is what will get them maimed. Quiet anger people will usually leave an area (and other people) when they are mad. Don't follow them! Let them go off and calm down. They can and will hurt you in this state. They will rip the shit out of any aggressive anger sort that continues to cross them. The extreme cases of this type of people not only get quiet when they get mad, their eyes go red. Run, for God's sake—just get the fuck out of there and take people with you. Anyone left is going to get maimed, and I mean this. These people are not to be messed with.

When hot meets cold, hot usually loses. The phrase that is heard most after the carnage is cleaned up is, "out of nowhere." This isn't exactly true. The signs were all there, just much, much subtler than people are used to. So watch your ass with quiet anger people. They look real close to passive aggressive, but they aren't. A P.A. will come after you in the name of revenge, later. A Q.A. will either relax and not do anything later, or rip your head off now.

If someone is a quiet anger type, let them go cool off. Talk to them later, when they are calm. I have seen people chase down a Q.A. type, trying to rationalize their behavior. I've also had to drag what's left of these fools out of it and patch them up (contrary to what you think, I don't like watching people get hurt).

A good physiological thing to know is that our bodies "telegraph" what's going on. If you see someone turn red in the face, you may think, "Oh fuck, he's going to kill me." Actually, the red-face person is less likely to attack than someone who goes white. White? That's fear! Wrong! Within us we have a thing called the "fight or flight" instinct. Either we are going to "boogie" or "rock and roll." Boogie means run for our lives. Guess what rock and roll means? (See the movie *Aliens* for Hollywood's best example ever of this.)

When someone goes white (or just pales, depending on his pigment), it means that the blood is rushing away from the skin and into the muscles, readying him for action. People in this state can take blows that would ordinarily drop them and not even feel it—as in, "keep on coming at you." Pain sensors get turned off. Adrenalin is pumped. The arms and legs go anaerobic. The pupils contract. Jaw and back muscles constrict. Trembling sometimes occurs. Basically, physiology aside, all hell breaks loose. So someone going white is like a gun; your safety depends on which end you're on.

Quiet anger people are not to be confused with "berserkers." Most berserkers are an extreme form of aggressive anger types. They want to take out their anger on you and hurt you. A Q.A. who goes white means he is not "human" for a period. They are biological machines of destruction, and you are their target.

Ever hear of an animal called a wolverine? It is the most ferocious beast that I know of. Pound for pound, there is no animal that can match it for sheer orneriness. It is the size of a small collie. Now, we all know about bears. Big bears, yeah, you don't mess with them. Yet a wolverine will tear the shit out of a bear in a fight. No lie; if you don't believe me, go ask a zookeeper or look it up. These little fuckers are mean and tough (the two not being synonymous). If an aggressive anger berserker is a bear, white faces are wolverines.

By the way, just in case you need something to lighten this up, another aspect of the "fight or flight" biological system is waste disposal—the bladder and sphincter release. This is for a good reason, but the end effect is you end up peeing in your pants. No lie, I've done it. The guy decided he was going to die and ran like hell, and I was left standing in a puddle of piddle.

The serious side of this is, if it looks like you have to fight, piss now. Do not wait, do not pass Go, do not collect $200—*do it now!* If you are struck in the bladder and it is full, it will bust like a water balloon. Urine in your bloodstream will poison you. It's called toxic shock syndrome. Any Vietnam vet will tell you that punji sticks were soaked in urine and feces. If you're lucky, it will leave you sicker 'n shit; unlucky leads to the morgue. A leading factor of death in auto accidents is people who, though they could survive the wounds alone, get nailed by the combo of wounds and poisoning. A system can heal itself; a polluted system can't because the healing will be polluted.

Anyway, let's look at a so-called "berserker." (actually the term is "berserk," but some English professor decided that was bad English. Since the word is Nordic in origin, that's sort of funny). Most berserkers are glorified temper tantrum throwers. This doesn't mean they aren't dangerous. They can be if you don't deal with them right. Somewhere, I can't remember where, I was told that all you had to do to these people was stand up to them. I really want to thank whoever said that to me. . .with a 2×4. That is about as good as telling someone that all they have to do is pull the pin on a grenade. The important part, throwing it, wasn't mentioned. With that "standing up to them" shit, they forgot to mention a very important part. Bullies are used to people standing up to them. These people are usually walked all over. If you just "stand up" to bullies, you're going to get used as traction. Standing up to a person only draws a line around your territory. Defending it is what keeps you safe.

My friend Oberon used to say, "A troll (bully type) doesn't try anything that they don't think that they can get away with." Somebody give that man a cigar! These people do shit because they think that they can get away with it! If you just stand up to someone and say, "this is my territory," he is just going to walk right over you. Why shouldn't he? Nothing is going to happen if he does. Yet, if you were to tell him, "If you cross this line, I am going to Super Glue your dick to a moving freight train" and mean it, do you think he would want to try? The part that is left out from the "standing up for yourself" teaching is that people need to understand that they can't fuck with you without paying a serious price.

What will warn these people off is the attitude: "If you reach into my space, you're going to pull back a bloody stump. I'm not attacking you; you're attacking me. You can go around, but if you try to walk over me, you're going to hurt, and you're going to hurt bad. The choice is yours." These people understand that. They understand that fucking with the wrong people is not conducive to their long-term survival. If what you say to them isn't a threat but a fact, they will think twice about messing with you. My stepfather used to tell me the way to deal with bullies was to get in and "give them three or four good ones, even if you get the hell beat out of you. After a while, the guy is going to forget what he did to you and remember what you did to him."

A threat is just that; it is something designed to scare you away. Will it happen? Usually, no. A threat is supposed to scare you. If you're scared, you can be bullied. In my family, you knew that you were in deep shit when the sentence, "That's not a threat, that's a promise" was heard. The difference is that a threat is a psychological weapon; a statement of fact is just that, a statement of fact, and can be much more dangerous. If you mean what you say about defending your territory, most people will not mess with you.

Incidently, someone threatening you is a backup form of bullying you. They think that maybe if you get nervous about their threat, they can try again later. Savvy? I once had some guy who was pissed off about backing down from me. He realized that he would lose if he kept on pushing my boundary. Bullying had proven to be ineffective, yet he wanted to get his way. I had told him that if he kept pushing it, I would stuff what was left of him into a trash can. So he tried the second step of bullying. His comment was to the effect of, I had better watch myself around shadows. Now this was not the brightest move he could of done. In fact, I am more lethal when surprised than when I think about it. Also, it pissed me off; being hunted is a pain in the ass. So I pulled a knife and started walking toward him. My comment to him was, "Well, if that's the case, it'll be easier for me to kill you now, because I don't want to fuck with you anymore." I swear to God, this guy's eyes got so big I thought his head would pop! With a statement that had to do with incest of the paternal variety, he ran from the place. I never saw him again.

The thing about this incident was, I meant what I said. I have been hunted before. It is not fun. (Yeah, yeah; excitement, adventure, danger, romance, etc. Bullshit. My mouth used to write checks my ass couldn't cover, alright? That is the truth of being hunted. Sorry, wanna-be Ramboites, but that's the way it is.) What I had said to that guy was a fact. I was not about to be hunted again, especially by some snot-nosed punk. That was the bottom line about my territory, and if he thought he could get away with stepping into it, he was sorely mistaken.

You have the right not to take shit like that from people. Unfortunately, you, and you alone, have to protect this right. Make sure that person knows that his behavior in regard to you has some consequences: like him licking his wounds.

Indignity will be a good place to start. Who the fuck is he to try and pull this shit on you?! How dare he! Most people think that indignity is some old prima donna clucking like a chicken. Put an edge to it. My indignity can result upwards to someone's head going through a wall. What about yours?

I once heard a good saying about bullies that, for the life of me, I can't remember where I ran across it. If I do, I'll give credit to whoever said it. "A bully doesn't want to fight you. In fact, a bully doesn't want to fight at all. He just wants to beat you up." Could be. There is a thunderin' herd of speculation as to what motivates bullies. Some say that bullies are really just sissies, and they are trying to prove something to themselves about their courage. Other theories exist along the line that they are insecure about their self-worth, and by bullying you are trying to protect themselves. Still others say that some people are just plum mean and like hurting others.

The thing is, *all* of these theories are right. The world is a big place, with a lot of room for variation. You can encounter all sorts, and more, out there. Yet you have to take a good look at your own situation and make a S.W.A.G. as to what is really going on. It's up to you to keep a bully from running amok on you. It's not your job to stop the bully from being a bully. If he's picking on your friend, and you feel that is your place to stop him, do it. Accept responsibility for your friend. If you try to stop the bully from doing his thing anywhere, then you are biting off more than you can chew. Maybe I'm wrong on that last statement; if you feel it is your place to do that, go ahead. Maybe your limitations aren't mine. If it works, great. If it doesn't work, you've just learned a lesson.

Most (not all) berserkers are just overly loud bullies. They have discovered that going wacko works. Few people want to tangle with someone who apparently doesn't give a shit. The thing is, they do. They think that they can get away with it, and with most people they can. It is here that you must make a decision. Is this a one-time event? Are you two hundred miles away from home and not coming back again? Or will this become a pattern if not stopped now? Will you have to deal with this person again and again? If you do, do you want to set a precedent of backing down and thus reinforce this person's behavior in regard to you? If it is a one-time event, apologize for whatever the guy is ticked about and leave. (Make sure he doesn't follow you. If he does, the only sure way out is to hurt him. Remember, though, what I told you about scum using the law when it's convenient. Make sure there aren't any witnesses. By the way, legally speaking, I didn't say that.) If, however, it is going to become a pattern (and yes, it will, Polly Anna), you're going to have to do something about it.

Now, before you go charging out and start knocking heads, study the situation. Is this guy a bully, or is he under a crisis deadline or something? I'm talking about the guy who is running to an emergency who shoves you vs. the prick who just feels like taking his impatience out on you. If it could evolve into a pattern, you must stop it now! You have to draw a line and let it be known that it will be defended a little more ferociously than his attacks. The old "I'll hit you twice if you hit me once." What's more he's got to believe it. If he knows that you'll both end up in the hospital if he goes berserk, it is a good incentive for him to keep his cool. If he goes nuts on you anyway, don't even try to reason with him. Do everything in your power to fuck him up as badly as he is trying on you, but add two points on your side.

The other type of berserkers—who aren't bullying you, but really are wacko—need to be taken out of the picture. There are some of you who just read "killed." I assure you that is not what I meant. You have to balance these things out. If the guy is gonzo, get him committed. Get a police restraining order on him. (Berserkers understand force, especially after they calm down.) Now comes the comment that gets the most "I can't do that!" responses. Which is absolute bullshit, of course, because you can. *Move!* Get out of the situation. If you don't want to frost the fucker, you can leave. Cover your trail; tell your friends where you can be found and tell them it is classified information. If you really can't—like if you're sixteen and your parents won't move (anything less is rationalization or a straight-out choice)—then you're going to have to face him down.

By the way, I have some experience with wackos, both on my own and bailing friends out from them. They do exist outside of *Fatal Attraction, Sophie's Choice,* and Pink Floyd's *The Wall,* etc. There is no overall law by which you can judge these people. On the surface they are intelligent, witty, fun, and agreeable. However, a very good warning sign is extreme and sudden mood swings. They go from feeling happy and good to viciously hurt and depressed in a matter of minutes. In that state, any amount of damage that they do to you is "justified," because you hurt their feelings or let them down.

Another thing that wackos do is they can "rationally" justify what by normal standards are "outrageous situations." Somehow, in these justifications, it all becomes someone else's fault. They never did anything wrong. The world is just so unfair and mean, to pick on little ol' them.

A final thing that they have is incredible insight on what is wrong with other people, including yourself. The problem about this is, because they think they're so right about other people, they must be right on you. "Arighty argh, Matey. Here be monsters!" If you let your self-assurance (later, self-worth) be cut out from under you, then anybody can walk over you. These wackos can and will do it, and quite well.

Anyway, you now have a general idea of what types of bullies there are out there and some possible ways to stop them. So, let's move on to the next subject—your own anger. I once heard that anger isn't a true emotion; rather, it is your reaction to pain. Well, if you look at expectations, limited world models, hurt from being lied to about what the world is all about, etc., I guess that could be true. So what does anger have to do with self-defense? Zip. Sorry, getting pissed and pounding somebody isn't defending yourself. You can get pissed off before you fight, but getting pissed off and fighting isn't where it's at. There are many different ways of dealing with your anger, but that shouldn't be one of them. If you get pissed off at something, go beat up a pillow. If you get pissed at someone, do something else (standing up for your territory is usually a good idea). When you are angry and you fight, you are more prone to be off balance and leave holes in your defense. This can lead to failure on your part. If you keep cool when you fight, you are less likely to make mistakes. Since your overall goal is to survive, I advise you to keep this in mind.

Sucker Punches, Low Blows, and Tricks

Son, if you hit me and I find out about it, you're going to be in a heapa' shit.

Doug "the Mighty" Ipock

What we got here is what most people who want to learn self-defense are afraid of—the cheap shot. I can't begin to tell you all the ways I know how to snake 'em in, namely because that would be giving away all my secrets. I can, however, tell you what they all have in common in regard to your self-defense: awareness and active exercising of it will keep you from getting caught "with your dick flapping in the wind."

The main thing to remember about this sorta thaing (things are things; a "thaing" is something disgusting and contemptible. Quick quiz. Complete this sentence: "That thaing looks like a piece of _____!") Where was I? Oh yeah; the thing to remember about these thaings is that they're designed to weaken you. Or, if you wish to be more egalitarian about it: these sorts of despicable acts are committed by people who wish to win by making you weaker rather than by being stronger themselves. Either way, a kick to the nuts can really ruin your day.

What do I mean by that weaken comment? Simple. These blows are usually used by people who want to win. The idea behind this is, if they can win without getting hurt too much themselves, all the better. Other than the million or so masochists that are running around, people don't like to get hurt. Pain hurts. Most people want to avoid it for this very reason. Getting stomped is a very good way of guaranteeing that you will be hurting in the morning.

If you're up against someone who wants his way but doesn't want to suffer too much for it, you're in a high risk area. These folks will use an incredible amount of creativity when it comes to getting one or two in on you. If they can start the fight with you by snaking in two Rattlers before you are ready, they definitely have an advantage, they think. You're in pain; you're confused; if he got in a good one, you're eyes are tearing. If you're not an experienced fighter, the boy does have the advantage.

Let's start with dispelling a myth. A big myth. A very big myth. A MYTH THAT IS HUGE! *I MEAN A MYTH YOU HEAR ALMOST EVERYWHERE!* That is the myth of ball shots. Yes, ladies and gentlemen, I do mean the male testicles. Someone once, with all sincerity, told me that a friend of his who was "good in the martial arts" had told him that all he had to do to survive a knife fight was a simple trick. The trick was, wave the blade above your head and kick him in the balls. I warned him, in advance and with sincerity, that what his friend had told him was utter and complete bullshit. Fortunately, it was I that proved this to him during a practice bout and not some thug on the street.

I will tell you this right now. No lie, no bullshit. Never, ever throw a ball shot as your first move. One, it's a waste of time. Two, it opens the door to all sorts of shit.

No one who has ever been around the block doesn't expect a shot to the balls. The weaker and smaller the opponent, the more likely a ball shot. Every man expects a woman to try and kick him in the nuts in a fight. If he doesn't, he also doesn't have much experience and therefore needs some. Certified Public Accountants are usually the type of people who don't have the experience. The sort of people who attack others are the type who do have this experience. Most of these guys expect the ball shot first, and often have a nasty counter in the wings waiting for those who try it. If you want to make it effective, punch him three times first, then knee him in the groin. Just don't waste your time by doing it first unless you're absolutely sure it'll work (like he's looking the other way and is drunker than a skunk).

Back to cheap shots and how to spot them. Ever watch a magician? His main trick is to get your attention away from what he's doing or what he is about to do. You now have the basic secret of cheap shots. There are multiple ways to do this. Usually they can be broken down into two categories: diversion and hiding. Let's look at them.

Not only was it the middle of a sentence when the son of a bitch hit me, it was in the middle of a word. I was caught, according to the term my friends and I use, with my dick flapping in the wind. While he had been talking, he had been setting up for a punch. I was so busy paying attention to what he was saying, I didn't see his body motion. My fault. Penalty point for lack of awareness. The main thing about this technique is that the person using it has all sorts of ways to get you to pay attention to something else other than what he's doing. The good news is that there are many ways to make most of what he can do ineffective.

The most common ways to distract people are speech, action, attention, or all of the above. The speech part you just read about. It happens, and the way to defend against it is the same as every other type of setup. We'll get into that in a bit.

Distraction by action: whop bop a lubop. Any motion that you either pay attention to or don't can be used. "Well, that's a lot of help!" I hear you saying. Okay let's look at it this way. Putting a beer down with the left hand can either be so you look at his left hand and he hits you with his right. Or it could be while you're not looking at his hand but at his face, he brings the beer mug upside your head. This is what I meant when I said it can be used for both. More often than not, though, these stunts look innocent. The "scratch of the cheek with the left hand, while the right hand curls up for the strike." The upper body shifting in the Italian "Aayyy" with the hands wagging up—this covers the shifting of weight that comes with most kicks. The hands being innocently put on the hips—that gets the hidden knife real close for the grab.

I was watching TV with my significant other (old lady pisses off some folks for some reason). On the boob tube comes a commercial for a movie. One guy, who is being chased, is confronted with someone in an unexpected area. I think it was his house, I'm not sure. The guy who shouldn't be there says, "My card" and hands the other guy a business card. When he did that, I said, "It's a setup!" Sure enough, the guy looks at the card, of which both sides are blank. He looks up in time to catch the Nighty Nite Bunny Rabbit between the eyes. My girlfriend looked at me and said, "Been there, huh?"

An action that would be proper in one situation but doesn't fit in another is a serious danger sign. If you're in a potential self-defense situation, everything that the motherfucker does is suspect! You have to remember that there isn't anything that can't be used as a setup while the guy is near you. You're not safe until he's across the room, out of striking distance. Even then it's sort of questionable.

Another thing: if you get into a serious jam with someone and they leave, wait a minute, or five, and then leave yourself, through another door. It may put a cramp in your evening's plans, but then so does the son of a bitch waiting in the shadows with a baseball bat. Remember passive aggressive? This is the street's version. When you get out into the darkness, step into the shadows and let your eyes adjust for a minute. Rubbing them helps. Then, if you are to pass through several light and dark areas, every time you get a light in your face, close one eye. This at least leaves you with some night vision. Circle around where you parked your car, if that is the situation, and sit still in the shadows for a minute. Watch wherever your car is. Look into the shadows; is he there? Stoop and get to your car if the coast is clear. Stay away from that place for a few days. If you return and he's there, acknowledge him if you think it will show that you hold no animosity towards him. If he doesn't mess with you, it's cool. But, if he sees you and immediately leaves, get out of there! It has all the stench of a setup, especially if he looks pissed when he walks out. It's better to be wrong and look silly than it is to be wrong and hurt. The flip side of this is, if neither of you leave, see how interested he is in your leaving when you do. If he is, get out of the area fast!

Back to setups for sucker shots, specifically attention as a setup. I used to have a border collie that was real fun for me and not so fun for others. Since I knew his whole family, I have to guess it was a genetic thing. This collie and his family had one thing in common: you knew they were about to attack when they weren't looking at you. They'd look at something else, and when you relaxed or looked, too...Whamo! This is attention distraction, and it is the most efficient form. Something about the way our little brains are wired makes us want to look, too. I and a biologist friend of mine call this the "turkey factor." Domesticated turkeys are so stupid that you can lose a whole flock of them in a heavy rainstorm. One turkey will look up, and the rest will follow suit. Because their mouths are open, they drown. *Don't be a turkey!* (Ohboyohboyohboy, I've been just waiting to say that!)

But seriously, folks, the thing about attention ruses is that they look like someone is going submissive or is thinking about something else. Most people will instinctively relax when they see these signs. (It is wired into us biologically somewhere in our little lizard brain. Honest folks, we got one. We have simply added a few ounces of grey matter to what was there originally.) This is why you sometimes can't trust a submissive signal. The best attention shots look exactly like the guy is going to agree that he's being a prick and back down.

The most effective counters for sucker shots are a blend between speech, action, and attention. Don't be distracted by what he's doing: *watch what he's really doing!* One of the best things to remember here is what I told you about "broadcasting" one's moves. A shifting of weight or the tightening of muscles will, in time, scream at you about setups. Practice moves in front of a mirror at home, and watch the shoulders. Watch for how the body moves when it is about to strike. If you're in a dojo, watch the others and learn how to read broadcasting. Fuck learning how to kick; if you learn how people move before a kick and combine it with what you know about dodging, it will save your ass.

I have just told you what took me damn near fifteen years to learn. Don't be distracted! It is not how slick the S.O.B. is that will get you sucker punched, it's you disregarding this advice. There are no rules in a fight for survival, so it is up to you to keep your eyes open. Shit happens! Learn this, and it will save your butt.

Now on to hiding. Remember what I told you about someone looking like they're going submissive, or carrying out an action that distracts you? Hiding is the same thing and more. Hiding consists of turning the body in such a way that you can't see what he's doing. *Never let his hands out of your sight!* Doing so is paramount to volunteering to be dogmeat. If he slips a hand out of sight, call him on it! This includes putting his hand in his pockets. I bullshit not on this. For one reason, you don't know what he's doing. The other reason I discovered later on, but it is a wonderful little fact. It isn't amateurs who spot the hand slipping out of sight, it's the pros. If you call the schmuck on his hand floating out of sight, it means only one thing; he's outclassed, and he knows it. There is nothing so disturbing as knowing that if you continue messing with someone who knows all your tricks and more, you're going to die. Again, I stress this: don't let his hands out of your sight!!!

Now I've never fallen for a sucker punch. Shit, I can't even say that with a straight face. I'm sure that my friends (those acknowledgment-mentioned types) are rolling around in helpless hysterics, kicking their feet up in the air. Okay, I lied; I've walked into a lot of traps. So, if I have walked into all these traps, how come I'm still breathing? Discounting dumb luck and the fact that most people really aren't that good at fighting (I just wrote off 90 percent), there are certain things that you can do to make them ineffective.

You now know what cheap shots are about, and various basics that they have in common. Most of the points I am about to mention will seem so obvious, now that you have a basic understanding, that I feel like an idiot for mentioning them. You'll shake your head and say, "no shit, Dodo." But I have to mention them anyway.

Most cheap shots, setups, etc., will only work once; after that, when you encounter something similar, you will be able to spot it. So awareness is your most important friend on this one. The second safety is range. If you have to look, step back out of range. If he follows, you can see it. The other thing is, turn your nuts (men only, of course) out of the way of a kick. The third thing is, wind up a serious Rattler before you look or do anything else dumb. That way you can counterpunch. The fourth; don't relax until he is across the room. Finally, if you pretend that there is a target in the middle of his chest that you would like to go for (like his left lung), most people won't even try the sort of shit I've mentioned in this chapter.

Bad Asses

If attitude was all it took, we'd all be famous.

Tupperware Kid

Bad asses are people who, depending how you look at them, can either scare you or reassure you. There are different types out there who can and will affect your life. What they are will (not should; will) affect how you deal with them. It is important to be able to scope out what you are dealing with. I can "spot" people a mile away, yet I'm blind when compared with my stepdad.

For many people, this "spotting" is a new concept. Actually it's an old concept that we aren't always aware of. You've got it tuned into your subconscious. Ever meet someone and like or dislike them immediately? Ever have an uneasy feeling about someone or something? Now that we know of what we speak, let's take a look at it.

Your subconscious remembers every detail that has happened in your life. It's been proven elsewhere; I don't have to argue that point. That means that you have in your little noggin a huge data bank. I do mean huge. Under hypnosis, a professional brick layer can recall the exact details of the sixth brick from the left, fifth row, of a wall he built twenty years ago. It's that big, this data bank. Your main problem is tapping into this reserve òf knowledge. If you could do this efficiently, you'd make Einstein look like an Irish setter.

Now you may be wondering why I bored you with that little dissertation. The reason is, you'll need access to your subconscious in this matter. Your rational mind is easy to deceive; it's got a short memory. Your subconscious doesn't.

The next little thing that you'll need is a category or eight. Wait! I remember all of that liberal training that said, "You shouldn't categorize people. Each person is unique and different." Yeah, that's true. Let's just widen it up a bit, shall we? Every rattlesnake is unique and different, as is each species. That doesn't mean that I want to get bit by the fucker. The problem that most people have with categories is that they are too specific, and they end up being married to them.

It is impossible to get through life without categorizing. If we didn't we'd go batshit. There are just too many details out there for us to cope with. You just have to remember that any category is a rule of thumb! Since we know that a thumb, when it isn't being used as a ruler, is an anal plug, we don't get "married" to these categories. An assumption that is not diffused with skepticism is no longer an assumption, it is a false law. Those suckers end up getting creamed because they aren't adaptable enough to deal with actuality.

To deal with bad asses, you must have loose categories of people. You can learn to "spot" certain types of patterns within people, and categorize them accordingly. Remember, in the introduction, I made the analogy about a flash of tiger stripes in the jungle? This is where we will bring it to fruition.

A rattlesnake falls under the category of poisonous snakes, and is dealt with accordingly. My friend in high school was studying to be a herpetologist. When I say "dealt with," I mean that in the sense of a snake handler, not someone who irrationally kills them on sight. You can handle poisonous snakes, if you know how, with little danger to yourself. This means you can relax around them. The same can be said for bad asses. Your main enemy is your own lack of awareness of who they actually are!

Now I'm sure that you're getting sick of me harping about being aware. Hell, I'm getting tired of carping about it. The truth still is, though, that awareness of different operating systems other than your own will keep you safe. Everything else is just trappings! Awareness is like a muscle: you must exercise it, and that is the hardest part of all. That is why I've made this book as funny and fun as possible. That's why I suggest at first you make a game of awareness-building. Look for things that are funny or that make you happy; that way it is less of a chore. But do it. For your own survival, don't blow this off.

Now, there is a very scary thing in this world—there are people who are professional killers. These people are experts at their jobs. I don't mean a professional as someone who gets paid just for doing a job. I mean people who are so good that if they come after you, you don't have a chance. End of conversation: you will be dead. There are so many ways to off someone, it isn't even funny. Walk out of your front door and scan distances. Where could a person with a high-power rifle get off a shot at your front door? Go out at least a half a mile. Bombs can be planted anywhere. What about your daily routine? General Yamamoto, the genius that designed the attack on Pearl Harbor, was wiped out during a bombing raid. Every week he flew at a certain time, to a certain destination, to fulfill a ritual that the army expected of him. The Americans found out about his little bus schedule, and boomie! Such habits are things that make damn near anyone a sitting duck for professionals.

Different cultures have different types of professionals. In Central and South America, it is knives. I once had a passing acquaintance with a guy. What was left of him was found by the side of the road in a Central American country. The guy(s) who had done it left his unfired machine gun next to him. (His wake lasted long into the night, and the number of hangovers...oh boy!) What I'm saying is that there are pros who are that good. The thing about it is, they are so rare and in such limited circles, you have more of a chance of getting hit by a meteor than having one of these guys come after you. They don't do it for fun or to prove anything; they do it for a living and aren't about to mess with someone if there isn't a profit in it. So, yeah, they do exist, but don't worry about them.

Another type is the retired hardass. Every year our military alone spits out thousands of experts in the fine art of destruction. Over three million U.S. service personnel were in the fiasco known as Vietnam (the fiasco was on the part of the government and brass, not the poor kid in the bush). While only a fraction of them saw actual combat, a fraction of three million is a fucking lot of people. Add that and the years since and you begin to realize that there are more than a few people out there who can, if provoked, wreak havoc.

There are also people out there who are just as good without the help of Uncle Sam's World Vacation Plan. The thing about most of these people is that they have "retired." They now have things like a wife and kids, a dog, and a mortgage. The straightforward all-American citizen. They're mellow, laidback sweethearts, but when you look deep into their eyes, you will see something that I can only describe as an ice cube. Somewhere in there lies a sleeping dragon. That killer instinct is there, only they have found, or are finding, better ways of dealing with the sort of problems that arise in life than offing the competition. If pushed to it, though, the beast will wake up. These people are usually easy to get along with. Often they are confident of their abilities. I mean, hey, if you had a pet dragon sitting there for backup, would you get scared of someone trying to threaten you? So look into people's eyes before you even think of doing something that might offend them.

The next type of bad asses are the wolverines. (Remember the creature that I told you about that will eat a bear for breakfast?) Unlike retireds, they are still active in the nebulous "borderlands" of realities. The thing about these people is, for the most part, they won't mess with you if you leave them alone. They have nothing to prove; they don't have to let you know how "tough" they are. They're also simple to spot. They have an air of coiled tenseness about them. Motion is something that is done deliberately and with great control, usually very slowly. Something about these people makes you just want to step out of their way when they approach. It's not that they want trouble; it's that they are trouble. When they look at you, it's like having a scope dropped on you; a little target is projected on you. It's incredible how people who don't even know about this get scared by them. It doesn't matter what they're wearing. They can be as well-groomed as any yuppie, and still that little targeting mechanism is there. In that sense they are like cyborgs: half man, half machine. They have little computers in their heads that look at a person and give them an instant readout as to strengths, weaknesses, operating systems, motivations, etc. The average tough will look at you and try to guess if they could take you out or not. These people look at you and know how they would take you out if they had to.

Fortunately, a great many of these people are nice. They are often caring people who have been stomped hard by life. They don't want to fight, but if you come pushing into their territory, or cross their world model, they will nail you not to your wall, but to your neighbor's—they throw the nail so hard that it would knock you through yours first. You will probably meet these people in your life. They cannot be mistaken for your average "tough." Unlike a tough, they just want to be left alone. They will, however, enter a fight with more control, but with the attitude that it is combat. That is part of the reason why they are so often left alone.

Another thing about these people is that they come in all sizes. In fact, many of these guys are medium to small in size. It doesn't matter if they're not six foot six. Most old-time fighters will all agree and nod their heads with comments like, "Look out for the little guys." So don't make the mistake wanna-be toughs often make and think size matters.

With practice, you will be able to spot a bad ass. If and when you meet one, my advice is, don't panic. Be polite, not grovelling, but polite. They aren't threatened easily, so if you remain calm, rational, and polite, you shouldn't have any problems. If you get threatened and start thinking that you have to challenge them, you will get seriously stomped. These people don't usually start fights, but they end them with stomach-churning efficiency. It's okay to be afraid of these people, just don't let your fear make you do something stupid. It's a big world out there; you don't have to walk on these people's toes.

The next group of people brings us closer to amateur status. In fact, we're at the hazy middle ground that I deem amateur, but others think is still professional. Remember "Lucky" and the machine-gunning of his hotel room? Those guys, as far as I'm concerned, were amateurs. They were probably paid; this is true. But the job was sloppy. Spectacular, but sloppy. They shouldn't have fired until they had a target in their sights. Also, machine guns without silencers? In a building? Come on, these guys watched too much TV. Even if it was to make an example of him, they should have been a whole lot tighter. Yet these are the people that the public think of as professionals. Bullshit! They're dangerous children wagging their dicks around! What they did wasn't "baaaaad," it was stupid!

The baddest dudes I have met are now either in jail or dead. They didn't give a fuck. Either they thought that they were so tough nobody would mess with them and were right, until some guy who didn't want to get hurt snuck up behind them and blew their brains out; or they just really didn't care and did someone in in front of twenty witnesses and are now doing hard time. That's stupid, man, I'm sorry. Being mean and vicious isn't where it's at unless you back it up with brains. The baddest of the bad either put themselves in areas where they can feed that thing inside of them, which is far from the normal flow of American culture, or they go to jail, or they end up dead in an alley, shot in the back. These guys are different from wolverines in the sense that they, unlike wolverines, are actively aggressive. The good news about these guys is you can usually outlast them. If you can keep from crossing them, sooner or later something will remove them from the picture. Dig in and let someone else take them out.

Most "toughs" are dick-waggers. "My dick is bigger than your dick!" seems to be their motto. They somehow miss the fact that it is okay to have a big dick, not to be one. The thing is, fear is what usually motivates these people. If they aren't constantly showing how tough they are, someone might come along and beat them up. What's worse is, down deep, this fear gnaws at their guts. It makes them wonder why, if they're so tough, are they still afraid? So they have to go out and prove to themselves how tough they are. If thy hand offends thee, cut if off; well, they think it should be your hand instead. This makes them aggressive. They have to prove something.

Knowing this little tidbit is fine until the first punch is thrown. Then it becomes irrelevant. I mean, hey, if he's got something to prove to himself, that's his problem—until he swings at you. The thing about it is, you can usually keep from making it your problem by looking objectively at the situation. Is it a one-time shot? Then what have you got to lose? Walk away—you can do that. Simply leave. Don't grovel or slink; that opens the door to other possibilities. Just say it isn't worth it to you to fight over this and that you are leaving. Nine times out of ten this will work; the tenth time, though, you might run across someone who isn't convinced he scared you enough (he would say, "you didn't learn your lesson") and will follow you. Sometimes you can convince the guy that he shouldn't have done it by snarling at him, but I am sorry to say that it took me many fights in parking lots before I got to that point. More often than not, if he keeps pushing, you'll have to stomp him. I don't mean fight; I mean stomp. This mentality understands getting stomped, because he pushed it. Usually, though, saying that you're leaving will do it.

The thing about being "tough" that most people don't think about is, there are a lot of people out there. If you choose to keep on crossing folk, sooner or later you will cross someone who will hand you your head on a platter to show you how amused he is about being crossed. Most toughs know this. Therefore, they don't try to shit on people if they don't think they can get away with it. It's true; a tough knows he will bleed if he tries the same shit on a wolverine that he pulls on the local junkie. Junkies are great for this; they whine and squeal nicely, and the tough can feel like a real man. The same, unfortunately, can be said about "straights." Most people go to pieces when confronted with a knife. That reaction gives toughs their ya-yahs. The thing about it is, every time they do this, they know that they are taking a chance. So they are nervous and scared. If you're calm about it, they might just get the idea that they have made a tactical error, along the lines of "Oops, maybe I just accidently crossed a wolverine."

I had one guy pull a knife on me in a laundromat. Since I was sorting my socks at the time, I didn't see him approach. I heard a "Gurgh...Gurgh!" sound from my girlfriend and looked up to see his knife in my face. At the time, I was teaching sword and knife fighting to a group of people I have association with. Instead of seeing a danger, what I saw was a person being careless with a knife in a way that someone might get hurt. I knew that I trained my students better than that. Without thinking, I reached up and snapped the knife out of the guy's hand while saying, "Give me that!" (I should mention; when I'm surprised my voice goes up, so it was an irritated, disgusted, squeaking voice.) I stood there for a moment, shaking my finger at him while berating him for his carelessness. Then it dawned on me that he wasn't one of my students; he was a mugger. He was backpedaling in terror. As far as he was concerned, he was going to be killed by this weirdo with his knife in one hand and a tube sock in the other. I stood there holding his knife in annoyed confusion while he ran out. I sort of felt stupid about lecturing him, but I got a new knife out of it.

So just remember: these toughs are scared shitless about just that sort of thing happening. I mean, hey, let's have a little sympathy for these people: here he had a nice thing going, and you messed it up by disarming and stomping him. Really, have you ever looked at what that does to his day? I don't know about you, but I feel the same amount of sympathy that I feel when a mad dog is offed.

Sometimes you can walk away. If you can't, figure out what sort of fight it is going to be, and resign yourself to winning it. Sort of like taking out the garbage; if ya gotta, ya gotta.

These folks have all sorts of things going on inside their head, so it depends on what the particular situation is before you can call it.

Most toughs are rather young and stupid. They think that a leather jacket and a slouch makes them tough. After going out and making a few judgement calls that weren't exactly on target, they usually unwind. How were they to know that the guy who bumped into them and apologized was a retired? I mean, "shit, only sissies apologize; you can really prove yourself on sissies." They also didn't know that the older guy that they buffaloed earlier was the sort that leaves first and is waiting for them with a baseball bat in the shadows. When the fight starts, a bad attitude isn't any help. These are the guys who cause the most trouble, and, if it's any consolation, they, not the general public, are the ones who get hurt the most.

Let's look at another type of bad ass—the old-timer. These are the biker types and ironworkers. These guys are a blend between wolverines and retired. You don't go messing with their space, and they will usually leave you alone. A large part of why they have such rotten reputations is that toughs go looking to prove themselves against them all the time. If you could get past the knee-jerk reaction that most people have and look objectively at them, you'd see that the Hell's Angels, the most feared outlaw biker gang of them all, actually very rarely starts a fight with "civilians." This is not to say that they don't fight among themselves; like everything else, it's a hierarchy, and fighting for position happens all the time. The thing is, they keep it contained. Most of the trouble that one hears about is actually instigated by young bucks outside of the biker community. Doesn't sound right, I know, but it is generally true.

In case you haven't noticed by now, except for a small part of the populace, most bad asses don't want to bother with you. If you don't give them a reason, they'd rather sit around, drink beer, and play Parcheesi than fight you. The simple truth is, they know something you don't. Fighting hurts; winning hurts too (it's the latter that they know so well). Even if they "win" they're going to hurt. Of the far too many altercations I've been witness to, or part of, I've never seen one where the cost of victory isn't pain on the part of the winner. Maybe not as much as the loser, but pain nonetheless. What Hollywood doesn't show too often is the week of hurting knuckles, swollen jaws, bruises, etc.,that the winner suffers. These people really don't want to mix it up without a good reason. Knowing this, you can relax about most of these people. They aren't going to attack you for no reason. There are systems here, and knowing that greatly increases your chances of not getting stomped.

Okay, now we get into the vicious types. These people are stone cold mean and like to hurt people. This type does exist, I am sorry to say. They can be anything from passive aggressives to bullies, or they can be psychotic. They vary in motivation, but the end effect is the same; they take it too far. These people are masters of blindshots. Oh, by the way, in case you haven't caught on:

> **Blindshot** (noun or verb)\often attributed to point of origin of this action\ 1. any blow that originates from an area where vision does not extend to 2. an ambush 3. an unexpected attack, especially from behind or the shadows, usually involving implements of destruction, i.e., lead pipes, baseball bats, beer bottles, etc. **to give/get a blindshot.** See: jump, bushwack, low blows, cheap shots.

The thing about vicious types is that most of them become mops when they get in a straight-out brawl. They get their asses kicked. Seriously, I've ricocheted more of these people off the walls than I want to remember. They are not worth spit in a fight and they know it. So the cockroaches back up on you and hit you when you're not looking. Sound scary? In one sense it is, *but* you have something on your side. Since you now know that a fight doesn't start with the first blow, you also know that it isn't over after the last blow. This is your main defense against these people, so *watch your back!* This is street combat, not a ring. There are no rules outside a certain point. If you get taken out by a blindshot in a dark alley three days after a fight, it's your fault for not keeping your guard up!

Don't think I'm telling you to be paranoid and afraid of your own shadow. The straights are always saying stupid shit like, "How can you live your life in such constant fear, looking over your shoulder all the time? That's a terrible way to live your life!" Bullshit. By being aware I can relax about it. It's like saying to a driver, "How can you live your life looking in the mirror all the time?" Is looking in the side-view mirror when you want to change lanes paranoid?

If you know that there are people who use your unawareness as a way to attack, what is the most logical thing to do? You got it. In time it will become as instinctive as looking in your car mirrors when you drive. It doesn't turn you into a gibbering paranoid, nor will it turn you into a gung-ho survivalist gun nut. (By the way, those people are just the ones who get the press. Real survivalists are quite sane and rather aware folks.) Blindshots are only effective for the first move. If you see someone coming at you with a baseball bat, you can take it away from him or run. If you don't see the guy hiding in the shadows, the bat will work.

Try to start looking around when you step through a door. When you walk down a street, if one side is dark and the other side is light, walk down the light side. If there are many shadows, walk as far away from them as possible. Keep scanning with your eyes. If you hear something, glance over your shoulder. Like when you drive, watch what is happening directly in front of you, a ways down the road, beside you, and behind you. Walk along the curb side if it's convenient. When you come to a car, look around it. In an empty parking lot, walk down the middle; anything that will make the fucker have to take extra steps to get to you. Extra steps for him means extra time for you! If one person steps out to speak with you, turn sideways, your back against something. It's hard to sneak up on someone over a car.

There are countless things that you can do to avoid being surprised, but the main thing is to be aware of your surroundings. Someone who specializes in blindshots is either out to avenge his "honor" or not get hurt. They always look at a situation from the aspect of whether they can get away with it. If they see that you are aware of your surroundings, and being the type of person they are, they know the odds of them getting seriously hurt have just increased tremendously. These people operate outside of the system of fights and move into the realm of combat. There are no laws in that land other than survival. Don't think that they don't know that that little fact is a double-edged sword. If their move doesn't work, they can expect no mercy. If you show them that the odds are against their success, nine times out of ten they'll back off.

That description of what to do with people who excel in blindshots is equally applicable to muggers. The difference is, muggers have a sort of limited world model. For thousands of reasons (rationalizations), the mugger usually "has" to mug. He's not a bad guy in his own eyes; he just needs money, and since you've got it and he doesn't...

The biggest bit of advice I can give you on how to keep from getting mugged, other than look like they'll only get hard knocks from you, is this: for a month, think like a mugger. Look into shadows and see if they're deep enough to hide in so you can jump out and mug someone. Figure out how you'd take someone out in your carport. How would you attack if you were a mugger? Once you have that down, begin to look in these places for muggers. Helpful hint: check out those goddamn Automatic Teller Machines for places where you'd attack someone from.

The thing about a mugging is, I can't tell you what to do. There are no fixed laws. I've been mugged myself; when I was younger, it happened two or three times. When I was older, I began to leave these people with gifts, like their lives. Yet I've never had anyone pull a gun on me when I was with someone I cared about. I'll risk my life without batting an eye, but I won't throw away someone I love because of my pride.

It is a situational call. I can tell you that most of these people are scared and not too bright. Others are getting off on the power that they have over someone else's life. (These are the guys that bug me the most. I like fucking them up.) If they are scared, you have a better chance; if you are slightly trained you can get away with it. If you do move on these people, remember *it is combat!* You go in with every ounce of energy you have trying to kill the son of a bitch. Maimers for the appetizers in this sort of situation. If he tries to run, though, let him go. You holding in your hand what's left of his ear will be a very good lesson.

Okay, women, let's talk about rape for a minute. I have had pseudo-feminists tell me that, because I'm a man, I can't possibly know what it's like to be raped. This is true, but what I can tell you about is the effect it has on people's lives. Not only yours, but the people who share it with you. I have had many lovers and friends in my time, and many of them have been raped. As far as I'm concerned, rapists deserve no mercy. I personally do not condone torture, but for rapists no death is too slow. I have had to deal with the wrecked emotions of women who have been raped. I know the shame and disgust that women feel after they have been raped. The thing about it is, it doesn't go away. It stays with people, down deep, and eats away at them. It not only hurts the woman but everybody who associates with her.

To this end, I say any attack on you should be dealt with as a combat situation. I know that some people say, "No! You shouldn't fight him! That's what he wants! He could get mad and hurt you!" My personal response to that is *bullshit!* It is my fervent hope that you do everything in your power to kill the son of a bitch! Go at the fucker with everything you have. Do not do it to hurt; do it to kill.

The thing about it is, if he is attacking you, that means he probably attacks or has attacked others. You may die on this, but if your death will stop the ruining of five more people's lives and avenge the same number, then my attitude is so be it. I have put my life on the line before for other people, so I know about all the rationalizations that go with why you shouldn't. I think that they are cop-outs. Kill him. I've seen too much suffering because of these people to have any remorse about their demise. When I was attending college, there was a rapist running loose on campus. He had managed to drag a woman off into a work room. A campus guard heard the noise and investigated. The rapist rose to attack the guard and the guard shot him dead. The school cheered. I would have liked it better if the woman had slit his throat, but I was happy.

My best advice to you on all of the charming people mentioned in this chapter is to go out and read some self-help books. Not that what they say will be applicable to you, but it might fit someone you know and/or will run across. Keep in mind that when you are learning about people, each individual will vary, but widely based, general categories can be a great aid. If you have a general idea of what is involved with people's way of thinking, things are less likely to pop out of the woodwork without warning.

Fights vs. Combat

*In species after species, natural selection has encouraged
social mechanisms which seem to ultimately exist for no other
reason than to provide conditions for antagonism, conflict, and
excitement.*

Ardrey's third rule of primate behavior

*Once more into the breach, dear friends, once more,
or close the wall with our good English dead!
In peace, there is nothing more becomes a man
as modest stillness and humility;
but, when the blast of war blows in our ears,
then imitate the action of the tiger;
stiffen the sinews, summon up the blood,
disguise fair nature with hard favored rage;
then lend the eye a terrible aspect.*

William Shakespeare

"Golly gee, Wally. Two whole quotes! One for fight; one for
combat!" As I've already mentioned several times, there is a
distinct difference between a fight and combat. If you're lucky
you will never get involved in the latter. I fought for years before
I got into my first combat situation. Anyone who has passed
through combat has something that is almost impossible to
describe, yet it is recognizable instantly by anyone who has it

himself. I was once visiting a dojo and was talking with the people there. One of them asked me how I had met all the experts that had trained me. I looked at her for a moment before my answer; "You know how the martial arts change you?" She agreed. "Well, combat changes you even more. What happens is, you find other people who have had that change, as well. They're the only ones who really understand."

When you have passed through life and death situations, especially combat, you are never the same again. It widens your horizons. People fresh from combat are often described as having a "thousand-mile stare," and it is true. Once you have been in combat, you will never look at people in the same light again. Oddly enough, for me, while it took me to the line of almost killing someone, it also showed how important loving people is.

I have to say right now that I have never killed anyone. I have been to the line where all it would take is a snap of my wrist, and yet I have always rationally stopped. For those of you who have never been there yourselves, yet think less of me for this, I have only two things to say. One, as a hand and knife fighter, it takes much more courage and skill to get to the point where you can kill someone than it does with a gun. This is due to the fact that, unlike with a gun, you are there and your ass is on the line. When you grab that guy's knife hand, it is the strength of your arm and how clever you are that is keeping you alive.

The simple fact is, by the time I got those people into a position to kill them, they were no longer a threat. So I would not have been killing out of self-defense; it would have been murder. Yes, they had tried to kill me, but that threat was past. Their life was mine; anytime that I wanted it, I could have had it. We both knew it. Therefore, it was unnecessary. (Also, I knew that they would be in the hospital for a while, anyway.) These incidents did not happen in the military or in military situations; they went down in the good old U.S. of A. In civilized circles, people get upset when you off someone. There are courts and cops to be dealt with. To be perfectly honest, not all those times was my breath pure. Like, what was I doing there in the first place?

The second reason why I never killed someone was one that eluded me for years. I knew that it was there, but I couldn't put it into words. Finally, my stepfather, who retired from the FBI after twenty-five years of active duty and never shooting anyone, summed it up in a succinct phrase (like he usually does): "The reason I never dropped the hammer on anyone was, it would be too easy to do the second time."

I have helped friends through their "first." It was not a pretty sight. It seriously fucks people up. It, in one sense, is the "nothing fails like success" syndrome. I try harder to find ways out of a situation knowing that I can kill someone but don't want to. If I have to kill, it means that I failed to find a better way. It is too easy to start failing instead of thinking. Understand?

My advice to you is the same; except for rapists, killing should be avoided, if possible. But, if faced with a combat situation, go in hard and fast. Don't wait, hesitate, or dance around. Forget Setups, etc. While feints still exist, it's straightforward maiming time. In a fight, you can hit him and step back to let him realize that he's hurt. In combat, you fake, then you bust his kneecap. By the time he realizes what happened, you're either long gone or you're crushing his thorax. (By the way, that's why you keep your chin down in a fight. A throat shot is dangerous. If you get a crushed thorax, you can suffocate right there unless someone knows how to do a tracheotomy. It doesn't take much impact to do this. Also, a serious strike to the side of the neck hurts as much as a kick to the nuts. Since it jams the spinal cord, it is basically the same thing.)

You can go through combat and merely cripple. Often, what happens is that your attackers aren't really ready for combat in the sense of spirit. They want to hurt you, yes, but they don't want to be hurt themselves. Since you are there for combat, you can easily defeat people. They may be fighting for whatever reason, but you are fighting for your life; that makes you, not them, dangerous. This includes groups. I personally have backed down a group of ten guys and their women. The reason I say it that way is because in some situations, men will fight when women are present, while they won't if there aren't any women. My first comment was, "I'm looking for an honor guard into Valhalla." The reason they backed down was that they wanted to fight; I was there for combat. Anytime that you are in a situation that could result in your death or maiming, be there for combat. If three guys come after you, it's combat. If a weapon is pulled, it's combat. If someone ambushes you, it's combat. If the guy is a sadist who likes hurting people, it's combat. These are situations where you can get seriously hurt. Don't dance around.

Combat is like a trap. You're there, and the only way out is to blast out. You're already going to get hurt, so you have to hurt them more, and *before* they hurt you. You're going to get hurt in combat; accept that. Nobody likes to get hurt, but like the shark analogy earlier, it's a choice between your arm and your life. When two tigers fight, one dies, the other is hurt. You be the one that is just hurt. In combat, you have to get mad-dog mean. There is no other way. Hurt the son of a bitch more than he ever dreamed of hurting you. That's combat.

If you are ready for combat, I mean truly ready—not as a game, but as a spiritual thing—nobody messes with you. Man, there are easier people to fuck with. The wolverines that I mentioned before are combat-ready. Most people would rather stick their dick in a blender than mess with someone who is combat-ready. The former causes less damage. So, in one sense, you become free of the threat by being ready for it.

I used to get the shit knocked out of me a lot when I believed that, "fighting never solved anyting." Dumb fucking liberals. Maybe in their world model fighting never solved anything, but not in all models. Then again, getting the shit knocked out of you doesn't solve much either. I say this right now, without any trepidation: there are some world models in which fighting is not only accepted, but an integral part of the system. So, when in Rome. . .

The first time that I encountered the "Good Ol' Boy"

mentality, I almost got my ass killed. I was coming from a place where fighting was to harm somebody. They thought fighting was a social past time! A friendly fight? *What the fuck is that?!* I almost didn't get out of that one alive. He moved, and I dropped him in three hits. Nothing fancy mind you, just three. The entire fuckin' bar turned against me! I haven't made that spectacular of an exit since her ol' man came home unexpectedly! I mean it was close! I'm good, but not that good. At least twenty people suddenly wanted to wring-out my little ass. All because a stranger left one of their own on the floor. Now, if I had slugged him around for a bit, and then bought him a beer, everything would have been fine. Ah yes, hindsight is 20-20. What I'm trying to tell you is, there are biological patterns in human beings that make fighting a way to establish order. Breaking these is inviting more trouble than you'd believe. No shit, no lie. It's weird but true.

Let's look at that strange puppy, the "friendly fight," first. Now I'm not exactly sure what all the dynamics are, but it is a creature that is sort of odd. I've seen it most in Texas, but it extends out from there. (And most people think *California* has brain rot...sheesh!) It seems that two people square off and pound on one another for some randomly specified time period. Then after some obscure point is passed, they both decide that the other is a "good ol' boy" and proceed to stop fighting and start drinking together like long-lost brothers. Fuckin' A.W.O.L. if you ask me, but it's true. The thing about it is, the fight, by some unspecified rules, has to be a tie or a marginal victory. If you wipe the guy out too efficiently, everyone in the room will turn against you. That's what almost cooked my goose. If you can figure out what the rules are on this one, call me; I'd love to know.

Then comes something almost as weird. It's when somebody just keeps on pushing you until he leaves you no choice but to fight. Okay, so you fight. You fight to either a standstill or you barely win. Suddenly this guy wants to be your best buddy. "Say what? Didn't we just fight?" It's another weirdo about the way some models work. My personal guess is that it is a matter of respect. For some reason, these people can't be friends with someone that they don't respect in the physical department. I have acquired three of my best friends in this manner. I wasn't looking for a fight, but they kept on pushing until I knocked heads with 'em. These are the types of friends that will ride through hell for you if you're in trouble. This is another "if you can explain it, call me" situation.

The thing about these types of fights is that they aren't full-bore. They are, in a sense, to establish dominance. With that out of the way, you can become friends. The thing to remember about these sort of fights is, *don't win by too much of a margin!* Allow the other person to save face! You may not agree with this sort of behavior, but unless you follow it you will get stomped! It is a world model that fighting is to establish order. In this situation, a fight is not combat unless you hammer on him too hard. Then the person will feel that in order to pro-tect his honor or to "save face," he must strike back at you. In this sense, what he is doing is protecting his place in the hierarchy. If you overkill in this sort of situation, either you will get no sympathy when you are blindsided or the entire surrounding group will turn on you. That's what happened to me; I was too efficient in the good ol' boy fight. I was lucky to get out of there with as little blood lost as I did.

Now comes a different form all together: the group mentality. There are certain types who feel, if you fight one and beat him too badly, the "honor" of the group is affronted. These are situations where an easy, quick victory is the surest way to lose. In order to truly "win," you must beat your opponent in a subtle manner so as not to get the rest of the herd uneasy. The group may not want to fight you, but if you stomp one of their members in such a way that they must take notice, they will. The thing about this one in particular is, groups are hierarchies. If you stomp someone too badly, you were at the wrong level. That means that someone higher up must face you. Since the person higher up really won't want to take the chance of losing their position, they'll sic the pack on you. So don't beat him (or lose to him) too badly.

The next group is not a group mentality, but a pack. If you fuck with one, you fuck with all. The group's name and honor are at stake, especially if you are not from another "recognized" group. The basis of this attitude is that it is "them" against the rest of the world. It doesn't have to be a gang, either. You punch a cop, and your life will be miserable in that city from then on. The pack mentality happens wherever people think that, as individuals, they are helpless. Their thoughts are that unless they band together they will be nailed by the "system." Any breach of the "all for one, one for all" mentality will seriously undermine the pack. Since this is a manifestation of their world model, you can see how it can get sort of tricky to deal with. There are ways out of this, but I don't want to tell you how, because it is an extremely delicate situation. Your best bet at this time is to run like hell and stay out of their way until some other poor schmuck gets the dubious gift of their attention. Take my advice on this. With seventeen years of this shit, I still run half of the time in this situation. It's not something to play with. John Wayne isn't around on this one, so don't try to be tough.

Now, there are some fights that you can get into so people know where you stand. You beat Fred, so Sam, Ralph and Joe will leave you alone. Bobby and Mark, on the other hand, will be wondering if you will try to take a shot for their positions. They will be watching for any behavior that they could interpret as an aggressive move. If they see something that they interpret as a challenge, you'll have another fight on your hands. If you beat Fred and are content to hold his position, nobody is going to bother you.

What is involved in most "fights" is something called the Alpha/Beta pattern. To find out more, turn the page...

Alpha and Beta

You cannot rely on your eyes when your imagination is out of focus.

Mark Twain

What I'm going to say here will send some students of anthropology and psychology, as well as liberals, through the roof. Mankind has built an operating system that allows for a hierarchy of dominant and submissive behavior.

I say this because our brains are built on the foundation (if you accept evolution) of what is called the "Lizard Brain." That means somewhere in the grey mess that we call our gourds is the same brain that started our ancestors on the road to our present condition. (Notice I didn't say supremacy. When the truth is told, the sperm whale has about three times the brain mass as we do. A porpoise has about a hundred cc's more brain than we do. Sorry, they could be smarter than us. Then again, they don't have to write books like this to protect the species, so they definitely are smarter. They just talk funny.) Anyhow, we have basic animal wiring that can be tracked back to other species. In one sense it is our own laziness that keeps us relying on this. We have enough brains to take us out of this mess, and yet we stick with it. That is the major thing for you to remember: adherence to the Alpha/Beta system is by choice, not instinct.

A wolf pack operates under a definite hierarchy. The top dogs (if you will excuse the pun) are called Alphas. The rest, submissive to them in a descending order, are called Betas. This means that there is an inherent order within the society. Those who are physically more capable are the leaders. In a wolf pack, only the Alpha male and Alpha female are allowed to breed. (Yes, it happens with women, too.) This ensures that the race will survive in its strongest form.

Leave it to mankind to take a perfectly good system and muck it up. Those few hundred cc's of brains had to go and get things all complicated. A hierarchy is built in such a way that each individual knows his or her place. Certain behavior is expected from certain levels. In the Western world, we have tried to abolish anything along these lines. "All men are created equal," etc. Yet, lest we forget, children, in the thousands of years that mankind has been calling himself the dominant species, it has only been in the last 200 years that this hierarchical assumption has been challenged. The caste system in India was the last one to bite the dust. In Europe there was Feudalism. In the East there was Confucianism. (Sorry, anybody who knows Eastern culture. I know that was a gross simplification, but it sort of works.)

The problem is that, in the smaller cosmos, the hierarchical system actually works. Maybe not in the bigger picture or in the long run, but right now and in the neighborhood, it works. So let's look at this local phenomenon. What is it and why? My personal belief, as previously stated, is that it is based on laziness. The universe, in case you hadn't noticed, is a rather big place. What we do is try to bring it down to scale. In attempting to do so, we fall back on certain patterns. The dominant/submissive one is relatively easy for us to drop into.

An Alpha is what we call a "natural leader." Somehow these people don't seem to be assailed by the same doubts and insecurities that cripple the rest of us. They just seem to jump out and do things that everybody else is afraid to try. Everything is easy for these people. People don't seem to cross them. I mean, nobody would dare yell at so-and-so—he'd tell them to go fuck off in no uncertain terms. If you call an Alpha an asshole, they just laugh it off. It doesn't hurt their feelings. These people are somehow just lucky in ways that the rest of the poor humans can't even begin to understand.

Betas, on the other hand, have to toil along. Nothing ever comes easy to them. There's always something standing in the way of success. Things are always too risky. It's impossible to do that, because the consequences are just too great. Nobody would willingly pay that high price. If someone yells at them, then they just have to take it, because if they fight back they'd be either fired or scorned. If someone calls them something insulting, it really hits home because it means that the person who called them that is somehow qualified to pass judgement on them. If they weren't, then why would the person call them that? There is where most poor humans have to toil their lives away—in this grey fog of mediocrity.

"Como say dee say bullshit?" as a Texas friend of mine would say. I mean, really, give me a break! Guess what? I'm considered, by so many people that if I said numbers you'd think me a liar, to be an Alpha male. Yet, at times, I feel all those things that I just described as Beta. Yet, I'm an Alpha male! Why? Could it be that the assumptions that people are using regarding the system are fraudulent? Could be, babycakes! Yet they don't know it! And God help you if you called them on it.

There is a story from India that I want to bore you with. It seemed that this town had a monster that was causing the people no end of worrying. Not that the monster actually did too much, just the people worried about it a lot. So, the people of the village, having the general I.Q. of a sponge, sent out word that they needed a hero to slay this terrible monster. Well who should show up but a bona fide hero, complete with brass balls and everything. Off he goes to kill the monster, with his nuts going "klackita-klackita." Well, old stud muffins rounds the corner and sees a watermelon patch, but no monster. "Klick-ity klack" he goes back to the village and says something to the effect of, "Where's da monster?" (Sub-heroes aren't renowned for brains. The I.Q. points usually go to the Alpha hero.) Well, the villagers take him off to the watermelon patch and point to the biggest, meanest watermelon of them all and say, "There is the monster!" Well, old numbnuts says, "You yo-yos. That's not a monster, that's a watermelon!" Whereupon, the villagers pick up rocks and beat the bejeebers out of the hero.

The ad is again run in the Sunday papers. Well, lo and behold, another hero shows up. This guy, unlike the first, has got something other than space between his ears. When he sees what these people are talking about, he backs up and says to them, "Yep, it's a monster alright. But I've dealt with these suckers before!" So he gets all the local yokels together and distributes nets and knives and off they go. At the end of the fight, the score was villagers one, watermelon zero. They paid the hero mucho gold and he went off to get laid or something, leaving a group of villagers very wise in the fine art of watermelon-slaying.

Take what you will from that story, but remember the bottom line: if people don't want to know about something, don't tell them about it. They'll pick up rocks and thump you with them. A lot of people don't want to know about Alpha and Beta behavior. Yet, after they tear the shit out of you for telling it to them, they go out and practice it anyway. While I agree it should be bullshit, it isn't with a thunderin' herd of folks. So keep your mouth shut and your eyes open on this one. Or, if you've gotta run out and tell someone, make hints about it before you come right out and say it. If someone picks up the hint and goes "yep," the odds are that they won't try to get you stuck into a padded room. If they don't catch on to the hints, don't say anything.

If you want a good example of this, ask people about full moons. Your average citizen will look at you like you've grown a second head when you say that people go nuts on the full moon. Yet anybody who has spent time dealing with the public (like cops, firemen, emergency room personnel, etc.) will tell you people go bonkers during the full moon. Statistics back this up, too. Sounds screwy, I know, but it's true.

Anyway, enough on how to keep from getting committed by well-meaning but dense relatives and friends, and back to social behavior. A hierarchy is designed to keep order. If you have a system that only allows three, instead of three hundred, fellas to take a shot at the leader, you eliminate quite a bit of time wasted in seeing who's going to be the boss. The army is a very good example of this. The orders are passed down from the top, and the bottom is supposed to do them. While there is supposed to be no room for disagreement between ranks (Como say dee say...), there is no real disagreement between large chunks of the ranks. While a sergeant can tell a lieutenant that it is undoubtedly the dumbest idea he's ever heard, a private can't. The same holds true for a lewie and a colonel.

Now here is where the old noodle comes into play. While you can't exactly out-and-out disobey a direct order, with a little flexing of the grey cells, you can come up with some surefire ways to put its dick in the mud. Ah yes, the joys of the military mind.

I have just given you an example of military hierarchy. You change it to wherever you're working or operating. Your boss's boss gives him/her an order. You can't say to old Big Dome, "That's stone cold stupid." You can, however, come up with some damn good reasons why it would fail in the field. Your boss knows about this and he, in many cases, agrees with you; that's how come he doesn't make more than a token effort to correct the problem.

Okay, that's an example of Alpha and Beta behavior that is known to most people. Let's look at it in other situations. You walk into a bar and for some reason some guy walks up to you and tries to pick a fight. The odds are that he thinks you're close enough to his level in the hierarchy for him to feel threatened. Until he knows where you stand in the system, he's going to be nervous.

So, it is up to you to figure out what to do. You could take the chump out, but if you take him out too fast, what does that do? Right, it scares the higher-ups. Or you could lose too quickly, which means that the people below him on the scale get twitchy. So, you end up rocking until you win a place for yourself. There is the option to convince him that he is outclassed and that you are above him on the scale. But if you go too far up, the Alpha is going to get annoyed or scared. Another option is to fight him but only beat him marginally. Not enough to get the higher-ups nervous, but enough to keep everybody happy, thinking they know where you stand.

In case you have any bright ideas about going after the Alpha in a long-term situation, can it. You might get away with it if all you're doing is trying to keep from fighting in a one-time situation. If, however, you're going to be in the neighborhood for a while, don't even think about it. Being an Alpha, in human terms, is more than just being able to fight; it also means having cranial capacity. In order to challenge the Alpha in a potentially long-term situation, you must work your way up the "ranks." If you aren't just trying to get out of a beating, to successfully challenge the Alpha you must first beat his lieutenants. That means both mentally and physically. If you win physically, you still may not advance at all. If you win mentally, that may mean that you're immune to physical attack from those down the line. They need you, the guy with the brains, to survive.

I have an ex who actually saw one of the best examples of what can come about from not following the system. An Alpha was challenged out of left field (as far as they were concerned) by some guy. The gang leader looked at the guy for a moment, snapped his fingers, and pointed at him. One of the lieutenants came forward and beat the shit out of the challenger, thus proving that the challenger was not of the caliber that it took to challenge the Alpha.

There are many levels to the hierarchy. It is, in fact, a massive pecking order. A person who is higher up the ladder has the right to "pick on" a Beta if the Beta does not show proper behavior. Behavior that is deemed inconsistent with one's social position is a surefire way to get a challenge. Whether it is too aggressive or too passive is immaterial. Behavior out of the norm can and will be challenged.

It *is* possible to work your way up the hierarchy. If you show sufficient brains and acceptable pattern behavior (model conformity), you can challenge the next higher-up. If you "win," you achieve higher status. If you lose, you will remain where you are until displaced by a challenger, retired, or victorious on your attempt at advancement. The higher up you get, however, the more you must take responsibility for the group. If you are trying to get up to the top with no consideration for the group's welfare, you will not get followers even if you defeat the Alpha. In fact, they will turn on you. A hierarchy exists to keep the group's well-being. If the "government" does not fulfill this requirement, the group itself will dissolve. If you look at the leaders of a group, they actually spend a considerable time helping their Betas out of trouble, even if it is just listening to complaints and giving advice. There is much more to this than being able to leave clawmarks higher in the tree than anyone else. It gets real complicated.

Most fights that I have seen, that weren't instigated by a third party, can be boiled down to Alpha/Beta behavior patterns. It is something that I really feel is out there and must be contended with. If you are consciously aware of it, you can be more alert to it than most people who are caught up in it. They may have a sort of hazy instinctive grasp of it, but you know what is going on.

Remember I said that many sucker punches come from someone being falsely submissive? With this system comes certain key signs of submission: the "Okay, okay! You're the Alpha!" signs that keep things clear for those who have the brains of a sponge. While they are too varied and numerous to list, they do exist. Go learn them.

Also understand, however, what some people have discovered about this submissive pattern. When some submissive signs are shown by the so-called Beta, the Alphas relax. When they relax—Ka-fuckin²-pow! That's why this theory, like everything in this book, is a rule of thumb.

We have the brains to abort this system if we want to. If someone is throwing submissive signals, wait until he's out of striking range before you relax. It is natural for the Alpha to relax when the Beta throws those signals. We have it wired in that if someone is throwing submissive signals (i.e., going limp), we stop attacking. The thing is, some people use this to their advantage. I once knew a guy who would give extreme amounts of verbal abuse, yet when you grabbed him, he'd go limp. Most people would let him go at this junction, but when they did, he'd leap back up and start it up again. He was unwiring, in these people's heads, the law about pounding passives. So, later on, if someone else really did go passive, these folks might just beat them anyway. That is why it is so necessary to keep your eyes and ears open. You don't know what has happened before you got there.

I feel it is only right to give you some ideas of what constitute dominant and submissive signals. Let's start with the biggest one of them all, the eyes.

Eye contact is one of the biggest forms of communication that we have. It can tell you everything: you're going to get stomped, you're going to get laid; this is a joke, this isn't a joke; we agree, we disagree; I'm amused, I'm not amused; I'm thinking deeply about something, I'm daydreaming. All of these and more are communicated by the eyes. In different circumstances, there are time limits on how long you can look at somone. There is also a certain number of times that you can look at someone, etc. The number of rules of "social etiquette" regarding eye contact is rather staggering. We're going to just touch on a few of them.

First and foremost, *eye contact is the primary signal of dominance!* It is what transmits the most information in this situation. I used to hear "civilians" cluck about the silliness of it, when the reason given for a fight was, "He looked at me wrong." Bullshit! That is a very real reason in human behavior. Lets look at some rules of not necessarily eye contact, but just looking at someone.

There is a time limit that you are allowed to look at someone. In our culture, if I remember right, it's about two seconds. There is leeway on this. If you are looking at an attractive member of the opposite sex (or, in accepted situations, the same sex), the time limit is bumped up a second or two. If it is someone who you don't wish to acknowledge, you don't even look at them when they are facing you. Another way is to pass your eyes over them with the same speed you would a telephone pole. This is looking at someone without making eye contact.

With eye contact, most glances can last somewhere between one and two seconds. Anything longer can and will be construed as a threat. Yes, boys and girls, we are talking a one second difference of eye contact can lead to a fight. This is no lie; I have the scars to prove it. If some tough guy looks at you with a "nasty glint in his eye," what is your usual reaction? Right; you look away quickly. That is the best example of what I'm saying. By looking away, you have (to him, at least) established that you are Beta to him. This usually tickles his dick, and he leaves you alone. He's happy, and, unless you know what's going on, you're nervous.

We now have a rough idea of how this system works. Let's look at things that you can do about it. First and foremost, you can ignore it. If the guy wants to pee on a tree, that's his problem; you're going to a movie. If you're just passing through, don't bite into it. It's like some tourist saying, "Look, Martha! There's a tough guy." "That's nice, George. Hurry up or we won't make it to the airport in time."

If the guy's concerned that you're going to challenge him over a street corner, he's got something seriously wrong with him. Let him alone. Give it the same amount of concern that you give some snarling dog that's on a leash. Step around it and keep on going. Don't get into a glaring contest with the dope. That can lead to a fight. Don't scorn him, either. That's taking it too far the other way. If you poo-poo it too badly, the guy will have to come after you because it is an affront to his world model. Instead, if you look at it in the light of, there is no profit for me to fight, it usually works. By that I mean, acknowledge that stud-lee there has something that he is willing to fight for, but you don't want it. There is no reason for a fight. You're not challenging him for whatever he has. The flip side of that is that he shouldn't challenge you for what you have, either.

The next type is a little rougher to blow off. You are in an area minding your own business and suddenly you notice someone giving you the evil eye. Don't panic! Slow down for a moment. Casually return your attention to the conversation (or whatever you're doing) for a few minutes. You also keep a bead on the fucker out of the side of your eye. Don't watch him, just keep his position marked. If he moves, you'll know about it. Then, with the same sort of disinterest a wolf has when a coyote is looking hard at him, look again. Is he still looking at you? Turn back to the conversation. If you can remain cool about someone looking hard at you, it will often get you out of trouble. The thing about this technique that makes it useful is that the message is the reverse of you going submissive. It is instead that you are so far above him on the Alpha scale that he isn't a threat. This is one technique that can work in some cases.

Another technique, which I often use, calls for a little more spirit. It is for use when you think that the guy isn't just looking for anybody, he's looking at you. For whatever reason, the guy is thinking of making a move on you. You're doing a casual scan of what is going around (Remember awareness? Periodic relaxed scans are part of it.) and you notice a hard look. Keep on scanning. Don't stop on him; go past. When you're past him, check to see if he's still looking at you. If he is, drop the sights on him. Before you were just doing a light computer scan; this time, computerized missile-lock drops on the chump. Go cyborg on the bozo. You're the Terminator and he's Sandra Conners. For reasons that would fill this book and ten like it, this usually works. It lets him know that he's going to get hurt if he messes with you.

A small thing that is almost microscopic but works quite well: instead of whipping back along the same line that your eyes went before, you drop them on him. Your eyes make an arc to where he's looking at you, like the way you drop a scoped rifle on a target. If you can make your head move slightly mechanical-like, it really improves the image. From there, if you intensify your glare like you're going to fly across the place and rip his throat out, it will be the finishing touch. If the guy was thinking about taking a shot at you, either there or in the parking lot, it might just change his mind. Real quick-like. You better be ready to rock and roll before you try it, however, because if the guy was looking at you for some other reason, it'll start it up right then and there. If the guy breaks eye contact, don't push it. Let him go. Either way, though, it's over.

The main thing about eyes is that you can tell a lot about a person by looking at them. If someone is lying, you can tell by the look in their eyes. If you've ever caught someone lying to you, the odds are that you noticed the subtle signals from their eyes. (Kids: important tip on how not to get caught!)

Another important thing to know about is glasses. Many people wear them. What do you do with them prior to a fight? Well, taking them off is a good idea, but not for the reason you'd think. Sincerity is conveyed by taking off the "shield" of glasses. You can prove a point regarding your sincerity by whipping off those little puppies. If your point is that you're going to rip his head off unless he backs off right now...well you get the idea.

Another thing about glasses is if you're blind as a bat without them you might make him chicken out. One of the most frightening things that can happen to a tough is when his signals of how bad he is are calmly disregarded. Not in the sense of you're so dumb you don't know that you're in trouble; rather, you're so Alpha to this chump, you're not concerned about him. If he can't read your nonverbals, like you're scared, he's going to get a little edgy. If you can't *see* his little nonverbals, you can't react to them, right?

Do I hear, "Yeah, but if I can't see, I'm gonna get punched"? In one sense this might help you. I used to sword fight with a guy who was blinder than a bat in a spotlight without his glasses, yet he was a damn good swordsman. The reason was, he didn't get distracted by the little things; he saw a motion and that's it. He didn't get nervous about seeing the blade coming at him (I do mean blade; these were real swords we were working with), so he'd block it without thinking. So if you wear glasses, relax about not being able to see. It might just help you out in ways you'd never expect.

There are all sorts of challenges that go on, and they aren't limited to eyes. When someone is walking toward you and they "drift" over to your side, five times out of ten that's a challenge. Four times it's either he needs directions, is going to his car, or is trying to bum money from you. The last time is when it's a setup for a two-man mugging. If he was stationary while watching your approach, check to see if anyone is suddenly behind you.

This form of challenge is taken to extremes by shoulder slams; neither party steps out of the way entirely, and the result is shoulders colliding. This doesn't mean that every time someone bumps into you, it's a challenge; hell, we're all klutzes now and then. Let it go if you can.

Another thing that I have to mention to men is, watch out for couples. I have experienced this many times: women "lean" against their men at just the right moment to push them into my path. It's not the man's fault. In fact, most of the time he doesn't even know what's going on. To him it appears that I stepped into his way. I have had this trick pulled on me in some of the worst necks of the woods to some of the richest and most prestigious areas in California. It isn't something that only happens in low class neighborhoods.

Spitting is another little act of defiance, especially among Hispanics. They look at you and then spit. Yeah, I think a lot of you too, guy.

These are just a few of the forms that can be construed as challenges. You should be aware of your own behavior and how it can be interpreted as a challenge. If you have a cold and are hawking and spitting, say "excuse me" when you spit. That way the guy knows it's not a challenge. If you're walking with someone and somebody is approaching, look to see if your party is taking up most of the sidewalk. If you are, drop back and let them pass. If you don't, your action could be interpreted as a challenge and you could end up getting socked in the jaw.

One thing about going passive: if you go too far, that means anybody has the right to beat on you. When I said, "leave, but not too passively," this is what I meant. The person might just figure you to be such a passive that he can beat up on you if he wants. Or there may be other people around who feel like picking on someone. They saw you back down; that means they can get away with directing shit at you.

I have explained why the Alpha/Beta behavior system works, and why it often doesn't. You have to always watch to see where you stand in it. It is always changing, but then again, so is our world. If you have the wits and the knowledge, you can get by.

Mistakes

If you don't learn from your mistakes, what's the use of making them?

My grandfather

Okay, I've bored you with tales of my deliciously misspent youth. The thing that I've tried to tell you is that I've blown it more than once. I have had spectacular victories, and I've also suffered some outrageous defeats. You have to understand that you're going to blow it now and then. Cut your losses and run if you can; if not, suffer the consequences. Either way, learn from what happened. I have learned more from my mistakes than I have from my victories. Don't berate yourself; evaluate. Get the critical voice out of the equation and try better next time. (By the way, a trick I use in regard to the critical voice is, when it gets too loud, just stop what you're doing and say to it, "Okay! Think you can do better? Go ahead, right now!" The critical voice is great at whining but it's not so hot at working.) The best way to view this is to look at what you've learned in the most positive outlook possible. In other words *"If you can't get a better outlook on life from something, you haven't learned the right lesson."* I'm not bullshitting you about this. The biggest mistake people make is they approach mistakes from the wrong perspective. It may hurt like hell, this lesson, but if you give in to bitterness over the pain, you've blown it.

This is obviously something that you have to do in regard to more than just fighting, but it does really work. Looking at mistakes this way takes out much of the sting. It really makes it easier on you. You're actually less likely to make the same mistake again if you try this.

Check out what is going on or what has just happened from other perspectives. Ask other people what they think went wrong. If some guy is about to bust your face, hold up your hands and say, "Hey, wait a minute! I didn't know I was stepping on your toes! Could you explain to me why that pissed you off?" Sometimes it works, if you're sincere and you don't know how you pissed him off. If you're using it as a cop-out to keep from getting stomped, it might not work. If it works, shit, buy him a beer and ask him his world view. He might give you some great insights on a different world model. Most situations aren't lethal, so you stand a very good chance of surviving. This will allow you some room to move and a whole bunch of room to learn. Learn from everything; if you made a mistake, learn from it. Don't do it again. What were the basic things that led up to that? Learn those so you don't step into it again.

And most of all remember what we professionals often say in regard to mistakes: "Oops."

Taking Punishment

"If all these things can get through armor, what good is it?"
"It covers your mistakes"
"Oh..."

A conversation overheard at the Armory.

My dick was so far out into the wind, the airport was using it as a wind sock. I mean this guy's punch caught me flatfooted. Right between the eyes. It was his version of a Nighty Nite Bunny Rabbit, and it should have worked. I was blown back two steps with the blinding flash in my head. I stopped and looked at him...and smiled. My words scared him so much, he immediately threw his hands up. Apologizing profusely, he at first backed away, then he ran. My words? "That's the best you can do? Heh, heh, heh."

That was the shortest fight that I've ever been in. I got punched once, and I won. I mean, hey, I'll take that sort of victory anytime. Take one punch and win? Yeah, no sweat. The thing that most people don't hear about that fight is that I walked away and sat down, whereupon my brains did the same thing those little dogs in the back of car windows do. You know the ones, with the spring in their necks and the stupid expression, whose heads go "bonga-bonga" when you hit a bump. Yeah, them.

Most people don't seem to realize, however, that pain goes

away. It is only a temporary thing and, like all temporary things, it can be tolerated. There are several methods of pain control. The one that works for me is called disassociation. I know the pain is there, sort of. It's somewhere else, though, someplace where it doesn't affect me until later. If you learn how to control the pain, you will not be afraid of it. If you know that the pain is eventually going to pass, it becomes less of a threat. It becomes a hassle instead of a juggernaut.

The thing to remember about pain in a fight is that you can't let it stop you. You can rewire pain. There are people, including myself, who the harder you hit, the madder they get. It is one of the most frightening sights to give someone a ball shot and have him glare at you. Someone like that knows the pain will go away. If they let it stop them now, they will be leaving themselves open for more. So they clench their teeth instead of throwing up and come after you. Later they throw up and cry (at least I do).

Don't waste time taking blows to prove how tough you are, but know that there will be blows that get through. If you've done your homework and found a pain control system that works for you, you will be less affected by these.

The other thing is, after a fight, go lick your wounds. Go curl up in a corner and cry if you want; it's okay. Be kind to yourself for a few days. Let yourself heal and recuperate. Take a hot bath, put vitamin E and C on your cuts and scrapes, massage the bruised areas and eight inches or so around them. Eat well, take vitamins, sleep, etc. It is now time to feel the pain. Pain is a message to you, warning you that something is wrong. Don't ignore it. If you pamper yourself for a few days, you will, in the long run, heal faster than if you were to go out and be butch about it.

Your body has just gone through a traumatic experience. It used resources that you don't usually have to use. So let it recoup, ya hear me?

Friends and Other Aggravations

If you do that again, I'll shoot you myself!

B. H. C.

You know, in the last eight years, none of the fights that I got into were mine. (I say actual fights, not skirmishes in the line of duty. I've been Security at certain events where alcohol and drugs abounded. I've also been the elected bouncer for a number of places. Nor do I mean confrontations—some guy screaming that he's going to rip my head off. It doesn't count until he moves.) Some may say that I'm trying not to take responsibility, but that isn't true. The times before that, I take full responsibility for the fights, but I got to a point where people sort of left me alone. But I still had "friends." Since this time, I have changed a number of acquaintances because of this little fact. My so-called friends figured that, since I was so good, they could mouth off to someone and I'd keep them from getting beat up. Thanks, pal.

Watch your friends' behavior often; they think that you knowing how to fight means they can be dickheads. Well, that just isn't so. It leaves a bad taste in my mouth to abandon friends, yet it also doesn't do my sense of humor much good to get in a fight because my buddy was being an asshole. The trick that I have discovered works for me is this: I simply tell my friend to back off. I further inform him that he is in the wrong, and if he continues to be aggressive about it, I will not back him. If he stops what he's doing and apologizes to the guy, I will back him against the guy trying anything from there on. But if he insists on his aggressive behavior, he will do it alone.

This has always worked. The other guys really aren't too hot to tangle with me, and this gives them a way out. My friend really isn't too keen on the idea of tying up with these guys if he doesn't have backup. The other party also knows that if they push after I pulled my friend back, they're being the asshole. Being an asshole around a little wolverine isn't the brightest thing to do, and they know it. So, by accepting an apology, nobody gets hurt. This approach has never failed; but then again, I don't associate with people who do this shit anymore.

There is another variation of this shit which I think you should know about. That's having a "pal" who gets in a jam with someone and, when you move to give him backup, it somehow ends up becoming your fight. There are a lot of people who do this when you're a good fighter. They set up the situation and sit back and watch you fight. Any problem should *stay* his problem. It shouldn't somehow end up being your fight. If you realize that he's sitting back and watching you jam with the person that he was having words with a moment ago, it could be a setup.

This is an example of friends who will misuse your skills. If a friend is in a serious jam, and it is a one-time event, help him out. If the sucker somehow always seems to get in jams when you're around, get a new friend.

Those are setups by your friends; there is another type that is far less pleasing but equally common. I have in my life gotten into more fights over pussy than I care to admit. The problem is, every time I fought over pussy I ended up not getting any! There is something wrong there! Yes, boys and girls, I am talking about fighting over women. I can't tell you the number of times that I or someone else has been sitting there talking to a woman when, from stage left, who should enter but a real knuckle

dragger. The conversation is usually close enough to:
 "Hey mutherfucker, whaddya think yer dooing?"
 "Pal, you're cutting in on me..."
 "Yer cuttin' on my woman."

Around this time, there is a little detail that you should notice. It's the woman. If she says, "George! I'm not your woman anymore!" it is a little obvious that the guy hasn't caught on the he's "ex." You may still have to fight the guy if he pushes it, but the odds are against it being a setup.

However, if we're talking about the standard eye contact, preening (messing with the hair, straightening the clothes, etc.), covert smiles in the exact direction that you're in, no mention of "Go away, my boyfriend..." but when the guy shows up, she says something to the effect, "Ernie! I was just sitting here and this guy just came up and started bothering me..." the odds are you have been set up! Provided you didn't actually do what she claims, you are about to experience first hand how ugly this sort of thing can get.

What is entailed in either example of the setups that I have mentioned is that the person who is doing the setting up is getting their yah yahs. It is a real dick-tickler for someone to know that they have enough power to get you into a fight. That means that you end up fighting to supply them with entertainment and power trips. What I have found to be an effective way out of this is to "call the ball." If you see a setup beginning to go down, stand up and holler about it. Tell the other guy in your most sincere tones what you believe is happening and do your best to decline to fight. Not that you're afraid to fight him, just you don't like to fight when you've both been suckered. From there you have a few options: walk away, buy him a beer, leave the place, or fight him.

I once got out of a setup like that because I noticed that the woman was egging the guy on. Moments before she had been wiggling to get into my pants; now she was thirsting for my blood. I got out of that one by looking at the guy and saying, "When I win I'm gonna fuck your woman!" He realized that in order for me to do that he would have to be hospital bait, and nobody who wasn't able to do that to him would tell him about it in that way. (Incidentally, she was a little less hot about his fighting me after that little statement. I mean, what if he really did lose?)

Whatever you choose to do, it might take the wind out of his sails enough so his heart isn't into fighting anymore. Even the dumbest brute doesn't like being manipulated by others. If you don't push it, he may decide to let it go. This isn't to say that you weren't in the right; it's just that being righteous about this means that you'll end up fighting. Once the first blow is thrown, right, wrong, blame, etc., go out the window. In other words, just because you're right doesn't mean you're going to win a fight.

Now ladies, don't get the idea that I'm saying men don't pull this sort of shit. It is a twisted aspect of our human sexuality that we as a species play this game. The fact remains, though, that when men pull this garbage on women, it results less often in a physical fight than when it is done the other way around. This is not to say that this sickening sort of shit is any less damaging, but this book is about physical fights and such. Therefore, I have to mention it in this context. What I'm not saying is that a man's breath is in any way, shape, or form, pure when it comes to pulling this kind of crap.

The first year I was at my high school we had a riot. Generically, it could be called a race riot. Actually what had happened was two girls, a black and Mexican, had gotten into a fight. It was solved to neither's satisfaction. So they went out to get their boyfriends. Both of the boyfriends were in gangs and the ensuing fight led to a gang fight. This, in turn, escalated into all black gangs against all Mexican gangs. The next step, logically, was a race riot. Maybe not logically, but actually. My point is that this whole thing, in which deaths and wounding were involved, was started by two women.

I'm sorry foks, Women's Lib hasn't hit the streets. America is becoming less and less white, which means there are different cultures around. Different cultures feel differently about women. In the "white" cultures that make up much of America, there are more variations about the place of women than you can shake a stick at. I have been dragged into more shit by women than I want to remember. I am not a sexist pig; I am, however, a realist. If the other guy doesn't think he should have to deal with women, he's going to come after me.

Women, please realize this: in some guy's model, what you think could amount to squat. I'm sorry if this offends anyone, but there are world models out there where women are second-class citizens. That means, in this person's world model, if you are an unknown or unattached woman, you are automatically a Beta. Unless he knows where your man stands in the hierarchy, he doesn't know where you stand. An Alpha female is above lower Beta males. So in these people's eyes, unless your man is seriously above them in the hierarchy (and they can tell by looking at him that he isn't), you have no fucking right to be mouthing off to them. According to them, it's "your man's" job to put you on a leash. If you keep on sassing them, they're going to beat the hell out of the man you're with.

I'm sorry if all of this offends you, but it is a reality that has to be dealt with regardless of your feelings on the subject. I had a "White Liberated Assertive Woman" for a lover once. That woman felt it necessary to give people a piece of her mind, regardless of the fact that it cost me pieces of my ass. There are world models that don't go for that sort of shit. Just in case you think I'm being a chauvinistic pig, I'd like to share an important fact with you. Most systems where women are considered second-class citizens are fighting societies! The people are not limited by the rules of civilized society. We're not talking about a world where, if you piss someone off, they won't invite you to the next "meet-another-up-and-coming-author" cocktail party. We're talking they'll slug you when they're pissed off.

If you're alone, you can prove to this guy that you are an Alpha female. This he understands. But if you're with a man, then your date must understand what the other guy expects of him. In some cases, as much as it might gall you, you have to let the man deal with it. In other situations, if you are with a man that can be considered an Alpha, and if he can keep a calm, slightly amused, and definitely unthreatened look about him, you can handle the problem by yourself. What that does is let the other guy know that the man really is an Alpha male and you are an Alpha female. By the hierarchy standards, he should have to back down, unless he wants to challenge the male.

Now men, here's the flip side of this. You have to back up the woman you're with, but you're responsible for her. If you don't "keep her on a leash," the locals are going to beat your head in. The woman I was lovers with used to get me into more shit because when I told her to lay off, she'd ignore me. The men that she was lipping off to took that to mean that I couldn't control her. This led to the assumption that if I couldn't control a woman, I really wasn't an Alpha. If I wasn't an Alpha male, then she wasn't an Alpha female, and therefore had no right to be giving them shit. By the time I managed to restore order, I had worked three times as hard as I should have had to. Her refusal to listen to me had dropped me in points on the scale, so I had to climb back up to their level and way beyond. This is not saying shit about if I thought she was right or not; this was just to avoid a fight. So, if you're involved with a woman who does this sort of thing, explain to her that her actions could easily lead to you getting beat up. If she doesn't want to accept this, I suggest that you either stay in polite society only, or seriously consider getting rid of her. (Watch out: she could be pissed off at men and know this stuff instinctively. She is then setting you up.)

I once experienced an almost comical example of what I have been talking about. I was having dinner with some friends. It was their anniversary, so I had taken them to a nice restaurant. At the time, we were doing traveling, unchoreographed "live steel" sword fight shows—we hacked wildly at each other with real broadswords in real armor. The dinner reservations were such that we had time only to change clothes and run. This meant that we were dirty, sweaty, and reeked of mud, blood, and beer. I freely admit, we looked like amphetamine-crazed werewolves after an extremely rough night. The other thing we looked was extremely dangerous, and to tell the truth, we were. The fact is, though, that we were having a quiet conversation with what we hoped would be a quiet anniversary dinner.

Well, we were sitting in the restaurant when out of the blue this woman storms up to us and starts ranting and raving on how we're disgusting and filthy. We sat there a moment watching her loudly proclaim her aversion to us. With a screech that she couldn't tolerate being in the same room with us, she beelined it out, presumably to the bar. I turned and looked at the man that she had been with to gauge his reaction. The poor guy, my heart went out to him. He was sitting there with one hand on his face and the air of a man convinced that some-one had just condemned him to death. The other impression that he gave was that these sort of occurrences happened often. When I returned my attention to my friend, he was returning his glance from the guy, as well. Our eyes met in understanding for a moment before we burst out laughing. The man, realizing he was not on the endangered species list, relaxed and finished his dinner. Bravo for him, I thought.

So, both men and women, listen up. You are responsible for each other's well-being. How you are at home, in polite company, or at the office has nothing to do with this. I may sound like a chauvinist, but my relationships with women are some of the most democratically balanced situations you will ever see. But we're talking about the streets. Out there if you fuck with their expectations you are outnumbered. If you don't listen on this one, don't come crying to me. I don't like those sort of systems, but the fact that they exist means they must be dealt with on their own terms. Don't let your emotions or pride set you up on this, because the ramifications can be serious.

Woofing

What we have here is a failure to communicate.

Cool Hand Luke

I should have named this chapter "Woofing and Face Saving." It is an indication that The Mighty Ipock was right when he said, "The line between teaching and intellectual sadism is awfully thin." I gather that most of you are wondering what "woofing" is. The face saving part is sort of a tip-off, but not a definition. Woofing is a black idiomatic term that I picked up in my little home town, namely Los Angeles. By the way, since we are talking about idiomatic phrases let's look at them for a minute. This book, in case you haven't noticed, is full of slang and colorful colloquialisms. I've traveled widely in the western United States, Mexico, and some in Canada. I've also worked and lived with people from all over the world. The thing is, American English is different than British English. Hell, American English is different from itself. Every location has a different dialect. By dialect, I mean different common usage words. To hell with English teachers' definitions of what constitutes a dialect or even a proper English period, what I'm talking about is communication.

I had a roommate from England, a rather pretty girl who was just as confused about the odd forms of communications we in America had as I was with hers. One day she walked into my room and the conversation went something like this:

"Animal, 'ave you seen the 'Oover?"

"The what?"

"The..." she slowed to pronounce it fully, "hoover."

"What's a hoover?"

"You know; the hoover, the sweep."

"Huh?"

"*The hoover! The sweeper!*" She pantomimed an action that took me a moment to figure out she wasn't masturbating someone, then I caught on.

"The vacuum?"

"The what?"

Eventually we got it figured out. Yes, she wanted the vacuum cleaner, what in L.A. is called a "vacuum." Unfortunately, each of us had different terms for the sucker, but no mutual terms. While we were speaking the same language, we weren't speaking the same dialect. To that end, we were confusing one another. We both assumed that we were speaking clearly. Since this happened in L.A., she was the one with the speech problem. If, however, it had happened in London, I'd have had the speech impediment. In New York, we'd both have Broca's Aphasia.

So different areas have different communication formats. What's more, so do different world models. Speech patterns reflect underlying assumptions and world models. It's the fastest way to "spot" someone's model. What is normal communication for you can be interpreted as snobby behavior elsewhere. My biological father used to get bent out of shape because he felt that I was using big words to try and impress people. What I was doing was talking normally for my social group at the time. (By the way, my current roommate is a Ph.D. in biology. As a kid I always liked animals, tide pools, bugs, snakes, etc. Since I don't want to quit doing something that gives me pleasure, I found a way to hang head down in a tide pool that "adults" feel comfortable with. Instead of hanging out at the tide pools, I go on biological expeditions. They don't get upset and I have fun looking at crabs. Socialize with people in a field that you like; you can get away with having fun and learn all sorts of neat shit while doing it.)

Okay, back to communications. When you are in an area where the language is "point and grunt," don't be talking the Queen's English. The natives get restless. This doesn't mean that you should get a frontal lobotomy in order to fit in. It means be, A) patient, B) careful of what and how you say something and, C) aware of how you will appear to others via speech.

If you are just passing through, you can exercise enough self-control not to outshine those poor illiterate masses with your brilliant wit. Be patient and keep your communications simple. Not simple, as in "to a simpleton." Rather, simple, as in not verbose. "When in Rome, babe. . ." If you don't know the local dialect, it's not their fault for not speaking like you do. You're outnumbered and in their territory, so either communicate in a manner that they are comfortable with, or shut up. There is no need to call attention to yourself in this manner. It doesn't matter if you're comfortable or not. If you will be leaving soon, you can wait it out. In other words, don't try to force your world model on them. Believe me, it's easier than having to fight your way out of a place.

The next part concerns what you say (or do). Some things have different definitions in different places. The best example that I know is the American okay sign. We all know it: index finger and thumb curled into a circle with the three remaining fingers extended upwards. Innocent, right? If you flash that to someone from a Mediterranean country, they might get torqued because that's the signal for asshole where they're from. To a southeast Asian, that means that they are zero. Ten is the best; zero is a bad insult. This is an example of miscommunication.

Examples of faux pas can be rather amusing. I had a friend who was in the Navy. He had spent his tour on what was then the toughest battleship in the Pacific Fleet. Home he goes to his nice Jewish family for his welcome home dinner. At the table, in a relaxed moment, he reverted to the language he had learned to relax with on the ship. A shocked hush fell over the entire table when he asked for the mashed potatoes. He looked around and realized everyone was staring at him. Quickly he replayed the tape and realized he had said, "Pass the fuckin' potatoes" without realizing he was no longer on the ship. On board that was a polite request. The family, however, was not amused.

I travel between world models quite regularly, and one of the hardest things to remember is to switch communication gears in this manner. Words that are perfectly acceptable when something goes wrong at work get shocked looks when I'm doing computer scans at UCLA. Now I usually get left alone to do my scans, so this can be used to your advantage.

The next part is that old bad penny, awareness. When you are in other world models, you must do a sonar bit. (Hell, do it in your own, but especially others.) If you have a pretty good idea of what their world model really is, stop and consider how you must look from their perspective. Do a quick scan on the reactions you are getting. If they are negative, change your ways. You must take responsibility for how your actions and words affect others. For those of you who are saying "It's not my job to worry how other people react," all I have to say is, can I have your stereo?

I mean really, how important is it to you that you *have* to be right? Me, if I somehow manage to be right 50 percent of the time, I'm happy. If I push it up to 75 percent, I'm ecstatic! This is reality here. If you don't take some responsibility for what's going on around you, you're going to get creamed if you step outside your world model. So either take some responsibility, or remain stuck in one area where you're tolerated. (By the way, since the world isn't a static place, you can guess what is going to happen sooner or later if you choose the latter.)

What I'm saying is, your world model is no more right than anyone else's. You may not agree with theirs, but unless theirs consists of nailing you somehow, leave them alone. "Don't frighten the taxpayers," as my stepdad says. You now understand about world models; they usually don't. That means you have an edge in survival. You noticed that I said survival, not "winning a fight." I'm talking overall here. Insisting on blatantly displaying your world model will call all sorts of attention to you. Since your overall goal is to get by, understand that attention sometimes may not be benign.

My friend Doc and I came close to getting into a jam with some guys over something that he was doing. I understood what he was doing, and I thought it was funny. My statement to him was, "I understand what you're trying to say, but they don't." We got out of a fight because he toned it down after that. (Also, I moved my jacket away from my knife for a quick draw. He moved his hand inside his jacket, unsnapped his knife in it's sheath, and then laid his hand on the table near that same spot. This is a good example of how subtle danger signals can be. Two of us and five of them made it closer to combat than a fight.) This, by the way, was in a nicer neck of the woods, so don't think that the price of real estate will save your butt.

You may have noticed that, up to this point, I haven't said anything about "woofing." Well, let's rectify that. There are two different definitions of woofing. One is making boisterous noise to save face after backing down. The other is making noise in hopes of either scaring your opponent away or working yourself up for a fight. Simple, eh?

Don't be upset if that makes absolutely no sense at all. It took me years to understand it myself. Let's look at the second definition first. The thing is, most people aren't ready to fight right off the bat. There are very few people who can suddenly go from doing something else to combat in a split second. I can do it, and I know others who can too. The thing is, we are all real careful about this. We can accidently hurt someone real bad if we don't keep it on a leash. So, in case you're curious, I don't advocate getting to this point, people; it can and does really fuck your life up. You're more likely to accidently take out your lover or spouse than you are to fend off a horde of attackers. All of the people I have lived with got into the habit of making recognizable noises when they entered an area that I occupied. This is no bullshit; I once threw my wife across the room and landed on her, ready to crush her skull, because she scared me out of sleep. I nearly killed the woman I loved because she moved into my space without positive confirmation of the recognition. I have never and will never strike someone I love in anger, yet I almost killed her before I woke up. So I mean this, don't try to get to that point. It's not good!

If most people aren't ready to just start rockin', that means they have to build up to that point. This is where woofin' comes into play. Either they try to work themselves up to fighting form or they try to puff up and scare you away. The difference is fear. If you look behind the eyes of someone who is doing the latter, you can see that they are scared. You should remain calm and don't aggressively scare him. Hold your ground, but don't go chasing him. If he leaves, leave him alone. It's that simple. Don't get loud and boisterous about what you're going to do to him. If he feels that you won't blow this off and you'll come hunting him or you'll hold this against him, he might panic and swing. The best phrasing for this situation that I ever heard was, "Get off my land." Those four words were so much more eloquent than, "Get the fuck outta my face and I'll let this slide," which is what it meant anyway. What it does is let the other person save face. He can back down and not get hurt without getting too much flack.

This type of woofing can also mean working up one's anger. The people who do this get louder and louder until they hype themselves up so much that they are ready to fight. There are many levels to this form of woofing. When someone is being just boisterous and pushy, they aren't ready to fight yet. When someone is boisterous and challenging, they're much closer. When they get to direct challenge and squaring off, they're ready. So someone can be woofing at a distance and the odds are that they're not really ready, or they can be closer and still not ready. Remember what I told you about the blood leaving the skin? This is when it comes into play. I can't tell you rules that will work every time here because every situation (as we all know so well by now) is different.

Now here is something that I can only describe in terms that will confuse most people. There is a moment when an altercation reaches critical peak. It is that moment when it hangs in the balance: back down or fight. If there will be a fight, it will start right there. While there is an exception, which I'll explain later, it is also the moment dominance is established. BAM! Someone backs down. He had the option to throw the punch and didn't. This is the turning point. What is hard to describe about it is that it's an energy change. One really doesn't want to fight the other and will begin the process of backing down. Since it took some time to get to that point, it will take some time to get away. This is where the first definition of woofing comes into play.

If the opponents are somewhat close to the same "rank," the person who just backed down has to save face. If you don't think it is important, I'll dance on your grave. If you are the dominant one, you have to allow this person to back away while you still retain dominance. Sound tricky? It is.

Here's the exception I spoke of: if you relax too much, the person might get the idea that you aren't really dominant to him and try to take another shot. If you get too heavy-handed and try to get him to back down too quickly, he'll have to come after you. Even if he knows that he will lose, he might not lose if you push him too hard. The very fact that you were in conflict means that he thought (or others did) that he was equal to or better than you. What has just been proven is that while you're of the same rank, you are a higher degree in that rank. In other words, you're both black belts, but you are 3rd degree and he is 2nd. The thing is, a black belt doesn't run away from another black belt. White and yellow belts run away from black belts; other black belts *back* away. If you push too hard for him to go submissive, he will have to fight you.

Once someone has gone truly submissive on you, and you are close to the same rank, let him go! Let him save face while he's backing away. He, in all probability, will still be making noise, but it is just that; noise! There's no need for you to get bent out of shape if he is truly submissive. If he is false submissive, then that is different. The only way that I can explain the difference is like a dog who is barking at you and backing away.

They keep going away and it's fine. If they get to a point just outside of kicking range and then increase their woofing again, it was false submissive.

If you push too hard to get this person to back down immediately, you've set yourself up for a fight. If that person backs down too quickly, everyone below him will want to take a shot at his position. This person knows this; he may fight you and lose, but nobody is going to challenge him. So he fights once and loses (or not, as the case may be; it's better not to find out) rather than having to fight twenty times because he backed down too quick. If you push someone to back down faster than their position warrants relative to yours, you've shot yourself in the foot. Allow him to save face in front of others, especially those below him.

In case you're wondering, this concept extends into polite society. One of the ways that you can tell if someone is a good manager is if they don't chew people out in front of spectators, especially the person's co-workers or, even worse, the person's work force. The concepts in this book are applicable to many more things than just keeping out of physical fights.

This is what woofing is. It has aspects in communication and Alpha and Beta behavior. It, like everything else, is part of a whole system that is interrelated. Each portion of reality affects, and is affected by, other portions. Things that by a linear logical form have nothing to do with one another become interrelated when viewed as aspects of a dynamic whole. If you keep your eyes and mind open, you can see a bigger picture, and if you can see more of what's coming, it's easier to put yourself in an advantageous position. You don't step into holes as often, which means you don't dent your nose as much. Makes sense when you look at it that way, doesn't it?

Mostly For Women
(but it wouldn't hurt men to know it, either)

It is useless for the sheep to pass resolutions for vegetarianism, as long as the wolves remain of a different opinion.
A quote I heard somewhere.

Ladies, if what I've been saying has offended you, I'm very sorry. It is not my intention to imply that women are second-class citizens in any way, shape, or form. This, I should point out, is in direct conflict with what I said at the beginning of this book about not apologizing for offending. It is, therefore, an indication of how strongly I feel about this. I don't usually apologize for the way I think, to man or God. The thing is, people who attack other people don't give a rat's ass about the way you think. So what I've been saying is raw, unpalatable truth. It may taste like hell going down, but not liking it isn't going to change the fact that it exists.

Let's look at it this way: the refusal to accept the existence of something doesn't make it go away. However, refusing to accept the existence of something as a qualification of its right to exist gives you one hell of an edge for combating it. This is a matter of accepting of what is, like it or not. *But you can still do something about it.* You can change the future, but right now you have to deal with what is happening.

Now I'm not saying you have to dumbly accept things, hell no! What you have to accept is that you have an uphill haul.

If you and I were to walk down the street together, it isn't the fact that I have a penis that would make you the more likely target. I have about me the aura that fucking with me is inviting a trip to the morgue for the fuckee, hereafter known as the fucked. That is what keeps me safe as I walk through the jungles.

Now there are certain things I do that convey this message to the dirtbags. If you take some of the things that I'm going to say to you and add them to your habits, you too can project the fact that there are easier people to mess with in this world. If you know (and show that you know) that the dirtbags are dangerous, it makes them less dangerous!

For those of you who protest, "Well, rapists and muggers know that, too!", I have one thing to say. If you know a tiger is dangerous, are you going to walk up with a stick and poke it? The only time a tiger is dangerous is when you're close to it. If you're away from the tiger, it won't hurt you. The bad guys know that, and they aren't going to poke you with a stick if they're going to bleed for doing it.

The line between training someone to be a victim and to endure shit until it passes is mighty fine. In fact, most people are unable to tell the difference. Another subtlety that escapes most people is that it's not bricks but rather one too many straws that wipes out the camel. You have to realize that it's not one thing that you can do but a collection of things that will lead to you being safer in this world.

I once knew a woman who felt destroyed when her sensei had told the class that they should expect to be defeated now and then. She claimed that it totally undermined her attempt to build self-confidence in her ability to defend herself. I called her reaction a cop-out. There are no guarantees in this world that something will work. There is, however, a bit of knowledge: the person who is looking for a guarantee will lose ninety-nine out of a hundred times to the person who is using their wits and always looking for a slight edge.

If you go around thinking that something is guaranteed, you're going to get creamed. Sooner or later the universe is going to make a liar out of you. The degree that you relied on the false guarantee is in direct proportion to how much damage you're going to take.

Once you get past the initial bullshit of helplessness and begin to do the grind of watching out for yourself, it becomes easier. For the most part, this is not a problem for women once they get past the first and biggest barrier. For some obscure reason, women seem to be able to accept responsibility of something that has to be done over and over better than men do. Must be the fact that men have short attention spans. (Usually the length of some other portion of their anatomy. Hey, just because I'm a man doesn't mean I don't realize that we can be assholes.)

So let's look at what you can do. The first thing is something that I have already mentioned. As a woman, any unprovoked altercation with a man should be considered combat. I will leave it up to your discretion as to what constitutes "unprovoked altercation." Mainly I mean someone jumping out of the bushes, but date rape is equally applicable. If you think that I just gave you carte blanche to mess anyone up that touches you, you're half right. It's carte blanche on anyone who attacks you. Kneeing the office molester at the first sign of a pass is somewhat of an overkill; telling him to keep his hands off you isn't, though. If, after that, he still pushes it, do what my lady did to one guy who was trying to fondle her at work. He had put his arm around her and she grabbed it, pinning it to her body. Then she spun around in such a way that he had a choice: he could try and resist and have his pinned arm disjointed by her body weight, or fly into a wall. He kissed the wall. She smiled sweetly and informed him that she didn't appreciate that sort of shit. What was he going to do; run to her boss and complain that while he was sexually harassing her, she threw him into a wall? It's somewhat more gratifying than spilling coffee on his crotch, although that works real well, too.

Basically, there are situations where just enough force to get your message across works fine. Mostly, though, these are social or work situations, where there are people who are watching the exchange. Any assault outside the view of others is combat. This is a damn good rule of thumb.

Now what that means is, when something happens, you go full tilt with everything that you have until either you can escape or your attacker(s) are dead or seriously hurt.

If you're still thinking that you can't do that for some reason or other (it's unladylike; what if he gets mad and hurts me; etc.), don't worry; the world will probably be better off without you anyway. I'm not shitting you on this; women are the victims of most crimes because the guy thinks he can get away with it without getting hurt. *Hurt him!* Better him than you!

You should go out and learn how to defend yourself; not fight, but defend yourself. In Los Angeles there is a group called "Model Muggings." I don't know if the program has spread elsewhere yet, but find an equivalent if it hasn't already come to your hometown. What they do is put guys in protective padding and have the women go at them full force. This teaches the closest to combat you can get without actually hurting someone. If something happens out in the street, you know what it feels like to go full force on someone, and that is important.

Thus far we have covered the most important barrier that you as a woman (although it wouldn't hurt for the men to know it either) will need to get past in order to defend yourself. I've known a number of women who have been raped. The thing about them that impresses me the most is that many will never be raped again. They will either kill the son of a bitch or die trying, and there is a good chance that they'd take the fucker with them. So anything short of "it *can* be done by me" from you is bullshit. If you want to be safe, you have to pay some dues. These dues are within you, nowhere else. Therefore, there is no excuse for not paying them.

The next step for you is awareness. Remember this old puppy? It's back. This manifestation is in a few parts, though the first one is awareness of the actions of others.

One of the reasons that someone of nefarious purpose is going to skip me is they know that they need ten steps to get away with whatever they are up to. If they try, I'll spot them on the first three steps, have them targeted by five, and if they keep it up they'll be dogmeat by seven. The first thing you need to do is learn how to spot something that is about to happen. This can be achieved by maintaining three stages of awareness.

Stage one is "Code Yellow." Every time that you are out of sight of immediate reliable help, you go to Code Yellow status. Code Yellow is first stage alert. It basically means, "Heads up, we might have a problem." There are two more stages: Code Red, which means "We got a problem," and Code Blue, which means "all hell's broken loose and the holocaust is happening." So don't panic when I say Code Yellow. It's not that bad, but you're on your toes. Capisce?

By immediate reliable help, I mean people that you know can and will help you if something happens. If you're at a bus station with two little old ladies, they aren't going to be much help if someone snatches your purse. Strangers aren't exactly known for the habit of going out of their way to help you when trouble begins.

This doesn't mean you have to be paranoid. After a time, Code Yellow will become second nature to you. If I may use an analogy here, mothers are the perfect examples of yellow alert. Ever notice how a mother of a baby can carry on a conversation while somehow knowing what the kid is up to? They'll be sitting there chatting away and casually reach out and snag the vase a half second before the little rug rat muckles onto it. Then, without breaking the stride of the conversation, she puts it out of the curtain climber's reach. That's awareness!

It's incredible how women, who can calmly save a priceless Ming Dynasty vase without losing a moment's concentration, will look me dead in the eye and say that they can't possibly muster this kind of awareness! For some reason they think it is an exotic form of magic that is beyond their understanding. I, in the meantime, am pulling my hair out in frustration. Women, hear me on this; you have an advantage over men in this department. Men have been bullied into ignoring their feelings and cutting off one of their best hopes of survival. That old saw about women being more intuitive than men is what I'm talking about here. If you have it, the hardest part of the job is done already!

If you leave a portion of your awareness free to scan your surroundings, you seriously reduce your chances being unpleasantly surprised. In time, if I may use another analogy, certain things will mean as much to you as when you suddenly realize that your kids are being too quiet. (I used to get pegged a lot by that one, until I learned to make some noise while doing something that I shouldn't be doing. Don't whisper; that attracts attention because it's out of the normal. Talk normally; that way nobody will notice what you're doing.)

By leaving part of your awareness free to scan, you begin to look for certain patterns. Anytime that someone is setting up a pincer move should send bells of warning off in your head. A pincer move is when you are caught between two people and have no place to go. The thing about them is they take time to set up. Usually, when you realize that you're surrounded it's too late. You need to spot the people trying to circle you while they are doing it, not after they've succeeded.

If you see someone trying to put you into a pincer move, move out of it. This has a two-fold effect; one, it means that they're going to have to do more work to get you into a vulnerable position. That means more time and a better chance of something going wrong. The other effect is that they know that you're onto them. If you can do this calmly, the message is clear. You're not afraid of them, and you're going to be more trouble than it's worth if they try anything because they don't have surprise on their side. This seriously decreases their chances of getting away with whatever they're planning. If you suddenly realize that you are caught in a pincer move, like between two cars, scream like hell. (If you've got the keys in your hands, throw them over a few cars. You can go looking for them later.) You've just made life real difficult for them. They can't just shove you into the car and drive away. They'd first have to go looking for the keys, and that scream might have attracted attention. If they don't immediately back off, attack. Bring the war to one of them. Try and blast through; just get away and back into a safe area. I don't care how good someone is; trying to prevent a person who is in combat mode from getting past you is damn near impossible.

By getting past, I don't mean through. I mean past. Fake left, then strike right with a maiming blow and keep on running. If you think that a person with experience can't recognize when someone opens up the conversation with a move that could crush their thorax, you've been reading the wrong kind of books. I don't care how good someone is, those sort of moves are unnerving. The first reaction is to back out of range until they can make the gear shift to combat level. By that time you should be long gone.

You need to know what constitutes a trap. I've already told you to pretend to be a mugger for a month. Figure how you'd ambush somebody anyplace that you go. This will teach you how to spot potential ambushes. Certain things should set off warning bells.

Some guy hailing you or stepping in your way may be a trap. Flash him for four things. One: are both of his hands in plain view? If not, go ahead and bump it to Code Red. This doesn't mean cream him, just get out of there now.

Two: how close is he, and where? Did he just pop out of nowhere and into easy striking distance? Are you in front of an opening that, if he were to lunge, he could push you into? Did he pop out from an area where he easily could push you into another? Again, if he did, Code Red. Most locations can be foiled if you keep on moving. Look and see if you would have to veer past an area where someone else might be hiding. Like the guy who said of the thirty-three types of snakes in Vietnam, thirty-two of which are poisonous, "You can't afford to be a little discriminating."

The third thing to flash on is a little harder to define, but I'll try. What kind of vibes is he putting out? Is he uptight? Nervous? Stoned? Slimy? What is your impression of the person approaching you? If something "tings" down deep, don't ignore it! Code Red! The most common mistake people make is they ignore those little bells that go off when a dirtbag is around. Yes, first impressions are usually correct! If you think that someone is a dirtbag the first time you meet them in normal circumstances, the odds are they really are a dirtbag! It may be the sort of dirtbag that you can deal with, in which case, fine, but the guy is still a dirtbag. Just because he doesn't fuck you over doesn't mean that he isn't slime.

There is something about the people's eyes that you should learn not to ignore. A bastard has a streak of mean way back there. A hustler will look at people, when they think nobody is watching, with eyes that are calculating whether or not they can get away with running a number on someone and how big of one. To hell with the smile, the eyes will give someone away faster than anything else. Someone once said that "eyes are the window to the soul," and man is that true. Check the feeling you get from this person, and if it isn't good, go Red! If you're wrong, you can feel like a fool when you're in a safe area. I'd rather look like an asshole than give some people a chance to get near me. I've spun on total strangers and growled in the middle of a crowd. While it usually cleared the crowd away, it also got the smegma-breathed pussbucket away from me, too. Don't deny this aspect of yourself; it's your greatest chance of survival.

The fourth thing to flash someone for is: are they alone? If you're using your awareness, you'll be able, in time, to sense when you're being dropped into a pincer situation. If the guy steps out of an area, and you have time, look over your shoulder. Has someone else come out of the shadows? Is he trying to herd you into an ambush?

Check these things when the situation arises. If any of them fail to pass muster, it's Code Red, possibly Code Blue. When things like this happen, you have to rely on your own sense of self-preservation. If the guy is legitimate, he won't get uptight about you reacting that way.

Flash everyone, even if you know the person peripherally, like the janitor of your apartment or something. If the guy pops out of the shadows, he's suspect. Great, he's your neighbor, but do you really know the guy past nodding and saying "Hi" in the hallway? If, after you've reacted negatively to them being in the shadows, they try to get close to you, *don't relax!* Proper response from someone who startles you is "sorry," and leaving, or keeping their distance while trying to converse with you. If they try to get close, don't turn your back on them. If your door isn't open yet, don't open it. If it is, close it and turn around to talk with the person. Do nothing that removes your attention from that person. Don't fumble with your keys, groceries, purse, or what have you. If you have been surprised by someone in the shadows, you are Code Yellow! There have been more than a few people taken out this way. Flash the person; I don't care if he is your neighbor, janitor, or co-worker.

Flashing is like radar. You go "beep," and if all is right with the world, it will go "boop." If you go "beep," and it goes "blip," that means something isn't right out there. Until you can identify what is wrong, you keep alert. That's why I say even if you are aquainted with someone in passing, you should occasionally send out your little flash. The advantage of this regarding self-defense is obvious. The extra sensitivity that you'll pick up about people can be worth its weight in gold. Just because you flash someone doesn't mean that you're a paranoid who's expecting to be attacked. In time it becomes as natural as breathing.

Another way of thinking about flashing is this: it's looking at the gaps between the images that people want us to see. Sort of like watching what people are doing in between the times they are talking. Try that as an exercise to increase your flashing skills. Sit back and watch people when they don't think anybody is watching them. You'll learn a lot about them that way. Another thing you can do is, once you've got that part down, try and guess what they're thinking. With people that you know, you can ask. With people you don't know, just try and guess what's going on with them. Make the answer about a sentence long. Don't worry about being right, just get into the habit of doing it. These silly sounding little exercises might be just the slight edge of awareness that you need to save your life.

Going back to Code Yellow when you are out of sight of immediate help, let's look at it a little more closely. There are a couple of things about this that you can profit by in the long run. The first thing is, when you are in Code Yellow, you are paying attention to where you are. You're not hashing over the fact that you had a fucked day at work. You're not worrying about if the puce blouse with the lime green sweater really would transcend all limits of good taste. You are paying attention to what is really going on around you at the time. This means that you are living in the "here and now." (Those of you with a philosophical bent will catch onto what I just said.) Wherever you go, there you are. That means that you are in the real world.

Look for things that you've never seen before; they may be important for self-defense, or they may just be interesting by themselves. I've found some great bargain stores while waiting for bus connections when my cars or motorcycles were broken down. The really important thing is that it's a relaxing technique. By being aware, you've bought yourself time in case something happens. You don't have to worry about something popping out of nowhere. You can now recognize real from imagined threats. So, by being alert, you've earned some space to relax. I know it sounds screwy, but it's true; and I don't know anybody who in this day and age can't use some relaxation.

Now let's look at how to keep from getting surprised. Ninety-nine percent of this is learning how not to leave yourself in a vulnerable position. I may seem extreme in some of my habits in this regard, but I've been through more shit than you have, and everything that I do makes sense to anyone who has passed through similar situations. For example, when getting frisky with my old lady, I will not leave my pants around my ankles. The reason for this is that there has been more than one occasion of *crisis coitus interruptus* that has gotten me out of the sack in a hurry. It only took me tripping over my pants once to get me out of the habit of leaving them around my ankles. You can get this extreme if you want, but what I'm going to be talking about here isn't that far-fetched. In fact, it's sort of dull and drab in comparison.

Okay, the first thing is, know your weak spot, or to be more precise, know your blindspot. That's right, folks, we're talking about "watch your back." You really need to realize that your back is your biggest weak spot. Most of the nasty shit that happens comes from behind. That's because we don't have eyes in the back of our heads, in case you hadn't noticed. That means nasty, icky people will want to sneak up behind us and do damage to our little bodies.

Now, knowing that we have this weak/blind spot, we can proceed to cover it! Right, we're now aware of the biggest chink in our armor. Keep this in mind at all times, because nobody's immune from a blindshot! Remember me saying that? Well it's still true. If you think of your back in this manner, you will be less inclined to make mistakes regarding its protection. You may think that just reminding yourself to turn around at Automatic Teller Machines is enough. It isn't. You may be great about turning around at ATMs—and get taken out while opening the trunk of your car. If you are aware of the greater theory, you can easily manifest it into specifics.

Think about it; anytime that your attention is directed at something for a period of more than a few seconds, you are vulnerable from behind. Awareness of this will make you take steps to prevent anybody from utilizing it to their advantage. At a pay phone? Turn around and put your blind side against something solid. Even if you're with a friend who's on the phone, put your back to the wall. You can look at her just as easily from that position as facing the wall and leaving your ass unprotected, and the odds of anything happening are less.

At ATMs, keep on looking around. Turn your body at an angle. Is it really necessary to watch all the little letters that say thank you for using your ATM card? The guy probably won't hit you at the beginning of the transaction. What's he going to do, knock you down and ask what your code is so he can finish the transaction? Easier to slam into you as you're reaching for the money, kiddo.

When you come to your car with your arms full of bags, look around before you do anything else. Set the bags down on the ground, then turn your back to your car before you root around in your purse for your keys. They tell you it's better to walk around with your keys in your hand, and maybe it is. One thing is for sure, though; if you forget to have your keys out, turning your back to your car before you go into your purse is a whole lot easier than getting jumped.

A security building? Aside from there being no such thing except in the minds of people who also believe in Santa Claus and the Easter Bunny, a security building is a great place to get nailed. When you approach the locked door, having forgotten to have your little keys ready, turn your back to the door instead of the bushes. Also, scan the bushes. If you hear anything, go to Code Red! When you go to your front door in an apartment building, check out the hallway before going for your keys. If your apartment door is at or near an intersection, look and see if there are evildoers slinking about around the corner.

Basically, it is awareness of how easy it is to approach someone from behind that will keep you from getting caught by it yourself. Don't expect a miracle about this. It isn't something that will suddenly pop full bloom into your head and you will know what to do in every situation. It's something that will take time to cultivate. First, be aware that your back is your blindest spot. Instead of scolding yourself when you forget, congratulate yourself for remembering. Even if you've been sitting there for fifteen minutes, you still remembered. In time it will become instinctive.

The next part that I want to cover, especially for women, is your home. Let's start by saying I'm against having a gun as your home defense. The main reason is because a gun is a purely offensive weapon. I don't care what they say: a gun can only shoot people, it can't protect you. That may sound weird, but I hope that by the time I'm done here you'll understand.

First, let's look at what you can do to make your house harder to get into. Most normal window locks suck. You know the type: on top of the lower window is the part that spins, and on the bottom of the upper window is the clasp. All you need to get through those suckers is a hacksaw blade and some patience. The crack between the windows is wide enough to slip the hacksaw blade through and to jimmy, not cut, the lock open. To do it silently is about a five minute operation, then slither right in through the open window. The guy doesn't need to know how to pick locks or anything, all he needs is about a buck fifty to get a hacksaw blade or something equally strong.

You can foil this type of break-in by installing the little sliding stops that sit further up the window frame. There are a few kinds; the ones I prefer are sort of hard to find but worth the search. The same knob that keeps the window from being opened tightens down so it can't be moved by the trick the guy used on the first lock. His only other option is to bust the window or, if he's a real sophisticate, cut the glass, either of which is sort of noisy. For sliding glass doors and windows, a simple long dowel laid the length of the runner will prevent the window or door from being opened quietly. Maybe he could get through after picking the lock, but he'd have to break the dowel with the door. The dowel should be long enough so someone can't slip their hand through and remove it.

The all-time worst form of security window is louvered window. You know the sort that they like to put in the bathroom, with slats that you control with a little lever. Those suckers are almost like asking to have your house broken into. All you have to do is jimmy them open, extremely easy, and remove the slats, even easier. There are only two things I can suggest other than getting the damned things replaced. One, if it's the bigger type that has two sections, superglue the slats into place on the bottom and, with wire, not string, wire down the lever to the bottom frame. That way you can still leave the top one free to be opened. Anyone trying to come in would have to bust out the slats, and that makes a lot of noise.

If you have the smaller type of louvered window with only one set of slats, take a board the size of the outer windowsill and drive a large number of nails and screws through it. (If insecticide somehow gets sprayed all over these punji sticks, I don't know how you got the idea.) Then screw or nail it to the outside of the sill (screws are better). Pour glue over the screw heads and along the side of the boards, which makes it real noisy to get off. Since this isn't a ledge that kitty usually sits on, you should have no problem. (This trick is a variation on what we called "Mexican barbwire." Years past, some of the more wealthy families built walls around their estates. Along the top of these walls were broken bottles set in concrete, making climbing over the wall rather difficult.) Getting through the window has now become a bit of a bother. Not only that, it lets whoever is trying to get in realize that there might be some bloodthirsty types who live there.

The next trick is a string of bells on the inside of your door. This way, if the door is opened you will hear it. After a time you'll become accustomed to the bell sounding. If it opens at the wrong time, your internal alarms will go off.

You may have noticed that what I have been talking about really won't stop someone who is determined to get in. That's true, but what I have done is brought you to a place where someone can't get in quietly. This is where I bring up the subject of home defense.

There are going to be a number of people who will think I'm nuttier than hell for saying what I'm about to say, but I'm going to say it anyway. Women, I think your best home defense weapon is a sword. There are a variety of reasons why I say this. The first and foremost is safety, not only for you but others. Whether you have roommates, boyfriends/husbands, or children, it all boils down to one thing; it's harder to accidently kill someone with a sword than it is with a gun.

In order for a gun to be effective, it has to be loaded. If it's loaded, the odds are greater that a loved one, rather than a burglar, will get shot. Unless everybody in the house has gun safety drilled into them so well that it's second nature, the odds for an accident are incredible. Unless everybody knows exactly what they're doing with a gun, it's inviting trouble. Shit, I know what I'm doing, and I once blew a hole in the fucking floor with a shotgun.

People don't realize how much damage a gun can do. A bullet

travels! I was in a house where they claimed to know gun safety, and I looked across the room and down the barrel of a loaded 9mm that was being casually examined by the owner and his brother. I nearly ripped their fucking heads off for that. I don't feel that a handgun is a good choice for home defense in the hands of someone who doesn't have a high level of competence with one.

What I mean by that level of competence is this: once I went to a range with some friends. Let's be polite; we had been drinking heavily. Nah, let's not; we were shitfaced drunk. I mean, we were so blotto that we staggered up to the firing line. *But*—the second we picked up a gun, all traces of drunkenness disappeared. Our hands ran through the loading, firing, and safety operations with ease and perfection. When we finished with our clips, we set the guns down and staggered away, utterly blasted. Now, I have no doubt that we weren't as tight as I would like to remember, but the simple truth was that, even drunk, the laws of handgun safety and handling were so well-ingrained that they overcame our inebriation for the time that the guns were in our hands. Unless everyone in the house is that good with guns, it's a bad idea to have them around. The families that have guns in the Midwest know how to use them. Little children are trained how to handle guns correctly from scratch. These are the only children I think are even close to safe around guns.

Now back to the sword as a home defense weapon for women. Aside from the fact that accidently hurting someone seriously with a sword is damn near impossible, the other advantage is that it's always ready for use. If you leave it lying under or behind your bed, it is always handy in case someone tries to break in. You don't have to fumble after bullets, etc. Once you have that blade in your hand, you are ready.

The next nice thing about a sword is, unlike a baseball bat, it's a bad idea for an attacker to rush it. A three and a half foot long straight razor is not something that you charge. Also, unlike a bat, it's not the brightest move someone can make to try and grab it away from you—unless they're really keen on the idea of getting busted down to raccoon status. You know: all the mischief, and no opposable thumbs to do it with. You can also lunge extremely effectively with a sword. Baseball bats don't get the point across as well. I don't care if he's got a leather jacket on, a lunge will go through it. All of this adds up and keeps any intruder at a serious distance from you.

In case you're going, "But what if he has a gun?" there are two points that I'd like to bring up. One, if he has the gun out already: ever tried to order your finger to pull a trigger when your hand is laying on the floor two feet away? Anywhere you strike with a sword will do enough damage that it's going to distract the son of a bitch a little. Two, if he has it in a holster or pocket, you know that you're never to let his hands out of sight. If he goes for it and you're within ten feet of him, he's worm food.

The final thing that I like about swords as home defense weapons is a matter of severity. One of the reasons that women don't like guns very much is that once you pull the trigger, you have no control over what happens. You can't control whether you're going to wound or kill an intruder. Wounding someone with a gun at point-blank range is a little hard to do. That bullet is traveling at some hellacious speed and the impact is rather fierce. If you're not quite ready to accept killing someone in the defense of self and home, you can just maim 'em with a sword. A foot and a half of steel through the gut will take the fight out of damn near anybody. Lop off his hand when he's reaching out to grab you—that'll teach him to keep his hands to himself. Laying some guy's thigh open with a ten-inch gash will make sure he hangs around until the police come. "Were you in fear of your life?" "He got close enough for me to nail him with a sword. He was obviously attacking, officer."

The real nice thing about swords is, unlike guns, if the guy is in the process of coming through the window you can just poke him. Three inches of steel through the shoulder will louse up the guy's career for a while. Incidentally, aim for his right side. Since most people are right-handed, any damage to that side of the body will usually prevent them from effectively retaliating. Try sticking your finger in your pectoral muscle (the muscle under your boob), and then try to raise your arm. If you're doing it right, it'll hurt. The same thing is applicable with blade wounds. If you're stabbed one place, it affects a whole different set of muscles that are connected in ways that you never noticed until you got stuck. This is going to be a constant reminder to the guy for about six weeks, if you do it right. So poke the guy in his right side and louse up his day.

You may have to take someone out in close quarters where there isn't much room to swing, like in a hallway. If this should occur, keep the flat of your blade horizontal when you lunge. That way it won't wedge between ribs and get stuck. If the guy manages to twist aside and the blade doesn't strike home all the way, he might be able to hang on long enough to do some damage to you. Remember: get out as fast as you went in.

In close quarters, like going around corners and such, hold the blade upright and close to your body, edge pointing the same way as your nose is. If the guy jumps out of somewhere and tries to grab you, you can sort of punch with the sword's edge. It's not as effective as a swing, but it'll still do damage. Whatever you do, don't lead through a door or around the corner with your weapon. Keep it tight and near to your body. This goes for guns, too.

The final thing that I like about swords is that you can pick up a decent quality blade for about $50 in some of the bigger gun stores. I recommend sabres for a variety of reasons. One, you can usually get the guy to throw in a sheath for only a little bit more or for free. Two, it's easier to get a quality blade. The charming, cheapo "Samurai" or "Cost Plus Toledo Specials" that abound don't hold an edge for spit because they aren't actual swords. Get a real sword and pay some key maker five dollars to put an edge on it. If you want to get real hi-tech about it, put black matte of primer on the blade after sharpening. That way light won't reflect off it. In the dark, the guy won't know what he's up against, which is definitely to your advantage.

Weapons

Heh, heh, heh. You guys and your guns. Give me a dark night and a knife, and your asses are mine.

Me, putting an end to a conversation
that had turned into defining manhood
by rounds per minute.

Here we get into undoubtedly the messiest portion of fighting. It is also the most confusing. The thing about weapons is, people forget that everything has weak points and blindspots. The most common mistake about weapons is that people are either too afraid of them or too reliant on them. The next most common mistake is using the wrong one—or using the right one incorrectly.

The "too afraid" part is obvious, but what about being "too reliant" on a weapon? Right weapon, wrong time. What? Let me bore you with another war story. I was shooting pool in a pool hall when some guy walked up and pulled a knife on me. Actually, it wasn't that arbitrary; there were about three lines of dialogue exchanged before he whipped open his knife. Since I was trying to line up a shot at the time, I was bent over the table trying to ignore the guy. Mind you, I had a pool cue in my hands. When he flicked open his Buck, I dropped the pool cue and seized his right hand with my left and grabbed him somewhere near his abdomen with my right. I then picked him up and slammed him down on the pool table. The fact that there had been no previous signal until the knife showed up meant that he had the thing in his hand when he approached me. They threw him out, and I went into the bathroom and threw up. I love surprises that get my adrenalin up like that. How come Clint Eastwood or someone like that never throws up after violence?

This story is a prime example of the two most common mistakes regarding weapons. First, his mistake. He wasn't expecting someone to fight *him,* he was expecting me to fight (or be frightened by) his weapon. I was fighting a man with a knife instead of fighting a knife. Do you see the difference? The best example of fighting the person instead of the weapon was when I saw my friend (I'm not saying who, because he'd still get in trouble) square off against some guy knife to knife. There was a momentary pause before my friend busted the guy's kneecap with a kick. End of fight. We went and had a beer.

Most people think a weapon makes them invincible and invulnerable. Bullshit. A weapon is nothing more than an extension. If you try and use it as anything else, you'll lose against anyone who knows what they are doing. All the rules of fighting don't suddenly cease to exist because someone decides not to be an ape and use a tool.

The second mistake in the poolroom incident is far less obvious. It involves range. I had a pool cue; why didn't I hit him with it? Simple; he was too close. He was about a foot and a half from me. From the position I was in and the distance he was from me, it would have taken more space (and more time) than I had available to make an effective strike. A pool cue is really effective from two to four feet. If I had tried to shift and strike with the cue, I would have ended up with a knife in the gut. I was in knife range, not staff range. So think: do you have enough time and space to bring something into play before the guy can stop you?

Every weapon has its effective range. A guy with a knife, who is four feet away, isn't really much of a threat. If he moves into range, yes, he's a threat, but not if you can keep him four feet away (barstools are a good way to convince people to keep

their distance). A guy with a baseball bat at four feet is
something to worry about—but have you ever tried to wrestle
while holding onto a baseball bat? Guns are rather interesting.
I can't deflect a bullet that is fired from across the room. I
can, however, deflect the gun itself if it's stuck in my face. A
gun in a grappling situation with a knife is not a good bet.
A knife against a gun from across the room isn't the best odds,
either. These are the two most common manifestations of a
much more serious mistake: lack of thinking.

You will encounter many people who think that a weapon
replaces thinking. A weapon is only good if you get a chance
to use it. This is why I dislike guns. Most people get a gun and
immediately go stupid. Having a gun in a shoulder holster is
fine, as long as you don't button your jacket. (Don't laugh, it
happens. Also, women, don't put a weapon in your purse. Think
of how long it takes you to find your wallet in there at times.
A mugger isn't going to wait while you rummage around trying
to find something to blow a hole in his chest.) This is what
I call the first of Animal's Laws of weapons: *A weapon doesn't
replace thinking!* Also, keep your mouth shut. If I know a
person has a weapon, he's never going to get a chance to get
to it. The second his hand goes for it, I'm going to land on
him—hard. If someone knows you have a weapon, they're going
to hit you from behind. The bigger the weapon, the harder the
hit. Nobody is immune from a shotgun blast while getting out
of their car. If you mouth off about your gun, that's what you
can get. People get extreme about guns; they get less extreme
about knives, but they still get extreme.

Law number two is: *Don't carry a weapon unless you really
know how to use it!* If we're talking about a gun, don't think
you know how to use it just because you go to the range.
Combat shooting is a little different from target. If it's in your
area, go play Photon. If not, Survival Games with paint balls
will put your dick in line real quick. If nothing else, grab an
air BB gun and go shoot it out with someone likewise armed.
They hurt like hell and put you in touch with how different
combat is from the range. Then you'll run out and take a

combat shooting course.

With a knife, unless you get real training, not just an after-noon reading a book, you can get it taken away from you. I *still* sit in front of the TV and twirl knives. After all these years, I keep up on my drilling. I've heard of another guy who would go home from school and practice throwing them. The other kids would go out and hang around; he'd go off and practice. What I'm saying is, unless you are as intimate with your weapon as you are with your dick, you're asking for trouble. That means that the use of whatever weapon you have should be damn near instinctive to you. You want to know how to spot a good knife fighter? He's the guy bored shitless in the laundromat who is drawing, twirling, and resheathing his knife without looking at the sheath. He instinctively and at all times knows where his weapon is.

Law number three: *Don't carry a weapon unless you're going to pull it. Don't pull it unless you're going to use it. Don't use it unless you're going to kill with it.* I think that this should be self-evident. Weapons are used to maim or kill. If you're going to carry one, be ready to use it in this manner. If you want to scare people with a weapon, you better put it away and go play with blocks instead, because you're not ready for weapons. You also better expect your weapon not to work now and then, or for your opponent to overkill on you because you scared him too effectively. This is a matter of accepting respon-sibility. When you strap on that weapon, you are accepting the responsibility of that action may be leading to the death of another human being or yourself. I've known the stench of blood in my nose too many times for me to try and make it soft. Weapons are all too real.

The fourth law I've already mentioned in the Fight vs. Combat chapter: *Don't kill unless it's absolutely necessary!* The reasons for this include a tendency towards mental laziness, guilt, a callousness of the soul that makes you unwelcome at cocktail parties, and a fucked up judicial system. Knowing that last one, you can make decisions regarding if you want to involve the police or not. A junkie turning up with broken knees and no witnesses is one of the best crime deterrents that I know of. Word gets around to leave you and yours alone. My cousin almost got busted for slamming the car door on some guy trying to steal his stereo. Yet the biker who manages the building next to his has had no problems ever since there were a number of gun shots that coincided with him walking down the alley back from a rock house with a baseball bat and .44 magnum. The thing is, this is outside of the law, and if you step out there, you can't go running to the police if it gets ugly. Hopefully, you live in a state where shooting a burglar won't end up getting you sued if he lives. In areas where that exists, I've known cops who say: waste him. Maybe you can wing him and drop him off somewhere else. That situation is a little tricky, and I can't really advise you on every situation. Like I said, though, your life will usually remain easier if you don't kill in a conflict.

Keeping these four laws in mind, you can keep from making the most common mistakes. After that, the boo-boos are a little less obvious but just as critical. After the two previously mentioned mistakes, the most common mistake I know of is lack of knowledge as to what really constitutes a threat. Let's look at knives in particular for this example. In this case, a real threat is a real knife fighter. Most people, when they grab a knife, either wildly slash or stab. When they are doing this they forget that if they only use the knife, they only have up to six inches that are effective. Six inches! That ain't shit! As a trained fighter, what makes you dangerous is this: spread your arms and spin around. Now add another foot to the radius of the circle for kicks. Figure in your height, and sum up all of that space. *That* is your immediate effective range. If you throw in mobility, the space that you are effective in is incredible. Next to that, six inches is nothing.

With an amateur, if you are outside of that six inch range, you're safe. If you're inside that range, he's in some deep shit. A wild stab is even less effective. The area you have to avoid is a two inch tunnel. Step aside and in against an amateur and it's over. Anybody who only uses the knife is setting themselves up for sudden disaster. Also, here's a rule of thumb. If you see the knife in the guy's hand, he's probably an amateur. With a pro, the odds are you'll never see the thing until it's too late. The Special Forces form I know hides the knife by the knee. A Chinese style hides the knife edge out along the back of the forearm. A Philipino hides the Balisong in the palms of his hands. All most people ever hear is the "clickity-clack" before they are cut.

Watch the subtleties of how a pro handles a knife. He will only be flashy when he wants to be, which has its advantages. I was once walking down a dark street when some guy stepped out of the shadows. He looked at me a stepped back into the shadows. I passed where he was hiding and continued on. He stepped back out and began to follow me. Since this was in Hollywood, the implications were obvious. I pulled my knife out of its sheath and spent about thirty seconds twirling and flipping it in my hand, then jammed it back into my sheath, all while still walking. When I looked back over my shoulder, the guy was gone. I wasn't making wild gestures—the knife was a shiny blur in a mobile two foot area. He just knew he was seriously outclassed.

The thing was, the guy was an amateur; he needed to be shown that little display before he realized he shouldn't mess with me. The motions were flashy, yes, but they were also tight. If I had swung my arms about and tried to make a bigger production, it might not have worked. If someone pulls a knife with a grand flourish that leaves them wide open and is of questionable hand work, that tells you something. If the knife somehow slides into their hand out of nowhere and is barely visible, that tells you to get the hell out of there now!

I once scared the shit out of a knife maker's assistant when he handed me back my blade. I twirled it and dropped it into my sheath while looking at, and talking to, his boss. His flinch at the speed and ease with which I had done it attracted both of our attention. That is how obvious—and subtle—these signs can be.

A good fighter works from the wrist and fingers; watch how they handle a knife from these points. Someone who carries a foot and a half long pigsticker and handles it like a club is less of a threat than the little Oriental guy who has a butterfly knife tucked into his pants. It doesn't mean that you can't get hurt; it just means that you have a better chance of surviving against the ape with the pigsticker. Also, watch how easily the person with a weapon holds it. Does he hold it like it is an old friend that he knows real well? If yes, throw something at him and run like hell. If no, maybe you have a chance.

By the way, there is a reason why I say to take a chance against an armed opponent. Up to now I have stressed, "Hey, run away. It's easier." While I still believe in that, there are times that you have to make a stand. If you are walking with someone and a mugger with a knife shows up, you have somewhat of a dilemma. You may have to hold the attacker off so the other person can make an escape. The only thing between someone you love and possible death sometimes boils down to one thing—you.

As an aside, anybody you are with should know what to do if a situation arises. I have nearly been killed more than once because the person I was with moved wrong and I had to bail us both out. When you move into action, they should know to get the hell out of danger. This doesn't mean turn around and run back the way you've both come. Since many bad guys work in pairs, turning around and running is going to put them in the arms of the backup. This means you have to be in two places at once. One is saving your ass; the other is saving theirs. They should boogie into the middle of the street and start running from there. (As another aside, don't yell "help," yell "fire" or something. People are less likely to help a mugging victim, because they think they can get hurt more than they can with fire. It's stupid, but true.) If you are in a confined area, blasting past while you're attacking the assailant might have to do. Don't brook any lip on this; unless they are trained, you'll end up covering their ass as well. They may want to help, but that kind of help can get you both killed.

Up to this point, I have pretty much told you in a weird, meandering way about my philosophy on weapons. Except for knives, I really haven't told you what to do about different kinds. People will tell you this weapon is great and that weapon is shit. The truth is, they all have serious weaknesses.

Nunchucks, those old Bruce Lee specials, are pathetically easy to disarm. Hit the chain or rope; that's it. The pivot point is the weakest point. I saw a wisp of a woman take a pair away from a hotshot black belt by snapping a towel into the chain. I've heard of an old guy who, while sitting cross-legged, leaned forward with his cane and basically snagged a pair right out of the hands of the kid swinging them. A handful of dirt in the eyes followed by a kick to the groin gets their attention, too.

Tonfas, those funny sticks with a handle rising out of them, are especially popular with the police. I won't be when I say just hit the guy's hand when he spins one. If he strikes, counterpunch into his hand. Don't block the stick. The hand is the weakest part of that operation. Go after it.

Clubs, sticks, baseball bats, etc.: figure out what their effective range is and get inside of it. The main impact of a baseball bat is out three or so feet. If you rush it and grab the person's hand as he swings, it seriously slows him down. The other option is to get out of range when they swing. If they swing expecting to connect with something (like your head) and miss, they often are off balance and continue on. By the time they stop all of that energy and try to turn it around, you can be inside their guard drumming a neat beat on their head. With most clubs, crossing is real good. Get out of the way long enough not to get hit, then step in.

A serious weapon in some people's hands is grandma's cane. I have seen cane-fighting before, and it is a bitch to deal with. If you're going to carry a weapon, check into this. In the hands of someone who knows what they're doing, you have a club, a hooking and trapping weapon, as well as a quarterstaff. Their only weakness that I know of is they take a whole lot of practice before they become effective close up. Up to that point, they are susceptible to being grabbed. There is a movie called *The Big Brawl*, which, aside from being a beautiful example of kung fu technique (God, I hate that phrase. The proper term is Gung

Fu, and it means time spent in study of something. Sorry, minor pisser of mine.), shows what a cane can do. The cane in the hands of the uncle is absolutely incredible as a weapon. Watch it and you can begin to see what you can do with one.

A butterfly knife is susceptible to a blow to the hand while it's being opened. As he's flicking it open, whap him one across the paw. Actually, this is true of all knives in the hands of amateurs. Get past the blade and grab the wrist from behind. Twist the knife hand while hitting the person. Twisting something out of someone's hand is incredibly easy if you know how the hand works. There's a thing to watch with knife fighters though: a good one uses the whole knife. If you try to disarm an expert the way I just told you, he'll rip you with the tip of the knife. Those are ragged and painful, because a backslash with the tip doesn't cut, it rips. If you're in a situation where you're up against someone with a knife, the safest (but not always possible) way to grab it is from the side where the blade isn't. If the person has the blade coming from the same side of his hand that his thumb is, you grab his wrist on the side that his pinky is on. This leaves you in less shit if your grab is less than accurate. If you try to grab on the top side, unless you muckle onto his wrist just right and immobilize it, you are leaving yourself open to a point rip. In the event that you have no choice but to grab the wrist on the blade side, a kick to the nuts or something equally unpleasant should land no more than a half-second later. This will prevent the person from getting you with the tip. If you realize that you've goofed and grabbed on too high, you can try sliding your grip down a bit, but do it fast.

Good knife fighters are also quick to use the handle as a Yara stick. A quick back blow from a knife handle can leave you on the floor out cold. So if it looks like the person has made a mistake and left himself open for a rush, keep your guard up when you go in.

As an aside, if you are the executive type, do what my friend Doc does. He carries a balisong in a neat, velcro-closed belt pack. It sits nicely under his suit jacket without a bulge. He can take off his jacket, and all he has is a little black vinyl pouch; no weapons that can scare people. Check it out in your state, though. In some places that's illegal and we all know *I'd never advocate doing anything wrong.* (Como say dee say bullshit?)

Chains, in the hands of the untrained, are first-strike weapons only. They have no defense advantages at all. If the person knows what he is doing, however, a chain can become a blend between a short staff, lasso, and garrote. If the person doesn't know what he is doing, either strike first or throw something at him. A frisbeed trash can lid can really ruin some guy's day.

Now that I mentioned trash can lids, let's look at them. Captain America! An impromptu shield! Shield fighting is an old trick—make a move and strike with the edge of your shield. If the block works, the shield is now inside the guard of the person who has just thrown a blow. That lid is just raring to go as a counterpunch (hint hint). Another aspect of this: plastic trash can lids can be punctured by a blade, but it's harder to get the blade out than it is in. A knife stuck in a trash can lid is just that.

Anything can be used along these lines. There was a guy named Miyamoto Musashi, who many people think was a sword saint. You hear them saying, "He was so good that he began to use wooden practice swords in his duels instead of real ones, and he always won." Yep, old Miyamoto was damn good. Not too many people realize, however, that a real sword will cut into a piece of wood and stick there. Then he'd brain the fucker with his other club while the guy's sword was trapped. Evil bastard—just the kind I respect. A great role model for students of PIBU.

Shuriken. Aside from dodging, your best defense is a heavy jacket. The thing to know about "stars" is that these days they are a setup move. Originally they were heavier and poisoned; they could kill you. Now, they are just a pisser. The thing hits you and it hurts; it also distracts you. Rip it out and throw it back at him. Let him worry about ducking it. If you're hit, ignore the pain, because if he knows what he's doing, he'll be following through with an attack.

There is also, of course, Hollywood's greatest gift, the broken bottle. The thing is, Hollywood doesn't show you how it's really done. You see the snarling coward grab a bottle and shatter the end against the table before he lunges toward the hero. Couple of basics here, kids. Nine times out of ten the bottle is going to bounce off whatever someone hits it against. Most tables aren't hard enough to bust a bottle. Most things in a house aren't either. Trying to bust a bottle off anything made of wood is a waste of time. Also, it is A) embarrassing when it bounces off, and B) dangerous, because the guy will know what you're up to and hit you hard and fast. So if you're going to use a bottle, hit concrete or something metal.

Another thing about breaking bottles is that you don't just use your arm; you have to snap your wrist to get up to speed. It's a whip, not the grand gesture that you see on the silver screen. The most important thing to know about using a bottle is that you're going to get hurt—glass is unpredictable when it breaks. You can smash a bottle and have it sliver down to nothing in your hand. In case you didn't catch what I just said, your "weapon" could disintegrate and slice you up real bad. The other thing is, when you bust a bottle, even if it doesn't completely fall apart, there will be glass shards flying. You *will* get cut! I once saw a guy without much experience bust a bottle, and then drop it in surprise—he caught glass in his eye. So look away when you do it. Nobody needs to be blind.

That's busting bottles. Using them as a club is another story. If a guy has a bottle in his hand and he shifts his grip so his thumb is against the body rather than the mouth, hit him. Hit him hard and fast, because he's getting ready to use it as a club. This isn't the only way to strike with a bottle, though. If the guy is holding it normally and crosses his body with that hand, he could be winding up for a backhand strike. The ballistics of a half-filled bottle are perfect for throwing, so watch somebody's partner.

You're likely to encounter all of these weapons and more. The thing is, most people don't want to dispel the mystique of weapons. You're supposed to go "Oooh!" when they show you how good they are with a weapon. You're not supposed to disarm them that easily. It kind of removes their "superiority" over you. When I started this chapter, I said that most people rely too much on a weapon. That is what I meant. You, with training and awareness, are superior over them, if you use what you have between your ears.

When dealing with weapons, it really depends on the situation. If you remember what I have told you and what you learn in your training, you'll increase your odds of surviving.

Martial Arts vs. Streetfighting

I'm looking for an honor guard into Valhalla, fuckers!
Me, while a bouncer, to about twelve rowdies
who decided I was serious and settled down.

Recently, I was watching the PKA (Professional Karate Association) Featherweight Championship title bout. It was so pretty I almost threw up. Those guys, with what they were doing, would be turned into dogmeat against a good street-fighter. This was the bout for the title.

Yet 90 percent of all good streetfighters I have ever met know some form of martial arts. This can include boxing, wrestling, military service, or the most common—plain old sparring with a number of other trained people. So, what gives? Are martial arts good for anything? The answer is yes—and no.

Martial arts are like a tool; good for some jobs and not for others. You wouldn't use a hammer to take off a nut. (Okay, okay, I've done it, too, but this is an analogy, alright.) Nor would you try to drive a nail with a socket wrench (yeah, I know, but let's stick with the analogy).

Anyway, when you study a "form" or "style" of martial arts, you have to realize that there are things that are not covered by it. The same goes with this book. There are aspects of self-defense that I didn't get around to mentioning. You, if you're fond of breathing, have to go and find out what I meant by things I've said here. Also, you have to find out about things I didn't say. This means you have to make the journey of discovery. I'm telling you that they are there; you have to find them. The reason I'm doing it this way is because when you're done, you'll really know these things. They won't be just intellectual concepts, they'll be part of your awareness. The same goes with your knowledge of what a style *doesn't* cover.

What I want to do with this chapter is cover the generic weak points of many of the martial arts. This will give you an idea of what you must protect yourself against when you learn them. A lot of it is rehashing of what I said earlier, but you now have a different awareness, so you can apply it differently.

I mentioned the chump...er...championship bout because I'm going to use it as an example. First off, I want to say, as sarcastic as I'm being about martial art bouts, they're better learning tools than "chop socky flicks" because they're real. The movies are nice, but they're choreographed. That means they throw in a lot of shit that looks good but is sheer, unmitigated horseshit. My old lady is amused by me when we watch them. (Ya know, sprawled on the couch on a rainy afternoon, beer in hand, with your feet squirreled away under her thighs to keep them warm.) She is amused because I sit there unconsciously going, "yep...nope...uuh-huh...well...yep... wrong." I do the same with the bouts.

The thing to remember about the bouts is *they have rules.* Break these rules and you're out; do it enough and you're out of the entire profession. Now there are rules with certain types of fights, as we've discussed earlier. If the guy feels too threatened, however, he'll break 'em and try to win. The problem is, that escalates it to serious shit. Those friendly fights in Texas have resulted in more people in prison for murder than you'd believe. The good ol' boy feels threatened and goes for his knife. That's how come you don't want to beat him by too much. The rules about streetfights are more often broken, and the results are much worse. Most people don't understand this. You do, so don't escalate it. If the other guy does, it's self-defense on your part. The courts are sort of twitchy even about that these days, though, so watch yourself.

Anyway, back to the bouts. One of the first things that I noticed about the bouts was that the participants were, by my standards, extremely sloppy about their footwork. By bout standards, their footwork was great. Problem: in bouts, ball shots are *verboten.* Same with dojo training. What does this lead to? Uuuh-huh, you got it. These guys weren't instinctively covering their nuts with their footwork. Wrongo, kiddies! That's one of the first things most streetfighters look for—a chance to snake one in on the old family jewels. Your footwork should always cover the old nuggets. (By the way, this applies to women, as well. Impact on the spinal cord by the pelvis is mostly what causes the pain that we all know and dread. This is also why a sharp blow to the muscles of the neck feels about the same as a kick to the nuts. Women are just as susceptible to crotch shots as men.) Your footwork should always protect you in this regard. Most people get about ten blows into a fight and forget their footwork. The eleventh blow ends the fight, with a serious case of nausea and tender McNuggets for a week. Until it becomes instinctive, and you've learned kick blocks (blocking a kick with a kick or other leg movement), pay more attention to protective footwork than kicking.

There *is* a difference between street and dojo. People think that they just shift over from one to the other. No you can't! The body has learned these moves, and it takes a long time (try years) to make the shift effectively. So when you go into the dojo, pretend you're in a streetfight, and always watch your footwork. The other thing about correct footwork is that it keeps you from getting a busted knee.

Before I go further, I'm going to have to explain something: by correct footwork, I mean the *concepts* involved in correct footwork, *not the form.* This is a subtle, but important, distinction. The concept of correct footwork is threefold: 1) it protects your balls at all times; 2) it protects your knees, feet, and ankles; 3) it retains your balance and mobility. Keep these concepts in mind, and whatever form your footwork takes, it will be correct, even if it mutates away from the footwork of your formal style. In a fight, the formal footwork of a particular style might have to be chucked out entirely if you're interested in surviving. In fact, I've only fought on open level ground a few times. All that neat footwork I had learned on a flat mat didn't do me a bucket of piss worth of good when I was fighting on an uphill slope or in a multi-level situation (driveway, curb, sidewalk, and street).

To this end, I suggest a few things. One is practice everywhere you can. This means on stairs, in alleys, in your front room (dance around between the coffee table and couch; it'll let you know about limiting your moves while not stepping on the cat), on slick surfaces and rough ones, and over surfaces with clutter that you could trip over. The other thing is, keep it in the back of your mind when sparring that the guy might throw a ballshot at any time. You begin to think this way, and you'll begin to protect one of your most valuable assets instinctively.

Another thing I noticed about the PKA boys is that clenching and throwing are no-nos. This means that the guys in the ring go way in the fuck off balance. I mean, any judo boy would dribble these chumps with the way they overextend themselves. This is something that you have to watch for in your training. If there is a move that puts you off balance or leaves you with your dick flapping in the wind, get rid of it, especially if it's an attack! Don't ever attack out of balance or overextended. If the style you study tries to promote something like that, drop it faster than an annoyed tarantula. Whenever you are learning an attack, run it by this criteria: A) Does it allow you someplace else to go in case something goes wrong? In other words, if it doesn't work are you left wide open? B) Does it put you in a position where someone can easily drag you off balance and onto your face? C) Does it require your opponent to do something special before it is effective? In other words, does the guy have to quack six times, hop to the left, and extend his left arm at a 45 degree angle before this move will work? If it does, forget it.

In a real fight, the guy hardly ever does the preamble work for you. You need to look for holes in his defense, not wait for him to move a certain way so that you can do a certain type of attack. This is why most martial artists lose in an actual fight. They're waiting for the guy to move in a way that they were trained to handle. The problem is, the guy doesn't know he's supposed to move just so; he goes off and does something entirely different and fucks up everything. Maybe you could explain to him that he's supposed to extend his arm a certain way so you can move in with a blinding blur of devastating kicks and blows that is guaranteed to bring any attacker to a state of bloody submission. Somehow, I don't think the guy's going to be sympathetic, though.

If the attack that you're learning doesn't pass those three points, file it in the round file. Trying to use stuff that fails this criteria will get you hurt bad in a real fight. Whenever you are taught something in the dojo, spend about half the time figuring out how to fuck it up. What can you do that would make that particular move ineffective? Don't get fancy; stepping back is often the best answer. When you practice this sort of thing, you'll get another benefit from it. If, when you make a move, you feel the guy begin to shift in a way that you know will counter the move, you can change your plans. That's another reason why so many martial artists lose in real fights; they were never trained to deal with the unexpected. I've taken out more than a few martial artists because they didn't know what it felt like when something began to go wrong. Many of these people were technically better than I was. What would happen, though, is they'd feel a shift that was different and keep going anyway. By the time they caught on that something had gone wrong, they were on the way out. Don't let this happen to you!

If something happens you don't recognize, *get out!* Trying to jam a square peg in a round hole isn't a good idea anyway; in a fight it can get you killed. If you know how a counter feels to a particular move, when you feel it, you can counter the counter. The concept is rather different than the way most people have been trained to think, but learning to understand what a move will mean three steps down the line is incredibly important in regard to fighting.

Another thing that I noticed about the PKA match I was watching was the participants utterly disregarded the rule about kicking above the waist. Add in turning their backs to their opponents and you have some wonderful habits. I do have to admit that I saw a rather humorous example of why you don't do those things. One of the guys threw a spinning heel kick to the head as his opponent stepped forward. What happened was, the kicker's leg wrapped around the other guy's shoulder. As the other guy walked forward, he caused the kicker to go into a split. The kicker fell over, and the ref stepped in and broke it up. In a fight, falling like that means you're going to get stomped real bad.

They don't allow trapping in the matches, either. That means that nobody does what is real common in streetfighting. Throw a high kick, and the guy catches your leg and lifts it. End of conversation. Either you get ripped groin ligaments and he kicks the shit out of you, or you go down and he kicks the shit out of you. Isn't that easy? All because you kicked high.

Another thing is that, since the kidneys and back of the head are off limits as targets, the participants are a little crazy about turning their back to opponents. It only takes one good kidney punch to let you know why you shouldn't turn your back. They were real bad about getting out as fast as they got in, too. That's because, in a match, you can't break someone's arm for staying exposed too long. You can in a fight. So keep on practicing these points; it might save your ass.

Here's something else that I've noticed about most fighting styles that is really bad news—padding. Now, I'm not exactly fond of the sight of my own blood. In fact, I'm really sort of allergic to it. Thing is, though, I've spilled more of my blood in practice and training than I have in actual fights. The reason for this is simple: I practice bare knuckles, no protection, and full speed. I also practice with people of equal or greater skill. We practice harder than most people fight, and go balls to the wall. What this ends up meaning is that we know what it means to get hit.

There's a double point about this. One, we aren't shocked when we are actually hit harder than one can with pads (like in a real fight, without gloves, when someone is trying to hurt you). Two, while we don't worry about getting hit as much, we're real wary about letting something through. In other words, we're more concerned about our own defenses than with beating the other guy up. Padding sort of makes people almost contemptuous about blows. Being able to take a punch with gloves doesn't mean you can take one without gloves.

The other thing about padding is you end up kicking only certain ways, and these types of blows are not as destructive as others. A kick with the top of the foot is what we call a "courtesy kick"; it does less damage than the same strength kick using the ball of the foot.

What you learn in most dojos is polite fighting. You don't learn how to maim people, and this is a serious weakness about what is taught in there. Fighting is a dirty business, and the niceties that are observed in dojos will get the snot beat out of you in a real fight. Padding and polite rules lead to a certain mental laziness about fighting. This is part of the reason why so many black belts get their ass kicked the first time they cross a streetfighter (not punks; streetfighters. Big difference).

There is only one fighting style I know of that uses elbows and knees. That's Muay Thai, commonly (if somewhat incorrectly) known in the states as Thai Kick Boxing. Most styles don't use these parts as well as they might, nor do they teach these tricks, but streetfighters use them with brutal efficiency. Someone who uses elbows in a fight can be wicked in a close space. What you don't learn in one style will cream you the first time you meet up with it, if you're not on your toes. The PKA doesn't like this sort of thing; nor do they like biting, gouging, binding, or ripping. These things do exist out in the real world, so you better learn how to deal with them in the dojo where it's safe. Otherwise, when you meet them on the street, it'll be fierce.

Another unrealistic aspect about bouts is that they last a long time. A lot of people are shocked when they discover that most of my fights have been "one punch" affairs. A serious fight shouldn't last longer than ten seconds. My old Sifu used to say that if the guy is still standing after three moves, get back and see what you're doing wrong. Now, this is serious "hurt the guy" fighting, not jockeying for position. Don't let a fight last a long time, because it increases your chances of getting hurt.

When I say that most of my fights have been one punch situations, I mean, we both swing and, afterwards, I step back and let him realize that I could and will do a whole lot worse if he keeps pushing it. Ususally the guy catches on, especially if his blow missed and mine didn't. This, however, calls for a certain amount of self-control on your part. You have to show him that you can and will hurt him if he keeps it up, but you won't push him into a corner. Let him woof his way out and save face. It's much trickier than it sounds, but it works a good portion of the time. If the guy still pushes it past that point, the ten second rule comes into play: it's quick and hard. That's for situations where you go often or with people you know. If it's on the street corner, and you don't know the guy, it's hurt him hard time.

By the way, if you really want to learn how to handle yourself, you'll need to practice in different states of consciousness. Practice while drunk, tired, high, wired, or whatever; just learn how to operate in all the states that you usually find yourself in. This is what really gives most streetfighters the edge. They can rock and roll anytime, with no preparation.

There are countless differences between streetfighting and martial arts. Most of them are small, yet relevant, but it mostly boils down to three points: 1) attitude and awareness; 2) streetfighters are more interested in results than in form; 3) streetfighters only expect what happens in a fight.

What I've been talking about here are most of the main differences between martial artists and streetfighters. There are others, but you can learn them on your own with what you now know. Having this information in your back pocket when you go into a dojo will keep you from making the most common mistakes that I've seen in a streetfighting situation. I said, "that I've seen." Remember that nobody knows everything about fighting, so I may have left out some concepts. Keep your eyes open for them, and they won't pop up and slap you in the face.

Teachers

*Undiscerning men who delight in the tenets of ritual lore
utter florid speech, proclaiming "There is nothing else!"*
Bhagavad Gita
2nd teaching

I have hinted throughout this book that the fighting style
you know doesn't really matter as long as you are aware of its
weaknesses, blindspots, and the habits of others. I believe this
is true. If you have a general idea of what you can encounter
in an altercation, you can go out and personally cover the holes
in whatever style you know. A Wing Chun fighter will cream
a Shao-lin stylist in a cramped alley. Of course, Wing Chun
was formed for fighting in the cramped alleys and doorways
of Hong Kong. The situation is going to be different if those
two fight in an open field. Most of the Shao-lin styles were
designed for fighting in wider spaces, and they use the space
with amazing efficiency. A boxer is going to eat a black belt
in karate. Most karate blocks are designed to stop Nighty Nite
Bunny Rabbits. They're way too slow to be effective for many
Rattlers and Setups. Yet, an aikidoist will dribble any boxer
who makes the mistake of committing his weight to a punch.
But God help any aikidoist who matches up with a Shao-lin
monkey stylist. Yet a boxer just might have a chance against
a monkey boy, if he knows that he's up against a maimer. A

Thai kick boxer will cream anybody who stays on the same line with him. They're weak against nonlinear styles, though, but don't let them get close to you unless you're an infighter who knows about blocking elbows and knees.

The point is, each style has its strong points and its weak points. Some styles have certain moves that there are no blocks for in other styles. Not that these blows can't be blocked, it's just that the blocking style never met up with that type of blow. The other ones are the Nighty Nite Bunny Rabbits that you shouldn't even try to block. Taekwon do is a style that I personally think relies on kicks too much. Many of the kicks are to the head, and most are done on the ball of the foot, which puts you in a precarious position in regard to balance. Yet they have one of the most powerful kicks that I have ever encountered. The thing is, until you begin to bounce around, you never hear about them.

Here is where we encounter what I consider to be the main flaw of most martial arts schools. Many teachers only know one style. That is okay. What's not okay is to tell people (whether verbally or nonverbally) that it is the greatest style ever invented. What's worse—and I don't know if this is intentional or not, but it happens—is the students get the idea that they know every type of blow they will ever encounter. This is complete hogwash. Those iron-bar blocks of karate are just not fast enough to stop two boxing jabs. Any boxer who doesn't get out of the way of the stick kick is history.

What I'm saying is that when you go out and select a style to study, first know that there is no system that is better than another. Each was designed for a specific setting. It is up to you to complete the holes in it. Don't let anyone tell you that one system is better than another. Any style that you study will be the one that you are most comfortable with. If it feels right, do it. Take it from there.

The next thing we're going to look at is teachers. Hey, I'm sorry but there are some serious dickslaps out there passing themselves off as teachers. Some of these people need to be dragged into a dark alley and stomped for the shit that they are pulling. What they are teaching is half-baked, dangerous bullshit. I once walked by one of those "franchised" karate schools and nearly had a stroke. They were teaching a yellow belt spinning heel kicks to the head! It was a young woman who was about as balanced as a three-legged mule in a kicking contest. I mean, really, remember rules of combat: never turn your back on your opponent, never kick above the waist, and always strive for balance! Yet they were teaching this poor woman something that any junior high school kid in my old neighborhood would take her out for. Then I remembered that I had been taught the same garbage in another dojo years ago.

There are teachers out there who have never been in a fight in their lives, yet they are teaching how to fight! EEEEK! There are also teachers out there who are arrogant and cocky. They are lousy teachers and abusive to their students. These people aren't teachers, they're loudmouths! They spout shit about what to do in a fight, yet it has no bearing to reality. Also, they get bent out of shape when you point it out to them. Forget these people; they're bullies who are being paid while pushing people around. There are also trophy hounds out there—schools that you walk into and they have three thousand eight hundred and fifty-two trophies in the prominently displayed display case. Even full-contact tournaments are for points. Three points and you're out! If you pulled any of the shit I've told you about, you'd be disqualified. Not only do you have to hit the guy, you have to look good while you're doing it. Is your form right? Is your hair perfect? That isn't fighting, that's dancing!

Shop around. Ask people what they've heard of this school or that one. Visit the school three or four times. Visit other schools. Ask the teacher what he thinks of other schools. Watch how the teacher interacts with his students. Are the students happy? Are they under stress? Is this a school or a boot camp? Does the sensei strike you as someone who has an overdose of testosterone? One of the best dojos I have ever visited, I ended up sitting on the floor with a little five-year-old girl coloring with crayons.

Remember that there are good and bad teachers out there.

Like the styles, teachers have their strong and weak points. You may get along with an instructor that nobody else does, or vice versa. The thing is, keep your eyes open in regard to who you pick as a teacher. Also remember that nobody knows everything, so it is up to you to go out and find out all you can.

Another real common flaw that I have encountered is perfectionist teachers. There is a subtle, yet important, distinction to be made here. Are you there to learn that particular style, or are you there to learn to defend yourself? In the beginning, it is my belief that there is no "both" answer. A formal fighting style does things a certain way surviving a brawl doesn't. When you go into a school, check to see what the guy is actually teaching. Is he so concerned about form that he's ignoring the fact that the block got there? Is he ragging on his students because they're doing a slightly different variation? Is he so wrapped up in doing things his way that he leaves out important facts regarding actual fighting.

The best example of this is that Tracy, my girlfriend, studies aikido. I watched her first sensei get bent out of shape because she was doing judo rolls instead of aikido rolls. He wasn't teaching self-defense, he was teaching aikido. He was so bent out of shape about the rolls being "wrong" that he was omitting critical information. The information he was leaving out is this. If you get thrown, fall and roll, then kick in some of your own energy and get up fast! He wasn't teaching that. He was so wrapped up in getting it done his way that he was putting his students in critical danger. Being an aikidoist, the instructor didn't teach what I and any other streetfighter would have noticed—the perfect opportunity to break a few ribs with a kick. It's not their style; it happens though.

So, when you go in, keep in mind that there is a big difference between the mat and an alley. If you take a streetfighter and put him on the mat, the odds are he will lose. If you take a straight dojo-trained martial artist into an alley, the same thing can be said about him. Unless you are in the school to study the "art" of a martial art form, remember that you will encounter the unexpected out there. If you spend too much time futzing over little details, a surprise package could settle your hash real well. Don't let the teacher bully you. When he gets too picky, ask, is this "form" or is this fighting? Form is good, but precedence is no excuse for failure.

Miscellaneous Tactics, Tricks, and Shit To Know

"There's no excuse for not thinking."
"Yeah there is; being dead."
"That is a pretty good one, now that you mention it."
A drunken conversation.

What I'm gong to do in this chapter is add those things that I either spaced out earlier, remembered as I wrote, or just couldn't find anywhere else to put.

With your newfound awareness, you're going to begin to see things that mean something to you. In the old days they didn't, but now something seemingly innocent to many people will scream warnings to you.

One thing that is a clear-cut danger sign is when two or more people walk into some place and split up. It doesn't always happen in the night clubs and bars, either. If you're alone in the laundry room of your apartment building and it happens, you're in trouble. I could be wrong and, yes, the world could also be flat. It depends on the setup. If you're alone in a place, one guy might stay by the door and the other(s) might approach you, or they might split up and come at you from either side. Your best defense at this point is simple: action! You may be wrong, at which point you can make a donation to the Boy Scouts to assuage your conscience, but better wrong than dead. If you see that trap being set up, don't sit there and eye the sons of bitches; charge! Get out of there! Throw something in their faces and boogie! Ever had laundry soap in your eyes? Soda pop? It hurts! In the meantime, you're out of the trap. You can either run like hell, or split to a place that they can only come at you one by one. Scream your fool head off as you blast past. These guys will suddenly realize that they will have to work to get you.

This sort of shit doesn't always happen in lonely alleys. I was in a pool hall in northern California (basically just up the road from San Quentin prison) the last time that it happened to me. For a variety of reasons, I was not in the best position. One: I was alone. Two: I was in a mellow mood, waiting for my lady to finish some business before we were to go out for the evening. I was dressed casually but nicely. Three: I was unarmed. Wearing a belt knife into a nice restaurant is a little déclassé. Two studs walked in and immediately split up. God knows why the dumb fucks walk in together, but they often do. They sat back, eyed the place, and spotted me. Great; my artillery was in the car. They weren't going to do anything in the pool hall; rather, the idea was to wait until I got outside, then follow me out and mug me.

What you do in that situation is really easy. You leave. In case you're wondering about it, yes, that is what they want. You just give them what they want, plus a little more. If you're in a bar, go up to the bartender or a bouncer and say, "Hey, those guys split up when they came in, and I don't like the way they've been eyeing me. I thing it's a setup. Rather than cause any trouble, I'm going to leave. If they try and follow me, could you slow them down until I can get to my car?" Bartenders and bouncers know this shit goes down all the time. Usually they'll help you out because a client getting mugged is bad for business. That's what I did with the pool hall guys. By the time that they got past the owner, I had reached the safety of my car.

If you're walking down the street and two people are leaning against the wall, it's suspicious. If one of them walks over and leans against the car as you approach, it's a setup. That's called a pincer move. One will distract you and the other will hit you.

The best way out of this is to cross the street. Don't worry about looking like you're scared. Hell, I still cross the street if I don't like the looks of something. John Wayne only exists on the screen. If you move to another location, that means they have to tip their hand in order to get close to you. If you cross the street and they follow, that gives you time to pick up a club or something to even the odds. They know this isn't good for them, and the odds are that they'll go back to waiting where they were. Why mess with someone that is not only going to fight back, but has spotted the attempt and readied himself for it? The reason that I have won most of my fights is because I don't fight on the other guy's turf, I make him come to mine.

There's also a puppy called "Close Convoy," which is real common. It takes two guys, one wearing tennis shoes, to pull it off. You'll be walking along and up ahead there is a dirtbag waiting. He's usually, but not always, in a "canyon" situation, which is an area where there are only two ways in or out: for example, a building on one side and a large truck on the other. He can be either in sight or waiting in the shadows. The other guy will fall out behind you as you're walking. The usual way of doing this is he will fall in step with you so you don't hear his footsteps. This way, the other guy will step out in front of you when you're in the canyon and the guy behind will either strike or back up the other guy's play.

Couple of things that you can do about it. One, if the guy is in view up ahead, cross the street. ("Gawd damn, ain't that easy?") The other thing is, if you see someone up ahead, look over your shoulder. If laughing boy has a partner, stop right there, and wait until the guy passes, or turn around and go another way. If he confronts you, nail him hard, before his buddy can come up to reinforce him.

Traps like this really are dangerous if you don't spot them. If you do spot them, you can either avoid them or blast through them. I advise the former. What you need to do is accept the fact that you're in an attempted setup and do something about it. When you see it being arranged, double-clutch the suckers. Let them know that you're on to them and not afraid! It is especially the "not afraid" part that will save your ass. These people are like animals in that they can sense fear. If you know that you're being followed and you run, you've just set off a signal flare that you're easy prey. If you cut down an alley and they follow, they're going to be a whole lot less interested in messing with you when you step out of the shadows swinging a club.

The number of times that I, and others, have gotten out of a jam by being like a cornered wolverine is unbelievable. I worked with a tiny little woman by the name of Gail. Two young punks decided she would be easy to mug. Not only did they not succeed, but she chased them across the street. If you get in a situation that looks ugly, start fighting first and harder than they could imagine.

Another thing along those lines is what is called a "Pyrrhic Victory." There was this old Persian king by the name of Pyrrhus who decided to rumble with the Romans. He won, sort of. The victory over the Romans was extremely costly; in fact, his army was damn near wiped out afterward. Upriver there were these nasty people called Turks who decided that, since Pyrrhus was in no shape to protect himself anymore, it was time to attack. They won; Pyrrhus lost. The term Pyrrhic Victory was given to any victory that ends up costing too much. Many will be the time that you can get out of a fight not by claiming that you'll win but rather by telling the rube the truth: he's going to pay too high a price for his victory.

Okay, we've covered how to spot a mugger or potential attacker. I want to point out a variation that I've learned over the years. Want to know how to spot a hustler? There are a couple of ways. The first is somewhat difficult to explain, but once you've caught on to it, it'll stand out like a nun in a whorehouse. Here it is: *the guy is just too damned smooth!* If you know what is normal for "smooth," when someone exceeds that he is a hustler. These people somehow just always seem to say the right thing, something that someone else wants to hear. If you listen to someone for a while, you'll notice that they will say one thing to one person, and flat out contradict it when speaking to someone else not five mintues down the line. The "smoothness" moves into "greasiness." This is something that you'll be able to see in time.

The other thing is; *they want to get too friendly too fast!* A strange person has no right to get that chummy. I'm not talking friendly; I'm talking about someone who acts like you've been bosom pals for twenty years. Only thing is, you've just met this guy, or you've only met him once or twice before. He isn't family! This leads to the next aspect.

Sooner or later, these people will try and tag you for money or services. The odds are that the request won't be big, just that it will happen often. That's right; ever had a friend who is always asking for favors. Little things, like running him/her across town, or can he/she borrow this, that, or the other thing? They don't ask for big things, but if you look at a cumulative tally, they have one hell of a bill. If you compare that with the amount of returned favors, and that sum is considerably less, you might have been hustled. If, for some reason, every time you try to get a return favor, they are too busy or it would really put them out of something that is critical for their survival ("I'd just die without my designer jeans!"), the sirens should go off in your little head.

They will always remind you how much they've done for you. "Don't you remember the time that I...?" But that was six months ago. Since then, they've borrowed your car twice, hit you up for a loan (they haven't paid you back yet—twenty dollars out of sixty doesn't cut it), and they've crashed on your floor six times since they've been thrown out by their roommates (wait until you get your phone bill, three weeks after they've split). This is actually the most common type of hustler; they won't take you for money *directly*, just your time. In case you haven't noticed, time is the one thing you can't get back after you've lost it.

The Money Hustler will come at you with a "sweet deal." In fact, that's the problem: it's too sweet. The returns are too high. In reality, things don't return that much for such a little investment. In my entire life, I have only encountered one deal that did. One deal out of an entire lifetime. That means that 99.99 percent of all the sweet high return deals that I have ever encountered have been hustles.

The final thing that will help you spot a hustler is *watch them when they don't think that anyone is watching.* There is something about the eyes of a hustler that can only be called "calculating." When they let down the facade, they look at people the way that they think about them, as targets. They will look at people the same way that a gambler will look at a racing form: a professional calculating odds and weighing possibilities. That is what will, in time, tip you off about these people. The reason that I tell you about this, aside from saving you from getting clipped, is because they can get you into some deep shit if you're not careful with them.

Okay, now back to keeping from getting jumped. When you enter a place that you're not sure of, for whatever reason that may be, crab along the wall. That means when you walk in, find a nice convenient wall and put as much of your back to it as possible. Walk along at a 45 degree angle, looking silly to those don't know any better. Those people who stand a better chance of quality donation to the gene pool (i.e., savvy people) will spot what you're doing real quick. When someone is doing the right moves naturally, people who like to do bad things usually look for easier, less aware targets. Wouldn't you?

By the by, one more way to spot potential trouble (boy will this sound redundant) is to pay attention to who's paying too much attention to you. Now, I ain't talking about flirting. I'm talking about if you're sitting somewhere and you notice someone watching you. If you "flash" now and then when you're sitting somewhere, you'll notice when someone is paying too much attention to you. I've spotted more shit about to come down by noticing when someone was sitting in a corner covertly watching me or someone else. Now I'm not talking about the evil eye that leads to a fight. I'm talking about the "size you up for a mugging" look. The way that a mugger looks at you is different than the way a tough guy will look at you. It's hard to explain, but there is a difference.

What follows is sort of a general restressing of facts that I've pointed out. It's just phrased differently this time. First, a lot of shit is opportunistic. That means that people who pull shit do it because they see a chance. If the opportunity presents itself and these people see a hole in your defenses, they'll go for it. If you learn how to cover those holes, you won't be such a tempting target. People who like to sneak up on others don't like to jam with people who sit with their back against the wall facing the doorway. Casual car thieves can't steal your car if you don't leave your car keys in the ignition ("just for a moment while I run in"). If you leave yourself open, someone is going to snake one in sooner or later. If you learn the casual habits of covering yourself, you seriously reduce the chances of being chosen as a target.

It's game time again. Look around and try to figure out how you'd rip someone off. Walk along and look at parked cars. It's unbelievable how many times you'll see keys in the ignition, doors unlocked, and windows down. When you begin to see these bad habits in others, you'll begin to weed them out in yourself. By the way, your significant other can drive you batshit at this time. I go into screaming meemies everytime my old lady leaves the keys in the car. Don't rag on him/her; get them to play the game too. My lady isn't as bad as she used to be with this. My awareness has started rubbing off on her. (I still have a slim jim squirreled away for when she locks the keys in the car, though.) Play the game for a while. See who you would try to mug, or wouldn't even consider trying something on. Then figure out what it is about those people that made you come to that conclusion. This will help you keep from becoming a target yourself.

Afterword

The meaning of life is living. The rest is just commentary.
A professor at Pierce College

It's 3:46 in the morning and my old lady, Tracy, is asleep on the couch. She wouldn't go to bed without me. She's happier 'n hell that this book is finished. For the better part of a month, I have been hunched over this machine writing, and I'm pretty close to going ga-ga. It's funny, but this book wouldn't let me not write it. It was supposed to just be ten or so pages that I would hand to my students so I wouldn't have to repeat myself. Well, now I'm sitting here drinking a beer and realizing: I have just poured my guts out in the hope that someone's path will be easier than mine was. This little booklet has grown into something serious. I could have made it three times as big, and still not scratched the surface. But that's okay, because I hope that what I have been able to do is impart critical information that can help you find yourself out there.

This book is to be used as an additional tool to your martial arts training. It, like any other book, is absolutely useless unless you practice. You can't learn it from a book; it just doesn't work that way. Learn everything you can by book and then get out there and get dirty. Test the theory in the real world. Correct your course as you go. You now have what it takes to be able to fly by the seat of your pants. Remember, as the greatest wild ones I have ever known have all said at some time or other, "Out of Control to Tower: What the Fuck! Over." These are the guys that make it, though. They have the blend that it takes—theory and practical. But theory only goes so far. By the same note, actuality is limited if you don't have the vision of theory to guide you through the forest. Learn to blend the two.

As I've said from the beginning, your greatest gift is your awareness of what is actually out there. It is a grand world for those who have the chutzpah to go out and get it. The thing it, it's up to you. I can tell you these things until I'm blue in the face, but until you go out and actually do them yourself, it won't matter. I've tried to point out that the style you choose to get there doesn't matter as long as you are aware of the bigger picture. I hope that I have shown you a way to free yourself from the invisible chains that seem to bind so many of us. If nothing else, I do hope you have learned that, in many cases, the way to get free from the chaos that crushes so many of us is to draw a line of territory and to defend it with all your might. That way, when you are no longer tripped by the petty things that cut us off at the knees, you can go out in the world and love and laugh fully.

Just remember, about this in specific and life in general: *it's a little theory and a whole lot of practice.* You are your own teacher in these matters; all anyone can do is give you road marks. You must make the voyage yourself. To this end, I give you my love and my blessings, and hope that you find how wonderful this world can actually be.

Suggested Reading List

These are some of the books that I have read and found useful. Not every one will be your cup of tea. That's okay. Like everything else, take what you can from where you can and let the rest be. Remember, information is where you find it.

Strategy

Book of Five Rings by Miyamoto Musashi. This is a seventeenth century book on sword fighting, if you only want to look that deep. In the wider sense, it's an extremely good book on strategy, enough so that Bantam made a mint passing it off as a secret to Japanese management. While it could be so, shop around for better translations.

Art of War by Sun Tzu. I know of two translations, one by a guy named Griffith. The other is the more readily available; that's by James Clavell. While I'm a little less than hot about that one, the quality of a man dead nearly two thousand years shines through. This guide is considered classic Oriental military strategy. It sort of explains why every time we go into the Orient, we have one hell of a rough time. They aren't dopes.

The Prince by Machiavelli. This guy has a bad rap through history for being carnivorous and sneaky. What worried me is I read it and it made sense. And you thought Texas politics were twisted; try Italian.

Winning Through Intimidation by Robert Ringer. It's a business book. Nonetheless, the guy has some sharp insights as to what motivates people when it comes to business (read: screwing you) and how to cover your ass when dealing with people.

Survival by Hugh C. McDonald. This is a nuts-and-bolts, practical guide on what to do if you're suddenly involved in a crime and/or a potentially violent place. He's got some real good advice as well as some stuff I'm a little twitchy about— mostly in the area of indicating that it is a law rather than a rule of thumb to be applied situationally. But since neither of us knows everything, it really behooves you to read this and get what you can out of it.

Attitude by Lisa Sliwa. This book was written (with a little help) by the wife of the head of the "Guardian Angels." It is a book of commonsense defense for women. She doesn't swear as much as I do, but she manages to get good ideas across anyway. The only thing that I disagree with is the physical section, not because it's wrong in content; rather it is the standard "this is the technique that you use in this situation" sort of shit. The reason that I have a hard time with that is it only gives people the intellectual concepts, not the practical understanding (like what to do if something goes wrong). I sort of suspect the publisher on that one. Other than that, I feel this book is a wonder and should be read by all women and as many men as possible.

Understanding People
Neurolinguistic Programming by Brandler and Grinder. There are several books in the series. NLP is one of the hottest psychiatric techniques to hit the fan in many moons. The first two are *Structure of Magic*, books one and two. These are good

for understanding how language affects the way we see the world. The next one is *Frogs Into Princes*. This one is an introduction to how the human mind models reality. I must say these books are very dry. There is a beginner's version called *Practical Magic* by some guy whose name I forget. It's easier reading but not as good.

Transactional Analysis. While this form of psychology is just glorified Freudianism, it takes away many of the loopholes Freud had. The main one is "I'm okay, you're okay." Even if it doesn't apply to you, it applies to a great many people, so it doesn't hurt to have it under your belt.

Looking Out For #1 by Robert Ringer. Same guy as before. Without a Ph.D. (piled higher and deeper), this guy has come up with some real world practical advice on how to get by out there. I highly recommend this as a beginning book.

End of Innocence by Sheldon Kopp. This guy can get a little depressing, but he is right on about having to take charge of your life, and how we were taught not to.

The One Minute Manager series by Kenneth Blanchard and Spencer Johnson. These are good books about how to deal with people who work for you (Betas) with as few problems as possible. The techniques, with a little adjustment for situational variance, really work.

How To Win Friends And Influence People by Dale Carnegie. This book has been around since before dirt, and for a good reason: it works. The guy wrote it before most people on this earth today were alive. Just because it's old doesn't mean it doesn't work. He wrote it before the academics got a stranglehold on how things were supposed to be written, so it's easy to read and understand.

Body Language by Julias Fast. This is an introductory book on how we "telegraph" what's going on in our heads by the way our bodies react. It's a good stepping-stone into the field of nonverbal communications, which, by the way, constitutes about 80 percent of our communications. Surprise!

Manwatching by Desmond Morris. My gay friends had a field day when they saw this title in my house. No, I hadn't changed my mind; I still was wildly into women. It's about body language around the world, thank you very much. It is a huge book, and it will give you an idea of how diverse mankind is in its nonverbal communications. If you are dealing with various ethnic communities on a regular basis (hell, even if you aren't), I strongly advocate this book. It's full of interesting items, like it's an insult to a Vietnamese person to sit with your feet pointing toward him. The thing about this book is it's hard to find outside of a public or an anthropologist's library.

Hell's Angels by Hunter S. Thompson. This is undoubtedly the finest book on the subject of bikers ever written. It is a calm, level-headed reporting of how these people think and act. Hunter S. Thompson is one of my favorite authors for a variety of reasons. "Uncle Duke" in the comic strip "Doonesbury" is a thinly disguised version of him. What makes this book interesting (aside from the fact that he really is objective about the subject) is that he gives their side of the story. While he was writing this book, he rode with the Angels, and cut through the media hype regarding these people. He points out with equal clarity their strengths and weaknesses.

Understanding Things Outside Ourselves
Tao Te Ching by Lao Tzu. Like many of the Eastern philosophical sutras (teachings), this book is in poetry form. There is a deep understanding about how the universe works. By the way, if you didn't know, Taoist monasteries are where Shao-lin kung fu comes from.

Bhagavad Gita. Yes, the book that the Hare Krishnas, those lovely people who bum money from you at major metropolitan airports, base their religion on. You don't have to shave your head or wear your bed sheets to read it. It is the God's counsel on war to Arjuna. Wait a minute...they're peaceful, yet it's counsel on war?

Miscellaneous Reading

Dune by Frank Herbert. Science fiction may not be your cup of tea, but this is one of the best books I have ever read for showing how another culture can work. These people make Machiavelli look like a piker. Get what you can from this book.

Chronicles Of Amber by Roger Zelazny. Another sci-fi series. Interesting in several aspects, but most of all the concept of "Shadow" travel—traveling through dimensions where the rules of reality aren't consistent—and what it does to people.

Myth Adventures by Robert Asprin. A comic version of the previously mentioned concept. The series is loaded with puns and jokes, but there are some serious concepts that are brought to light in a humorous way.

Illusions by Richard Bach. A book dealing with reality and how much we make of our own. Somewhat hippyish in format, but some practical concepts regarding mystical goo.

Early Autumn by Robert Parker. TV made Spenser a rather watered-down version of the books' hero. This is a book where Spenser has to teach a young boy how to survive for and by himself. Even though it is in the "private eye" genre, the man comes out with some provincial wisdom that is right on. Also, the fun and games between Hawk and Spenser are hysterical, if you enjoy that brand of humor.